Journal of the Early Book Society
for the study of manuscripts and printing history

Special Focus: *Women and Book Culture in Late Medieval and Early Modern France*

Edited by Martha W. Driver, with Cynthia J. Brown
Volume 4, 2001

Copyright © 2001
Pace University Press
One Pace Plaza
New York, NY 10038

All rights reserved.
Printed in the United States of America

ISBN 0-944473-56-3 (pbk: alk.ppr.)
ISSN 1525-6790

Member

Council of Editors of Learned Journals

♾™ The paper used in this publication meets the minimum requirements of American National Standard for information Sciences—Permanence of Paper for printed Library Materials, ANSI Z39.48—1984.

The *Journal of the Early Book Society* is published annually. JEBS invites longer articles on manuscripts and/or printed books produced between 1300 and 1550. Special consideration will be given to essays exploring the period of transition from manuscript to print. Articles should not exceed 8000 words or thirty typed pages. Authors are asked to follow *The Chicago Manual of Style*. A Works Cited list at the end of the text should include city, publisher, and date. Manuscripts are to be sent, in triplicate, along with an abstract of up to 150 words, to Martha Driver, Early Book Society, Department of English, Pace University, 41 Park Row, New York, New York 10038. Only materials accompanied by a self-addressed, stamped envelope (or international reply coupon) will be returned. Members of the Early Book Society who are recent authors may send review books for consideration to Susan Powell, Reviews Editor, Department of Modern Languages, University of Salford, Salford M5 4WT, England. Brief notes on recent discoveries, highlighting little-known or recently uncovered texts and/or images, may be sent to Linne R. Mooney, Department of English, University of Maine, Orono, Maine 04469. Subscription information may be obtained from Martha Driver or from Pace University Press.

Those interested in joining the Early Book Society or with editorial inquiries may contact Martha Driver by post or e-mail (MDriver@Pace.edu). For ordering information, call Pace University Press at 212-346-1405 or visit http://www.pace.edu/press. Institutions and libraries may purchase copies directly from Ingram Library Services (1-800-937-5300).

The editor wishes to thank Patricia Godfrey, Stephanie Elliott, and Mark Hussey of Pace University Press for their help and advice on this issue.

Journal of the Early Book Society
For the Study of Manuscript and Printing History

Editors:
Martha W. Driver, *Pace University*
with Cynthia J. Brown, *University of California, Santa Barbara*

Associate Editors:
Linne Mooney, *University of Maine, Orono*
Sue Powell, *University of Salford*

Editorial Board
Beatrice H. Beech, *Western Michigan University*
Norman F. Blake, *University of Sheffield*
Julia Boffey, *University of London, Queen Mary and Westfield College*
James Carley, *York University*
Joyce Coleman, *University of North Dakota*
Mary Erler, *Fordham University*
Vincent Gillespie, *Saint Anne's College, Oxford University*
Avril K. Henry, *University of Exeter*
Stanley S. Hussey, *Lancaster University*
Daniel W. Mosser, *Virginia Polytechnic Institute and State University*
Ann Eljenholm Nichols, *Winona State University*
Joanne S. Norman, *Bishop's University*
Judy Oliver, *Colgate University*
Michael Orr, *Lawrence University*
Myra D. Orth, *independent scholar*
Steven Partridge, *University of British Columbia*
Derek Pearsall, *Harvard University*
Robert Raymo, *New York University*
Pamela Sheingorn, *Baruch College and
   The City University of New York Graduate School and University Center*
Toshiyuki Takamiya, *Keio University*
John Thompson, *Queen's University, Belfast*
Ronald Waldron, *King's College, University of London*

Contents

Introduction
Women and Book Culture in Late Medieval   1
and Early Modern France
    CYNTHIA J. BROWN AND MARTHA W. DRIVER

Articles
Women and the Circulation of Books   9
    BRIGITTE BUETTNER

Charlotte de Savoie's Library and Illuminators   32
    ANNE-MARIE LEGARÉ

Family Values: Manuscripts as Gifts and Legacies
among French Renaissance Women   88
    MYRA DICKMAN ORTH

Christine de Pizan and the Book: 112
Programs and Modes of Reading, Strategies for Publication
    JACQUELINE CERQUIGLINI-TOULET

The Patroness and the Poet: 127
The Religious Allegories of Gabrielle de Bourbon and Jean Bouchet
    JENNIFER BRITNELL

Les Albums Poétiques de Marguerite D'Autriche: 150
The Dynamics of an Early Renaissance Court
    JANE H. M. TAYLOR

Grief, Rape, and Suicide as Consolation for the Queen: 172
Ambivalent Images of Female Rulers in the Books of Anne de Bretagne
    CYNTHIA J. BROWN

Reinventing the Roman de la Rose for a Woman Reader: 202
The Case of MS Douce 195
    DEBORAH MCGRADY

Louise de Savoie, "Bibliophile"   228
    MARY BETH WINN

Nota Bene: Brief Notes on Manuscripts and Early Printed Books
Highlighting Little-Known or Recently Uncovered Items or Related Issues

Two Fragments of Lydgate's Troy Book in the Bodleian Library   259
    LINNE R. MOONEY

A New Manuscript Fragment of the Northern Homily Cycle   267
    OLIVER PICKERING

Descriptive Reviews
Susan Powell, Review Editor

Marie Axton and James P. Carley.   281
'Triumphs of English': Henry Parker, Lord Morley, Translator to the Tudor Court
    SUSAN POWELL

Elizabeth J. Bryan.   284
Collaborative Meaning in Medieval Scribal Culture: The Otho Laȝamon
    CAROLE WEINBERG

A.S.G. Edwards, Vincent Gillespie, and Ralph Hanna, eds.   288
The English Medieval Book: Studies in Memory of Jeremy Griffiths
    SUSAN POWELL

Susanna Fein, ed.   292
Studies in the Harley Manuscript: the Scribes, Contents, and Social Contexts
of British Library MS Harley 2253
    JASON O'ROURKE

Jean-François Gilmont, ed.   296
The Reformation and the Book
    BRIAN CUMMINGS

Andrew Hunter, ed.   304
Thornton and Tully's Scientific Books, Libraries and Collectors
    GEOFFREY CANTOR

Ann Eljenholm Nichols, Michael T. Orr, Kathleen L. Scott, & Lynda   306
Dennison, eds.
An Index of Images in English Manuscripts from the time of Chaucer to Henry VIII
c.1380–c.1509
    MALCOLM JONES

Helen Phillips. 309
An Introduction to the Canterbury Tales: Reading, Fiction, Context
   SIMON HOROBIN

Notes on Libraries and Collections

The Chapin Library 311
   MERADITH MCMUNN

Innerpeffray Library 313
   MARGARET CONNOLLY

Penn State University Library
   JEANNE KROCHALIS AND SANDRA STELTS 315

About the Authors 317

Women and Book Culture in Late Medieval and Early Modern France

CYNTHIA J. BROWN AND MARTHA W. DRIVER

Et des poetes dont tu parles, ne scez tu pas bien que ilz ont parlé en plusieurs choses en maniere de fable et se veulent aucunefois entendre au contraire de ce que leurs diz demonstrent? Et les peut on prendre par une figure de grammaire qui se nomme antifrasis qui s'entent, si comme tu scez, si comme on diroit tel est mauvais, c'est a dire que il est bon, aussi a l'opposite. Si te conseille que tu faces ton prouffit de leurs dis et que l'entendes ainsi, quelque fust leur entente es lieux ou ilz blasment les femmes.[1]

[As far as the poets of whom you speak are concerned, do you not know that they spoke on many subjects in a fictional way and that often they mean the contrary of what their words openly say? One can interpret them according to the grammatical figure of *antiphrasis*, which means, as you know, that if you call something bad, in fact, it is good, and also vice versa. Thus I advise you to profit from their works and to interpret them in the manner in which they are intended in those passages where they attack women.][2]
— Christine de Pizan, *La Cité des Dames*

In June 2000, ten scholars from various disciplines participated in a colloquium titled *Women and Books in Late Medieval and Renaissance Europe: Female Readers, Owners, and Makers*, held at the Château de la Bretesche in Missillac, France. During this three-day round table discussion, a number of questions were raised. While some begin to be addressed in the papers presented here, others remain unanswered. It is our hope that the questions raised at the colloquium will inspire future research. Indeed, we look forward to engaging in further dialogue about the roles of women in late medieval and early modern book culture. As many scholars know, the reconstruction of late medieval and Renaissance libraries, and reading and writing networks, is a particularly difficult task, for the incomplete and disparate nature of available documents offers only partial insight into these cultural dynamics. To reconstruct women's libraries and collections,[3] and trace their reading and writing patterns, is an even more extraordinary act of recovery, because of the legal, social, ideological, and cultural strictures governing these activities.

The questions raised at the Bretesche Colloquium include the following: When did women become empowered to own, create, and produce books? How did their ownership and possession of books differ legally and culturally from collections owned by men? The suggestion that medieval property laws acted to conceal book ownership among women leads, in turn, to a host of other queries: How did laws concerning property affect actual ownership? Did women have title to their own property? Did they have private means of owning books? It is the state of widowhood that frequently makes visible for the first time the contribution of women, galvanized by financial (Christine de Pizan) or political (Marguerite d'Autriche, Louise de Savoie) necessity, to the history of the book.[4] And yet, in certain cases, such as that of Charlotte de Savoie, married aristocratic women participated actively in book collecting behind the scenes well before their husbands' demise. While noble men's deaths typically precipitated the creation of official inventories of their book collections, these documents did not necessarily shed light on the contents or existence of the libraries of their widows.

A related theme that arose repeatedly throughout our discussions was the problem of identifying female ownership, which has often led medieval and modern bibliographers alike to misattribute or incorrectly catalogue books under men's names. While it is clear that women played a vital role in the book culture of late medieval and early Renaissance Europe, a contradiction emerges between this reality and cultural stereotypes that appear to have discouraged a discourse about a woman's accumulation of books. Because noble women's libraries, such as that of Anne de Bretagne, either were not considered an official part of men's book collections or were commonly absorbed into them, documents tracing the history of libraries after the death of the female book collector are much rarer than those detailing collections of their male counterparts. It is astonishing, for example, that accounts of the libraries of certain prominent female intellectuals, such as Marguerite de Navarre, have still not been recovered.[5] In the end, women's libraries apparently constituted more of a private than a public phenomenon.[6]

How, then, do we identify a book or a manuscript owned by or intended for a woman, especially when many such works have often been assumed to have belonged to men? Moreover, how do we understand and define the movement of texts among cultural networks involving women, such as those associated with Gabrielle de Bourbon, Marguerite d'Autriche, or Anne de Bretagne, when official documentation of these very networks is lacking? Was there a difference between books acquired through inheritance and books less formally handed down, from mother to daughter, for example? What works were considered treasured *objets d'art* as opposed to books commissioned or purchased especially for their contents? Did women acquire these as often as men? In other words, was there a difference between collecting and using books among men and women? Were women's reading practices and strategies different from those of men?

In analyzing the contents of the books that women owned, can we faithfully determine what kinds of works and the manner in which women actually read? How do we learn what kinds of books they wanted to read? Were books that women received as gifts, such as the devotional texts that typically dominate women's libraries, a response to personal or social predilections? How did authors and artists address the interests and desires of female readers? And what about the contributions made by female authors themselves? For whom did they write? How involved were they in the production of their own books?[7] What tools do modern scholars need to adopt in interpreting the visual and verbal signs in books made for, by, or about women?[8] To recover women's contributions to book history, scholars are examining old evidence in new ways, striving to uncover heretofore concealed evidence in new places, and reading the evidence differently.[9] Since the dates of inquiry of our Bretesche discussions included late medieval to early modern France,[10] we find it particularly appropriate to adopt Christine de Pizan's concept of *antiphrasis*, an interpretive tool she employed in the rereading of antifeminist texts, as a metaphor for our own reinterpretation of inventories, bibliographies, literary texts and images, and issues surrounding authorship and ownership. Reading historical, literary, and cultural documents through such a lens will better enable us to recover women's contributions to the history of the book and to discover those who have traditionally been absent from cultural accounts.

To this end, Brigitte Buettner ("Women and the Circulation of Books") suggests that in order to understand the cultural dynamics of women's acquisition and reading of books in late medieval and early modern Europe, we must look to other domains than those that have been traditionally explored, such as patronage, which tends to provide a partial view of the role of females in the establishment of their libraries. Through her preliminary typology for the modes of circulation of women's books, based on the probability that their libraries had a different function, size, and content from those of their male counterparts, Buettner encourages scholars to explore more conscientiously patterns of the transfer, exchange, and loan of books among women and between husbands and wives, as well as the category of books acquired as wedding gifts and brought into a household in a bride's trousseau or through her dowry.

Anne-Marie Legaré's reconstitution of the library of Charlotte de Savoie, queen of France through her marriage to Louis XI ("Charlotte de Savoie's Library and Illuminators"), provides an excellent model of the deductive methods of detection and fine-tuned rereading of existing inventories and archival documents that this endeavor requires. Her careful reinterpretation of the 1484 inventory made of Charlotte's library upon her death exposes the difficulties of such a complex task, as she compares the 1484 inventory with royal acquisitions the queen bequeathed to her son, the future king Charles VIII, and with two reconstituted accounts of the library of the husband (Pierre de Beaujeu, duc de Bourbon) of her daughter, Anne de France, through whose hands many of Charlotte's books must have passed. Unraveling the intertwined threads of those books owned by husband and wife, passed down to son and daughter, commissioned for the queen's own interest, or received as gifts, through exchange, or on loan, Legaré helps modern scholars better understand Charlotte of Savoie's patterns of acquisition, personal predilections for reading, and patronage of contemporary artists, scribes, and authors.

Tracing similar dynamics, Myra Orth's study of book networks among Renaissance women focuses on the importance of family gifts in the creation and circulation of book manuscripts in sixteenth-century France ("Family Values: Manuscripts as Gifts and Legacies among French Renaissance Women"). Women authors such as Marguerite de Navarre, Catherine d'Amboise, and Anne de Graville, all raised in families of bibliophiles, often dedicated or offered copies of their own works, reproduced in luxury manuscripts whose pictorial programs typically featured them as central figures, to female family members. These women tended, then, to disseminate their own writings to relatives through private manuscript "publication" rather than to larger audiences through print like their male counterparts. Orth also provides several examples of Books of Hours offered as gifts to women by their husbands as well as the famous *Hours of Catherine de Médicis*, whose probable passage down through the female line of the Lorraine branch all but confirms that this book was the dowager queen's personal possession.

Owning and reading books were activities intimately associated with the act of authoring itself, as the case of Christine de Pizan makes abundantly clear. Jacqueline Cerquiglini-Toulet ("Christine de Pizan and the

Book: Programs and Modes of Reading, Strategies for Publication") extrapolates with great finesse from Christine's own words how her early associations with books, men of letters, and princely libraries gave rise to her intense interest in both the material fabrication of her books and the very materiality involved in the act of writing. Often generated from scenes of reading, Christine's allegories are edifying architectural constructs whose multiplication and dissemination consciously ensure the author's place in posterity.

Drawing too from her reading experiences, particularly from the devotional books in her library, Gabrielle de Bourbon penned at least four spiritual writings (three now extant), and thereby occupies a unique place among the small number of lay writers of pious texts in the early sixteenth century. Her works, particularly *Le Voyage espirituel entreprins par l'Âme Devote pour parvenir en la Cité de Bon Repoux* (c.1510?), are examined by Jennifer Britnell ("The Patroness and the Poet: The Religious Allegories of Gabrielle de Bourbon and Jean Bouchet"), who makes a strong case for reversing conventional assumptions about the direction of male-female literary influences. Britnell convincingly proposes that, despite significant differences between Gabrielle de Bourbon's writing and Jean Bouchet's *Triumphes de la noble et amoureuse dame* (1530), differences that can be attributed to the changing religious climate with the advent of Lutheranism, Bouchet drew inspiration from his former sponsor. From her he not only learned that royal and aristocratic women constituted a substantial reading public to whom he could offer religious instruction through his printed works, but he also borrowed and elaborated upon the themes, motifs, and metaphors of Gabrielle's more contemplative works.

A similar intertextual process characterizes Marguerite d'Autriche's association with individuals at her court in Malines in the early sixteenth century, where she reigned as duchesse de Savoie until her husband's death in 1504. Through a study of her *Album poétique* (Brussels, Bibliothèque Royale MS 10572), Jane Taylor reconstructs networks of poetic practice at this vibrant early Renaissance center dominated by a woman ("Les Albums Poétiques de Marguerite d'Autriche: The Dynamics of an Early Renaissance Court"). This poetic anthology of rondeaux and ballads composed by courtiers, diplomats, advisers, privy council member, and *demoiselles* in the entourage of Marguerite, who contributed in her own hand a work to the collection, figures as one of the duchesse de Savoie's extensive library holdings, which rivaled the book collections of late medieval and early Renaissance princes.

In an effort to understand more fully women's reading of both texts and images in works created for them by male artists, Cynthia Brown uncovers the apparent unease with which Queen Anne de Bretagne must have perused manuscripts dedicated to her in the early sixteenth century ("Grief, Rape, and Suicide as Consolation for the Queen: Ambivalent Images of Female Rulers in the Books of Anne de Bretagne"). In the manuscript copy of the *Voyage de Gênes* (B.N. f.fr. 5091), for example, offered to the queen by her secretary Jean Marot about 1507, overt and implicit allusions to grief, rape, and suicide by means of the author's and artist (Jean Bourdichon)'s allegorical reconstruction of historical events through an antifeminine lens undermine the stated goal of pleasing and comforting the royal dedicatee. The verbal and pictorial rhetoric of other works offered in homage to Anne de Bretagne suggests that she was sometimes not such an "honored" recipient of the books created in her name.

Figuring centrally in any discussion of women's association with the collection and reading of books in early modern Europe is Louise de Savoie, duchesse d'Angoulême, whose patronage of authors and artists and involvement in the book trade following her husband's death in 1496 are well known. Deborah McGrady, however, seeks to expose earlier evidence of Louise's participation in the manuscript and print culture ("Reinventing the *Roman de la Rose* for a Woman Reader: The Case of MS Douce 195"). She suggests that Robinet Testard, illustrator of the *Roman de la rose* manuscript presumed to have been made for duke Charles d'Angoulême (Bodeleian Library, MS Douce 195), anticipates Louise de Savoie as a recipient as well, both by inscribing models of female readers within its elaborate miniature program and by visually revising antifeminist passages in the text to accommodate the tastes and sensibilities of a noble female clientele.

In her examination of Louise de Savoie's book-collecting activities in the context of late medieval and early modern bibliophilia, Mary Beth Winn ("Louise de Savoie, 'Bibliophile'") demonstrates that the notion of bibliophilia was not even being formulated until the early sixteenth century. One impetus for this development comes from savvy, profit-seeking publishers like Antoine Vérard, who was newly motivated by economic aims with the advent of print. But it was above all Vérard's association with avid book collectors such as Louise de Savoie, driven herself to acquire luxury books by political and educational goals centering upon the future of her son, François 1er, that significantly contributed to the rise of book collecting. Despite that fact that Louise figures as one of the first real female bibliophiles, the epitaphs redacted in her honor and dedications found in her books bear little if any reference to this role.

These typologies of book circulation among women and profiles of individual female contributors to book culture—as collectors, authors, manuscript organizers, and dedicatees—together form only a small part of the still incomplete reconstruction of female textual communities of late medieval and early modern France. It is our hope that the essays presented

INTRODUCTION

here will stimulate further research into the many unanswered questions that remain.

NOTES

1. Cited from Earl Jeffrey Richard's edition of Christine de Pizan's *La Cité des dames* (Milan: Luni, 1998), 48.
2. Cited from Earl Jeffrey Richards' translation of Christine de Pizan's *The Book of the City of Ladies* (New York: Persea, 1982), 7.
3. Susan Groag Bell's article "Medieval Women Book Owners: Arbiters of Lay Piety and Ambassadors of Culture," *Signs* 7 (1982): 746-68, remains the classic reference for a discussion of medieval women book owners, but with the passage of nearly two decades, her work needs to be expanded. See also the recent collection *Commanding Women in Honor of Charity Cannon Willard*, in *The Profane Arts/Les Arts Profanes* VII, 2 (Autumn 1998), for one of the few insightful discussions of French women writers, readers, and book collectors, in particular the articles by Meradith McMunn, Mary Beth Winn, and Christine Reno. Another pertinent essay, "Women in Command, Women in Demand," by Nadia Margolis, appeared in a subsequent issue of *The Profane Arts/Les Arts Profanes* VII, 2 (Spring, 1999): 100–110. Research on related questions in England is further advanced, as attested by the books recently edited by Felicity Riddy [*Prestige, Authority and Power in Late Medieval Manuscripts and Texts* (Woodbridge, Suffolk; Rochester, NY: York Medieval Press, 2000)], June Hall McCash [*The Cultural Patronage of Medieval Women* (Athens and London: The University of Georgia Press, 1996)], John Carmi Parsons [*Medieval Queenship* (New York: St Martin's Press, 1993)], and Carol Meale [*Women & Literature in Britain* 1150-1500 (Cambridge: Cambridge University Press, 1993)].
4. For details on one of the largest libraries of a woman during the late medieval and early modern period, that of Marguerite d'Autriche, twice a widow and a reigning sovereign in her own right (regent of Netherlands from 1507 to 1515, then governor from 1518 to 1530), see Marguerite Debae's *La Bibliothèque de Marguerite d'Autriche* (Louvain and Paris: Peeters, 1995).
5. To date, no documentation on the library of Marguerite de Navarre has been uncovered. Pierre Jourda published a list of most of the manuscripts and the printed works dedicated to Marguerite (see his *Marguerite d'Angoulême, duchesse d'Alençon, reine de Navarre* (1492-1549): *Étude biographique et littéraire* [Paris: Champion 1930]), but this is not the same as a reconstitution of her library. The fact that some of the manuscripts dedicated to Marguerite were housed in the French Royal Library with low *fonds français* numbers suggests that they were considered to be royal holdings. We are grateful to Myra Orth for these details.
6. Similar questions are being raised about women's libraries in Spain and Catalonia about the same time. See, for example, Araceli Guillaume-Alonso, "Des Bibliothèques féminines en Espagne (XVIe–XVIIe siècles): Quelques Exemples," and Dominique de Courcelles, "Recherches sur les livres et les femmes en Catalogne aux

XVe et XVIe siècles: Figures de lectrices," both in *Des Femmes et des livres: France et Espagne, XIVe-XVIIe siècles*, ed. Dominique de Courcelles and Carmen Val Julián (Paris: École des Chartes, 1999), 61–74, 95–114.

7. Much research has been carried out recently on these issues in the cases of Christine de Pizan and Marguerite de Navarre, but more attention needs to be paid to other female authors of the period. For a recent assessment of Renaissance writers such as Gabrielle de Bourbon, Jeanne Flore, Louise Labé, Marie Le Gendre, and others, see *Women's Writing in the French Renaissance*, ed. Philip Ford and Gillian Jondorf, Proceedings of the Fifth Cambridge French Renaissance Colloquium, 7-9 July 1997 (Cambridge: Cambridge French Colloquia, 1999).

8. One of the few recent attempts to provide interpretative models of visual signs in books made for, by, and about women is *Women and the Book: Assessing the Visual Evidence*, ed. Jane H. M. Taylor and Lesley Smith (London: The British Library, 1996).

9. Anne-Marie Legaré's "Reassessing Women's Libraries in Late Medieval France: The Case of Jeanne de Laval," *Renaissance Studies*, 10, no. 2 (June 1996): 209–36, is one of the few examples of this new effort of archival recovery in the reconstitution of women's book communities.

10. Discussion also included papers dealing with a wider European context. Patricia Stirnemann of the Institut de Recherche et d'Histoire des Textes, Paris, addressed the question, "Who Makes a Renaissance?" Martha Driver's paper, "Representations of Saintly Women in Late Medieval Woodcuts," will appear in *The Image in Print*, a book manuscript she is currently preparing for publication by the British Library.

Women and the Circulation of Books
BRIGITTE BUETTNER

In 1982, Susan Groag Bell published a pioneering article, "Medieval Women Book Owners: Arbiters of Lay Piety and Ambassadors of Culture."[1] In it, she contended that women acquired books through "inheritance, commission, and patronage," and identified a total of 242 women who owned at least one book from c. 800 to 1500—a list that, twenty years later, could be expanded quite substantially thanks to the increased efforts scholars have made to identify female owners of books and to make visible their possessions, which had all too often been left "buried" in the belongings of their husbands. What has not changed, however, is the validity of Bell's argument that from the middle of the fourteenth century onward the libraries of women at the top of the social ladder swelled just as steadily as those of their male counterparts. What I propose to do here is to expand on the categories put forward by Bell and at the same time to question the pertinence of patronage—understood as the commission, dedication, or purchase of a book—as the generally dominant, often exclusive, category by which we account for the ways in which books circulated in late medieval French court milieus in general, and among women in particular. Yet while the case for women's vigorous sponsorship of artistic and literary activities no longer needs to be made, the other ways in which books circulated have not been charted in any systematic fashion; what follows will therefore only offer a preliminary overview of topics that need more sustained and detailed attention elsewhere.

A few general remarks first. Despite our understandable enthusiasm at unearthing so many women who played a catalyzing role as patrons of artists and writers, it cannot be denied that women's libraries remained on the whole much more modest than those of their husbands.[2] Partly this was due to the fact that the acquisition of books held a different value for men than for women: in the first case, assembling a library already fell within certain expectations about the public duties of a ruler and that, in turn, endowed their libraries with an official or at least semi-official role. Conversely, most women's libraries were considered strictly personal, even in a legal sense—unless, that is, a particular woman enjoyed a degree of political and financial autonomy, sometimes as consort, more often as regent or dowager. What happened to the substantial library owned by Anne de Bretagne (d. 1514) is revealing in this regard.[3] Anne was an energetic patron who engaged artists and commissioned important books in her own right; yet the most significant part of her huge library of about 1,500 volumes was inherited, either from her ancestors and brought to Blois as part of her trousseau ("livres autrefoiz apportés de Nantes," says her inventory), or from her two royal husbands, Charles VIII and Louis XII. Specifically, Charles had given her a staggering collection of 1,140 manuscripts, looted from Naples during his Italian campaign in 1494, perhaps as a belated wedding gift. The manuscripts previously owned by her husbands were regarded, however, as belonging to the embryonic royal collection, and remained at Blois after her death; by contrast, all others, including the manuscripts of Italian origin, were considered her own property and as such they were bequeathed to her short-lived daughter Claude de France (d. 1524). In the absence of any comprehensive study detailing the legal definition of property as it affected books and other valuables, it would be premature to infer any general patterns from this case. All what can be said is that it was not an isolated instance, for Anne de Bretagne's predecessor, Queen Charlotte de Savoie (d. 1483), wife of Louis XI, who owned a considerable library of more than one hundred volumes, had drawn a similar distinction: the most substantial portion of her personal library went to her daughter Anne de France, dame de Beaujeu and duchesse de Bourbon, while she expressly reserved a coffer containing thirty-three mostly unillustrated Latin books for study inherited from her deceased husband, as well as such a choice manuscript as Jean de Berry's *Grandes Heures*, inherited from her parents, for her son Charles VIII, thus already ensuring the continuity of a nucleus of the royal library.[4]

    Art historians are notoriously reluctant to deal with numbers, but our assessment of women's involvement in cultural affairs would surely be enhanced if we sometimes took into account the economics of collecting. In particular, it needs to be remembered that women, at least until widowhood, remained financially dependent on their husbands—who were the de facto managers of dotal funds as well. Financial restrictions not only account for the smaller size of women's collections but also explain why, and despite some spectacular exceptions, the manuscripts women commissioned or bought were less lavishly illustrated and thus less costly than were their husbands'. (Printed books will make a difference, and it is no accident that many early printers were patronized by women). Take, for instance, Margaret of York (d. 1503), the third wife of the Burgundian duke Charles le Téméraire, whose discriminating patronage was highlighted at a conference held in 1990 at the Getty Museum.[5] There is no question that Margaret was an important patron, supporting printers, such as Caxton, and commissioning some richly illuminated manuscripts, often graced with innovative iconographies. And yet, when one looks at the sheer numbers, only twenty-four manuscripts—including eight that she commissioned herself—have been ascertained to have belonged to her personally, whereas almost one thousand were owned by her husband, most of which, it is true, he inherited from his ancestors. What is even more telling is that once retired from court life, the duchess ceased to acquire manuscripts altogether, except for a handful that she gave away as gifts to the religious foundations she had endowed or, more exceptionally, a copy of *Les Fais d'Alexandre*, jointly commissioned with her stepdaughter Marie de Bourgogne, offered to their common friend Sir John Donne.

As is well known, the content of women's libraries tended to be more restricted, though there are exceptions to this rule too, especially in the case of larger collections.[6] Margaret of York may have been uncommonly pious, yet it is undeniable that the most common books owned by women were Books of Hours—decorated, in richer versions, with the portrait of the owner, say, at the beginning of the Office of the Virgin—as well as other liturgical, paraliturgical, and devotional texts.[7] In an examination of wills made by roughly one thousand owners of books in England in the fourteenth and fifteenth centuries, Susan Cavanaugh found that only fifty-three were women; but of these, thirty possessed a Book of Hours as opposed to just twenty-eight men.[8] This shouldn't come as a surprise given that piety was one of the few sanctioned cultural areas in which women could nurture their intellectual aspirations, often setting innovative trends by commissioning either new works or translations into vernacular languages of existing treatises.

Does this mean that in late medieval and early modern court society women's patronage of books is, in the end, a relatively marginal phenomenon? I would answer both yes and no. Yes, that is, if book ownership continues to be approached from the perspective of patronage alone; no, if one takes a larger view and includes the many other ways in which books were passed along and came, as it were, to life. In fact, both for men and women such alternative channels of book acquisition were more important than is generally said. Take Jean de Berry, held to be the quintessential art patron; yet between 1401 and 1416, the dates of his first and last inventory, he purchased and commissioned only about 119 objects, whereas he received 358 as gifts. And among these gifts were 78 manuscripts; that is, almost a third of his library.[9]

Yet numbers alone can hardly give an adequate sense of the meaning that books held for a collector. Queen Isabeau de Bavière (d. 1435), for example, possessed a modest library compared to that of her husband Charles VI and is not especially known for her patronage. She must nevertheless have taken a very personal interest in some of her books, because in addition to commissioning a translation of a Passion of Christ for herself, she bought several volumes, little psalters and primers, for her children as well as for various ladies attached to her court, thus in a sense creating her very own textual community.[10] This is not to say that books were, by contrast, only a matter of social prestige for men, but it is safe to assume that the smaller the library the more personal the relationship with each individual book.

Books as Inheritance
In addition to variations in size, scope, and function, distinct modes of acquisition further colored the relationship a woman had with her belongings. And even though wills, postmortem inventories, and marks of ownership offer partial and ambiguous evidence, patterns of inheritance remain one of the most fruitful ways to study how women acquired books other than by patronage. First, the fact that women outlived men and, under normal circumstances, inherited their predeceased husband's libraries explains why women, though they made fewer testaments, bequeathed books much more frequently than did their male relatives.[11] Secondly, wills are revealing not only in terms of what but also to whom one gave. Of course religious and charitable bequests as well as the provisions that had to be made for the funeral, burial, and commemorative masses, often ate a significant portion of one's fortune, whether of women or men, wealthy or not. But after settling spiritual matters, women typically designated other women as heirs of their movable property—dresses, jewels, plate, small items of furniture, books, and the like.[12] Though occasionally they went to female friends, ladies-in-waiting, or even to simple servants, daughters, followed by other close female relatives, were the usual recipients of books. In fact, Bell refers to a passage from the *Sachsenspiegel*, an early-thirteenth-century collection of Saxon customary law, which specifically enjoined mothers to bequeath their devotional books to their daughter(s).

Thus among the selection of testaments registered in Paris during the reign of Charles VI (1380–1422) published by Alexandre Tuetey, the one drawn in 1416 for Marguerite de Bruyères, a lady of the minor nobility, allocated to her two female cousins and to a niece her most prized possessions, including two books—a Book of Hours and a prayerbook in French—in the hope that she, Marguerite, "may be remembered."[13] Sometimes books contain within their own pages the evidence of their history, like the Dutch Book of Hours, inscribed with the names of six generations of female owners, mentioned by Bell. The little-known *Hours of Marguerite Crohin* (before 1552), studied by Anne-Marie Legaré, also lists at the beginning its successive owners, attesting that it was passed from mother to daughter across five generations.[14] One of the most eloquent examples of the ways in which a specific manuscript was transmitted along the female line concerns an English psalter (Leiden, Rijksuniv. Libr. MS BPL 76A). Presumably made for one of Henry II's sons, it became the property of Louis VIII; he gave it to his wife, Blanche de Castille, who used it as a primer for her son Louis IX. Less known is the subsequent history of the so-called *Psalter of St. Louis*, although it is actually spelled out in the wonderfully loquacious testament of Blanche de Navarre (d. 1398), second wife of Philippe VI de Valois, who had "inherited" it from Philippe's first wife, Jeanne de Bourgogne, who in turn got it from her mother, the Great Duchess Agnès de Bourgogne, one of the daughters of Louis IX. And the entry further affirms that the manuscript was authenticated by some ladies of Jeanne de Bourgogne's entourage, and that Blanche, who remained childless, decided to bequeath it to her step-grandson Philippe le Hardi, exhorting him to preserve this history-laden manuscript for his own successors.[15]

This is an excellent example of how books moved along a tight network of interrelated people and events, clustered for the women around education, marriage, and inheritance. Forging links across generations through meaningful objects must have been especially important for them insofar as they were increasingly excluded from the official and patrilineal chains of transmission of landed property and kinship identity, and generally only had complete authority over personal valuables, which they could pass along as they pleased.[16] Personal objects, chief among them books, thus participated in larger commemorative strategies: studded with lineal memories and special associations like the jewels that adorned their covers, books in that regard were never truly private but bore witness to a collective mode of ownership.

Along with the transmission of actual books and their familial incrustations, women would have set a model for book collecting to younger women as well. Hence veritable dynasties of female book owners, such as the now well-known English example of the FitzAllan ladies, the most conspicuous of whom, Eleanor of Bohun (d. 1399), commissioned many of the high-quality manuscripts previously ascribed to her husband Thomas, duke of Gloucester. Like her sister Mary, Eleanor inherited manuscripts from her mother, the active patron Joan FitzAllan, and in their turn, both Eleanor and Mary bequeathed a number of books to their own daughters, who continued the practice to the fourth generation of FitzAllan daughters.[17] Similarly, most French queens since Blanche de Castille (d. 1252) and, in the fifteenth century, the Burgundian, Savoy, Breton, and Bourbon duchesses in particular both set an example of patronage for their daughters, granddaughters, nieces, or stepdaughters, and passed actual books along the female line. The Burgundian case is particularly impressive, for bibliophile interest stretches without a break from Marguerite de Flandre (d. 1405), wife of the first duke of Burgundy, Philippe le Hardi, to Mary of Hungary, who along with the regency of the Netherlands, inherited the huge library of her aunt Margaret of Austria. Even Isabel of Portugal (d. 1472), third wife of Philippe le Bon, is now known, thanks to the work of Charity Cannon Willard and Claudine Lemaire, to have been more interested in books than had previously been thought. She not only commissioned some books—mostly works of piety or ones related to her Portuguese ancestry—but also introduced Christine de Pizan's *Livre des trois vertus* to her niece Isabel, queen of Portugal, who had it translated into Portuguese.[18] And she repeatedly borrowed books from the ducal library for her own use, which allows me to mention, at least in passing, that this too was another common avenue for increasing if not book ownership then at least one's access to a wider spectrum of texts.

In addition to designating individual legatees, testaments allowed a testator to attach particular requests to the bequest. The injunction to "remember me" appears most frequently; but clauses could be more specific. In 1514, Lady Elizabeth Scrope named her sister the heir of two books, a primer and a psalter, on condition that her daughter, Elizabeth Scrope's niece, "be brought up virtuously and never disagree unto the marriage to be had between her and John Cutte."[19] While in this case the possession of a book was linked to the obligation to marry, the opposite could occur just as well. Jeanne de Laval, wife of René d'Anjou, for instance, stipulated in her 1498 will that her "breviary and psalter, and her books of hours and all other books"—that is, her personal library—be entrusted to the care of the head of the chapter of the church of Laval so as to be made available to the female heirs of the counts of Laval "for as long as they are unmarried and live in that city."[20] It appears that Jeanne thought it more important to build a patrimonial (or, for that matter, matrimonial) library than to remain individually present to her female successors, yet it is interesting that this passage again forges an explicit link between women, book ownership, and marriage. By contrast, it was much more typical for men to have the right to accede to their inheritance hinge upon the successful completion of their studies or professional training.

A father could of course also designate a daughter to inherit his books, which would most typically occur in the absence of a male heir.

Though it cannot be taken as the norm, the destiny of Jean de Berry's succession is nevertheless revealing. The duke had reserved many liturgical books for religious foundations, but the better part of his splendid collection and library had essentially to be sold wholesale upon his death in 1416 in order to pay his many debts. Chief among his creditors was one of his own daughters, Marie, duchesse de Bourbon (d. 1434), herself a discriminating patron of art, who had received several manuscripts during her father's lifetime. At his death, he still owed her 70,000 livres of her dowry; it must therefore have been her very own decision to grab a lot, valued at 40,000 francs, comprising forty-one among the best of her father's manuscripts, with an agreement to forgo any further claims to her inheritance.[21] Berry's other daughter, Bonne, comtesse de Savoie, as well as his wife, Jeanne, also took some books, as did another female relative, Yolande d'Aragon, wife of Berry's nephew Louis II d'Anjou, who seized the occasion to enrich her library with the splendid *Belles Heures*, and possibly the *Très Riches Heures*. (It can here be noted parenthetically that buying lots from deceased, or confiscating them from disgraced, collectors offered another opportunity for women as for men to handily expand their holdings—looting, by contrast, appears to have been gender-specific.)

In addition to inheriting books from parents, women normally took over the books that had belonged to their predeceased husbands as well (the reverse case was far less frequent). Thus Marguerite de Flandre left at her death in 1405 more than 150 manuscripts, some of which she had brought into the conjugal fund by inheritance from her father, Louis de Mâle, count of Flanders, and her mother, Marguerite de Brabant; others which she had acquired herself; the remaining and most substantial part, however, had belonged to her husband.[22] The most impressive case remains that of Margaret of Austria. Regent of the Netherlands between 1507 and 1515 for her nephew Charles V, then governor until 1530, the two-time widow owned one of the most extensive and prized collections in her day and age. As Marguerite Debae, the publisher of her inventories, has shown, it was for the most part a "bibliophile's collection," for about 300 of the 392 books (348 manuscripts and 44 printed books) that she left at her death were medieval, that is, made before her lifetime. And while she bought a substantial lot of 78 manuscripts from Charles de Croy, a courtier who had fallen into disgrace, Margaret inherited most of the remaining 200-odd manuscripts. In addition to acceding to what remained of the library of her Burgundian ancestors upon the death of her brother Philip the Handsome, she brought back to the Netherlands ten manuscripts and nine incunabula given by her Spanish husband Juan of Castile, as well as the qualitatively excellent library of about thirty manuscripts that had belonged to her second husband, Philibert de Savoie, a transfer which had been expressly stipulated in the marriage contract.[23]

To round out our picture, we need to add those books, like Blanche de Navarre's Leiden psalter, which a woman took over from the former wife of her husband. Modern technologies, such as infrared photography, allow us to detect these often covert transfers of ownership—or, perhaps more accurately, of usufruct—and reveal how the arms and mottoes of the second wife have been superimposed onto those of the first, a palimpsest emblematic of their actual interchangeability.

Books as Gifts: Weddings

Weddings were unquestionably the single most important formal occasion on which a woman could receive a book as a gift properly speaking. It is therefore surprising that books as wedding gifts, while often mentioned in the literature, have not been studied in any depth. Yet even if in most cases the relationship has to remain conjectural, one can be certain that these books—chief among them the ubiquitous Books of Hours—must have held just as special a meaning as those that one inherited.

Most famous of all are the *Hours of Jeanne d'Évreux*, painted by Jean Pucelle (New York, Metropolitan Museum of Art, The Cloisters, MS 54.1.2). This amazing pocket-size marvel was in all likelihood given to the fourteen-year old Jeanne by Charles IV le Bel when in 1324 he took her as his third wife. The manuscript has most recently been studied in some detail by Joan Holladay, who argues that its iconography was designed to remind the young queen of the need to perform works of charity, as well as by Madeline Caviness, for whom the miniature cycle and border decorations emphasize the young queen's duty to procreate, especially pressing since Charles' previous wives had left him no male heir. Though the manuscript is, in Caviness' view, sprinkled with aggressively redundant sexual symbols, Jeanne, albeit continuously pregnant, ended up without bearing a son either, with the fatal dynastic consequences we know. (She was, however, not only exemplary in her charitable activities but also a successful patron, who, for instance, secured a portion of the books left by her predecessor Clemence of Hungary).[24]

The equally superb *Bedford Hours* (London, British Library MS Add. 18850) are thought to have been made on the occasion of the wedding of John of Lancaster, duke of Bedford, regent of France, to Anne de Bourgogne in 1423.[25] But like many others of its kind, this manuscript is strewn with the emblems and portraits of both spouses, and it blends allusions to events past and present that would have mattered to Anne and John alike, thus leaving open the question whether in fact the book was a gift from husband to wife (I know of no example of any such gift from wife to husband) or a joint commission, commemorating their wedding, to be used in the family chapel. And to complicate matters further, some scholars believe that the manuscript may in fact have been commissioned as a wedding present by Anne's brother Philippe le Bon, a hypothesis that is, as in most cases, hard to prove or disprove conclusively.

But let me continue to assume that most wedding manuscripts were in fact offered by the bridegroom, and ask why it is, after all, that books were deemed an appropriate wedding gift? Christiane Klapisch-Zuber's work on Florentine marriage customs can help us in formulating an answer, for she has best brought to light the cultural and symbolic transactions that were woven into this most crucial rite of passage in the life of a woman.[26] According to her, Florentine husbands were compelled by custom to cover their new brides with finery and jewels of a value that could be substantial when compared to the dowry brought to the marriage by the woman. Yet these gifts—a counter-prestation for obtaining both dowry and wife—were normally of a temporary nature and could be taken back from the bride even before her death. (I like to think that this disposition accounts for those manuscripts that, offered as wedding presents, were subsequently passed on to the husband's lineage, as was precisely the case with the *Hours of Jeanne d'Évreux*: the old queen bequeathed the precious manuscript to the then-reigning king, Charles V of Valois, as opposed to the other precious objects for which she expressly designated heirs, and which all went to female relatives.[27]) Klapisch-Zuber further persuasively argues that the function of such wedding gifts, peppered with the emblems of the bridegroom's family, was to proclaim the aggregation of the bride into the new lineage. Because books offer a wonderfully malleable medium, one that can be shaped to advertise the most diverse messages, it makes sense to imagine that they were similarly enlisted to proclaim the symbolic incorporation of the bride, as well as to allude, more or less heavy-handedly, to the bride's duty to procreate. Among many other examples, the portrait of Isabella Stuart in the Hours now bearing her name is in this regard particularly vivid, for she is literally coated with her father's arms of Scotland impaling those of her husband's Brittany. The irony here lies in the fact that Isabella was the second owner of this manuscript. Painted by the Rohan Master, the manuscript is thought to have originally been commissioned by Yolande d'Aragon (the same one who bought some of Jean de Berry's best manuscripts) on the occasion of the marriage of her daughter, Yolande d'Anjou, to François I de Bretagne—but as in a *damnatio memoriae*, Yolande has been scratched out to make space for Isabella, François's second wife.[28]

This manuscript thus is an example of a mother giving a book as a wedding gift, and it is possible that Yolande d'Aragon also commissioned the celebrated *Hours of Rohan*, this time for the projected wedding, which in the end never materialized, of her youngest son, Charles, with a daughter of

Alain IX de Rohan.[29] Bell in fact surmised that "there may have been a general practice of mothers commissioning books as wedding gifts for their daughters," though she unfortunately failed to adduce any evidence.[30]

One can assume that when a mother gave her child a book upon her marriage, this parting gesture was equivalent to a pre-mortem bequest, a way to encapsulate in a concrete object a bond that might otherwise be marked by lifelong physical separation. At the same time, powerful mothers, such as Yolande d'Aragon, particularly when as widows they were primarily in charge of their offspring, were just as likely as fathers to use their children as capital to be invested in the highly competitive aristocratic marriage market. Manuscripts dotted with heraldic emblems of both the bridegroom's and bride's families, then, also proudly publicized the newly contracted alliance between two lineages.

A comparable figurative logic governs manuscripts that were offered as wedding gifts by true marriage brokers, the ambassadors that rulers dispatched across Europe to negotiate profitable marriage contracts for their children. A prime example is the richly illuminated collection of French romances commissioned by John Talbot, first earl of Shrewsbury, which he gave to Marguerite d'Anjou when she married King Henry VI in 1445 (London, British Libr. MS Royal 15.E.VI). Marguerite (d. 1482) was the daughter of the enlightened art patron King René d'Anjou, and it is therefore not altogether surprising that Talbot, who had spent over twenty years in France and knew the bride well, would choose a manuscript for this purpose. Yet Michel-André Bossy has rightly stressed how the manuscript's content and iconography, while flattering the queen's taste, were massaged in such a way as to serve Talbot's self-promotion as well; how, for instance, in the miniature prefacing Christine de Pizan's *Le Livre des fais d'armes et de chevalerie* he willfully replaced the expected presentation miniature with a male-to-male exchange showing the king in the act of giving him the sword of his office as marshal of France. How also, and more disturbingly, in the opening genealogical page, Marguerite's portrait, which should have appeared next to that of her husband, has been elided, supplanted by her emblems and a bunch of daisies, penetrated by a tentacle that spouts from the main stem.[31]

Francisco de Rojas was another courtier who, like Talbot, offered a book, the so-called *Isabella Breviary* (London, British Library, Add. Ms. 18851), as a wedding gift. Unusually, however, in this case the manuscript was presented not to the bride but to the mother, Queen Isabella the Catholic, simply because she was Rojas's patron and had charged him, presumably in return for a fitting reward, with the task of negotiating the double wedding of two of her children—John of Asturias and Joanna, later known as the Mad, to Margaret and Philip of Austria respectively.[32]

Our picture of books offered on the occasion of a marriage would not be complete if we did not include those books that were brought into the marriage by the bride as part of her trousseau, and which, in principle at least, remained her personal property, though in practice they were often integrated into the dotal fund, and thus fell under the husband's administration. This is the category that most fully bears out Bell's characterization of women as "cultural ambassadors," for the trousseau was composed of objects from a bride's country of origin, as was famously the case with Anne of Bohemia and the Bible in German and Czech that she brought to England upon her marriage to Richard II. Yet any woman of some means carried at least one book—yes, the unavoidable Hours, perhaps received from her mother—in her wedding "basket."[33] In the case of aristocratic women, dowries and trousseaux could be of staggering proportions. A well-documented example concerns Valentina Visconti, who in 1387 was married to the brother of the French king Charles VI, Louis d'Orléans. The marriage contract stipulated that she bring 300,000 golden florins in addition to a wealth of precious objects, including no less than 150 diamonds, 28 emeralds, 310 sapphires, 425 rubies, and more than 7,000 pearls—an enormous dowry, which had been extracted for the most part from the subjects of Giangaleazzo Visconti, Valentina's father and ruler of Milan. We are so well informed in this case because when Valentina finally arrived in Paris, two years after the marriage had been celebrated by proxy, an official inventory of the goodies that had accompanied her was taken. This survives, along with a Latin copy sent by an obviously delighted Louis to his father-in-law. Valentina also brought along twelve books, all but one of which were devotional; some in Latin, others in Italian, two in German. Once in France, Valentina steadily added to this personal collection, for the inventory taken upon her death registers at least twenty-six items, including manuscripts dedicated to her, like Honoré Bouvet's *Apparition de Jean de Meung* and possibly Christine de Pizan's *Livre de la description de la prudhomie*.[34]

Though there now is ample literature on the subject of late medieval dowries and trousseaux in Italy, those in France have not been studied much at all, and at this point it is often unclear what the legal status of particular objects was: the famous *Belleville Breviary*, painted by Jean Pucelle for Jeanne de Belleville about 1325, for instance, is described in sources as being "given" by Charles VI to his daughter Isabelle's bridegroom, Richard II, on the occasion of their marriage (Richard's second) in 1395—but given as a wedding gift? Or was it part of her dowry? Her trousseau?

Book as Gifts: "Étrennes"

In addition to weddings, there was at least one other major formal occasion on which books were offered: New Year's Day or the *étrennes*. Functionally equivalent to our Christmas, this was the single most important date for exchanging gifts among nobles from the latter part of the fourteenth century onward.. Because the *étrennes* provide a well-documented if not much examined sampling of gift-giving practices, they enable us to cast a glance from yet another perspective on gender-specific patterns in the circulation of books. In general, it appears that women participated in this official exchange of gifts in a more sporadic fashion than men, and when they did, they found themselves, as with wedding gifts, more often than not on the receiving end. According to the statistics established by Jan Hirschbiegel, who has provided a systematic study of New Year's gifts for the reign of Charles VI, among the 144 named donors of *étrennes*, only 22 were women (that is, about 15 percent); conversely, of 298 named recipients, 67, or 22.5 percent, were women, headed by Valentina Visconti and Queen Isabeau de Bavière.[35]

Somewhat unexpectedly, books, including de-luxe copies, were not a very popular New Year's gift among peers of the ruling elite; instead they preferred to offer jewels and plate made of precious materials. If we refer to Jean de Berry once more, we can see that according to his inventories he received 22 manuscripts on New Year's Day but 178 *joyaux*; still, that put him easily above anyone else, presumably because donors, well aware of his bibliophile appetites, sought thus to curry favor with him and secure his patronage. For while only a small fraction of books were exchanged among the nobility, they were significant gifts in asymmetrical relationships, and the better part of the manuscripts offered as *étrennes* came from the various ranks of courtiers—secretaries, counselors, household members, important prelates, or merchants dealing in luxury products. And that accounts in part for the fact that no manuscript was either given or received by a woman as an *étrenne*, leaving aside, for the moment, Christine de Pizan. It needs to be remembered that a woman's household was still predominantly staffed with men, save for the low-skilled servants (nannies, wet nurses, chamber women, laundresses) or the equally low-skilled if ceremonially crucial ladies-in-waiting. Obviously there were no female clerics; but there were no female doctors, top household officials, or major merchants either. And while it is true that Anne de Bretagne, ahead of her time, employed women as secretaries, and that others could be entrusted with the care of books—Catherine de Villiers, a lady-in-waiting of Isabeau de Bavière or Valentina Visconti's keeper of manuscripts, Marguerite de Solier, come to mind—these women seem not to have offered books; unlike, say, Gilles Malet, the distinguished librarian of Louis d'Orléans and Charles V, who was a regular donor of manuscripts. I remains unclear if the rule that, as argued by Pierre Cockshaw, women were "prevented from receiving gifts of manuscripts other than from their husbands or close relatives"[36] is why they were not offered books during one of the most public settings for gift exchanges; certainly, it agrees with Mary Beth Wynn's findings, explored in this volume, about contemporaries' appreciation, or rather lack thereof, of Louise de Savoie's role as a "bibliophile."

The lonely and formidable exception to the absence of women from the *étrennes* is, not altogether surprisingly, Christine de Pizan. It is obvious that Christine realized the importance of this occasion, for she presented four books to Jean de Berry on New Year's Day (the *Livre des fais et bonnes meurs de Charles V* in 1405, redirected to Berry after the one who commissioned it, Philippe le Hardi, had died before its completion; an allegorical commentary on the Seven Penitential Psalms in 1410; the *Livre des fais d'armes et de chevalerie* in 1413; the *Livre de la paix* in 1414); to Philippe le Hardi, she gave as an *étrenne* in 1404 the *Livre de la mutacion de Fortune*; and a copy of the *Débat des deux amants*, dedicated to Louis d'Orléans, to Charles d'Albret. Yet belying the uniqueness of a gift, Christine knew how to protect herself—and the considerable financial investment that an illuminated manuscript represented for a writer—by repeatedly issuing her books in multiple copies that she sent to different patrons.[37] And like her contemporary Eustache Deschamps, she also resorted to the financially altogether safer strategy of composing and dedicating poems in a genre that came later to be known as *étrenne*, poems that made gifts out of words.[38] The fact that Christine de Pizan was the only woman to offer books within the framework of such a highly visible avenue for the giving of gifts must have contributed in no small way to singling her out even more as a "novelty."[39] At the same time, she must have been well aware of the greater resources men commanded as patrons, for how else are we to explain that all of her dedications, save for a few exceptions, were addressed, and gift copies offered, to men?

Besides being a consummate practitioner of gift giving, Christine was an equally fine theorist of largesse, a topic that she revisited in writings throughout her life. Drawing in particular on Cicero, she commended Charles V for understanding that the true meaning of liberality consists in a mixture of material benefits and behavioral norms. Chapter XIV on the "liberality of princes" in the *Livre du corps de policie* similarly argues for a moral meaning of largesse, the magnanimity of the soul, as when a ruler forgives prisoners and enemies, or tries to alleviate the pains of the sick and the poor. In the female pendant to the *Livre du corps de policie*, the *Livre des trois vertus*, Christine likewise includes a chapter (XX) on a princess's need to practice largesse. Her advice closely follows the precepts she espouses for men, such as the key requirement to give in a measured way, one that is equidistant from the two excesses of avarice and prodigality. And she also reiterates the belief that generosity consists not only in material gifts but can express itself in comforting words to someone in distress, wise counsel, the ability to forgive, and generally in a charitable attitude as an outward manifestation of the munificence of one's mind. But as a public virtue, largesse comes rather late in her compendium of desirable virtues for noble women, late especially when compared to the more prominent place it occupies in the male treatise.[40]

To some degree, then, Christine followed her contemporaries in endorsing a gender-specific conception of gift giving along the public-private axis. And though never absolute, this polarity remains a helpful conceptual tool, for it encompasses not only the ways in which women read and interpreted texts and images differently from men, or even the kinds of texts that where available to them, but also the ways in which they actually obtained books. Moreover, the public-private paradigm, which of course structured much of late medieval and early modern social life along gender lines, nicely resonates with what anthropologists have observed about gift giving in general, namely that "transacting is the political activity of men *par excellence*;"[41] that the distribution of wealth tends to be played out in a public arena for men, whereas it is much more likely to be confined to the private sphere for women, even when the same kinds of objects are used in both contexts; and, finally, that social and political power is generated only by those exchanges that a society considers to be public. Feminist critiques of anthropological theories of exchange and, in particular, Annette B. Weiner's influential *Women of Value, Men of Renown*, have gone further, however, by arguing that gift giving is a practice where *different* forms of power and control over resources, both real and symbolic, are exerted.[42] Thus, in her studies of the Trobriand Islands, Weiner has highlighted how women are in charge of "the regeneration of matrilineal identity" at particularly crucial junctures of the life cycle, of which birth, marriage, and death are the foremost. And it is during these highly charged events that women engage in intense exchanges of "women's wealth"—skirts and bundles of banana leaves, objects redolent of associations with sexuality, reproduction, and nurture. As such—and this is the crucial insight—women's exchanges become a structuring principle of the society as a whole, and therefore acquire the kind of sociopolitical and economic dimension usually associated only with men's transactions.

Even though much more work is needed to refine the picture I've sketched, it remains unquestionable that, statistically speaking, European women, too, circulated books and other valuables not so much through official channels of exchange but in relation to such salient events in their lives as the education of children, marriage, and death. Yet it does not follow that they could not simultaneously occupy the more prestigious and, I would say, more male position of a patron. What is unfortunate is that this latter model has eclipsed all others—not so much historically, but in modern accounts of past book ownership. Seduced by the narratives that one can plot between individual patrons and authors and artists, male or female, the study of patronage has largely been oblivious of the more subterranean networks of relatives, friends, and allies among which the majority of books, some new, many old, were passed along on significant occasions.

Smith College

NOTES

1. Susan Groag Bell, "Medieval Women Book Owners: Arbiters of Lay Piety and Ambassadors of Culture," Signs 7, no. 4 (1982): 742–68; repr. in Women and Power in the Middle Ages, ed. Mary Erler and Maryanne Kowaleski (Athens: University of Georgia Press, 1988), 149–87.
2. This seems to have been less true in the 14th than in the 15th century. Clemence of Hungary (d. 1328), for instance, owned 18 books in Latin and 21 in French; by contrast, the library of her husband, King Louis X, numbered only 30-odd titles and was not as diversified (see Léopold Delisle, Le Cabinet des manuscrits de la Bibliothèque impériale [Paris: Imprimerie Impériale, 1868–81], 1:12, and the Bulletin du Bibliophile, 2d ser., 16 [1837]: 561–63, for her inventory). The library of Clemence's contemporary Mahaut d'Artois (d. 1329) was one of the most celebrated, though in the absence of an inventory it is hard to judge its extent beyond the 25 books attested in a partial listing (see Jules-Marie Richard, Une Petite-nièce de saint Louis, Mahaut, comtesse d'Artois et de Bourgogne, 1302–1329: Étude sur la vie privée, les arts et l'industrie, en Artois et à Paris au commencement du XIVe siècle [Paris: H. Champion, 1887], 99–106.)
3. Pascale Thibault, Les Manuscrits de la collection d'Anne de Bretagne (Blois: Amis de la Bibliothèque de Blois, 1991), and esp. Michael Jones, "Les Manuscrits d'Anne de Bretagne, reine de France, duchesse de Bretagne," Mémoires de la Société d'Archéologie de Bretagne 55–56 (1978): 43–81.
4. See Anne-Marie Legaré in this volume. Also Ursula Baurmeister and Marie-Pierre Laffitte, Des Livres et des rois: La bibliothèque royale de Blois (Paris: Bibliothèque Nationale, 1993), 74–75.
5. Margaret of York, Simon Marmion, and "The Visions of Tondal," ed. Thomas Kren (Malibu: The J. Paul Getty Museum, 1992), catalogue no. 24. See also Muriel J. Hughes, "Margaret of York, Duchess of Burgundy: Diplomat, Patroness, Bibliophile, and Benefactress," Private Library 3d ser., 7 (1984): 2–17 and 53–78.
6. A little-known but very interesting exception is offered by the richly eclectic library, comprising more than 200 titles, personally owned by Gabrielle de La Tour (d. 1474), wife of Louis de Bourbon, comte de Montpensier, and mother of the Gabrielle de Bourbon discussed here by Jennifer Britnell. Published by Louis de la Trémoille in Annuaire-Bulletin de la Société de l'Histoire de France 17 (1880): 269–309.

7. See Geneviève Hasenohr, "L'Essor des bibliothèques privées aux XIVe et XVe siècles," in *Histoire des bibliothèques françaises*, vol. 1, *Les bibliothèques médiévales du VIe siècle à 1530*, ed. André Vernet (Paris: Promodis, 1989), in part. 249.
8. Quoted after Sandra Penketh, "Women and Books of Hours," in *Women and the Book: Assessing the Visual Evidence*, ed. Lesley Smith and Jane H. M. Taylor (London: British Library, 1997), 266–81.
9. His inventories were published by Jules Guiffrey, *Inventaires de Jean duc de Berry, 1401–1416* (Paris: E. Leroux, 1894–96). See also Delisle, Le Cabinet, 1:56–68.
10. Auguste Vallet de Viriville, *La Bibliothèque d'Isabeau de Bavière, femme de Charles VI, roi de France* (Paris: J. Techener, 1858); originally published in the *Bulletin du Bibliophile*, 3d ser., 14 (1858): 663–87.
11. Joel T. Rosenthal, "Aristocratic Cultural Patronage and Book Bequests, 1350-1500," *Bulletin of the John Rylands University Library of Manchester* 64 (1982): 522–48, analyzing wills made by English nobles between 1350 and 1500, shows that while 48 percent of women bequeathed books only 18 percent of men did.
12. Martha C. Howell, "Fixing Movables: Gifts by Testament in Late Medieval Douai," *Past & Present* 150 (1996): 3–45.
13. Alexandre Tuetey, *Testaments enregistrés au Parlement de Paris sous le règne de Charles VI* (Paris: Imprimerie Nationale, 1880), 341.
14. The manuscript is now Copenhagen, Kongelige Bibliothek MS Thott 542 4o. See Anne-Marie Legaré, "Livres d'heures, livres de femmes: Quelques exemples en Hainaut," *Eulalie* 1 (1988): 53–68, with further useful insights on female book ownership.
15. "Item nous laissons à nostre très chier fils le duc de Bourgongne le psaltier où monseigneur saint Loys aprint; et fu à madame la grant duchesse Agnès, duchesse de Bourgogne, sa fille; et depuis la duchesse Agnès vint à nostre dicte dame la royne Jehanne de Bourgongne, sa fille; et en après à nostre dit seigneur et espoux qui nous le donna, et nous tesmongna, et aussi firent les femmes de la dicte madame la royne qu'il [sic] nous bailla que c'estoit icellui vraiement. Si desirons qu'il soit à la ligne. Et pour ce prions à nostre dit filz que il le vueille garder et faire tenir à ses successeurs et en sa ligne, pour l'amour de ceulx dont il est venu." Léopold Delisle, "Testament de Blanche de Navarre, reine de France," *Mémoires de la Société de l'Histoire de Paris et de l'Île-de-France* 12 (1885), no. 200. See also Patrick M. de Winter, *La Bibliothèque de Philippe le Hardi, duc de Bourgogne (1364–1404): Étude sur les manuscrits à peintures d'une collection princière à l'époque du "style gothique international"* (Paris: Éditions du Centre National de la Recherche Scientifique, 1985), 260–61. Notwithstanding Blanche's injunction, the manuscript disappeared from the Burgundian library after the death of Charles le Téméraire.
16. Carol Meale, "Laywomen and Their Books in Late Medieval England," in *Women and Literature in Britain, 1150–1500*, ed. Carol M. Meale (Cambridge: Cambridge University Press, 1993), 130–31.
17. Karen K. Jambeck, "Patterns of Literary Patronage: England, 1200–ca.1475," in *The Cultural Patronage of Medieval Women*, ed. June Hall McCash (Athens: University of

Georgia Press, 1996), 228–65. She describes some other such families, including the powerful female descendents of Joan Beaufort.

18. Charity Cannon Willard, "The Patronage of Isabel of Portugal," in *The Cultural Patronage*, 306–20; and Claudine Lemaire, "Remarques relatives aux inventaires de la librairie de Bourgogne réalisés en 1467–69, 1477, 1485, 1487 et aux manuscrits des duchesses," *Scriptorium* 48, no. 2 (1994): 294–98.

19. Rosenthal, "Aristocratic Cultural Patronage," 549. For a similar wording in bequeathing small possessions to a female servant and a niece, see the testament of Simonette La Maugère published by Tuetey, *Testaments enregistrés*, 383.

20. Published by Anne-Marie Legaré in "Reassessing Women's Libraries in Late Medieval France: The Case of Jeanne de Laval," *Renaissance Studies* 10, no. 2 (1996): 209–36.

21. Delisle, *Le Cabinet*, 1:64–65. The dowry was, of course, generally considered to be a daughter's pre-mortem inheritance.

22. Patrick M. de Winter, *La Bibliothèque de Philippe*, 142–74, and Muriel J. Hughes, "The Library of Philip the Bold and Margaret of Flanders, first Valois duke and duchess of Burgundy," *Journal of Medieval History* 4 (1978): 145–88.

23. Marguerite Debae, *La Bibliothèque de Marguerite d'Autriche: Essai de reconstitution d'après l'inventaire de* 1523–24 (Louvain: Peeters, 1995). On the Savoyard library, see Agostino Paravicini Bagliani, ed., *Les Manuscrits enluminés des comtes et ducs de Savoie* (Turin: Allemandi, 1991).

24. Madeline H. Caviness, "Patron or Matron? A Capetian Bride and a Vade Mecum for Her Marriage Bed," Speculum (April 1993); repr. in *Studying Medieval Women: Sex, Gender, Feminism*, ed. Nancy F. Partner (Cambridge, Mass.: Medieval Academy of America, 1993), 31–60; and Joan A. Holladay, "The Education of Jeanne d'Évreux: Personal Piety and Dynastic Salvation in Her Book of Hours at the Cloisters," *Art History* 17, no. 4 (1994): 585–611.

25. Janet Backhouse, *The Bedford Hours* (London: British Library, 1990).

26. For instance, Christiane Klapisch-Zuber, "The Griselda Complex: Dowry and Marriage Gifts in the Quattrocento," in *Women, Family, and Ritual in Renaissance Italy*, trans. Lydia G. Cochrane (Chicago: University of Chicago Press, 1985), 213–46. Also of fundamental importance is Diane Hughes Owen, "From Brideprice to Dowry in Mediterranean Europe," *Journal of Family History* 3 (1978): 262–96. And, for a discussion of visual artifacts as part of marriage transactions, see Adrian W.B. Randolph, "Performing the Bridal Body in Fifteenth-Century Florence," *Art History* 21, no. 2 (1998): 182–200.

27. Her inventory, comprising 20 books, was published by Paulin Paris in the *Bulletin du Bibliophile*, 2d ser., 16 (1837): 492–94.

28. The manuscript is now Cambridge, Fitzwilliam Museum MS 62. See John Harthan, *The Book of Hours: Illuminated Pages from the World's Most Precious Manuscripts* (New York: Thomas Y. Crowell, 1977), 114–17.

29. Paris, Bibl. Nat. de France MS lat. 9471. See most recently François Avril and Nicole Reynaud, *Les Manuscrits à peintures en France, 1440–1520* (Paris: Flammarion,

1993), 26, as well as *The Rohan Book of Hours*, introduction and commentary by Marcel Thomas (London: Thames and Hudson, 1973).
30. Bell, "Medieval Women Book Owners," 165.
31. Michel-André Bossy, "Arms and the Bride: Christine de Pizan's Military Treatise as a Wedding Gift for Margaret of Anjou," in *Christine de Pizan and the Categories of Difference*, ed. Marilynn Desmond (Minneapolis: University of Minnesota Press, 1998), 236–56.
32. Janet Backhouse, *The Isabella Breviary* (London: British Library, 1993), and Thomas Kren, ed. *Renaissance Painting in Manuscripts: Treasures from the British Library* (New York: Hudson Hill Press, 1983), 40–48. Rojas also commissioned two copies of the marriage treaty itself.
33. *Corbeille* was the common name for the trousseau. On Florentine trousseaux, see Christiane Klapisch-Zuber, "Les Corbeilles de la mariée," in *La Maison et le nom: Stratégies et rituels dans l'Italie de la Renaissance* (Paris: Éditions de l'École des Hautes Études en Sciences Sociales, 1990), 214–27.
34. Valentina's dowry has been discussed most extensively by Jules Camus in *La Venue en France de Valentine Visconti, duchesse d'Orléans, et l'inventaire de ses joyaux apportés de Lombardie* (Turin: François Casanova, 1898). For her library, see Pierre Champion, *La Librairie de Charles d'Orléans* (Paris: H. Champion, 1910), lxxii–lxxiii.
35. Jan Hirschbiegel, "Étrennes: Untersuchungen zum höfischen Geschenkverkehr im spätmittelalterlichen Frankreich der Zeit König Karls VI (1380–1422) am Beispiel der Neujahrsgeschenke," 2 vols., Ph.D. diss., University of Kiel, 1997, 1:142–49. It will be available shortly in published form, as will my "Past Presents: New Year's Gifts at the Valois Courts, ca. 1400." For 16th-century examples, see Lisa M. Klein, "Your Humble Handmaid: Elizabethan Gifts of Needlework," *Renaissance Quarterly* 50, no. 1 (1997): 459–93, as well as Myra D. Orth in this volume.
36. Pierre Cockshaw, "Some Remarks on the Character and Content of the Library of Margaret of York," in Thomas Kren, *Margaret of York*, 57.
37. For a study of how different dedications affected the decorative program of a particular work, see Sandra L. Hindman, *Christine de Pizan's "Epistre Othéa": Painting and Politics at the Court of Charles VI* (Toronto: Pontifical Institute of Mediaeval Studies, 1986). Natalie Zemon Davis, "Beyond the Market: Books as Gifts in Sixteenth-Century France," *Transactions of the Royal Historical Society*, 5th ser., 33 (1983): 69–88, mentions only one women in the 16th century who dedicated books, the Lyonnais printer Antoinette Peronet, who, like Christine de Pizan, was widowed with children to support. On women dedicating manuscripts, see Myra D. Orth, "Dedicating Women: Manuscript Culture in the French Renaissance, and the Cases of Catherine d'Amboise and Anne de Graville," *Journal of the Early Book Society* 1, no. 1 (1997): 17–47.
38. Christine de Pizan, *Œuvres poétiques*, 3 vols., ed. Maurice Roy (Paris: Firmin Didot, 1886–96), 1: nos. 16, 18–21, and 36; and Eustache Deschamps, *Œuvres complètes*, 11 vols., ed. Auguste Henry Edouard Queux de Saint-Hilaire and Gaston Raynaud (Paris: Firmin Didot, 1878–1903), 3: nos. 496 and 531.

39. This is how she explains her meteoric success as a writer in *Lavision-Christine*, ed. Louis Towner (Washington, D.C.: Catholic University of America, 1932), 165; trans. Glenda K. McLeod, *Christine's Vision* (New York: Garland, 1993), 120.

40. Christine de Pizan, *Le Livre des fais et bonnes meurs du sage roy Charles V*, ed. Suzanne Solente (repr., Geneva: Slatkine, 1977), 1:79–82; *Le Livre du corps de policie*, ed. Angus J. Kennedy (Paris : H. Champion, 1998), 23–26, trans. Kate Langdon Forhan, *The Book of the Body Politic* (Cambridge: Cambridge University Press, 1994), 25–28; *Le Livre des trois vertus*, ed. Charity Cannon Willard in collaboration with Eric Hicks (Paris : H. Champion, 1989), 77–80, trans. Charity Cannon Willard, A *Medieval Woman's Mirror of Honor: The Treasury of the City of Ladies* (New York: Bard Hall Press, 1989), 115–17.

41. As formulated by Lisette Josephides in *The Production of Inequality: Gender and Exchange among the Kewa* (London and New York: Tavistock, 1985), 220.

42. Annette B. Weiner, *Women of Value, Men of Renown: New Perspectives in Trobriand Exchange* (Austin: University of Texas Press, 1976). See also her more recent *Inalienable Possessions: The Paradox of Keeping-While-Giving* (Berkeley: University of California Press, 1992).

WORKS CITED

Avril, François, and Nicole Reynaud. *Les Manuscrits à peintures en France, 1440–1520*. Paris: Flammarion, 1993.

Backhouse, Janet. *The Bedford Hours*. London: British Library, 1990.

———. *The Isabella Breviary*. London: British Library, 1993.

Baurmeister, Ursula, and Marie-Pierre Laffitte. *Des Livres et des rois: La bibliothèque royale de Blois*. Paris: Bibliothèque Nationale, 1993.

Bell, Susan Groag. "Medieval Women Book Owners: Arbiters of Lay Piety and Ambassadors of Culture." *Signs* 7, no. 4 (1982): 742–68. Reprinted in *Women and Power in the Middle Ages*, edited by Mary Erler and Maryanne Kowaleski, 149–87. Athens: University of Georgia Press, 1988.

Buettner, Brigitte. "Past Presents: New Year's Gifts at the Valois Courts, ca. 1400." Forthcoming.

Bossy, Michel-André. "Arms and the Bride: Christine de Pizan's Military Treatise as a Wedding Gift for Margaret of Anjou." In *Christine de Pizan and the Categories of Difference*, edited by Marilynn Desmond, 236–56. Minneapolis: University of Minnesota Press, 1998.

Bulletin du Bibliophile, 2d ser., 16 (1837): 561–63 (inventory of Clemence of Hungary).

Camus, Jules. *La Venue en France de Valentine Visconti, duchesse d'Orléans, et l'inventaire de ses joyaux apportés de Lombardie*. Turin: François Casanova, 1898.

Caviness, Madeline H. "Patron or Matron? A Capetian Bride and a Vade Mecum for Her Marriage Bed." In *Studying Medieval Women: Sex, Gender, Feminism*, edited by Nancy F. Partner, 31–60. Cambridge, Mass.: Medieval

Academy of America, 1993. Originally published in *Speculum* (April 1993).

Champion, Pierre. *La Librairie de Charles d'Orléans*. Paris: H. Champion, 1910.

Cockshaw, Pierre. "Some Remarks on the Character and Content of the Library of Margaret of York." In *Margaret of York, Simon Marmion, and "The Visions of Tondal,"* edited by Thomas Kren, 57. Malibu: The J. Paul Getty Museum, 1992.

Davis, Natalie Zemon. "Beyond the Market: Books as Gifts in Sixteenth-Century France." *Transactions of the Royal Historical Society*, 5th ser., 33 (1983): 69–88.

Debae, Marguerite. *La Bibliothèque de Marguerite d'Autriche: Essai de reconstitution d'après l'inventaire de 1523–24*. Louvain: Peeters, 1995.

Delisle, Léopold. *Le Cabinet des manuscrits de la Bibliothèque impériale*. Paris: Imprimerie Impériale, 1868–81.

———. "Testament de Blanche de Navarre, reine de France." *Mémoires de la Société de l'Histoire de Paris et de l'Île-de-France* 12 (1885): 1-64.

Deschamps, Eustache. *Œuvres complètes*. 11 vols. Edited by Auguste Henry Édouard Queux de Saint-Hilaire and Gaston Raynaud. Paris: Firmin Didot, 1878–1903.

Guiffrey, Jules. *Inventaires de Jean duc de Berry, 1401–1416*. Paris: E. Leroux, 1894–96.

Harthan, John. *The Book of Hours:Illuminated Pages from the World's Most Prrecious Manuscripts*. New York: Thomas Y. Crowell, 1977.

Hasenohr, Geneviève. "L'Essor des bibliothèques privées aux XIVe et XVe siècles." In *Histoire des bibliothèques françaises*, vol. 1, *Les bibliothèques médiévales du VIe siècle à 1530*, edited by André Vernet, part 249. Paris: Primodis, 1989.

Hindman, Sandra L. *Christine de Pizan's "Epistre Othéa": Painting and Politics at the Court of Charles VI*. Toronto: Pontifical Institute of Mediaeval Studies, 1986.

Hirschbiegel, Jan. "Étrennes: Untersuchungen zum höfischen Geschenkverkehr im spätmittelalterlichen Frankreich der Zeit König Karls VI (1380–1422) am Beispiel der Neujahrsgeschenke." 2 vols. Ph.D. diss., University of Kiel, 1997.

Holladay, Joan A. "The Education of Jeanne d'Évreux: Personal Piety and Dynastic Salvation in Her Book of Hours at the Cloisters." *Art History* 17, no. 4 (1994): 585–611.

Howell, Martha C. "Fixing Movables: Gifts by Testament in Late Medieval Douai." *Past & Present* 150 (1996): 3–45.

Hughes, Muriel J. "Margaret of York, Duchess of Burgundy: Diplomat, Patroness, Bibliophile, and Benefactress." *Private Library*, 3d ser., 7 (1984): 2–17 and 53–78.

———. "The Library of Philip the Bold and Margaret of Flanders, First Valois Duke and Duchess of Burgundy." *Journal of Medieval History* 4 (1978): 145–88.
Jambeck, Karen K. "Patterns of Literary Patronage: England, 1200–ca.1475." In *The Cultural Patronage of Medieval Women*, edited by June Hall McCash, 228–65. Athens: University of Georgia Press, 1996.
Jones, Michael. "Les Manuscrits d'Anne de Bretagne, reine de France, duchesse de Bretagne." *Mémoires de la Société d'Archéologie de Bretagne* 55–56 (1978): 43–81.
Josephides, Lisette. *The Production of Inequality: Gender and Exchange among the Kewa*. London and New York: Tavistock, 1985.
Klapisch-Zuber, Christiane. "Les Corbeilles de la mariée." In *La Maison et le nom: Stratégies et rituels dans l'Italie de la Renaissance*, 214–27. Paris: Éditions de l'École des Hautes Études en Sciences Sociales, 1990.
———. "The Griselda Complex: Dowry and Marriage Gifts in the Quattrocento." In *Women, Family, and Ritual in Renaissance Italy*, translated by Lydia G. Cochrane, 213–46. Chicago: University of Chicago Press, 1985.
Klein, Lisa M. "Your Humble Handmaid: Elizabethan Gifts of Needlework." *Renaissance Quarterly* 50, no. 1 (1997): 459–93.
Kren, Thomas, ed. *Renaissance Painting in Manuscripts: Treasures from the British Library*. New York: Hudson Hill Press, 1983.
———. *Margaret of York, Simon Marmion, and "The Visions of Tondal.": Papers Delivered at a Symposium Organized by the Department of Manuscripts of the J. Paul Getty Museum in Collaboration with the Huntington Library and Art Collections, June 21-24, 1990* Malibu: The J. Paul Getty Museum, 1992.
La Trémoille, Louis de. "Inventaire des bijoux, vêtements, manuscrits et objets précieux appartenant à la comtesse de Montpensier, 1474." *Annuaire-Bulletin de la Société de l'Histoire de France* 17 (1880): 269–309.
Legaré, Anne-Marie. "Livres d'heures, livres des femmes: Quelques exemples en Hainaut." *Eulalie* 1 (1988): 53–68.
———. "Reassessing Women's Libraries in Late Medieval France: The Case of Jeanne de Laval." *Renaissance Studies* 10, no 2 (1996): 209–36.
Lemaire, Claudine. "Remarques relatives aux inventaires de la librairie de Bourgogne réalisés en 1467–69, 1477, 1485, 1487 et aux manuscrits des duchesses." *Scriptorium* 48, no. 2 (1994): 294–98.
Meale, Carol. "Laywomen and Their Books in Late Medieval England." In *Women and Literature in Britain, 1150–1500*, edited by Carol M. Meale, 130–31. Cambridge: Cambridge University Press, 1993.
Orth, Myra D. "Dedicating Women: Manuscript Culture in the French Renaissance, and the Cases of Catherine d'Amboise and Anne de Graville." *Journal of the Early Book Society* 1, no. 1 (1997): 17–47.

Owen, Diane Hughes. "From Brideprice to Dowry in Mediterranean Europe." *Journal of Family History* 3 (1978): 262–96.
Paravicini Bagliani, Agostino, ed. *Les Manuscrits enluminés des comtes et ducs de Savoie*. Turin: Allemandi, 1991.
Paris, Paulin. "Livres de Jeanne d'Évreux, Reine de France, Femme de Charles le Bel, de 1325 à 1370." *Bulletin du Bibliophile*, 2d ser., 16 (1837): 492–94.
Penketh, Sandra. "Women and Books of Hours." In *Women and the Book: Assessing the Visual Evidence*, edited by Lesley Smith and Jane H. M. Taylor, 266–81. London: British Library, 1997.
Pizan, Christine de, *Œuvres poétiques*. 3 vols. Edited by Maurice Roy. Paris: Firmin Didot, 1886–96.
———. *Lavision-Christine*. Edited by Louis Towner. Washington, D.C.: Catholic University of America, 1932. Translated by Glenda K. McLeod as *Christine's Vision*. New York: Garland, 1993.
———. *Le Livre des fais et bonnes meurs du sage roy Charles V*. Edited by Suzanne Solente. Reprint, Geneva: Slatkine, 1997.
———. *Le Livre des trois vertus*. Edited by Charity Cannon Willard in collaboration with Eric Hicks. Paris: H. Champion, 1989. Translated by Charity Cannon Willard as *A Medieval Woman's Mirror of Honor: The Treasury of the City of Ladies*. New York: Bard Hall Press, 1989.
———. *Le Livre du corps de policie*. Edited by Angus J. Kennedy. Paris: H. Champion, 1998. Translated by Kate Langdon Forhan as *The Book of the Body Politic*. Cambridge: Cambridge University Press, 1994.
Randolph, Adrian W.B. "Performing the Bridal Body in Fifteenth-Century Florence." *Art History* 21, no. 2 (1998): 182–200.
Richard, Jules-Marie. *Une Petite-nièce de saint Louis, Mahaut, comtesse d'Artois et de Bourgogne, 1302–1329: Étude sur la vie privée, les arts et l'industrie, en Artois et à Paris au commencement du XIVe siècle*. Paris: H. Champion, 1887.
The Rohan Book of Hours. Introduction and commentary by Marcel Thomas. London: Thames and Hudson, 1973.
Rosenthal, Joel T. "Aristocratic Cultural Patronage and Book Bequests, 1350–1500." *Bulletin of the John Rylands University Library of Manchester* 64 (1982): 522–48.
Thibault, Pascale. *Les Manuscrits de la collection d'Anne de Bretagne*. Blois: Amis de la Bibliothèque de Blois, 1991.
Tuetey, Alexandre. *Testaments enregistrés au Parlement de Paris sous le règne de Charles VI*. Paris: Imprimerie Nationale, 1880.
Vallet de Viriville, Auguste. *La Bibliothèque d'Isabeau de Bavière, femme de Charles VI, roi de France*. Paris: J. Techener, 1858. Originally published in the *Bulletin du Bibliophile*, 3d ser., 14 (1858): 663–87.
Weiner, Annette B. *Inalienable Possessions: The Paradox of Keeping-While-Giving*. Berkeley: University of California Press, 1992.

———. *Women of Value, Men of Renown: New Perspectives in Trobriand Exchange*. Austin: University of Texas Press, 1976.

Willard, Charity Cannon. "The Patronage of Isabel of Portugal." In *The Cultural Patronage of Medieval Women*, edited by June Hall McCash, 306–20. Athens: University of Georgia Press, 1996.

Winter, Patrick M. de. *La Bibliothèque de Philippe le Hardi, duc de Bourgogne, 1364–1404: Étude sur les manuscrits à peintures d'une collection princière à l'époque du "style gothique international."* Paris: Éditions du Centre National de la Recherche Scientifique, 1985.

Charlotte de Savoie's Library and Illuminators
ANNE-MARIE LEGARÉ

Charlotte de Savoie (c. 1442-1483), the second wife of Louis XI, had a sizable personal library. The majority of the manuscripts that have been identified as belonging to her are housed today in the collections of France's Bibliothèque Nationale.[1] But these constitute only a very small portion of her library, as is shown by the inventory made after her death and other archival documents. They confirm that she had her own book collection, distinct from that of her husband. In this, the queen followed the example of other princesses and high-ranking ladies of France.[2] The goal of this paper is threefold: to bring together the different archival sources concerning Charlotte de Savoie's book patronage, to give an account of the research on this subject, and to add some new elements to the long-standing but meager dossier on the reconstitution of her library. It is worth noting that there are gaps in the documents, especially between 1523 and 1673, which make it difficult to confirm beyond doubt attributions that are already weakened by the absence of owners' marks on most of the preserved manuscripts.

State of the Question

In the inventory of Charlotte de Savoie's property, more than one hundred books are listed. The extracts concerning her library are part of the document estimating her moveable assets, which was written in Tours in 1484, a year after her death.[3] It was first published in 1865 by Alexandre Tuetey.[4] The archivist suggested, without taking a definitive stand, relationships between certain articles in the inventory and manuscripts in the collections of the Bibliothèque Nationale de France. These are Paris, B.N.F., MSS Fr. 997, 1821, 1841, 1875, respectively nos. 85, 32, 58, and 34 in the Table of Concordances and Identifications appended in this paper. Three years later, Léopold Delisle,[5] in the process of reclassifying the books in a methodical manner, recognized four works that were undeniably executed for Charlotte de Savoie: Paris, B.N.F., MSS Fr. 407-408 (Fig. 1), 449 (Fig. 2), 1813, and 2222 (Fig. 3), respectively nos. 89, 92, 84 and 109 in the Table.

Other manuscripts have since been identified: a Vie de saint Julien dedicated to Charlotte de Savoie by Guillaume Danicot [49],[6] studied by Charles Samaran;[7] a Vie et office de sainte Radegonde [31] in which François Avril recognized a portrait of the queen and her coat of arms (Fig. 4);[8] a sumptuous book of hours called the Heures de Charlotte de Savoie, containing, in eleven of the thirteen miniatures, the coats of arms of France, Savoy, and France impaling Savoy, probably added after 1451, the year of Charlotte's marriage to the future Louis XI (Fig. 5);[9] a prose Pèlerinage de vie humaine [77] by Guillaume de Digulleville, bearing the queen's coat of arms, which recently reappeared on the market (Fig. 6).[10]

Several authors have attributed to the queen's personal library a Vie de saint Adrien that has a full-page miniature depicting Louis XI and Charlotte de Savoie kneeling before Saint Adrien and which bears the arms of France and Savoy.[11] It is more likely that the king rather than the queen would have appreciated a book containing the life of a warrior saint; in any case, the book does not figure in the inventory of the queen's library. A Book of Hours bearing the arms of France and Savoy as well as those of the abbey of Saint Victor of Paris was acquired by Chicago's Newberry Library in 1991. Here again we have a book of prayers that was probably destined for the king.[12] And finally, a Livre des trois vertus a l'enseignement des dames to the arms of Urfé, written by Jehan Gardel of Tours "serviteur de madite Dame" cannot be identified with the one in Charlotte's inventory in which it is said to be richly illuminated ("bien historié") [30]. A close examination of this manuscript shows that it was never intended to be illustrated.[13]

Thirteen new manuscripts that correspond to the inventory of Charlotte de Savoie's library were identified by François Avril in the collections of the Bibliothèque Nationale: MSS Fr. 300, 316, 445 (Fig. 7), 916 (Fig. 8), 1009, 1045, 1801, 1835, 1836, 2101 and 2234, Lat. 919 and Lat. 10525, respectively nos. 1, 80, 12, 87, 79, 20, 91, 101, 96, 27, 19, 97, and 6 in the Table appended. These unpublished findings, generously communicated by Mr. Avril, have served as the basis for my own research at the Département des Manuscrits.

My own contribution was aided by a judicious remark[14] formulated in 1878 by A.-M. Chazaud at the beginning of his new edition of the inventory of the library of the dukes of Bourbon in Moulins dated September 19, 1523.[15] The archivist suggested that the queen's books must have "passed through the hands of her daughter, before entering the library of the château de Moulins."[16] Thus I have taken up my research based on this edition, without, however, overlooking the edition published a few years earlier by Leroux de Lincy.[17] The two editions complete and correct each other, but even a collation of the two does not give the full picture, having both gaps and errors.[18] Chazaud indicated with an asterisk thirty-five items that were also present in the queen's inventory but failed to correctly identify any surviving manuscript. A careful reading of the two inventories enabled me to identify fourteen manuscripts belonging to the queen and housed today in Chantilly, Musée Condé, MSS 36, 37 and 38 [15 and 38 in either order], 138 [39], 143 [56], 145 [26], 153 [76], 154 [48], 158 [72], 159 [43], 615 [47], 685 [13] and 741 [42] and in the Bibliothèque Nationale (MS Fr. 12538 [21]).

The Library in the Château of Moulins
Many but not all of the manuscripts mentioned in Charlotte de Savoie's inventory passed through the hands of her daughter Anne de France and Pierre de Beaujeu into the Bourbon library at the château of Moulins. At least four manuscripts, however, remained at Amboise under Charles VIII, for they ended up in the library installed at Blois by Louis XII: Paris, B.N.F., MSS Fr. 300, 316, 449 (Fig. 2) and Latin 919, respectively 1, 80, 92 and 97 in the Table.[19] Another forty or so do not figure at all in the inventory of the Bourbon library. At present only two of these have been identified: the Psalter of Saint Louis [6] which Charlotte had borrowed from a "dame de Poissy" and which was to be returned to her by Anne (B.N.F., MS Lat. 10525); the *Pèlerinage de vie humaine* in prose [77] which is now the property of Heribert Tenschert (Fig. 6). We can assume that those of Charlotte's books that are mentioned in the Moulins inventory remained in the Bourbon family until 1523, when following the execution of the Connétable de Bourbon for treason, François Ier immediately transferred the choicest pieces into the royal library. The queen's manuscripts, however, do not seem to figure among these initial confiscations. Indeed, none of them are described in the inventory made in 1544 when the royal library was transferred from Blois to Fontainebleau.[20]

Those of Charlotte's books that came into the royal collections were probably kept apart. A small number, for example, have the classification marks and titles characteristic of the manuscripts that were placed in the personal library of François Ier (Paris, B.N.F., MSS 2099, 2101 and 2222 (Fig. 3), respectively nos. 49, 27, and 109 in the Table).[21] Most of the books appear for the first time in the king's inventory that was made at the end of the sixteenth century, when the royal collections were transferred to Paris.[22]

After the royal confiscations, the remnants of the library at Moulins seem to have been quietly forgotten until 1660, when they were appropriated by the Grand Condé (Louis II de Bourbon), to whom the Peace of the Pyrenees had given Bourbonnais in exchange for Albret. They figure in the inventory of the Hôtel de Condé drawn up in Paris in 1673.23 This explains their presence today at Chantilly.[24]

It is worth noting that none of these works contains a mark of ownership and that only a few bear traces of their passage through the Bourbon library. Not surprisingly, these books are all modest productions, transcribed on paper and mostly without illumination. It seems that in 1660 the prince de Condé only found leftovers. One exception is the *Livre de la Passion*, which has thirteen miniatures. The most beautiful items had already been appropriated for the royal collections or had found their way into other hands. This is the case of *La Vie et office de sainte Radegonde* [31] (Fig. 4) and the illuminated *Pèlerinage de vie humaine* in prose [77] (Fig. 6), and no doubt other prayerbooks today in various collections, containing the arms of France and Savoy.

A Portrait of Queen Charlotte[25]

Charlotte was the youngest daughter of Louis, duc de Savoie, and of Marie de Chypre. Born about 1442, she was married at the age of eight in 1451 to the Dauphin Louis XI, widower of Mary Margaret of Scotland. The marriage took place despite the opposition of her father and of Charles VII but was not consummated until she passed her fifteenth birthday. Unfortunately for Louis XI, this new union did not bring him the promised dowry of 400,000 écus d'or, but rather the modest sum of 15,000 livres and a pension of only 5,000 écus d'or.[26]

The queen gave Louis XI six children. Her first-born, Joachim, died in the year of his birth, 1459. Similarly, her second child, Louise, was born and died in 1460. The following year saw the birth of Anne, future Dame de Beaujeu. She was raised with the greatest of care, loved books, and proved to be well-informed and wise—"la moins folle femme de France" according to her father–but of a haughty and imperious temperament.[27] In 1474 she married Pierre de Beaujeu, youngest son of Charles I of Bourbon and Agnès de Bourgogne. Louis XI expressed total confidence in his daughter and son-in-law, and on his deathbed he entrusted them with management of his affairs.

The queen's other daughter, Jeanne "dite la Boiteuse," born in 1464, was sickly and hunchbacked, and did not receive the same favors as her older sister. Separated from her mother at a young age, Jeanne knew the sorrow of abandonment and isolation at the château of Lignières where she resided until the death of her father, when Charlotte was able at last to procure her a room at Amboise.[28]

Charles, the long-awaited son, was born June 30, 1470, followed by François in 1472, who died of the plague a year later.[29] Of delicate health, the future Charles VIII was sent by his father to Amboise, which was less exposed than Tours to the dangers of the plague. There he was raised by Madame des Tournelles[30] and Jean Bourré. When Louis XI died, on August 30, 1483, thirteen-year-old Charles was placed under the tutelage of his sister and brother-in-law, Anne and Pierre de Beaujeu. Charlotte de Savoie died a few months after her husband, on December 1, 1483, and was buried with him at Cléry.

It is the fine portrayal of Charlotte de Savoie by Alfred Gandilhon that has served subsequent historians of the court of Louis XI in their descriptions of the gentle and loving wife of a fairly inconsiderate husband. "Small and brunette, without any great beauty," according to Commynes, she was not a woman "in whom one would take great pleasure," but she was simple, not extravagant, and played her role as "une honneste et noble dame". Her contemporaries found her looks rather unprepossessing,[31] leaving us the image of a fairly unattractive woman whose features were certainly less regular and serene than in the portrait recognized by François Avril in her personal copy of the Vie de sainte Radegonde[32] (Fig. 4). We have a few other early pictures of the queen. One is a miniature on the first folio of the Douze Périls d'enfer [92], where she is supposed to represent the wife of Charles VII, Marie d'Anjou, to whom the volume is dedicated (Fig. 2). Another is a drawing in the famous collections of portraits in the Recueil d'Arras.[33] Finally, there are two eighteenth-century watercolors executed for Gaignières[34] depicting Charlotte de Savoie in a dress embroidered with the arms of France and Savoy. These are copies of a stained-glass portrait of her in the Ave Maria Convent which she founded in Paris toward the end of her life.[35]

The chronicles do not show any trace of political activities on the part of Queen Charlotte, except her royal entries into Amiens in 1464 and Paris in 1467, her visit to the home of the duc de Bourgogne in Hesdin in 1464, and her presence at the reception for the Hungarian ambassadors in 1466. In fact, her only recorded activities were those of aiding the disinherited and educating children at her own expense. She appears as a very timid woman, self-effacing, spending little, and then only on good works rather than countless luxuries. The inventory of her personal possessions does not let us imagine any excesses in clothing, jewels, or precious objects. Despite her status as spouse of the king of France, she received a pittance for her household expenses. Nicolas de' Roberti, an Italian ambassador visiting in Touraine, mentions "her poverty," saying that when she wanted to visit a church, she had only two carts covered with leather and a dozen horsemen, which was apparently unusually austere compared to the royal standards of the time.[36] Her pleasures, as deduced from her belongings, included needlework, card games, chess, marbles and spillikins,[37] whereas her preferences in reading ran to works of devotion, moral treatises, and the lives of saints.

Charlotte de Savoie's Inventory

Paul Chauvin and Guillaume Bourdaize, sworn notaries from Tours, took several months in 1484 to compile the postmortem inventory of the queen's possessions. The whole of her belongings had been transported to the townhouse of Sir Jean Briçonnet, which explains their being regrouped in several locked leather trunks.

The manuscripts were placed in some of these trunks, along with other objects.[38] Nestled among numerous black dresses and their accessories, we find the second volume of Jean Mansel's Fleur des histoires [1], bearing the arms of Charlotte's son-in-law, Pierre de Beaujeu. In another trunk, among an assortment of dresses, sheets, velvet and fur collars, blankets and rugs, bedclothes, small amber and ivory boxes, and coral-decorated ribbons, we find objects of more personal value: a papal hat,[39] "a picture of the Nativity, with the queen's arms, not estimated," and "a large ivory table," possibly for playing games.[40] There are also three books in this lot, which I gather were probably more intimately linked with the daily life of the queen: a "small Psalter, not estimated" [2], a "large book on paper, entitled Boucasse, Des Cas des nobles hommes" [4], and her most sumptuous prayerbook, "a Book of Hours covered with black velvet, with gold fittings and four little pearls and four little rubies, not estimated" [3].

The inventory of Charlotte de Savoie's books gives almost no information about their value; only one of the manuscripts described had been appraised: "Item, une heures, couvertes de veloux noir a fremouers d'or, extiméees XXV escuz"[41] [110]. The mention of material—whether parchment or paper—is not systematic. However, the surviving manuscripts on paper are described in the inventory as "sur papier," whereas the support of the surviving manuscripts on parchment is not always mentioned.[42] According to the statements of the inventory, forty manuscripts are on paper, thirty-two on parchment, one on paper and parchment, and thirty-eight have no mention of the material used. If those for which no material is specified are on parchment, one can estimate that more than half of her books (63 per cent) were on parchment.

Little attention is paid to the aesthetic quality of the manuscripts: only six books (five of which still survive) are described as being historiated (ystoriés [6, 87, 104]), well historiated (bien ystoriés [30, 92 (Fig. 2)]), or fully historiated (tout ystorié [83]). Nevertheless, we can confidently assume that the descriptions that stress certain elements of the binding[43] (like the clasps or ornaments of precious metal), or the fact that they were preserved in a leather bag, or bore coats of arms, concern books with decorated elements.[44] Only one printed book, "ung livre en pappier, escript en mosle, nommé le Nouveau Testament, couvert de cuir fauve"[45] was itemized in the queen's inventory [*11 bis].

Louis XI's manuscripts

Apart from her personal manuscripts, Charlotte's inventory includes the description of a certain number of books that clearly belonged to Louis XI. The inventory is quite precise in this respect: "Item, ung grant coffre, a fest, couvert de cuir noir, ferré de fer blanc, estant en la gallerye de dehors a Amboyse, ouquel coffre estoient les livres du feu roy Loys, et en icelluy la feue royne que Dieu absoille n'y vouloit toucher, mais vouloit qu'ils feussent baillez et renduz au roy son filz."[46] Thus we see that Charlotte had gathered together books from her husband's collection to be given as heirlooms to her son, Charles VIII. The inventory itemizes thirty-three manuscripts in the trunk. The list of these manuscripts was published by Léopold Delisle, but it does not concern us here.[47]

Another twenty-two books apparently belonged to Louis XI.[48] Not only are they gathered together in a small trunk along with other objects bearing the royal colors, but three of them also bear the king's arms.[49] The trunk also contained a purse of red and white satin in which were found "... une gibeciere de sainct Jacques, et plusieurs enseignes de plomb, et ung petit lingot d'argent ..." as well as "... l'ordre du roy, d'or, en laquelle pend ung sainct Michiel,[50] lequel est en ung estuy de cuir roge, poisant six onces deux gros, extimé LIIII écus," and little paper packets whose contents are not specified. The "order of Saint Michael" surely belonged to the king, as probably did the badges, for Louis was more keen on pilgrimages than the queen, who was disinclined to travel. Should we follow the lead of Delisle[51] and include these books in the list of the queen's possessions, or should we consider them as a separate group belonging to the king? We could consider those books containing Louis XI's arms as gifts to Charlotte. However, the deaths of the king and queen were separated by only four months, which may expain why books apparently belonging to Louis are listed in Charlotte's inventory.

La Congratulation et graces de la nativité de Charles aisné fils du roy Loys unziesme de ce nom [109][52] is listed as found in a trunk, along with items of silver (a saltcellar, candle holder, small dish, burning mirrors,[53] a bracelet that protected against poisoning, and other pieces), a few crystal rosaries, a mother-of-pearl cross, a "small silver inkstand covered in black, weighing two ounces, estimated at 11 écus," and the like. The author of *La Congratulation*, Guillaume Danicot, a monk from Saint-Julien in Auvergne, was Louis XI's historian, but he dedicated to the queen his translation of *La Vie de saint Julien de Vienne* [49].[54] Charlotte so appreciated Danicot that she asked Pope Paul II to provide him with a secular benefice so that he could devote himself to preaching, for which he had a natural aptitude.[55]

La Congratulation is an official dynastic text, whose contents relate to prince Charles and his parents. The arms on the shield painted on folio 1 are " parties de France et de Savoie,⁵⁶ supported by two angels, indicating the union of the king and the queen (Fig. 3). However, Christian de Mérindol has refused to accept La Congratulation as belonging to the queen, believing this to be an erroneous attribution that originated with Delisle.⁵⁷ He considers the work to be exclusively a reflection of the king's preoccupations, noting that Louis had a particular devotion to "the Virgin's belt," a relic especially venerated by barren women, housed at the church of Puy-Notre-Dame, near Saumur.⁵⁸ It hardly seems likely, however, that Charlotte would have been left out of the picture. Indeed, a few years later, Anne de Bretagne borrowed the Virgin's belt, in September 1495, in order to enhance the fertility of her union with Charles VIII.⁵⁹ It is quite probable that Charlotte de Savoie, who had already lost two sons in infancy, was closely associated with the devotional activities of her husband. In 1470, the king went to Puy-Notre-Dame at least twice during Charlotte's pregnancy and again at the birth of Charles (on pilgrimage February 28, again in April, and in July-August). On the July 15, two weeks after the birth, he gave 160 écus d'or (equivalent to 220 livres tournois) for the fabrication of a statue in silver representing his infant son, which was to be placed on the high altar. Given the price paid, André Lapeyre has deduced that the weight of the statue, five kilos, corresponds with that of a two-month-old infant.⁶⁰

The arguments that seek to invalidate the attribution of the manuscript to the queen are even less convincing, given that the book appears in the inventory of Moulins, among the books that Anne de Beaujeu most probably inherited from her mother, and not in the library of Charles VIII.⁶¹

I have certain reservations about the last two articles in the inventory [**110 and **111], which were placed in the same trunk with La Congratulation. This is why I have marked them with a double asterisk. Les Heures [**110], bound in black velvet with gold clasps, could ultimately have belonged to Charlotte de Savoie. But what should we make of the Vie de saint Servais [**111], which on the one hand contains the king's arms, and on the other does not appear in the inventory of Moulins?

Loans and Gifts

Charlotte de Savoie's inventory attests to the practice of lending books. The queen had borrowed three manuscripts: the superb Psautier de saint Louis [6], which she intended to return to the nun at Poissy, from whom she had borrowed it, after her death; a small book in parchment, called Le Livre des Espitres et Euvangilles de tout l'an [99], bound in leather, which belonged to Madame de Segré;⁶² and a copy of the Miroir historial by Vincent de Beauvais [80], lent to her by Louis de Laval, seigneur de Châtillon. Louis de Laval had apparently recovered the manuscript from among the books of Jacques d'Armagnac, duc de Nemours. The inventory states that the queen had ordered the work to be returned to the seigneur de Châtillon, but the order was not respected and the manuscripts remained in the royal collections.[63] This is not the only one of Louis de Laval's manuscripts to figure in Charlotte de Savoie's inventory: three other volumes of Froissart's *Chroniques* owned by the duke, are also found among Louis XI's books.[64]

Among the possible gifts given to the queen, one notes *La Fleur des histoires* by Jean Mansel (B.N.F. MS Fr. 300 [1]), bearing the arms of Pierre de Beaujeu, the queen's son-in-law.[65] The work was not returned to its owner by his wife, Anne of France, but passed into the royal collections, as is attested by the topographical inscription used at Blois, which still exists in this manuscript.[66]

Also in the queen's library were the *Grandes Heures du duc de Berry* [97], which passed into the hands of her son, Charles VIII, after her death.[67] Another gift is mentioned in the inventory, a "large book bound in red, that Monseigneur de Maillé gave her" [93]. The donor is Hardouin IX, baron de Maillé, seigneur of Rochercorbon, Montils-les-Tours, counselor and chamberlain to the king, still in service in 1487. It is he who gave Louis XI's mother "... ung dour de licorne que le roy donna et envoya a la royne sa mere par Monsgr de Maillé, non extimé"; that is, a unicorn's horn, which Charlotte de Savoie seems to have inherited, since it is found in her inventory.[68]

Some of the extant manuscripts that I believe should be attributed to Charlotte de Savoie's library bear coats of arms other than her own, which can cast doubt on their having belonged to the queen. However, they fit in perfectly with the practice of loans or gifts that has been well attested in the inventory. Whereas, for example, the *Lamentations de saint Bernard* [87] (Fig. 8), "bound in black velvet and historiated," was written by a scribe who worked for Jacques d'Armagnac, the remains of black velvet on the inner sides of the binding covers are enough to dispel any doubts about this being the manuscript in Charlotte's library. How did it come into the queen's hands? Two hypotheses have been advanced by Nicole Reynaud: either the book was unfinished at the time Jacques was put to death for treason in 1477, and was available on the market, or it may have passed to Charlotte from her son-in-law, Pierre de Beaujeu, who was in charge of confiscating the deceased duke's library at Carlat.[69] Considering the queen's modest means, the latter hypothesis seems more probable.

Other books came to the queen by various means. One of the copies of the *Château Périlleux* [12] (Fig. 7) was transcribed for Messire Estienne Chotard, bursar for "Mesdames de Saint-Laurent," nuns of the Benedictine abbey of Saint Laurent in Bourges. The *Passion de Jésus-Christ* in French at Chantilly bears the arms of Louis of Bourbon-Montpensier and his wife, Gabrielle de La Tour, flanked by their initials.[70] No other manuscript owned by the couple seems to have come into the Bourbon library. The book must either have been a gift from Gabrielle before her death in 1477, or from Louis, who survived his wife by a dozen years.

Le Livre qui parle du prêtre de l'église et de la messe [43] appears in the 1523 inventory of Moulins, and also at the Hôtel de Condé in 1673.[71] The parchment flyleaf contains an elegantly calligraphed dedication stating that Catherine d'Alençon[72] ordered it for the queen: "Ce present traicté a esté compousé par frere Olivier Le Rouyer, frere mineur de l'observance [indigne (crossed out)] professeur en theologie, demourant ou couvent de Laval. A la requeste de tres redoubtee dame madame Katherine de Alençon, contesse de Montfort, lequel traité donné a la Raigne. A la Raigne."[73] Clearly, the queen referred to here is not Anne de Bretagne, as was asserted in the Chantilly catalogue, but Charlotte de Savoie.[74]

The Queen's Favorite Reading
The libraries of other great ladies of the late medieval aristocracy do not greatly resemble that of the queen, where ascetic spirituality and religious morality take precedence over literature or history. This contrast is readily visible in the comparative table established by Geneviève Hasenohr for twelve French princesses. Almost three quarters of Charlotte de Savoie's books are religious works. Only the inventories of Blanche of Navarre (inventory of 1398) and of Margaret of York (manuscripts recorded in 1503), with works of morality and spirituailty constituting 74 per cent and 83.5 per cent respectively, exceed the percentage of 71.5 per cent in the inventory of Queen Charlotte.[75]

Geneviève Hasenohr has also stressed the role the queen played in encouraging the composition of devotional literature, calling upon Jean Saulnier, Jean Henri, Pierre des Arpentis, Robert Ciboule, an innovator in the genre, and many others.[76] Dominated by works on asceticism and spirituality such as the Montagne de contemplation by Jean Gerson [22], the Visions de sainte Catherine de Sienne [42], the Horloge de sapience by Henri Suso [12], or Ludolphe de Saxe's Vita Jesu Christi [89], Charlotte's collection was undoubtedly one intended to bring daily solace to a reclusive soul.

The queen seems to have enjoyed religious theater, a taste she shared with her sister-in-law Yolande de Savoie.[77] Charlotte owned a "Livre de la Resurrection Nostre Seigneur en pappier, couvert de roge et par personnages" [47], which corresponds with the Mystère de la Résurrection, a mystery play in 10,000 lines lasting three days and involving 105 roles. It was performed at Angers in 1465 in the presence of René d'Anjou.[78] Her "Livre de la vie de sainct Vincent" [21] matches a Vie et mystère de saint Vincent en vers et par personnages at the Bibliothèque Nationale (MS Fr. 12538), a mystery play in 15,000 verses, lasting three days and involving fifty-nine roles, which was performed in 1471, again in the presence of king René and his wife, Jeanne de Laval.⁷⁹ This attribution is based on the following observations. No "life" of Saint Vincent is attested in French, and it is quite common for mystery plays of saints' lives to be referred to as *"livre de la vie. . ."* in late medieval inventories. Furthermore, in the Moulins inventory, the text is described as *"La Passion sainct Vincent*, rythmé, en papier, a la main," and indeed the mystery is rhymed.⁸⁰ Finally and perhaps most conclusively, MS Fr. 12538 is the only copy of the text.

On folio 213v,⁸¹ the canon of Angers and abbot of Mélinays⁸² René De la Barre gives his authorization for the play to be performed in 1476 in the Benedictine "prieuré" of Le Lude, also called Raillon, under the supervision of prior Johannes Jousbert.⁸³ The manuscript, although today housed at the Bibliothèque Nationale, comes from the collection at Moulins and passed through that of Bourbon-Condé, as attested by the binding; it was probably seized at the Revolution and was never returned to the duc d'Aumale.

We can also detect in a variety of books the queen's maternal preoccupations: the panoply of the "mirrors of princes" is nearly complete, from the treatises of Gilles de Rome [37] and Jacques de Cessoles [51] to the recent *Jardin des nobles* [98] by the Cordelier Pierre des Gros. Similar titles appear in the royal collections, but also in more modest libraries of the period.

The presence of *Enseignements* written especially for women is quite predictable, including Geoffroi de La Tour Landry's *Enseignements à ses filles* [54] and three works by Christine de Pizan, *Le Livre de la cité des dames* [29], *Le Livre des trois vertus a l'enseignement des dames* [30], and *L'Epistre d'Othea* [70]. Christine was the most frequently represented fifteenth-century author in women's libraries at the end of the Middle Ages.

It is more difficult to discern the areas of interest in secular literature. Charlotte's library contains no chansons de geste, no romances in verse from the twelfth or thirteenth centuries, no *Roman de la Rose* or Arthurian romances. It does, however, contain several "romans" from the west of France—*Ponthus et Sidoine* [23], *Cleriadus et Meliadice* [40], *L'Abuzé en court* [65]—as well as works inspired by folklore like *La Belle Mélusine* [24] or *Pierre de Provence et la belle Maguelonne* [45]. There are also two French translations of the *De casibus* by Boccacio [4 and 9], whose success was widespread. As for translations of classical texts, they are practically nonexistent, except for *Le Livre de Boece de Consolation* [41], a work that was found in the libraries of several princesses.⁸⁴

"Escripvains" and Artisans of the Book

As we have seen, the queen's dowry was modest. However scanty, the accrued income enabled her to maintain her books in good condition. On

August 31, 1463, she paid the "escripvain" Jean Goislart forty-five sous tournois for having trimmed thirty-five parchment leaves for holding pilgrimage badges, and having then sewn and bound them between two boards covered with dark leather; the payment was also for having copied the "Heures de la Madeleine" and other prayers on five quires of parchment that he had himself supplied the preceding year (Appendix, 1).[85] Charlotte not only saw to the repair of her frequently used books, but also ordered new ones. In October of 1469, Louis Pigault, *sommelier* of her chapel, was paid twenty sous tournois for having bought ruled paper to be used to write two books for her.[86] Four months later, in March 1470 (N.S.), he was given twenty livres tournois for having written several books "at the request of the aforementioned lady" (Appendix, 2.1 and 2.2). In this same month and in April, Frère Pierre Thiery cleaned, repaired, and rebound the queen's Book of Hours, described as "completely falling apart" (Appendix, 2.3 and 2.4). In August, Guillaume Geobault had a burse made in black leather for her book of hours (Appendix, 2.6). In September, she bought from Regnault Fylolle, who also worked for the king, "two dozen parchments" for a scribe in her employ (Appendix, 2.7).[87] In 1482, shortly before her death, she paid fifteen sous to Jean Villet for having written and illuminated two quires of prayers that he would insert into her Book of Hours (Appendix, 3.2). Given the modest cost of the project, the "illumination" surely means ornamentation of the initial letters only. Finally, in 1483, Jean de Manseul, chief clerk to the queen, was paid "for the writing of several small books of devotion..." (Appendix, 7).

Unfortunately, none of the manuscripts just described in the accounts can be identified with those that still exist today. Nevertheless, the latter give indications (literary, stylistic, prosopographic, codicological) that point toward specific areas of production. Several of Charlotte de Savoie's contemporary manuscripts, whether richly illuminated or soberly conceived, have some relationship (composition, fabrication, provenance, etc.) with Laval, Tours, or Bourges.

Laval
Chantilly, Musée Condé, MS 159, *Le livre qui parle du prêtre, de l'église et de la messe* [43]; composed by Frère Olivier Le Rouyer, living in the convent of Laval.

Tours
Paris, B.N.F., MS Fr. 407-8, Ludolphe de Saxe, *Vita Christi*, French translation [89], Tours, 1482 (Fig. 1). These two volumes are particularly well documented thanks to two lists of the queen's expenses dated 1482 (Appendix, 3.1 and 4), which mention Thibaut Bredinc "bookmaker liv-

ing in Tours," and Guillaume Piqueau "illuminator living in Tours."[88] The second volume was illuminated by Jean Colombe probably in Tours.[89]

Paris, B.N.F., MS Fr. 449, Robert Blondel, *Les Douze Périls d'enfer* [92], illuminated by Jean Colombe in Tours or Bourges, about 1480 (Fig. 2).

Paris, B.N.F., MS Fr. 916, *Lamentations* of Saint Bernard, followed by various spiritual treatises [87], executed in Tours, c. 1470. The thirteen miniatures are by the Master of Jean Charpentier, an illuminator who was no doubt from the Touraine and whose style is closely related to that of Jean Fouquet (Fig. 8).

Paris, B.N.F., MS Fr. 1813, *Préparation du saint Sacrement de l'autel* [84], a text which begins with a decorative border frame by an artist from the Touraine, including, in the lower part, the arms of Charlotte de Savoie in a lozenge-shaped medallion.

Paris, B.N.F., MS Fr. 1821, *Le Réducteur de l'âme* [32] with decorative elements indicating that the manuscript was executed in the Touraine c. 1470-80.

Paris, B.N.F., MS Fr. 1835, Jean Gerson, *Le Secret Parlement de l'homme à son âme* [101], a treatise on spiritual mendicancy, followed by *La Montagne de consolation*; the penwork decoration seems to be by the same hand as MSS Fr. 407 (Fig. 1) and 408, which would situate its execution at Tours c. 1480.

Bourges

Chantilly, Musée Condé, MS 138, *Le Legiloque* [39], a copy with very elegant decoration, was written by Estienne Fauvre, priest, October 12, 1476. The only watermark on the paper is attested at Bourges (medallion with the arms of the Coeur family) in 1470 in the *Délibérations capitulaires de la cathédrale* and later in the accounts of the Sainte-Chapelle.[90] The paper comes from a mill established near the abbey of Saint-Sulpice in Bourges; at the time, the abbot was the archbishop Jean Coeur, son of Jacques Coeur. Papers from this mill were used for a long time in Bourges and the area.[91]

Paris, B.N.F., MS Fr. 445, Robert le Chartreux, *Le Château Périlleux* [12], which according to the colophon (fol. 215v) was copied by Thomas Valery, priest in Bourges, for the bursar of the Benedictine nuns of Saint-Laurent in Bourges, and illuminated by a certain Jean Pion, who is otherwise unknown (Fig. 7).[92] It is tempting to agree with Paul Chenu, who suggested that this is the same Jehan Pion whose daughter married, on March 20, 1499, Geoffroy de Tuffon, a stained-glass painter living in Bourges.[93]

The Manuscript Painters

Like other queens and princesses, Charlotte de Savoie was an important patron of the arts, calling upon such illustrious painters as Jean Colombe,

CHARLOTTE DE SAVOIE'S LIBRARY 45

Jean Poyer (Poyet) and Jean Bourdichon. On the other hand, certain artists who are only mentioned in the archival sources have little chance of ever emerging from the shadows. Such is the case of the Touraine painter Jean de Launay, paid for having executed ten miniatures in 1470. He illustrated a *Livre des aveugles* [33] that belonged to the queen but remains unknown to this day. It is interesting that this manuscript does not appear in the queen's inventory. Jean de Launay also painted a "pourtraicture de deux visaiges" at her request (Appendix, 2.5).

Jean Colombe
We have already seen that Jean Colombe illustrated at *least two* manuscripts for Charlotte de Savoie: *Les Douze Périls d'enfer* [92] (Fig. 2) and the second volume of a *Vita Christi* [89]. The queen's interest in this artist appears in a letter on his behalf, addressed to Monsieur Dubouchage in Bourges (Appendix, 5). This letter is perhaps the basis of the painter's success, unless it reflects an already established renown, thanks notably to the patronage of Louis de Laval, one of his best clients.[94] It is signed by the queen and by René Tardif, her secretary who remained at her service at least ten years, from 1469 to 1479.[95] The document is undated, but it is known that Ymbert de Batarnay, Seigneur du Bouchage, received a commission from the "governor of Bourges" in the spring of 1478. Thus it dates, at the very earliest, from this period and probably not after 1479, but it refers to the queen's previous numerous requests to the municipality. It is likely, as Louis Thuasne showed some time ago,[96] that she profited from Batarnay's recent commission to renew her request, which means that Jean Colombe was working in Bourges at the time, and had already been working for some time, on one of the manuscripts destined for the queen. It may have been the *Douze Périls d'enfer* [92], completed about 1480, one of the most elaborate works executed for the queen, with a frontispiece and pictures placed at the beginnings of each of the twelve chapters (Fig. 2).[97]

Charlotte de Savoie may have placed another substantial order with Jean Colombe while he was in her service between 1469 and 1479. This would have been the *Heures d'Anne de France*, painted in Bourges between 1473 and 1475 by Jean Colombe and assistants. The inclusion of the arms of France, as well as the richness of the painted decorations (107 full-page miniatures, 24 calendar illustrations), has led some scholars to consider this manuscript a gift from the queen to her daughter shortly before her marriage to Pierre de Beaujeu in 1474, since the arms of her future husband are not included.[98]

Finally, a *Vie de nostre benoit Seigneur Jésus Christ* also includes *La Sainte Vie de Nostre Dame* and *L'Exposition du Miserere mei Deus*, illustrated with 130 miniatures attributed to the artist's early period, perhaps patterned after a model sent from Savoy to the queen.[99] This hypothesis advanced by François Avril is based on the existence of another copy of the text, copied in October 1473 for Antoine d'Orlier, one of the chief counselors of the duchesse de Savoie, Yolande de France.[100]

After the queen's death, Jean Colombe was employed by her brother, Charles I, duc de Savoie. The duke may have done so on the recommendation of Charlotte, a decision which he was not to regret, since as soon after as 1486 he granted Colombe the title of "son familier et enlumineur de livres." The duke asked him to complete two superb manuscripts that had come into his possession: the *Très Riches Heures de Jean de Berry* (Chantilly, Musée Condé, MS 65), for the illumination of which Colombe received payment in 1485, and a splendid *Apocalypse* (Escorial, MS E. Vit. 5), bearing the arms and emblems of the Savoy dukes, for which he was paied four hundred florins in 1490.[101]

Jean Poyer[102]

The work of Jean Poyer seems to have dominated illumination in Tours during the period 1480-1520. His work has been reconstructed by François Avril and Nicole Reynaud, as well as by Janet Backhouse and John Plummer.[103] Our knowledge of his activities, which formerly relied mainly on sources published by Charles de Grandmaison and Jules Guiffrey,[104] has recently been enriched by Roger Wieck[105] and by Pierre-Gilles Girault's publication of new documents.[106]

One of these documents shows that Jean Poyer, along with a mysterious "Johannes, illuminator," were among Queen Charlotte's favorite artists. We learn that "Jean Poyer, paintre" received three lengths of black cloth in order to make himself a mourning robe and cape, a third more than allowed for lower members of the royal household, thus distinguishing him as a favored member of the court (Appendix, 6.7). As for Johannes, he received three and a half lengths of the same fabric. The document confirms that, contrary to what had been previously believed, Poyer held, and no doubt had held for a long time, a considerable place in the household of the late queen.[107]

Unfortunately, none of this early activity of Jean Poyer appears in the illuminated manuscripts of Charlotte de Savoie or in her accounts. But this document is precious for another reason: it shows two artists benefitting from special favors in the household of the queen, Jean Poyer, and perhaps even more, the mysterious Johannes. Who was he? We may dismiss Jean Colombe, who did not belong to the royal household. The queen's documents suggest two possible candidates Jean de Launay, but he is called "painter" in the documents (Appendix, 2.5); or Jean Goislart, "escripvain" who already in 1463 had been paid for binding and writing, but who has left no evidence of being an illuminator.[108]

Jean Bourdichon

In 1483, Jean Bourdichon (c. 1457-1521) executed "deux hystoires de sainct Gregoire et deux de Notre-Dame de Piété" for queen Charlotte (Appendix, 6.1). None of these miniatures has survived, but their style is surely reflected in the Getty Hours, illuminated between 1480 and 1485. Here, the freshness of the youthful Bourdichon is manifest, with well constructed, well anchored figures that nonetheless still lack the monumental solidity of his mature works.[109] At that time, Bourdichon, who was only twenty-six, was already a confirmed master. He succeeded Jean Fouquet as the king's official painter in 1481, having been in his service since 1479.[110]

Bourdichon's apparent attachment to Charlotte in satisfying her requests during her final illness is further attested by the attention he gave to decorations for her funeral. Asked to prepare a life-size statue of the queen in wood, for her "lit de parement," he was directed to portray her face as realistically as possible. Three or four designs were made, showing the queen in different costumes. Bourdichon even took a trip from Amboise to Blois in order to consult with the elder Madame d'Orléans, namely Marie de Clèves.[111] Among other adjustments, he reworked the arm of the statue so that is would hold a scepter (Appendix, 6.2 and 6.3).

Conclusion

The evidence presented here suggests that Charlotte de Savoie was an active reader and gave much interest to her books and to the artists who illustrated them at her request. Her library truly reflects her personality and the devotional occupations that probably filled most of her sedentary life. As the following Table of Concordances and Identifications shows, it is possible that still more manuscripts will be identified. Some books might have made their way to the Savoy family which we know had a long tradition of patronage in this field. At least thirty titles from Charlotte's inventory are lacking in the inventory at Moulins. Anne de Beaujeu would have had the time, between 1483 when she inherited her mother's collection, and 1522, when she died, to sell or give away some of Charlotte's manuscripts. What I have presented is a state of the current research, which will, it is hoped, be complemented in the near future.

        Université de Rennes 2 – Haute-Bretagne
        Institut de Recherche et d'Histoire des Textes, Paris (CNRS)

APPENDIX

I: Documents related to illuminators, book artisans and manuscripts

Currency abbreviations
l.: livre
s.: sou
d.: denier
t.: tournois

1. Paris, B.N.F., MS. Fr. 26089, pièce 208 [31 August 1463]
" En la presence de moy Regnault Farmeau clerc notaire et secretaire du Roy nostre seigneur, Jehan Goislart escripvain a congnieu et confessé avoir eu et receu de Pierre Brette naqués argentier et maistre de la chambre aux deniers de la Royne la somme de quarante cinq solz tournois pour avoir taillé, cousu, relié ens deux ays et couvert de cuir noir xxxv feuillets de parchemin pour servir a mectre et actacher les enseignes de la dite dame et pour avoir escript en parchemin les heures de la magdelaine et autres oroisons qui contiennent cinq cahiers et pour avoir fourny dudit parchemin le tout ou moys d'aoust que l'on disoit mil CCCC soixante et deux. De laquelle somme de XLV s. audit Goislart s'est tenu et tient pour contant et bien payé et en a ... ledit Piere Brette et sous avis tesmoing mon seing manuel cy mis a la requeste dudit Goislart le derrenier jour d'aoust l'an mil cccc et soixante et troys. Signé R. Farmeau. "

2. Paris, Archives Nationales, KK 68 "Compte commun de la despense ordonnee de l'ostel de la royne Charlote pour un an commencé le premier jour d'octobre mil CCCC soixante neuf et finissant le derrenier jour de septembre ensuivant l'an revolu mil CCCC soixante dix. . ."

2.1 "Du mois d'octobre mil CCCC LXIX" [October 1469]
"A maistre Loys Pigault, sommelier de la chapelle de ladite dame, pour quatre mains de pappier riglé qu'il a achecté du commandement de ladite dame pour escripre deu livres a la plaisance de ladite dame, pour ce XX s. t."
Fol. 105

2.2 "Du mois de mars ensuivant oudit an" [March 1470 N.S.]
"A maistre Loys Piguault, sommelier de la chappelle de ladite dame pour avoir escript durant ceste annee plusieurs livres a la plaisance de ladite

dame la somme de vingt livres tournoy a luy ordonnee par ladicte dame et par son roole dudit mois pour la cause dessusdite donné par la quictance cy rendue appert pour cecy XX l. t."
Fol. 110-110v

2.3 [March 1470 N.S.]
"A frere Pierre Thiery pour avoir relié et mis a point cy cedit mois les heures de la dame, XV s. t."
Fol. 110v

2.4 "Du mois d'avril ensuivant mill CCCC LXX" [April 1470]
"A frere Pierre Thiery pour avoir relyé et nectoyé en cedit mois les heures de ladite dame qui estoient toutes rompues par marché fait a luy XV s. t."
Fol. 112

2.5 "Du mois de juillet ensuivant l'an devant de mil CCCC LXX" [July 1470]
"A Jehan de Launay, painctre demourant a Tours, la somme de unze livres cinq sols tournois a luy ordonnee par ladicte dame et par son roole dudit mois pour les parties qui s'ensuivent et est assavoir pour dix hystoires par luy faictes en cedit mois a la plaisance de ladicte dame en ung livre appellé le *Livre des aveugles* au pris de VI s. chacune hystoire, pour ce LX s. t.
(...)
pour la pourtraicture de deux visaiges par lui faiz et painctz a la plaisance de ladite dame durant cedit mois pour ce XXX s. t."
Fol. 115v-116
Cited by Gandilhon, " Contribution à l'histoire, " 378 n. 1.

2.6 "Du mois d'aoust ensuivant l'an dessusdit mill CCCC LXX" [August 1470]
"A Guillaume Geobault pour une bourse de cuir noir de luy achectee ledit jour pour servir a mectre les heures de ladicte dame pour ce par vertu d'icellui soole II s. VI den. = 256 d."
Fol. 118

2.7 "Du mois de septembre ensuivant l'an devantdit mil CCCC LXX" [September 1470]
"A Regnault Fylolle pour deux douzaines de parchemin de luy achecté ledit jour et baillé a ung escripvain que ladicte dame fait escripre au pris de XXXV s. la douzaine, LX s. X d."
Fol. 119v

3. Paris, B.N.F., MS Fr. 26098, pièce 1983-2: Rôle des dépenses de la reine Charlotte de Savoie, Dépenses communes pour janvier 1482 [January 1482]

3.1 "A Thibault Bredinc, libraire demourant a Tours, pour avoir fait escripre XXXV cayers d'un livre de *Vita Christi*, fleury et relyé ledit livre pour ce par marché fait L livres.
A Guillaume Piqueau enlumineur, demourant a Tours, pour avoir enluminé ledit livre et fait plusieurs lettres et paraffes par marché fait XII livres."

3.2. "A Jehan Villet pour avoir escript et enluminé certaines oroisons en deux cayers mys et reliez es heures de ladite dame, pour ce XV s."
Edited by Bibliothèque Nationale, *Le Livre* (Paris, 1972), p. 140, no. 435.

4. Paris, B.N.F., n. a. lat. 2308, fol. 11 Rôle des dépenses de la reine Charlotte de Savoie pour août 1482 [August 1482]
"A Thibault Bredinc, libraire demourant au dit Tours, pour l'escripture du second volume de Vita Christi contenant quarante kayers en parchemin par marché fait avecques luy la somme de L livres."
Partially edited by Bibliothèque Nationale, *Le Livre* (Paris, 1972), p. 140, no. 435.

5. Letter of Charlotte de Savoie to Monsieur Dubouchage (Ymbert de Batarnay) in favour of Jean Colombe, her illuminator in Bourges.
" De par la Royne.
Monsieur Dubochage, j'ay ung povre enlumineur a Bourges, nommé Jehan Coulombe. Par plusieurs fois ay escript et prié a ceulx de la ville, que en ma faveur ilz le tenissent exempt des charges de la dite ville, ce neantmoins ilz le contraignent de faire le guet a la porte, par quoy il ne peut vacquer en mes affaires. Je vous prie que en vueillez escrire a ceulx que verrez estre a faire, car je suis lasse de plus les requerir. Et croyez que me ferez ung bien singulier plaisir se vous le faictes descharger desdites charges, car il me faict beaucoup de services. Et a Dieu, Monsieur Dubochage, qui vous doint ce que desirez. Escript a Amboise, le 12e jour de juing. Charlotte. – René Tardif."
Cited by Louis Paris, ed., *Le Cabinet historique*, Vol. 2, Part 1, *Documents* (Paris, 1856), 123-24 who mistakenly read "Joseph" for "Jehan"; see corrected edition by Louis Thuasne, " Note sur Jean Colombe, " 61-62.

CHARLOTTE DE SAVOIE'S LIBRARY 51

6. Paris, Archives Nationales, KK 69, Accounts from the treasury of the queen Charlotte de Savoie (1483-84)

6.1 "A Jehan Bourdichon, enlumineur de ladite dame, la somme de VI l. X sous a lui ordonnee par ladite dame durant sa maladie pour quatre ystoires qu'il a faictes pour le plaisir de ladite dame, c'est assavoir deux ystoires de sainct Gregoire et deux de Notre Dame de Pitié, pour cecy par quictance dudit Bourdichon, cy rendue ladite somme de VI l. X s. t."
Fol. 63v
Edited by A. Betgé, "Fragments d'un compte du receveur général des finances du Languedoïl," in *Mémoires de la Société des sciences et des arts du Loiret-Cher*, Vol. 2 (1930), and Guiffrey, " Peintres, ymagiers ", 195.

6.2 [January 8, 1484]
"A Jehan Bourdichon, enlumineur et paintre du Roy notre seigneur, demourant a Tours, la somme de XXXII l. X s. t. pour ses paine et sallaire d'avoir fait faire de boys la stature, representacion et figure de ladite feue dame et le visaige de ladite figure, paint selon sa semblance et de la grandeur de ladite dame, au mieulx que possible lui a esté, et selon le devis a lui fait pour mectre sur le lit de parement a l'entrée de Cléry, ou ladite dame a esté enterree, pour cecy, par quictance dudit Bourdichon, signee du seing manuel de maistre Anthoine Bayart, notaire et secretaire du roy nostre sire, le 8e jour de janvier mil CCCC IIII^{xx} et troys (1484), cy rendue, montant LV l. XV s. t., cy employe pour lad. somme de XXXII l. X s. t. et en la partie ensuiv. pour XII l. t., pour cecy lad. somme de XXXII l. X s. t.

Audit Bourdichon, la somme de XII l. t. tant pour avoir fait troys ou quatre patrons au plus prés de la semblance de ladite feue dame et selon le devis a luy ordonné, en divers habitz, pour ce que bonnement on ne savoit en quel estat seroit faicte ladite stature, que pour ung voyage par ledit Bourdichon fait d'Amboise à Bloys devers madame d'Orléans l'aisnee[112] pour avoir son advis desdites choses, tant aussi pour reffaire ung des bras de ladite stature pour tenir le septre royal, que pour avoir fait une saincture de noir en la voulte ou est en sepulture le corps de ladite dame, et y avoir mis ses armes, pour cecy, par quictance dudit Bourdichon rendue sur la partie precedente, montant LV liv. XV s. t., illec employee pour XXXII l. X s. t., cy pour ladite somme de XII l. t., et encores cy apres pour le reste montant XI l. V s. t. pour cecy ladite premiere somme de XII l. t."
Fol. 116v
Edited by Guiffrey, " Peintres, ymagiers," 195–96.

6.3 "A Jehan Bourdichon, paintre demourant a Tours, la somme de 11 l. 5 s. t. pour ung grant chasseiz de boys pour tendre ledit poele, et quatre lances

qu'il a envoyé querir de Cléry a Orléans pour porter ledit poele, et icelles semees de fleur de liz et des armes de ladite dame, et pour avoir painct de noir lesdits chasseiz, pour cecy, par quictance dudit Bourdichon randue sur la 28e partie precedente, ladite somme de 11. l. 5. s. t."
Fol. 122v
Edited by Guiffrey, " Peintres, ymagiers," 196.

6.4 "A luy [Pierre Morin, maître de la chambre aux deniers de la reine, échevin puis maire de Tours] la somme de XI^c XLIII l. XII s., VI d. t. pour troys cens quatre vingt dix aulnes troys quart de drap noir [en marge au pris de LXX. s. t. l'aulne], par led. Morin baillees et delivrees a plusieurs officiers, damoiselles, femmes et serviteurs de l'ostel de lad. Dame pour faire leurs robes et chapperons de dueil, duquel drap la distribucion a esté faicte en la maniere que s'ensuit. C'est assavoir
A Bazille [*crossed and replaced by* Blaise] Savary, eschanson, III aulnes et demye."
Fol. 169

. . .

"A Maistre Jehan Desquartes, III aulnes et demye
A Jehan Poyer, paintre, III aulnes
A Jehan du Boys, III aulnes
A Johannes, enlumineur, III aulnes et demye
A l'escuier tranchant de Madame d'Orléans,[130] III aulnes
A son eschanson, III aulnes
A son escuier de service, III aulnes "
Fol. 171
Edited by Girault, " Jean Poyet, " 78, document no. 1-1483.

7. Expense of Queen Charlotte de Savoie, 1483
"A Jehan de Manseul clerc des offices de ladicte dame, pour l'escripture de plusieurs petits livres de devocion et autres charges qu'il a eue depuis ladicte dame, par don a lui faict par icelle, la somme de XXX f."
Edited by Leber in *Collections des meilleurs dissertations, notices et traités particuliers relatifs à l'histoire de France*, (Paris, 1838), 19: 250.

II. Books of Louis XI that were included with the manuscripts of the inventory of Charlotte de Savoie by Delisle (Cabinet des manuscrits: 91-93) The list was assembled by me from Tuetey's edition ("Inventaire des biens," 430-32).

1. Ung livre en pappier, ou il y a des pappes figurez, avecques meschentes petites figures, et ne scet on se led. pappier s'appelle le livre pappal, ou non.
2. Ung livre couvert de drap d'or, bandé, garny et relyé d'argent doré et neslé aux armes du roy, commancant en lettre roge Ad ultrississimum principii [sic]; ledit livre estant en ung estuy de cuir roge, aux armes du roy, et une sainture garnye d'argent doré.
3. Ung livre couvert de veloux cramoisi, fermant a esguillectes de soye jaune.
4. Ung autre petit livre couvert de veloux cramoisi, a ung fremouer de laton, escript ou couvercle L'istoire Merlin.
5. Ung livre de Conditor[113] et de Noez, couvert de jaune.
6. Ung livre qui gueres ne vault, marché de rayes.
7. Ung petit livre, couvert de gris, fermant a esguillets de chevrotin, et y a sur le couvercle escript De essencia et motu signifficacionem [sic].
8. Ung messel couvert de veloux cramoisi, a fremouers d'argent doré aux armes du roy.
9. Ung autre livre en pappier, faisant mencion d'inventoires.
10. Ung petit livret, couvert de veloux violet, ouquel a au comancemant Revelaciones sancte Brigide.
11. Ung autre petit livret en parchemin, couvert de parchemin, ouquel a au commancement une S, dedans les armes du roy.
12. Ung armenac en parchemin.
13. Ung cahier en pappier, ouquel a au commancement coppié Nycollas Erlaut.
14. Unes heures couvertes de veloux cramoisi.
15. Ung petit calendrier, couvert de veloux cramoisi.
16. Unes autres heures, couvertes de veloux cramoisi, commançant Domine labia.
17. Ung petit livre, couvert de veloux cramoisi, dont n'y a que ung fueillet et demy escript.
18. Ung autre petit livre escript de la quizielle.[114]
19. Ung autre livre, couvert de veloux, escript comme dessus, et deux calendriers dedans.
20. Unes heures couvertes de veloux cramoisi, commançant In principio erat Verbum.
21. Ung petit livre couvert de veloux cramoisi, ouquel a des quizielles.
22. Petites oraisons en parchemin.

NOTES

1. I am especially indebted to Mr. François Avril, chief curator of the Manuscript Department at the Bibliothèque Nationale de France in Paris, who gave me generous access to his copious dossier devoted to the library of Charlotte de Savoie. For their encouragement of my work and several improvements, I am indebted to Professor Geneviève Hasenohr, University of Paris-Sorbonne (Paris IV) and to Patricia Stirnemann, Codicological Section of the I.R.H.T. in Paris. I would like to thank Roxanne Lapidus and Patricia Stirnemann, who aided in the translation of the French version of this essay that was presented at the symposium Women and Books in Late Medieval and Renaissance Europe: Female Readers, Owners, and Makers organized by Prof. Cynthia Brown at the Château de la Bretesche, Missillac, France, June 25-28, 2000.
2. For example, Jeanne de Laval, second wife of René d'Anjou, with whom Charlotte and Louis XI seem to have had bibliophilic affinities. On Jeanne de Laval's library and illuminators, see Anne-Marie Legaré, "Reassessing Women's Libraries in Late Medieval France. The Case of Jeanne de Laval," Renaissance Studies, 10, no. 2, *Women Patrons of Renaissance Art* (1996) 209-36; and "Livres et lectures de la reine Jeanne de Laval," in *Bretagne, Art, création, société. Mélanges en l'honneur de Denise Delouche*, edited by J.-Y. Andrieux and M. Grivel, 220-34. Rennes: Presses Universitaires de Rennes, 1997.
3. It is preserved in Paris, B.N.F., MS Fr. 15538, fols. 64-101.
4. Alexandre Tuetey, *Inventaire des biens de Charlotte de Savoie*, Bibliothèque de l'École des chartes, 26: 338-66 and 423-42, Paris, 1865. The citations from the queen's inventory in the present article come from this edition.
5. Léopold Delisle, *Le Cabinet des manuscrits de la Bibliothèque impériale* [nationale], 1: 91-3 (Paris, 1868).
6. The numbers in brackets are those I have assigned to the items in the Table of Concordances and Identifications at the end of this article.
7. B.N.F., MS Fr. 2099. See Charles Samaran, "Un Ouvrage de Guillaume Danicot, historiographe de Louis XI," *Mélanges d'Archéologie et d'Histoire de l'École française de Rome. Moyen Âge*, 45: 8-20 (1928). *Dictionnaire des Lettres françaises du Moyen Âge*, ed. Michel Zink and Geneviève Hasenohr (Paris, 1992) 1343-44 (hereafter DLF).
8. Paris, B.N.F., MS Fr. 5718, vellum, 135 fols., 195 x 125 mm. The *Vie de sainte Radegonde* (fols. 1-65) is an anonymous text. It is followed by an account of the saint's actions during her life and the miracles that occurred after her death, written by Baudonivie, a nun at the convent of Sainte-Croix in Poitiers (fols. 65-104), and by two epistles addressed to Radegonde by Césarie d'Arles (fols. 110-124). See François Avril, "Un Portrait inédit de la reine Charlotte de Savoie," in *Études sur la Bibliothèque Nationale et témoignages réunis en hommage à Thérèse Kleindienst* (Paris, 1985), 255-62.
9. New York, Pierpont Morgan Library, M. 1004, Paris, c. 1420-25. See John Plummer, *The Last Flowering: French Painting in Manuscripts, 1420-1530*, exhibition catalogue, Pierpont Morgan Library, New York, Nov. 1982-Jan. 1983 (New York and London:

Oxford University Press, 1982), 2-3, no. 2. Plummer also suggests that the arms might have been added later, after 1452, when Amédée de Savoie, the brother of Charlotte, married the dauphin's sister Yolande.

10. Ramsen, Heribert Tenschert: see Eberhard König, with the collab. of G. Bartz and H. Tenschert, *Vom Heiligen Ludwig zum Sonnenkönig: 34 Werke der Französischen Buchmalerei aus Gotik, Renaissance und Barock*, Leuchtendes Mittelalters: Neue Folge 3, no. 13, 210-28 (Ramsen, Heribert Tenschert, 2000). I am currently preparing a monograph on this lavishly illuminated manuscript.

11. Vienna, National Library. MS ser. nov. 2619, fol. 3. On this manuscript illuminated by the workshop of the Master of Mary of Burgundy, see Georges Lieftinck, *Boekverluchters mit de omgeving van Maria Bourgondie c.1475-c.1485* (Brussels,1969): 152-56, no. 11, and Sheila Edmunds, "Catalogue des manuscrits savoyards: II, Manuscrits liés à d'autres membres de la maison de Savoie," in *Les Manuscrits enluminés des comtes et ducs de Savoie*, A. Paravicini Bagliani, ed., (Turin, 1990), 213-14 (no. 64).

12. I thank Roseline Harrouët for pointing this out to me.

13. Tours, Municipal Library, Ms. 2128. Acquired in 1975 from Giraud-Badin Library, Sale Catalogue *Livres Anciens et Modernes*, October 23-24, 1975, lot 20, ill. (Paris, Hôtel Drouot). Cf. *Catalogue des Manuscrits en Écriture latine*, edited by Charles Samaran and Robert Marichal, 8: Ouest de la France et Pays de Loire, Paris, 1988: 541. Pierre Gasnault, keeper of the Bibliothèque Nationale, reached the same conclusions in a private letter sent on March 16, 1976 to Madame Liebert, keeper of Tour's Municipal Library. On the manuscripts owned by the Urfé family, cf. André Vernet, "Les Manuscrits de Claude d'Urfé (1501-1558) au château de la Bastie," in *Comptes rendus de l'Académie des Inscriptions des Belles-lettres* (Paris, January-March 1976), 81-97.

14. Also mentioned by Avril, " Portrait inédit, " 258, n. 9.

15. Alphonse-Martial Chazaud, *Les Enseignements d'Anne de France, duchesse de Bourbonnais et d'Auvergne à sa fille Susanne de Bourbon* (Moulins, 1878), 211-58. This edition relies on the Dupuy MS, vol. 488, fols. 210-19v, original copied by Bouhier, vol. 21, fols. 178-92 (Paris, B.N.F., Lat. 17917).

16. Chazaud, *Enseignements*, 211. Chazaud marked with an asterisk the works enumerated in Charlotte de Savoie's inventory that are found in the 1523 inventory.

17. Antoine-Jean-Victor Leroux de Lincy, *Catalogue de la bibliothèque des ducs de Bourbon qui sont en la librairie du chasteau de Molins*, Mélanges de la Société des bibliophiles français (Paris, 1850), 73-111.

18. In fact, the two editions rely on different sources. The source for Chazaud's edition (MS Dupuy, vol. 488) seems more reliable than Leroux de Lincy's source (Carpentras, Bibl. Mun. MS 1769; Peiresc, *Catalogi varii codicum manuscriptorum*, fols. 6-17v, 16th century), since it inventories three additional books, including one of Charlotte de Savoie's manuscripts (Chazaud no. 46, *Le Livre des miracles de saincte Catherine*) and two printed books (Chazaud nos. 239 and 240), which are missing in the edition of Leroux de Lincy. The latter skipped three items in the inventory, which luckily were included by Chazaud no. 218 "Deux grans vollumes nommés

Pantheologlorum, en molle, papier [printed on paper] "; no. 232 "*Ambrosius, De officiis*, en molle, papier"; and no. 233 "Le *nouveau testament* corrigé, en molle, papier." Certain titles that were mistranscribed or incomplete in Leroux de Lincy's edition are also corrected by Chazaud. On the other hand, not only did Chazaud omit an article concerning Charlotte de Savoie's library that appears clearly in the inventories ("*Livre des anges*, en papier, a la main", Leroux no. 276) but he also mistakenly copied twice the entry of "*Le livre de la Maison de conscience*" (nos. 145 and 146). Thus both editions are necessary in order to retrace Charlotte de Savoie's manuscripts in the Moulins library.

19. Cf. Henri Omont, "Répertoire de la librairie de Blois (1518)," in *Anciens Inventaires et catalogues de la Bibliothèque Nationale. La Librairie Royale à Blois, Fontainebleau et Paris au XVIe siècle*, volume 1 (Paris, 1908) 12-13, no. 88 (MS Fr. 300); 10, no. 75 (MS Fr. 449); 26, no. 161 (MS Fr. 316); no. 325 (MS Latin 919). For this manuscript, see Ursula Baurmeister and Marie-Pierre Laffitte, *Des Livres et des rois. La bibliothèque royale de Blois* (Paris, 1992), 82–83, no. 14. These manuscripts have been identified independently by both François Avril and me, and our identifications agree.

20. Idem., "Inventaire de la librairie de Blois lors de son transfert à Fontainebleau (1544)," in ibid., 155-264.

21. Marie-Pierre Laffitte, conservateur en chef at the Bibliothèque Nationale, is currently reconstructing the library and marks of ownership of François Ier.

22. Omont, "Catalogue des bibliothèques du Roy à Paris," in *Anciens Inventaires*, 265-475.

23. Paris, B.N.F., Fonds Fontette, Portefeuille LXI-A, Belles-Lettres, fol. 174 ff. The inventory has been published by Le Roux de Lincy in the *Bulletin du Bibliophile* (1860).

24. Henri d'Orléans, duc d'Aumale, *Chantilly: Le Cabinet des livres. Manuscrits*, Vol. 1, (Paris, 1900): 35 (hereafter *Chantilly: Le Cabinet*); Ernest Picot, *Le Duc d'Aumale et la bibliothèque à Chantilly* (Paris, 1897), 19 ff.

25. Most of the following information on the life of Charlotte de Savoie is borrowed from Gandilhon, *Contribution*, 374-82 and Pierre Champion, *Louis XI*, 2: 223-25. See also Roman d'Amat, "Charlotte de Savoie," in *Dictionnaire de biographie française*, (Paris, 1959) 8: col. 596.

26. During the reign of Charles VII, the écu d'or was equal to 25 sous tournois. In 1475, Louis XI created the écu au soleil, which was equivalent to one livre and 13 sous tournois. Cf. *Encyclopédie Universalis, Thesaurus-Index*.

27. On Anne de Beaujeu, see Pierre Pradel, *Anne de France, 1461-1522* (Paris, Publisud, 1986).

28. Cited by Alfred Gandilhon in *Contribution à l'histoire de la vie privée et de la cour de Louis XI (1423-1481)*, Mémoires de la Société Historique, Littéraire et Scientifique du Cher, 4th ser., 20 (Bourges, 1905): 375, n. 1. On Jeanne la Boiteuse, see René-Alphonse-Marie Maulde La Clavière, *Jeanne de France* (Paris, 1883), a realistic and unsparing description of whom is given in Bernard Quillet's *Louis XII* (Paris, Fayard, 1986), 67-68.

29. Gandilhon, *Contribution*, 378-382, Pierre Champion, *Louis XI*, Vol. 2, (Paris, 1928): 225.
30. The daughter of the seigneur de Crussol, the "fidèle gouverneur" of Poitou under Louis XI. Cited by Gandilhon, *Contribution*, 335.
31. This negative opinion, first formulated by Philippe de Commynes in his *Mémoires*, was accepted by Champion, *Louis XI*, 1: 223 and 2: 203, and by Paul Murray Kendall, *Louis XI* (Paris, 1974) 79, 218. Cf. Philippe de Commynes, *Mémoires*, ed. Jean Dufournet (Paris, 1979), 2: 271.
32. Paris, B.N.F., MS Fr. 5718, fol. 2. It is, however, the only true portrait of Charlotte that is preserved, but her features are no doubt too idealized for us to rely upon. On this subject, see Avril, " Portrait inédit," 260.
33. Paris, B.N.F., Cabinet des Estampes, *Recueil des dessins d'Arras*, Nª 28d, fol. 5. For a reproduction of this portrait, see Champion, *Louis XI*, 2: 224, pl. XIV.
34. Paris, B.N.F., Cabinet des Estampes, *Recueil Gaignières*, Oa^{15} fol. 4; cf. H. Bouchot, *Inventaire des dessins exécutés pour Roger de Gaignières* (Paris, 1891), nos. 707 and 7095. Avril, " Portrait inédit, " 257 n. 4, and 260 n. 13; see also Paris, B.N.F., MS Clairambault 633, fol. 144.
35. See Gandilhon, *Contribution*, 375 n. 2.
36. Dispatch from Nicolas de' Roberti (*Mélanges de l'École Française de Rome* [1904] 154) cited by Gandilhon, *Contribution*, 377 n. 1
37. For example "Item, ung mestier d'yvyere ouquel a des billars, billes et jonchez tous d'yvyere [Item, an ivory box containing billiards, marbles, and spillikins, all in ivory]" (Tuetey, *Inventaire des biens*, 426); "Item, ung autre coffre de Chipres, de grandeur d'un pyé et demy, fermant a clef et ouvré par le devant, ouquel a esté trouvé ung espinglier de drap violet, ung escheveau de layne roge, et des jonchez, et une fuzee de layne blanche, le tout non extimé " [Item, another trunk of Cypress wood, one and one-half *pyé* wide, having a lock and opening in the front, containing a pin cushion of violet material, a bundle of red wool, and some knitting needles, and a spool of white wool, none of which was assessed]" (Ibid. 356). Note that according to the context, " jonchez " either means spillikins or knitting needles.
38. Objects that one valued tended to be kept in trunks. Even if the inventory gives no indication of where objects were kept, one can assume that in many households the bedroom served also as the study and was supplied with furniture for reading and writing, and was a repository for books. Cf. Geneviève Hasenohr, "L'Essor des bibliothèques privées aux XIVᵉ et XVᵉ siècles," in *Les Bibliothèques médiévales du VIe siècle à 1530*, vol. 1 of *Histoire des Bibliothèques françaises*, André Vernet dir. (Paris, 1989), 216-20.
39. It was most probably the papal hat of Duc Amédée VIII de Savoie, the grandfather of Charlotte, who was elected as antipope in 1439 under the name of Felix V and presided over the Council of Basle from then until his abdication; Cf. J. Helmrath, *Das Basler Konzil, 1431-1449: Forschungsstand und Probleme* (Cologne and Vienna, 1987), 233-37.

40. See Tuetey, *Inventaire des biens*, 352 n. 2, where he refers to the glossary that accompanies the *Notices des émaux du Louvre*, by the Comte de Laborde.

41. "Item, a Book of Hours, covered with black velvet with gold fittings, estimated at 25 écus"; Tuetey, *Inventaire des biens*, 429.

42. It may thus be possible to deduce that where the support is not specified, it is, by default, parchment.

43. Nearly all of the manuscripts have lost their original binding. Those in the Bibliothèque Nationale were covered with 17th century bindings of red morocco leather with the royal arms, while most of those at Chantilly are bound in marbled calf, with the arms of the Bourbon-Condés—"trois fleurs de lis avec bâton en bande or"—which corresponds to stamp no. 7 in the classification of Eugène Olivier, Georges Hermal, and R. de Roton, *Manuel de l'Amateur de reliures armoriées françaises* (Paris, 1935), pl. 2635.

44. The mention of coats of arms is often juxtaposed with the description of bindings. Did the clasps really have coats of arms? The fact that the bindings no longer exist makes it impossible to answer this question, but it is quite possible that the mention of coats of arms refers simply to those contained in the manuscripts themselves. This could be true, for example, of the book *Congratulation et graces de la nativité de Charles aisné* [109] or of *La Fleur des histoires* [1].

45. "A book on paper, written with type and named the New Testament..."; Tuetey, *Inventaire des biens*, 358.

46. "Item, a large trunk with a rounded top, covered with dark leather, with tin fittings, standing in the outer gallery at Amboise, containing the books of the late king Louis, and which the late queen—God rest her soul—did not touch, but wished that they be wrapped and taken to the king, her son". Ibid., 423.

47. Tuetey, *Inventaire des biens*, 430-32; this list was integrated by Delisle into the manuscripts of the queen's inventory, *Cabinet des manuscrits*, 1: 91-93. See the list of these books at the end of this article.

48. Tuetey, *Inventaire des biens*, 430-32; this list was integrated by Delisle into the manuscripts of the queen's inventory, *Cabinet des manuscrits*, 1: 91-93. See the list of these books at the end of this article.

49. Cf. Tuetey, *Inventaire des biens*, 430-31.

50. The order of Saint Michael was founded by Louis XI on the first of August 1469, and led to the creation of one of those rare illuminated manuscripts ordered by the king himself: the *Statuts de l'ordre de saint Michel* painted by Jean Fouquet (Paris, B.N.F., MS Fr. 19819). See François Avril, *La Passion des manuscrits enluminés. Bibliophiles français, 1280-1580*, (Paris, Bibliothèque Nationale, 1991), 62-63, no. 24.

51. Delisle, *Cabinet des manuscrits*, 1: 91-93

52. Paris, B.N.F., MS Fr. 2222. Cf. Charles Samaran, "Un Ouvrage de Guillaume Danicot, historiographe de Louis XI," *Mélanges d'Archéologie et d'Histoire de l'École Française de Rome*, 45 (1928): 8-20.

53. A burning miror is a concave miror that concentrates the sun's rays at a focus, and causes them to set fire to objects (OED).

54. Paris, B.N.F., MS Fr. 2099. See Samaran, " Un ouvrage, " and DLF, 1343-44.
55. Cf. J. Lesellier, "Un Historiographe de Louis XI demeuré inconnu, Guillaume Danicot," *Mélanges d'Archéologie et d'Histoire de l'École Française de Rome*, 43 (1926): 1-29.
56. The shield has been painted over, as can be seen from the verso, which suggests that originally it was "écartelé aux armes de Savoie et de France" and not "parti."
57. Christian de Mérindol, "Louis XI et le Puy-Notre-Dame. Mise au point, nouvelles lectures, nouvelles perspectives," in *Mémoires de l'Académie d'Angers* (n. p.,1996); offprint.
58. Not the shrine of Notre-Dame du Puy-en-Velay, as Charles Samaran believed. Cf. Mérindol, " Louis XI. "
59. Cf. Célestin Port, "Puy-Notre-Dame" in *Dictionnaire historique, géographique et biographique de Maine-et-Loire*, Vol. 2, Paris, 1874-78: 202. See also Timothée L. Houdebine, *Le Puy-Notre-Dame, l'église et le pèlerinage de la Sainte-Ceinture* (Angers, 1924), 35.
60. André Lapeyre, *Louis XI, mécène dans le domaine de l'orfèvrerie religieuse* (Paris, 1986), 81-82 n. 3 and 4.
61. "La Congratulation et Grâces de la nativité du roy Charles VIIIe de ce nom, ensemble de Nostre Dame du Puy en Auvergne, a ung fermaut d'argent doré. *Nota*, que le fermaut n'y soit point." See Leroux de Lincy, *Catalogue*, 76, no. 16.
62. According to Tuetey, a mention of Commynes's *Mémoires* (he used the edition by the *Société de l'Histoire de France*, vol. 3), documents this lady in a letter addressed to the deputies of the town of Amiens, concerning the marriage of the Dauphin. See Tuetey, *Inventaire des biens*, 364 n. 3.
63. It can be identified in the 1518 inventory. Cf. Omont, " Répertoire, " in *Anciens Inventaires*, 1: 26, no. 161.
64. Those found among Louis XI's books are described as follows: "Item a large book on parchment that begins, 'Here follows the table of contents of the second book of the Chronicles of Jean Froissart,' bound in crimson velvet, placed in a red and white leather bag" (Paris, B.N.F., MS Fr. 2652). "Item another book in parchment, bound in crimson velvet, which begins, 'Here begins the third main part of the *canoniques*'" (Paris, B.N.F., MS Fr. 2653). "Item another volume of Froissart, bound in crimson velvet, in a red and white leather bag" (Paris, B.N.F., MS Fr. 2654). See Tuetey, *Inventaire des biens*, 424. These manuscripts remained in the royal collections and seem recognizable in the 1518 inventory of Blois. This information comes from unpublished notes by F. Avril that I was able to consult.
65. Three fleurs-de-lys on a field of blue, with a bend of gules, the whole shield held up by two angels.
66. " Des histoires et livres en françoys. Pulpitre 5 contre la muraille de devers la Court Bloys. " It appears in the 1518 inventory of Blois (Omont, " Répertoire ", in *Anciens Inventaires*, Vol. 1: 12-13, no. 88) and in that of 1544 (Id., " Inventaire de la librairie, " in *Anciens Inventaires*, Vol. 1: 224, no. 1366).
67. Baurmeister and Laffitte, *Des Livres et des rois*, 82-83, no. 14, with one color reproduction.

68. Tuetey, *Inventaire des biens*, 429 n. 2.
69. François Avril and Nicole Reynaud, *Les Manuscrits à peintures en France, 1440-1530* (Paris, 1993), 288-89, no. 158.
70. Chantilly, Musée Condé, MS 36. For a color reproduction of one of the thirteen miniatures in the work, see Frédéric Vergne, *La Bibliothèque du Prince. Château de Chantilly. Les manuscrits* (Paris, 1995), 118.
71. Chantilly, Musée Condé, MS 159. Cf. *Chantilly: Le Cabinet*, 1: 156.
72. Catherine d'Alençon was the daughter of Jean II, duc d'Alençon, and was married January 8, 1461, to Guy de Laval, 14th of that name, but called Guy XV, comte de Laval and of Montfort (1435-1500). She died without posterity on July 17, 1505.
73. The inscription appears on the reverse of the endleaf at the beginning of the work.
74. *Chantilly: Le Cabinet*, 1: 156.
75. The percentage of the religious works contained in either the inventories or manuscripts of the ten other princesses is as follows: Mahaut d'Artois (books in 1329), 17.5%; Clémence de Hongrie (inventory of 1328), 50%; Marguerite de Flandre (inventory of 1405), 28%; Valentine Visconti (inventory of 1408), 39%; Marguerite de Bavière (inventory of 1423), 23%; Marguerite de Bretagne (inventory of 1469), 50%; Gabrielle de La Tour (inventory of 1474), 29.5%; Yolande de Savoie (inventory of 1479), 54%; Marie de Clèves (inventory of 1487), 33.5%. See comparative table in Hasenohr, " L'Essor, " 1: 249, table 6.
76. Id., 252 ff., which I summarize here.
77. Of the works in the postmortem inventory (1479) of Yolande de Savoie, sister of Louis XI, 11.5% were mystery plays. Id., 249.
78. Cf. DLF, 1046, and Gustave Macon, "Note sur le Mystère de la Résurrection," *Bulletin des Bibliophiles* (1898): 1-21.
79. On this anonymous mystery play, see DLF, 1351-52; Graham A. Runnalls, "René d'Anjou et le Théâtre," *Annale de Bretagne et des Pays de l'Ouest (Anjou, Maine, Touraine)* 88 (1981): 171-73, and more recently Gilles Roussineau, "La Représentation du *Mystère de saint Vincent*, joué à Angers en 1471," *Revue d'Histoire du Théâtre*, 1-2 (1991): 27-42.
80. Leroux, no. 231; Chazaud, *Les Enseignements*, no. 256. It is worth mentioning that the same type of description applies to the *Mystère de la Résurrection*: "*La Résurrection Nostre Seigneur*, rithmee, par personnaiges, comme elle fut jouee a Angiers, en papier, a la main." Leroux, no. 244; Chazaud, no. 269.
81. Fol. 213v: "Data est licentia ludendi presens misterium apud Ludium ad relationem curati dicti loci ac magistri Johannis Jousbert, prioris prioratus de Raillon, in theologia baccalarii, qui nobis viccario subscripto certifficarunt quod nichil in eo continetur contra articulos fidei. Actum apud Ludium die prima mensis Augusti anno domini millesimo IIIIC septuagesimo sexto. René Delabarre." René de la Barre was the son of Jean de la Barre, second of this name, and of Jeanne de Croisay. He was "seigneur de Vaudusson et d'Anon et bailli de Lude." A famous professor of law, he was abbot of Mélinays from at least 1477 and canon of Saint-Maurice à Angers.

He died on September 1, 1502, and was buried in the chapel of the knights of the cathedral of Saint-Maurice. Cf. Carré d'Hozier, under "Barre, de la," piece 27-28, and Port, *Dictionnaire hystorique*, 2, 20.

82. Augustinian abbey founded in 1138 by Saint Regnault, disciple of Blessed Robert d'Arbrissel, diocese of Angers. Cf. Dom L. H. Cottineau, *Répertoire Topo-bibliographique des abbayes et prieurés*, (Mâcon, 1939), 2: col. 1811.

83. Le Lude is not the city of Lude, as Runnalls ("René d'Anjou," 173) and Roussineau thought (" La Représentation, " 27) but the priory of Saint-Aubin at Saint-Vincent au Lude, also called Raillon. Cf. Cottineau, *Répertoire Topo-bibliographique*, col. 1674. Johannis Jousbert (d. 1503) could be Jean Joubert, a professed religious of Angevin origin at the abbey of Saint-Aubin at Angers, a monk reportedly very learned in the law, in 1502. He was also titular bishop of Arcusance. Cf. Port, *Dictionnaire historique*, 2, 411 and Roussineau, " La Représentation, " 28 n. 5.

84. Marguerite de Flandres, Marguerite de Bavière, Gabrielle de La Tour and Yolande de Savoie each had copies. Cf. Hasenohr, " L'Essor, " 1: 252 n. 326, who notes that "the only collection where they [the classics] are well represented is that of Gabrielle de La Tour, where their amazing abundance equals, in the secular domain, that of Charlotte de Savoie's library in the religious domain."

85. Cited by Gandilhon, *Contribution*, 377 n. 6.

86. The *sommelier* was an officer charged with the transport of baggage during royal travels. He had an important responsibility, since he was in charge of the safekeeping of the most precious objects from the chapel and personally oversaw their security, especially when they were moved from place to place. Cf. Frédéric Godefroy, *Dictionnaire de l'ancienne langue française* (Geneva-Paris, 1982), 7: 467.

87. Regnault Fylolle copied and illuminated four books four the king in 1481. Cf. Paris, Archives Nationales, A.A. 64: Louis IX, *Menus plaisirs* (1478-81), fols. 161v and 169-169v.

88. Cf. Delisle, *Cabinet des manuscrits*, 3: 342-43.

89. The attribution to Jean Colombe has been made by François Avril in his unpublished notes.

90. Cf. C. M. Briquet, *Les Filigranes. Dictionnaire historique des marques du papier dès leur apparition vers 1282 jusqu'en 1600*, 2d ed. (Paris 1923; repr. New York 1966), no. 1468: "écu à la fasce chargée de 3 coquilles, à trois cœurs, posés 2 en chef et 1 en pointe."

91. I am grateful to Mr. Pierre-Yves Ribault, former director of the Archives du Cher, for this information. According to him, the name of Fauvre is attested to in Bourges.

92. On Thomas Valery, see J. W. Bradley, A *Dictionary of Miniaturists, Illuminators, Calligraphers, and Copyists from the Establishment of Christianity to the Eighteenth Century*, (London 1887; repr. New York 1958), 3: 69, 75.

93. On folio 215v, the following mention is written in red ink: "Ci fine l'orreloge de sapience escripte de la main Thomas Valery prestre a Bourges en Berry que fist escrire messire Estienne Chotart procureur de mesdames de Saint-Laurent. Priez Dieu pour eulx." A bit further down, there is written in blue ink: "Anluminé de la main ... Jehan Pion." This mention is decorated with a flowering branch, which suggests

once more that the illuminator was more likely the author of the penwork initials and line endings in the form of stylized fleurs de lys, executed in gold leaf and blue paint. Cf. Paul Chenu, *Note sur un manuscrit de la bibliothèque de l'archevêque Guillaume de Cambray*, Mémoires de la Société des Antiquaires du Centre, 41 (Bourges, 1923): 256 n. 3. The author refers to the Archives du Cher, Min., Dujat E 2521, fol. 130.

94. Avril and Reynaud, *Les Manuscrits à peintures*, 325-26. One thinks of the *Heures de Louis de Laval*, which contain more than a thousand illuminations (ibid., 328-332, no. 179), or of Sébastien Mamerot's *Les Passages d'outremer*, with its 64 miniatures (ibid., 332, no. 180), two prestigious commissions executed by Jean Colombe for the great bibliophile.

95. René Tardif is mentioned as secretary in the "Estat des officiers domestiques de l'hostel de la reyne Charlotte, du premier juillet 1478 au premier juillet 1479," with a salary of seven *livres* a year. Cf. Tuetey, *Inventaire des biens*, 342 and Louis Thuasne, "Note sur Jean Colombe, enlumineur," *Revue des bibliothèques* (January-April 1904), 60, n. 2.

96. See Thuasne, "Note sur Jean Colombe," passim. My thanks again to Mr. J.-Y. Ribault for communicating to me his views on the possible date of the letter.

97. See the detailed notice in Baurmeister and Laffitte, *Des Livres et des rois*, 84-85, no. 15, with color reproductions.

98. New York, Pierpont Morgan Library, M. 677, Bourges, c. 1470, illuminated by Jean Colombe and other members of his atelier. See Claude Schaefer, "Les Débuts de l'atelier de Jean Colombe: Jean Colombe et André Rousseau, prêtre, libraire, et 'escrivain,'" *Gazette des Beaux-Arts* 2 (November 1977): 142, and John Plummer, *The Last Flowering*, 53-54, no. 70.

99. Paris, B.N.F., MS Fr. 992. See Avril and Reynaud, *Les Manuscrits à peintures*, 332, no. 181.

100. Paris, B.N.F., MS Nouv. Acq. Fr. 10823, *Vie de Nostre benoît Sauveur Jhesus Crist et la Sainte Vie de Nostre Dame*, indicated by G. Hasenohr, "A propos de la *Vie de Nostre Benoît Sauveur Jhesus Crist*," *Romania*, 102 (1981): 352-91. Cf. Avril and Reynaud, *Les Manuscrits à peintures*, 332, no. 181

101. Cf. D. MacGibbon, *Jean Bourdichon* (Glasgow, 1933), 42; Avril and Reynaud, *Les Manuscrits à peintures*, 326.

102. The spelling "Poyer" (as opposed to the usual "Poyet") is justified by the fact that it appears in the 15th century archival documents, while "Poyet" was adopted only in the 16th century. For this observation, I would like to thank Mara Hofmann who is currently preparing a doctoral thesis entitled *Jean Poyer*, under the direction of Eberhard König at the Free University of Berlin.

103. Avril and Reynaud, *Les Manuscrits à peintures*, 306-318 ; Janet Backhouse, "A Book of Hours by a Contemporary of Jean Bourdichon," in *Manuscripts in the Fifty Years after the Invention of Printing*, ed. J. B. Trapp, (London, 1983), 45-49; also her "French Manuscript Illumination 1450-1530," in *Renaissance Painting in Manuscripts: Treasures from the British Library*, ed. Thomas Kren, exhibition cat., New York, 1983 (New York:

Hudson Hills Press, 1983), 143-92 (cf. 150 and 175-80, no. 23); and her "The Tilliot Hours: Comparisons and Relationships," *British Library Journal*, 13 (1987): 211-31. For further bibliography, see her "Poyet, Jean," in *The Dictionary of Art* (New York, 1996), 25: 405-06, ill. ; John Plummer, *The Last Flowering*, 85-89, nos. 111-114.

104. Charles de Grandmaison, *Documents inédits pour servir à l'histoire des arts en Touraine* (Paris, J. B. Dumoulin, 1870), 10-11, 139-40; Jules Guiffrey, "Peintres, ymagiers, verriers, maçons, enlumineurs, écrivains et libraires du XIVe et du XVe siècles," *Nouvelles Archives de l'Art Français*, 7 (1878): 157-221 (cf. 197-99). See also, despite the frequent absence of indication of his sources, Ernest Giraudet, *Les Artistes tourangeaux*, Mémoires de la société archéologique de Touraine, 33 (Tours, 1885), s.v. Pohier, 332, and s.v. Poyet, 338-39.

105. Roger S. Wieck, *The Prayer Book of Anne de Bretagne*, Pierpont Morgan Library, MS M. 50 (Lucerne: Faksimile Verlag Luzern, 1999), especially 85-94.

106. Pierre-Gilles Girault, "Jean Poyet peut-il être l'auteur des heures du Tilliot?" *Revue de l'Art*, 110 (1995): 74-78.

107. Girault confirms that Jean Poyet was active before 1483, the year that he executed 1,031 escutcheons for the funeral of Charlotte de Savoie, which took place on December 1, 1483 (Paris, A.N., KK 69, *Comptes de la trésorerie de la reine Charlotte de Savoie*, fols. 123v-124). See Guiffrey, " Peintres, ymagiers, " 198-99. This new dimension of Poyer's career allows Girault to propose that the painter Jean Poyer mentioned in 1465 in the municipal accounts of Tours (*Archives historiques*, 37, fol. 102v) is the artist himself, and not a relative, as Avril had suggested (Avril and Reynaud, *Les Manuscrits à peintures*, 306). He was charged by the town's aldermen with making armorial flags for the town's gates, painting a standard, and accomplishing other tasks that, according to Girault, would only be entrusted to a recognized and esteemed artist. Wieck (*Prayer Book*, 85) suggests that he could have been twenty years old in 1465, situating his date of birth about 1445. In light of this new document, one could even push back his date of birth to 1435, especially since Girault extracts from literary sources celebrating Poyer, convincing arguments that situate his death before 1503, and not after 1515, as one was obliged to do on the basis of works attributed to him without solid documentation. See Girault, " Jean Poyet, " 74 and 76.

108. I did not include Jehan Villet, paid 25 sous for certain writing and illumination work in the queen's Book of Hours (Appendix, 3.2).

109. Los Angeles, J. Paul Getty Museum, MS 6. Cf. Avril and Reynaud, *Les Manuscrits à peintures*, 293-94, no. 161. On Jean Bourdichon's illuminated manuscripts, see ibid., 292-305.

110. For a good résumé of the artist's life, cf. Nicole Reynaud, "Bourdichon, Jean," in *The Dictionary of Art* (New York, 1996), 4: 569-72.

111. Marie de Clèves, duchesse d'Orléans, daughter of Adolphe de Clèves and Marie de Bourgogne. Only the date of her death, 1487, is known. Her postmortem inventory made that same year at the château de Chauny describes twenty-six books (Paris, B.N.F., MS Fr. 22335, fols. 263-64 ; edited by Pierre Champion, *La Librairie de*

Charles d'Orléans (Paris, 1910) : 116-17). She was the third wife of Charles (1391-1465), duc d'Orléans and Milan, peer of France, comte de Valois. She married him in 1440 and among their children were Marie d'Orléans, who married Jean de Foix, comte d'Étampes (d.1493), and Anne d'Orléans, abbess of Fontevrault in 1478 (d.1491). Cf. Louis Moreri, *Le Grand Dictionnaire historique*, Vol. 8, Paris, 1759 (Geneva: Slatkine Reprints, 1995): 107-08.
112. See above note.
113. Delisle (*Cabinet des Manuscrits*, 91 n. 5) transcribes " conviteor " which according to him ought to read "confiteor".
114. A book that speaks of armors.

WORKS CITED

Avril, François. *La Passion des manuscrits enluminés. Bibliophiles français*, 1280-1580. Paris: Bibliothèque Nationale, 1991.
———. "Un portrait inédit de la reine Charlotte de Savoie." In *Études sur la Bibliothèque Nationale et témoignages réunis en hommage à Thérèse Kleindienst*, 255-62. Paris: 1985.
Avril, François and Nicole Reynaud. *Les Manuscrits à peintures en France, 1440-1530*. Paris: Flammarion, 1993 (reprint, 1995).
Backhouse, Janet. "A Book of Hours by a Contemporary of Jean Bourdichon." In *Manuscripts in the Fifty Years after the Invention of Printing*. Edited by J. B. Trapp, 45-49. London: The Warburg Institute, 1983.
———. "French Manuscript Illumination 1450-1530." In *Renaissance Painting in Manuscripts: Treasures from the British Library* Edited by Thomas Kren, 143-92. Exhibition catalogue, New York, 1983, 143-92. New York: Hudson Hills Press, 1983.
———. "Poyet, Jean." In *The Dictionary of Art*. Vol. 25. New York, 1996.
———. "The Tilliot Hours: Comparisons and Relationships." *British Library Journal* 13 (1987): 211-31.
Baurmeister, Ursula and Marie-Pierre Laffitte. *Des Livres et des rois. La bibliothèque royale de Blois*. Paris, 1992.
Bouchot, H. *Inventaire des dessins exécutés pour Roger de Gaignières*. Paris, 1891.
Bradley, J.W. *A Dictionary of Miniaturists, Illuminators, Calligraphers, and Copyists from the Establishment of Christianity to the Eighteenth Century*. Vol. 3. London, 1887. Reprint, New York, 1958.
Briquet, C.M. *Les Filigranes. Dictionnaire historique des marques du papier dès leur apparition vers 1282 jusqu'en 1600*. 2d ed. Paris, 1923. Reprint, New York, 1966.
Catalogue des Manuscrits en Écriture latine. Edited by Charles Samaran and Robert Marichal, 8: Ouest de la France et Pays de Loire, Paris, 1988.
Champion, Pierre. *La Librairie de Charles d'Orléans*. Paris, 1910.
———. *Louis XI*. 2 vols, Paris: Honoré Champion, 1928.

Chazaud, Alphonse-Martial. *Les Enseignements d'Anne de France, duchesse de Bourbonnais et d'Auvergne à sa fille Susanne de Bourbon.* Moulins, 1878.
Chenu, Paul. *Note sur un manuscrit de la bibliothèque de l'archevêque Guillaume de Cambray.* Mémoires de la Société des Antiquaires du Centre, 41 (Bourges: Société des Antiquaires du Centre, 1923): 248-56.
Commynes, Philippe de. *Mémoires.* Edited by Jean Dufournet. Vol. 2. Paris, 1979.
Cottineau, Dom L. H. *Répertoire Topo-bibliographique des abbayes et prieuré.* Vol. 2. Mâcon, 1939.
D'Amat, Roman. "Charlotte de Savoie." In Dictionnaire de biographie française. Vol. 8. Paris, 1959.
Delisle, Léopold. *Le Cabinet des Manuscrits de la Bibliothèque impériale* [nationale]. Vol. 1 and 3. Paris, 1868 and 1881.
Dictionnaire des Lettres françaises du Moyen Âge. Edited by Michel Zink and Geneviève Hasenohr. Paris, 1992.
Edmunds, Sheila. "Catalogue des manuscrits savoyards: II, Manuscrits liés à d'autres membres de la Maison de Savoie." in *Les manuscrits enluminés des comtes et ducs de Savoie.* Edited by A. Paravicini Bagliani, 213-14, no. 64. Turin, 1990.
Gandilhon, Alfred. *Contribution à l'histoire de la vie privée et de la cour de Louis XI (1423-1481).* Mémoires de la Société Historique, Littéraire et Scientifique du Cher, 4th series, Vol. 20 (Bourges, 1905): 335, 375-82.
Giraudet, Ernest. *Les artistes tourangeaux,* Mémoires de la société archéologique de Touraine 33 (Tours, 1885).
Girault, Pierre-Gilles. "Jean Poyet peut-il être l'auteur des heures du Tilliot?" *Revue de l'Art* 110 (1995): 74-78.
Godefroy, Frédéric. *Dictionnaire de l'ancienne langue française et de tous ses dialectes du IXe au XVe siècle.* Vol. 7, Geneva-Paris: Slatkine, 1982.
Grandmaison, Charles de. *Documents inédits pour servir à l'histoire des arts en Touraine.* Paris: J.B. Dumoulin, 1870.
Guiffrey, Jules. "Peintres, ymagiers, verriers, maçons, enlumineurs, écrivains et libraires du XIVe et du XVe siècles." *Nouvelles Archives de l'Art Français* 7 (1878): 157-221.
Hasenohr, Geneviève. "A propos de la Vie de Nostre Benoît Sauveur Jhesus Crist." *Romania* 102 (1981): 352-91.
Helmrath, J., *Das Basler Konzil, 1431-1449: Forschungsstand und Probleme.* Cologne and Vienna, 1987.
Houdebine, Timothée L. *Le Puy-Notre-Dame, l'église et le pèlerinage de la Sainte-Ceinture.* Angers: Société française d'Imprimerie et de Publicité, 1924.
Kendall, Paul Murray. *Louis XI.* Paris, 1974.
König, Eberhard, with the collab. of G. Bartz and H. Tenschert, *Vom Heiligen Ludwig zum Sonnenkönig: 34 Werke der Französischen Buchmalerei aus Gotik,*

Renaissance und Barock Leuchtendes Mittelalters: Neue Folge 3, Ramsen, Heribert Tenschert, 2000.
Lapeyre, André. *Louis XI, mécène dans le domaine de l'orfèvrerie religieuse*. Paris, 1986.
Legaré, Anne-Marie. "Livres et lectures de la reine Jeanne de Laval." in *Bretagne, Art, création, société. Mélanges en l'honneur de Denise Delouche*. Edited by J.-Y. Andrieux and M. Grivel, 220-34. Rennes: Presses Universitaires de Rennes, 1997.
———. "Reassessing Women's Libraries in late Medieval France. The Case of Jeanne de Laval." *Renaissance Studies* 10, no. 2, *Women Patrons of Renaissance Art* (1996): 209-36.
Leroux de Lincy, Antoine-Jean-Victor. *Catalogue de la bibliothèque des ducs de Bourbon qui sont en la librairie du chasteau de Molins*. Mélanges de la Société des bibliophiles français, 73-111.Paris, 1850.
Lesellier, J., "Un Historiographe de Louis XI demeuré inconnu, Guillaume Danicot", *Mélanges d'Archéologie et d'Histoire de l'École française de Rome Moyen Âge* 43 (1926): 1-29.
Lieftinck, Georges. *Boekverluchters mit de omgeving van Maria Bourgondie c. 1475–c. 1485*. Verhandelingen van de Koninlijke, Vlaamse Academie voor Wetenschappen, Letteren en schone Kunsten van Belgie: Klasse der Letteren 31, Brussels, 1969.
Livres Anciens et Modernes. Sale catalogue, Paris, Hôtel Drouot, October 23-24, 1975.
Macon, Gustave. "Note sur le Mystère de la Résurrection." *Bulletin des Bibliophiles* (Paris, 1898): 1-21.
MacGibbon, D. *Jean Bourdichon*. Glasgow, 1933.
Maulde La Clavière, René-Alphonse-Marie. *Jeanne de France*. Paris, 1883.
Mérindol, Christian de. "Louis XI et le Puy-Notre-Dame. Mise au point, nouvelles lectures, nouvelles perspectives." In *Mémoires de l'Académie d'Angers*. N.p. 1996 (off-print).
Moreri, Louis, *Le Grand Dictionnaire historique*. Vol. 8, Paris: Les Libraires associés, 1759 (Genève: Slatkine Reprints, 1995).
Olivier, Eugène, Georges Hermal, and R. de Roton. *Manuel de l'Amateur de reliures armoriées françaises*. Paris, 1935.
Omont, Henri. *Anciens inventaires et catalogues de la Bibliothèque Nationale. La Librairie Royale à Blois, Fontainebleau et Paris au XVIe siècle*. Vol. 1, Paris, 1908.
———. *Catalogue général des Manuscrits français, nouvelles acquisitions françaises*. Vol. 2. Paris, 1900.
Orléans, Henri d', duc d'Aumale. *Chantilly: Le Cabinet des livres. Manuscrits*. Vol. 1. Paris, 1900.
Picot, Ernest. *Le Duc d'Aumale et la bibliothèque à Chantilly*. Paris, 1897.
Plummer, John. *The Last Flowering: French Painting in Manuscripts, 1420-1530*. Exhibition catalogue, Pierpont Morgan Library, New York, November

1982-January 1983. New York and London: Oxford University Press, 1982.
Port, Célestin. Dictionnaire historique, géographique et biographique de Maine-et-Loire. Vol. 2, Paris, 1874-78.
Pradel, Pierre. Anne de France, 1461-1522. Paris: Publisud, 1986.
Quillet, Bernard. Louis XII. Paris: Fayard, 1986.
Reynaud, Nicole. "Bourdichon, Jean." In The Dictionary of Art. Vol. 4. New-York, 1996.
Roussineau, Gilles. "La Représentation du Mystère de saint Vincent, joué à Angers en 1471." Revue d'Histoire du Théâtre 1-2 (1991): 27-42.
Runnalls, Graham A., "René d'Anjou et le Théâtre." Annale de Bretagne et des Pays de l'Ouest (Anjou, Maine, Touraine) 88 (1981): 157-180.
Samaran, Charles. "Un ouvrage de Guillaume Danicot, historiographe de Louis XI." Mélanges d'Archéologie et d'Histoire de l'École Française de Rome 45 (1928): 8-20.
Schaefer, Claude. "Les Débuts de l'atelier de Jean Colombe: Jean Colombe et André Rousseau, prêtre, libraire, et 'escrivain.'" Gazette des Beaux-Arts 2, (November 1977): 137-150.
Thuasne, Louis. "Note sur Jean Colombe, enlumineur." Revue des bibliothèques, Paris, Librairie Emile Bouillon (January-April 1904): 59-62.
Tuetey, Alexandre. Inventaire des biens de Charlotte de Savoie. Bibliothèque de l'École des chartes, 26: 338-66 and 423-42. Paris, 1865.
Vergne, Frédéric. La Bibliothèque du Prince. Château de Chantilly. Les manuscrits. Paris, 1995.
Vernet, André, director. Les Bibliotheques médiévales du VIe siècle à 1530. Vol. 1 of Histoire des Bibliothèques françaises. Paris, 1989.
Vernet, André. "Les Manuscrits de Claude d'Urfé (1501-1558) au château de la Bastie." In Comptes rendus de l'Académie des Inscriptions des Belles-lettres, 81-97. Paris, January-March 1976.
Wieck, Roger S., The Prayer Book of Anne de Bretagne. Pierpont Morgan Library, Ms. M. 50. Lucerne: Faksimile Verlag Luzern, 1999.

TABLE OF CONCORDANCES AND IDENTIFICATIONS

The text of the inventory is transcribed in its totality but I have isolated the portions concerning the binding in the column BINDING. When possible, I have given in the second column the author and title of the work, sometimes with question marks. Mentions of vellum (V) or paper (P) are indicated in the column SUPPORT. They appear in bold when the information comes from the identified manuscript and not from the inventory.

TABLE OF CONCORDANCES AND IDENTIFICATIONS

INVENTORY OF 1484	AUTHOR AND TITLE	SUPPORT	BINDING	MOULINS 1523 Leroux	MOULINS 1523 Chazaud	SHELF MARKS
1. Ung livre... appellé le second volume des Ystoires.	Jean Mansel, La Fleur des histoires	V	...couvert de veloux gris a fermouer de leton, aux armes de mons' de Beauju...	Inventory of 1518		B.N.F., Fr. 300 (Avril)
2. Ung petit psautier, non extimé.	Psalter					
3. Une Heures... non extimee.	Book of Hours		...couvertes de veloux noir, a fremouers d'or, ou il y a quatre petites perles et quatre petiz grenez de rubiz...			
4. Ung grand livre en pappier nommé Boucasse, des cas des nobles hommes.	Boccacio, Du cas des nobles hommes et femmes, trans. by Laurent de Premierfait	P				
5. Unes petites heures...	Book of hours...		garnies d'argent doré a l'environ, et couvertes de veloux cramoisi a deux fremouers.			
6. Ung sautier historié... appellé le sautier saint Loys, lequel lad. Dame avoit emprunté de la dame de Poyssy, et estoit son entencion le luy rendre, ainsi que ont rapporté les femmes de chambre de lad. Dame, lequel sera baillé es mains de madame de Beaujeu pour le rendre.	Saint Louis' Psalter	V	...couvert de satin figuré vert et roge, a deux fremouers...			B.N.F., Lat. 10525 (Avril)
7. Une Legende doree en parchemyn...	Jacques de Voragine, La Légende dorée, trans. by Jean de Vignay	V	...couverte de cuir blanc.	168	179	
8. Ung second volume de la Cité de Dieu...	Saint Augustine, La Cité de Dieu, trans. by Raoul de Presles...		couvert de cuir blanc a deux fremouers d'argent dorez.	17	17	
9. Ung livre de Boucasse des nobles hommes malheureux...	Boccacio, Du cas des nobles hommes et femmes, trans. by Laurent de Premierfait		fermé a deux fremouers	160 "deficit"	171 "deficit"	
10. Ung livre ... nommé Tresor en ligue (sic) francoyse.	Brunetto Latini, Le Trésor or Robert le Chartreux, Trésor de l'âme		...couvert de veloux bleu, garny de boyllons et de deux fremouers dorez, qui est en ung sac de cuir blanc...	76 or 162	81 or 173	

V = VELLUM; P = PAPER; **IN BOLD** = INFORMATION SUPPLIED BY THE MANUSCRIPT.

TABLE OF CONCORDANCES AND IDENTIFICATIONS

INVENTORY OF 1484	AUTHOR AND TITLE	SUPPORT	BINDING	MOULINS 1523 Leroux	MOULINS 1523 Chazaud	SHELF MARKS
11. *Ung livre... appellé Le Proprietaire*	Barthélemy l'Anglais, *Le Livre des propriétés des choses*, trans. by Jean Corbechon		...*couvert de trippe de veloux...*	66	71	
*11 bis. *Ung livre en pappier, escript en mosle, nommé le Nouveau Testament...*	New Testament	P	...*couvert de cuir fauve*			
12. *Ung autre livre en parchemyn...appellé l'Orloge de Sapience, le Chasteau perilleux.*	Henri Suso, *L'Horloge de sapience*, anonymous trans.; Robert le Chartreux, *Le Château périlleux*	V	...*couvert de cuir rouge...*	10	10	B.N.F. Fr. 445 (Avril) (Fig. 7)
13. *Ung livre des secretz d'Aristote en pappier qu'il envoya a Alexandre.*	[Book of versified and prose texts...]	P		266	290	Chantilly 685 (Legaré)
14. *Ung livre de Pellerinaige de vie humaine, en parchemyn...*	Guillaume de Digulleville, *Le Pèlerinage de vie humaine*	V	...*couvert de noir.*	142	152	
15. *Ung livre de la Passion Nostre Seigneur en pappier... translaté de latin, en françoys* (cf. no. 38)	*La Passion de Jésus-Christ*	P	...*couvert de roge...*	236 or 268	261 or 292	Chantilly 37 or 38 (Legaré)
16. *Ung livre des Merveilles du monde en pappier...* (see no. 52)	Marco Polo, *Livre des merveilles?*	P	...*couvert de jaune.*	240	265	
17. *Ung Livre du roy Alixandre en pappier...*	Quinte-Curce, *Faiz d'Alixandre*, trans. by Vasque de Lucène	P	...*couvert de cuir jaune.*	35	38	
18. *Ung livre de la Mortification de l'ame escript en pappier...*	René d'Anjou, *Mortifiement de vaine plaisance*	P	...*couvert de roge.*	269	293	
19. *Ung livre en parchemin, nommé le Debat des quatre dames...*	Alain Chartier, *Livre des quatre dames*	V	...*couvert de roge.*	117	125	B.N.F., Fr. 2234 (Avril)
20. *Ung livre de Miracles de saincte Katherine en parchemin*	*Miracles de Madame sainte Catherine de Fierbois*	V	...*couvert de roge.*	Omitted	46	B.N.F. Fr. 1045 (Avril)

*Printed book
V = Vellum; P = Paper

CHARLOTTE DE SAVOIE'S LIBRARY

TABLE OF CONCORDANCES AND IDENTIFICATIONS

INVENTORY OF 1484	AUTHOR AND TITLE	SUPPORT	BINDING	MOULINS 1523		SHELF MARKS
				Leroux	Chazaud	
21. *Un livre de la vie sainct Vincent en pappier...*	Guillaume Danicot, *Vie et Mystère de saint Vincent en vers et par personnages*	P	*...couvert de blanc et de roge.*	231	256	B.N.F., Fr. 12538 (Legaré)
22. *Ung livre en pappier de la Montaigne de contemplacion*	Jean Gerson, *La Montagne de contemplation*	P	*...couvert de taffetas changent.*	265	289	
23. *Ung livre de Ponthus en pappier...*	*Ponthus et Sidoine*	P	*...couvert de cuir vert.*	248	273	
24. *Ung livre de Melurine en prose, en pappier...*	Jean d'Arras, *Histoire de la belle Mélusine*	P	*...couvert de cuir noir.*	235 or 241	260 or 266	
25. *Le livre de l'Exposition des Euvangilles de tous les dimenches de l'an, en pappier...*		P	*...couvert de cuir roge.*			
26. *Le livre du Sermon de maistre Jehan Jarson, en pappier...* (cf. no. 50)	Jean Gerson, *Sermons*	P	*...couvert de cuir roge.*	256	281	Chantilly 145 (Legaré)
27. *Le livre de la vie de sainct Jousse, en pappier...*	*Vie de saint Josse*, in verse	P	*...couvert de cuir noir.*	85	90	B.N.F., Fr. 2101 (Avril)
28. *La Confession avec la Passion, en parchemyn...*		V	*...couvert de cuir roge.*			
29. *Le Livre de la Cité des Dames, en parchemyn...*	Christine de Pizan, *Livre de la Cité des dames*	V	*...couvert de cuir noir.*			
30. *Le livre des Troys vertuz a l'enseignement des dames, en parchemyn, bien ystorié...*	Christine de Pizan, *Livre des trois vertus à l'enseignement des dames*	V	*...couvert de cuir roge, a deux fremouers de cuivre doré.*	120 or 124	129 or 133 "deficit"	
31. *Ung livre ... de la Vie de saincte Arrogonde...*	*Vie et office de sainte Radegonde*	**V**	*...couvert de velouz noi..., fermant a esguilletes ferrees d'or.*	134	143	**B.N.F., Fr. 5718 (Avril) (Fig. 4)**
32. *Le Réducteur de l'ame...*	*Réductoire de l'Ame*, trans. by Etienne des Arpentiz	V	*...fermant a esguilletes, couvert de satin violet.*	79	84	B.N.F., Fr. 1821 (Tuetey)

V = VELLUM; P = PAPER; **IN BOLD** = INFORMATION SUPPLIED BY THE MANUSCRIPT.

TABLE OF CONCORDANCES AND IDENTIFICATIONS

INVENTORY OF 1484	AUTHOR AND TITLE	SUPPORT	BINDING	MOULINS 1523		SHELF MARKS
				Leroux	Chazaud	
33. Le livre que le roy de Secille envoya au duc de Bourbon, avec la Dance aux aveugles, en pappier...	Pierre Michault, Dance aux aveugles	P	...couvert de cuir roge.	278	302	
34. Ung livre de la Vie contemplative... en pappier.	Traité de la vie contemplative	P	...couvert de cuir roge...	118	126	B.N.F., Fr. 1875 (Tuetey)
35. Ung Livre de L'Instruction d'un jeune prince, en parchemin...	Gilbert de Lannoy, Instruction d'un jeune prince	V	...couvert de roge.			
36. Le Livre des herbes et abres, en parchemin...		V	...couvert de roge.	42	45	
37. Le Livre du Gouvernement des roys et princes, en parchemyn...	Li Livre du gouvernement des rois, trans. by Henri de Gauchy	V	...couvert de cuir blanc, et a boillons.	108	115	
38. Le livre de la Passion Nostre Seigneur en pappier et en françoys... (cf. no. 15)	La Passion de Jésus-Christ	P	...couvert de cuir roge.	236 or 268	261 or 292	Chantilly 37 or 38 (Legaré)
39. Le Livre nommé le Legigolle, en pappier...	Legiloque or Dialogue du père et du fils	P	...couvert de cuir roge.	255	280	Chantilly 138 (Legaré)
40. Le Livre de Cleriadus en pappier.	Roman de Cleriadus et Meliadice	P		262 and 284	287 and 308	
41. Le livre de Boesse de Consolacion, en françoys et en pappier...	Livre Boece de Consolation. anon. trans.	P	...couvert de roge.	157	167	
42. Le Livre de saincte Katherine de Sayne en pappier...	Visions de saincte Catherine de Sienne	P	...couvert de cuir fauve.	219	245	Chantilly 741 (Legaré)

V = Vellum; P = Paper

CHARLOTTE DE SAVOIE'S LIBRARY

TABLE OF CONCORDANCES AND IDENTIFICATIONS

INVENTORY OF 1484	AUTHOR AND TITLE	SUPPORT	BINDING	MOULINS 1523 Leroux	MOULINS 1523 Chazaud	SHELF MARKS
43. *Le Livre qui parle que c'est du prebstre, de l'église et de la messe... et en pappier.*	Olivier le Royer, *Le livre qui parle du prêtre, de l'église et de la messe... et en pappier.*	P	*...couvert de cuir roge...*	260	285	Chantilly 159 (Legaré)
44. *Le livre de plusieurs miracles de Nostre Dame, en parchemyn.* (cf. no.74)	Gautier de Coinci, *Miracles de Nostre Dame*	V		129	138	
45. *Le Livre de Maglonne en pappier...*	Pierre de Provence et la belle Maguelonne	P	*...couvert de vert.*	285	309	
46. *Le livre de Paris et de Vienne en pappier...*	Pierre de la Cépède, *Paris et Vienne*	P	*...couvert de cuir blanc.*	257	282	
47. *Le livre de la Resurrection Nostre Seigneur en pappier... et par personnages.*	*Mystère de la Résurrection*	P	*...couvert de roge...*	244	269	Chantilly 615 (Legaré)
48. *Le livre de la Maison de conscience en pappier...* (see no.76)	Jean Saunier, *La Maison de conscience*	P	*...couvert de cuir roge.*	216 or 243	242 or 268	Chantilly 153 or 154 (Legaré)
49.*Le livre de la Translacion de latin en françoys de sainct Julian...*	Guillaume Danicot, *Vie de saint Julien*	**V**	*...couvert de roge, fermant a deux esguilletes.*	90	96	B.N.F. Fr. 2099 (Samaran)
50. *Le livre des Sermons maistre Jehan Jarson en parchemin...* (cf. no.26)	Jean Gerson, *Sermons*	V	*...couvert de roge.*	132	141	
51. *Ung livre des eschecs en pappier...*	Jacques de Cessoles, *Le jeu des échecs moralisés?*	P	*...couvert de roge.*	259	274	
52. *Le livre des Merveilles du monde, en parchemin...* (see no. 16)	Marco Polo, *Livre des Merveilles?*	V	*...couvert de roge et a boillons.*			
53. *Le sautier en françoys, en pappier... par pseaulmes.*	Psalter in French	P	*...couvert de parchemyn...*			
54. *Le livre que fist le chevalier a la Tour pour enseigner ses filles, en parchemyn......*	Geoffroi de La Tour Landry, *Le livre pour l'enseignement de ses filles*	V	*...couvert de vert.*	84	89	

V = VELLUM; P = PAPER; **IN BOLD** = INFORMATION SUPPLIED BY THE MANUSCRIPT.

TABLE OF CONCORDANCES AND IDENTIFICATIONS

INVENTORY OF 1484	AUTHOR AND TITLE	SUPPORT	BINDING	MOULINS 1523		SHELF MARKS
				Leroux	Chazaud	
55. *Le Livre de Confession, en pappier...* (cf. no.71)	Jean Gerson?	P	*...couvert de noir.*			
56. *Ung Livre des Anges, en pappier...*	Francesc Eiximenis, *Livre des Anges*	P	*...couvert de jaune.*	229 or 276	254 omitted	Chantilly 143 (Legaré)
57. *Ung livre de la Vie Nostre Dame et plusieurs sainctes, en pappier....*		P	*...couvert de roge.*			
58. *Ung livre qui parle du Traictié de perfection, en parchemin...*	Robert Ciboule, *Livre de perfection*	V	*...couvert de cuir roge.*	62	144	B.N.F., Fr. 1841 (Tuetey)
59. *Ung livre de certains laiz et coustumes pour passer le temps, en parchemin...*	Guillaume Alecis, *Passetemps des deux Alecis* or *Passe-temps de tout homme* or Michault Taillevent, *Le Passe temps* or *Lois et comptes à passer le temps*	V	*...couvert de cuir roge.*			
60. *Ung Traictié de l'ame devote, en parchemin...*		V	*...couvert de cuir roge.*			
61. *Ung livre en pappier, qui parle au commencement pourquoi Dieu fist l'omme a sa figure...*		P	*...couvert de roge.*			
62. *Le Livre de la vroye ystoire de Troye, en pappier....*	Raoul Lefèvre, *Recueil des histoires de Troie?*	P	*...couvert de roge.*			
63. *Le livre de Pierre Chastellain, en parchemin...*	Pierre Chastellain, *Le temps perdu, Le temps recouvré?*	V	*...couvert de roge.*			
64. *La Bible en parchemin, aveques les exposicions des Euvangilles et plusieurs autres choses...*	Bible	V	*...couvert de roge.*			
65. *Le livre de L'Abbuzé en court, en parchemin...*	*L'Abuzé en court*	V	*...couvert de roge.*			

V = Vellum; P = Paper

TABLE OF CONCORDANCES AND IDENTIFICATIONS

INVENTORY OF 1484	AUTHOR AND TITLE	SUPPORT	BINDING	MOULINS 1523 Leroux	MOULINS 1523 Chazaud	SHELF MARKS
66. *Le Livre du Pellerinaige en prose, et en pappier...*	Guillaume de Digulleville, *Pèlerinage de vie humaine?, de l'Âme?, de Jésus-Christ?* in prose	P	...*couvert de roge*.			
67. *Ung autre livre de La Passion, en parchemin...* (cf. no. 100)	*La Passion de Jésus-Christ?*	V	...*couvert de roge et a bouillons*.	55	59	
68. *Le Temple de Boucasse, en parchemin*	Georges Chastellain, *Le Temple de Boccace*	V	...*couvert de roge*.			
69. *Le livre des Troys filz de Roy, en parchemin...*	*Roman des trois fils de roi*	V	...*couvert de roge*.	57	62	
70. *L'Espitre que la deesse Ostea fist a Hector de Troye, en pappier...*	Christine de Pizan, *L'Epistre d'Othea*	P	...*couvert de vert*.	270	294	
71. *Ung livre qui parle de Confession, en pappier* (cf. no. 55)	Jean Gerson?	P	...*couvert de vert*.			
72. *Ung livre envoyé a une novice de Frontevaulx, en pappier...*	Jean Henry, *Livre d'instruction pour religieuses novices envoyé à une novice fontebriste*	P	...*couvert de vert*.	234	259	Chantilly 158 (Legaré)
73. *Le Livre de Sapience qui enseigne a bien mourir; en parchemin...*	Jean Gerson, *Science de bien mourir?*; part of *Tresor de Sapience?*	V	...*couvert de noir*.			
74. *Ung livre de plusieurs Miracles de Nostre Dame, en parchemin...* (cf. no. 44)	Gautier de Coinci, *Miracles de Nostre Dame*	V	...*couvert de cuir roge*.	129	138	
75. *Troys ou quatre cahiers en pappier, qui parlent de la resurrection des mors*		P				
76. *Le Livre de la Maison de conscience, en pappier...* (cf no. 48)	Jean Saulnier, *La Maison de conscience*	P	...*couvert de roge*.	216 or 243	242 or 268	Chantilly 153 or 154 (Legaré)

V = VELLUM; P = PAPER

TABLE OF CONCORDANCES AND IDENTIFICATIONS

INVENTORY OF 1484	AUTHOR AND TITLE	SUPPORT	BINDING	MOULINS 1523 Leroux	MOULINS 1523 Chazaud	SHELF MARKS
77. Ung livre ... aux armes de la royne, faisant mencion du Pellerinaige de vie humaine...	Guillaume de Digulleville, Le Pèlerinage de vie humaine in prose	V	...couvert de veloux violet, ferment a deux fremouers d'argent... remis en ung estuy de blanc et de roge.			Ramsen, Antiquariat Heribert Tenschert (Sotheby's **(Fig. 6)**
78. Ung livre de la mort du duc de Bourgoigne, en parchemin...	(Maybe John the Fearless, according to Tuetey)	V	...couvert de vert.			
79. Le livre de Chasteau perilleux et Tulle de vieillesse...	Robert le Chartreux, Le Château périlleux ; Cicero, De Senectute, trans. by Laurent de Premierfait	V	...couvert de roge.	96	102	B.N.F., Fr. 1009 (Avril)
80. Plus le premier volume du Myrouer ystorial que lad. Dame emprunta de Monsgr de Chastillon, et ordonna qu'il luy feust rendu	Vincent de Beauvais, Le Miroir historial, trans. by Jean de Vignay	V		Inventory of 1518		B.N.F., Fr. 316
81. Petiz cahiers en pappier et parchemin...		V P	...non reliés.			
82. Ung livre ... nommé de plusieurs renvoys.			...couvert de drap d'or sur satin figuré a grans figures...			
83. Ung livre de la Passion tout ystorié...	La Passion de Jésus-Christ in prose	V	...couvert led. Livre de satin figuré cramoisi a fons d'or, et les fremouers et boillons d'argent doré estant en une bourse de cuir noir.	15	15	Chantilly 36? (Legaré)
84. Ung autre livre ... comançant en lectre roge : <u>Comment on se doit pre-parer</u>.	Préparation du saint Sacrement de l'autel	V	...couvert de satin vermeil, non fermé...	131	140	B.N.F., Fr. 1813 (Delisle)
85. Ung autre livre... appellé Le Livre du Jardin de contemplacion...	Jean Henry, Jardin de contemplation		...couvert de cuir roge... lequel est en ung sac de cuir violet.	140	150	B.N.F., Fr. 997 (Tuetey)

V = VELLUM; P = PAPER; **IN BOLD** = INFORMATION SUPPLIED BY THE MANUSCRIPT.

TABLE OF CONCORDANCES AND IDENTIFICATIONS

INVENTORY OF 1484	AUTHOR AND TITLE	SUPPORT	BINDING	MOULINS 1523 Leroux	MOULINS 1523 Chazaud	SHELF MARKS
86. *Ung autre livre ... parlant des vices et vertuz.*	Frère Laurent, *La Somme le Roi* or *Livre des vices et des vertus*		*...de semblable couverture...*	83	88	
87. *Ung autre livre ... ystorié, nommé Les Lamentacions Monsgr sainct Bernard...*	*Lamentations de saint Bernard*, followed by various treatises	V	*...couvert de velours noir...fermé a fremouers de cuivre doré.*	139	149	B.N.F., Fr. 916 (Avril) **(Fig. 8)**
88. *Ung autre livre .... appellé Les Espitres et Euvengilles, translaté de latin en françoys.* (cf. no.99)	*Des Epîtres et des Evangiles* for a whole year, trans. by Jean de Vignay??		*...couvert de cuir roge...*	86	91	
89. *Deux grans volumes de Vita Christi...*	Ludolphe de Saxe, *Vita Jesu Christi*, anon. trans.	V	*...couvers de roge.*	21-22	21-22	B.N.F., Fr. 407-408 (Delisle) **(Fig. 1)**
90. *Ung petit livre de l'effect d'orasions...*	*Des biens qui viennent d'orisons*		*...couvert de roge.*	93	99	
91. *Ung autre petit livre des Revelacions que fist Nostre Dame a saincte Elizabel...*	Book of ascetic and spiritual texts	V	*...couvert de roge.*	128	137	B.N.F., Fr. 1801 (Avril)
92. *Ung autre livre, intitulé le Livre des perilz d'enfer... et bien ystorié.*	Robert Blondel, *Les Douze Périls d'enfer*	V	*...couvert de roge...*	Inventory of 1518		B.N.F., Fr. 449 (Delisle) **(Fig. 2)**
93. *Ung autre livre...que Monsgr de Maillé luy donna.*			*...couvert de roge...*			
94. *Ung petit livre de dames et d'amours...*	[Book with songs?]		*...ataché a esguilletes, couvert de vert.*			
95. *Ung petit livre appellé Triboulet...*	*Les Vigilles Triboulet?*		*...couvert de noir, ataché a esguilletes.*			

V = VELLUM; **IN BOLD** = INFORMATION SUPPLIED BY THE MANUSCRIPT.

TABLE OF CONCORDANCES AND IDENTIFICATIONS

INVENTORY OF 1484	AUTHOR AND TITLE	SUPPORT	BINDING	MOULINS 1523 Leroux	MOULINS 1523 Chazaud	SHELF MARKS
96. Ung autre petit livre en parchemin, appellé L'Examen de conscience, et le Sainct Pierre de Luxembourg...	Jean Gerson, L'examen de conscience, L'Art de bien mourir; L'ABC des simples gens ; Pierre de Luxembourg, La Diete de Salut	V	...couvert de roge.	133	142	B.N.F., Fr. 1836 (Avril)
97. Ung autre livre en parchemin, appellé Les Heures de Monsgr de Berry, bien ystorié.	Grandes Heures du duc de Berry	V		Inventory of 1518		Paris, B.N.F., latin 919 (Avril)
98. Plusieurs cahiers en parchemin, faisant mencion du Jardin des Nobles.	Pierre Des Gros, Jardin des nobles	V				
99. Ung petit livre en parchemin, appellé le Livre des Espitres et Euvangilles de tout l'an... qui est a madame de Segré (cf. no. 88)	Des Epîtres et des Évangiles for the whole year, trans. by Jean de Vignay	V	...couvert de cuir tanné.			
100. Ung livre ... parlant de la Passion Nostre Seigneur. (cf. no. 67)	La Passion de Jésus-Christ		...couvert de roge poinssonné.	55	59	
101. Le livre de la Complainte de l'omme a son ame....	Jean Gerson, Le Secret Parlement de l'homme à son âme	V	...couvert de roge.	143	153	B.N.F., Fr. 1835 (Avril)
102. Ung autre petit livre en pappier, de saincte Clere...	Vie de saincte Claire?	P	...couvert de cuir roge.			
103. Ung petit livre.... commençant : Humane beate Marye virginis.			...couvert de cuir jaune....			
104. Ung petit livre... ystorié, et commance : Tres noble.		V	...couvert de jaune....			
105. Ung autre petit livre comançant : S'ensuit une petite et briefve contemplacion...			...couvert de cuir noir.			

V = Vellum; P = Paper

CHARLOTTE DE SAVOIE'S LIBRARY

TABLE OF CONCORDANCES AND IDENTIFICATIONS

INVENTORY OF 1484	AUTHOR AND TITLE	SUPPORT	BINDING	MOULINS 1523		SHELF MARKS
				Leroux	Chazaud	
106. *Unes heures de lad. Dame...*	Book of Hours		...*couvertes de veloux noir, aveques ung fremouer d'or, ouquel est empraint une Nostre Dame de Pityé.*			
107. *Ung petit livre... appellé Le Chappellet Nostre Dame.*	*Chapelet Notre-Dame*		...*couvert de veloux noir, fermant a esguilletes...*			
108. *Plusieurs lectres missives et plusieurs autres pappiers de devocion.*						
109. *Ung petit livre plain d'oraisons et choses contemplatives de la nativité du roy... aux armes de la royne.*	Guillaume Danicot, *Congratulation et graces de la nativité de Charles aisné filz du roy Loys unziesme de ce nom...*	V	...*couvert de veloux noir a ung fremouer d'argent doré...*	16	16	B.N.F., Fr. 2222 (Delisle) (Fig. 3)
**110. *Unes Heures... extimees XXV escuz.*	Book of Hours		...*couvertes de veloux noir a fremouers d'or...*			
**111. *Ung petit livre... de la vie de sainct Servays... non extimé.*	*Vie de saint Servais*		...*couvert de veloux bleu, aux armes du roy... estant en ung sac de velous noir...*			

V = Vellum; **IN BOLD** = INFORMATION SUPPLIED BY THE MANUSCRIPT.

** Books which might have been the king's property.

Figure 1. Paris, B.N.F., MS Fr. 407, Ludolphe de Saxe, *Vita Jesu Christi* [89], fol. 1; Guillaume Piqueau, 1482; Annunciation, Nativity, and Adoration. Cliché Bibliothèque Nationale de France.

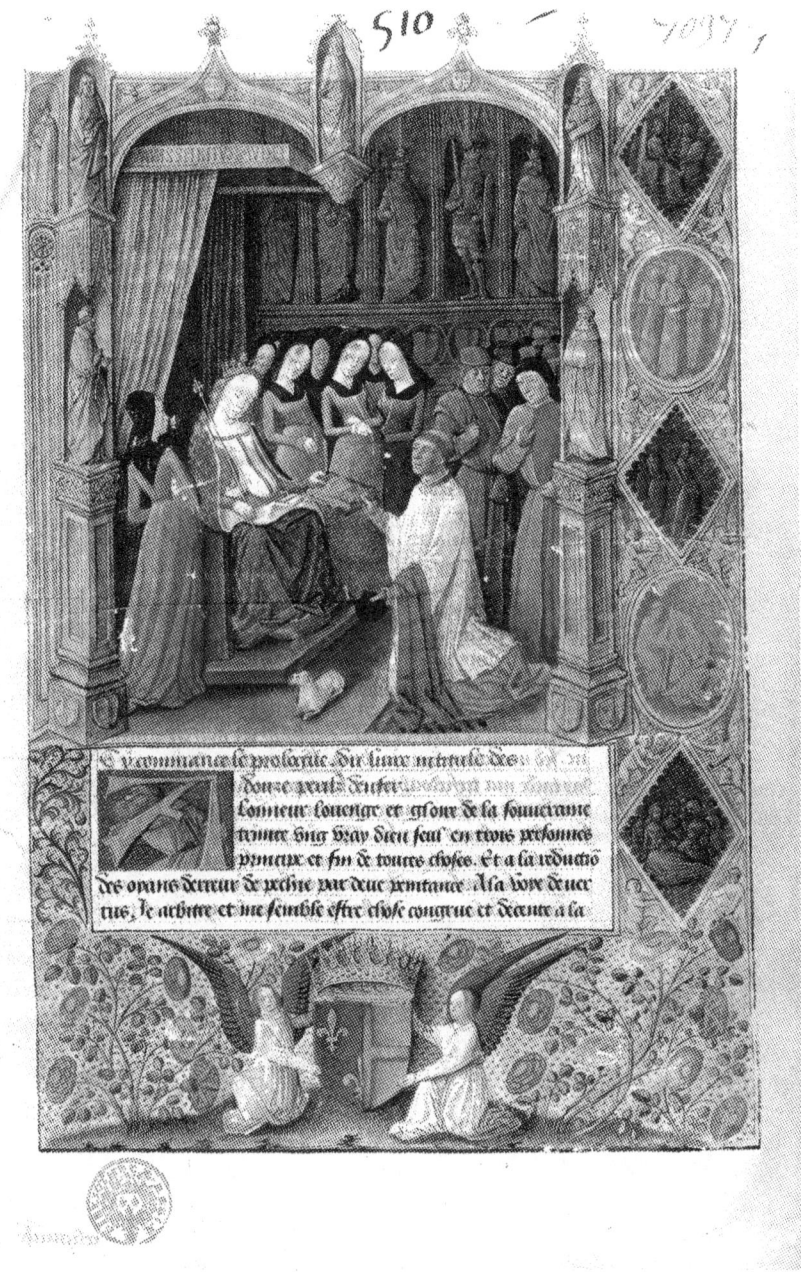

Figure 2. Paris, B.N.F., MS Fr. 449, Robert Blondel, *Les Douze Périls d'enfer* [92], fol. 1; Jean Colombe; Robert Blondel offering his book to Charlotte de Savoie. Cliché Bibliothèque Nationale de France.

Figure 3. Paris, B.N.F., MS Fr. 2222, Guillaume Danicot, *La Congratulation et graces de la nativité de Charles aisné fils du roy Loys unziesme de ce nom* [109], fol. 1; unknown artist; The arms of Charlotte de Savoie held by two angels. Cliché Bibliothèque Nationale de France.

CHARLOTTE DE SAVOIE'S LIBRARY

Figure 4. Paris, B.N.F., MS Fr. 5718, *Vie et office de sainte Radegonde* [31], fol. 2; unknown artist ; Charlotte de Savoie kneeling in front of saint Radegonde. Cliché Bibliothèque Nationale de France.

Figure 5. New York, Pierpont Morgan Library, M 1004, *Hours of Charlotte de Savoie*, fol. 44v; follower of the Boucicaut Master, Paris, c. 1420-25; Funeral service. By permission of the Pierpont Morgan Library.

Figure 6. Ramsen, Heribert Tenschert, Guillaume de Digulleville, *Le Pèlerinage de vie humaine* in prose [77], fol. 1v; unknown artist; The Heavenly Jerusalem and the arms of Charlotte de Savoie held by two angels. By permission of Heribert Tenschert.

Figure 7. Paris, B.N.F., MS Fr. 445, Robert le Chartreux, *Le Château Périlleux* [12], fol. 4; unknown artist; Robert le Chartreux and his cousin Rose with seven Virtues in front of the Château Périlleux. Cliché Bibliothèque Nationale de France.

Figure 8. Paris, B.N.F., MS Fr. 916, *Lamentations de saint Bernard* [87], fol. 13 ; The Master of Jean Charpentier, c. 1475; saint Bernard kneeling before the Christ of the Last Judgment. Cliché Bibliothèque Nationale de France.

Family Values: Manuscripts as Gifts and Legacies among French Renaissance Women

MYRA DICKMAN ORTH

French Renaissance illuminated manuscripts from the period 1515-70 demonstrate time and time again their continuing importance as family gifts. The persistence of such manuscripts in the era of the printed book is a surprising fact, but many in Renaissance aristocratic society, particularly women, still appreciated limited editions for the same reasons collectors have always preferred the rare and the beautiful. In addition, the luxury manuscript, with the strength of tradition behind it, still served as a powerful and private family memorial. By understanding the familial, personal genesis of the manuscripts chosen for discussion here, we can clarify the possible reasons for the gift and speculate—there is a great deal of speculation in this paper—why and to whom these manuscripts were gifts. For books as gifts in the Renaissance period, an article by Natalie Zemon Davis remains the only signpost, although it addressed printed books and a more public and political repertoire.[1]

This paper includes much information from my forthcoming catalogue of French Renaissance manuscripts and from my already published articles.[2] Here I will set aside art-historical information and codicologial detail and instead stress women's family history and its relevance to the manuscripts under study. I will downplay politics, including dynastic politics, although this is an important aspect of several of these manuscripts, most notably those of Catherine de Médicis. Two kinds of texts structure the discussion: poetry and Books of Hours. There is a mixture of manuscripts—some were gifts tied to family events and some are relevant because they were passed down through the female line.

Poetry

Marguerite de Navarre, *La Coche* (Chantilly, Musée Condé, MS 522 [1848]).[3] Marguerite de Navarre (d. 1549) wrote this highly personal poem in 1541, carefully planning illuminations that picture her as the main protagonist. A document describes her sending her chaplain, with funds from her duchy of Berry, to Paris to see to the final steps of illumination and binding in January 1542 (NS). We assume that the document concerns the prime copy, that at Chantilly, and probably a second illuminated copy made by an assistant of the Chantilly artist (Oxford, Bodleian, MS Douce 91).[4] Both were made for presentation to the family of the duchesse d'Étampes, the mistress of Marguerite's brother, King François I. Three other manuscript copies, with Marguerite's long descriptions of the illustrations carefully written in the text block, can be dated to 1543.[5] The actual title *La Coche* was only used slightly later in the *Suyte des Marguerites de la Marguerite des princesses*.[6] Like the lesser women poets, Marguerite mainly left the print publication of her works to others with the result that relatively few editions appeared in her lifetime.[7]

La Coche is a completely secular and personal poem that can be understood on several levels.[8] Its status as a gift is of most interest to this essay. The poem opens with Marguerite fleeing the court, bemoaning the loss of her desire to write and thus the loss of her creativity and of love. She encounters three weeping, lovesick women on the edge of the forest and offers to record their grief, which is poured out at some length. A storm provoked by their tears drives them into the queen's *coche*, in which they return to court. The eleven miniatures are striking in the insistent and repeated presence of the black-garbed women, who are visual clones of Marguerite, moving like shades or shadow puppets across the narrow stage of the verdant field that borders a forest lit by a progressively declining sun. The women are never identified. It is hardly credible that at court no one would have speculated about their identities. Even if they do not stand for specific individuals, Marguerite gave the reader every chance to think that they did. Possibly they were meant to represent general situations or three states of mind. In the poem the three complaining women and Marguerite debate the choice of a reader who can judge the poem. They decide on the duchesse d'Étampes, hoping she will like the poem enough to describe it, but not show it directly, to the king. The final miniature shows Marguerite presenting the manuscript to the duchess. This is a rare image of gift-giving, since the poem was neither dedicated to her nor commissioned by her. Looking again at the miniatures, I am struck by the fact that the male figures—whether they are peasants in the first illustration or courtiers in the tenth—not only have a subordinate role, but are very small in size. Thus the pictures emphasize an obvious point often overlooked in analyses of the poem, the importance of female solidarity and friendship.

Marguerite's mood of despair, which is reflected so specifically in this poem, has been traced to a low point in her personal and political power and, not incidentally, to the fact she was about to turn fifty. The disputed (and later repudiated) marriage of her daughter Jeanne to the duke of Cleves set Marguerite against her brother; 1540-41 was also the period of deep division in the court between the pro- and anti-imperial factions, a division that set the constable of France, Anne de Montmorency, against the duchesse d'Étampes.[9] Marguerite and the duchess were on the same side, and Marguerite badly needed her support in more than literary matters. It is tempting to think that Marguerite meant *La Coche* as a gift to the duchess in thanks for her political influence and success in disgracing Montmorency.

Although the subject matter of the poem is not exactly suitable for a wedding present, it seems probable that both manuscript copies were intended to commemorate marriages in the duchess's family. Heraldic evidence connects the Chantilly and Oxford copies to the families of Avaugour, counts of Vertus, the bastard line of the dukes of Brittany. A folio with a full-page coat of arms was added to the front of the Chantilly copy by François III de Bretagne, whom Charlotte de Pisseleu married in 1537. She was the duchess's much younger sister, to whom, Marichal suggested, it may originally have been offered.[10] The arms in the Oxford manuscript were added by Guy I, baron de Caylus-Castelnau, lord of Clermont, whom Louise d'Avaugour-Bretagne, sister of François III de Bretagne, married in 1542.[11] An inscription by Aldonce de Bernuy, who married Guy II de Caylus-Castelnau in 1565, attests to the family's continued possession of the Oxford manuscript in the sixteenth century.

We do not know the destination of the other three extant copies (those with descriptions in place of miniatures) but it is safe to suppose that they were intended as gifts. It is worth adding here that author's copies, time and time again in this period, turn out to be the "fair copy" or a recopied draft (usually on paper), rather than one of the carefully copied vellum manuscripts.

Catherine d'Amboise, *La Complainte de la Dame pasmée contre fortune* (BNF, MS nouv. acq. fr. 19738).[12] Catherine d'Amboise's autobiographical allegory is unpublished. Although the text is never mentioned in literary history in connection with Catherine (d. 1550), it is surely hers. More than Marguerite's *Coche*, Catherine's work is closely involved with her family affairs, and I suggest that her immediate family was its audience. Biographical information and heraldry in two other illuminated copies of the same text (but missing in MS nouv. acq. 19738) make the attribution of the text to Catherine a certainty.[13] These copies also suggest a possible date in the second half of the 1520s. The Amboise family was second only to the royal family in art patronage in the first decade of the sixteenth century.[14] Nevertheless in her writings Catherine found much to complain about: she laments the death of her brothers: *"dont cardinal l'un. ..aultre estoit grand maistre de France et gouuerneur de Milan et lieutenant general es guerres ytaliens Liguriens et venetiens...au service du roy decedé."*[15] These brothers were Louis II, cardinal-archbishop of Albi (d. 1517), and Charles II d'Amboise (d. 1511); the king was Louis XII (d. 1515). The cardinal-archbishop of Rouen Georges I d'Amboise (d. 1510) is explicitly named as her uncle. Both manuscripts contain other references to family events and long passages about marriage, sickness, and growing old.

Catherine was the daughter of Charles I d'Amboise, the cardinal-archbishop's brother. Charles II, Catherine's brother, and his son Georges inherited most of the cardinal-archbishop's very considerable worldly possessions.[16] Her nephew Georges's mother, Jeanne Malet de Graville, was the sister of Anne de Graville, another noble woman author discussed here. Catherine had inherited the Amboise family château of Chaumont (near her husband's château of Lignières [Cher], where she resided), but there is no evidence, direct or indirect, that she was familiar with the French manuscripts that the cardinal-archbishop had willed to Chaumont. Could the sad news referred to in the La Dame pasmée have been the unexpected death of her nephew Georges in 1524/5 at the battle of Pavia? Catherine, along with her niece Antoinette, dame de Barbezieux, eventually inherited Georges's estate, probably because they were the only living direct heirs in the Chaumont and Amboise lines. The theme (and image) of Fortune and its inconsistencies was a popular one also exploited by Catherine's half-brother, Michel d'Amboise, Antoinette's secretary.[17] The shared inheritance would also explain why Catherine gave Antoinette three of her major châteaux (Chaumont, Meillant, and Lignières) at the time of the death of Catherine's husband Philippe de Beaujeu in 1540. By a trick of fate, both women lost their fortunes in subsequent marriages.[18]

Like Marguerite in La Coche, Catherine appears in almost every miniature of La Dame pasmée. The story begins when bad news conveyed by a letter causes Catherine to collapse. She is rescued from her faint by Reason, who teaches her patience in her travails and instructs her concerning Fortune and Sadness, which they confront together. They meet Patience (the Virgin), ending their pilgrimage at the park of Divine Love, where the Virgin awaits them at the foot of the Crucifix. Although all three known copies of Catherine's text were probably made in Paris, it is significant that none of them is by the same artist, nor were the compositions copied from one manuscript to the other, even though their quarto formats and heavy parchment are very similar. In short, there is no evidence of the author's direct involvement with the making of the manuscript. Unlike Marguerite, Catherine evidently provided no written instructions for the artists.

That Catherine used the three known copies of La Dame pasmée as family gifts is speculation on my part. The lack of autobiographical detail and blank first bifolio in the BNF copy are puzzling, but may indicate a redaction not meant for close family. The other two copies, however, decorated with family heraldry and replete with personal asides, seem likely to have been intended for family members, such as Catherine's niece Antoinette. That would have been particularly appropriate if I am correct in linking both texts to the death of Catherine's nephew Georges. Perhaps SMAF MS 79-7 was given to Georges's mother, Jeanne Malet de Graville. It is inscribed with the monogram and written ex-libris of Léonor de Rohan, princess of Guemené (c.1560-70), who could have inherited it through the Balsac family, to whom Jeanne willed her estate.[19]

Catherine's writings were never printed in their time. In fact, not until 1531 was any work by a living Frenchwoman published in print.[20] Catherine's first known work, dated 1509, is the ambitious *Livre des prudens et imprudens des siecles passés* (Paris, Bibl. de l'Arsenal, MS 2037), with seventy-six miniatures of allegorical and historical figures and events. Despite a preface in which she regrets that women cannot be educated as men are,[21] the text is generally impersonal, although Catherine is frequently pictured in it. The last miniature (fol. 133) shows her as Dame Philosophy discoursing with Boethius, whose *Consolation of Philosophy* informs the text of *La Dame pasmée*.[22]

Catherine d'Amboise, Dévotes Epistres (BNF, MS fr. 2282).[23] The Epistles to Christ and the Virgin composed by Catherine d'Amboise plead for forgiveness for unspecified transgressions. These pious, meditative verses are constructed of familiar mystical and penitential metaphors and Catherine wrote them in "trembling tearfulness," affirming her authorship in several places and stating that she wrote the poem in her "secret place" (at the Château de Lignières).[24] Three similarly composed miniatures show the pious author presenting her book first to Christ and then to the Virgin through the intermediary of an angelic messenger, and finally receiving from Christ a ring as a sign of peace and remission of sins. The kneeling figures in a landscape combine the dedication image of kneeling author with the devout kneeling donor. If the miniatures reflected the text accurately we would see Catherine not primly at prayer, but weeping, face down on the ground. Souchal, in her study of the Amboise family, has suggested that Antoinette is the girl kneeling behind Catherine in all of the miniatures. Catherine had no living children.[25]

I would suggest that Catherine meant the manuscript of the *Dévotes Epistres* as a gift for her niece Antoinette and therefore that the manuscript dates from the later 1520s, when their shared inheritance from Georges was settled. His death may have caused the mourning referred to on fol. 13. Catherine never had her poem published, although it is possible that at one time there were other copies. It finally saw print in 1861 under its present title, Dévotes Epistres.

Anne de Graville, *Roman de Palamon et Arcita*, her translation of Boccaccio's Theseida (Paris, Bibl. de l'Arsenal, MS 5116).[26] The translation-adaptation of Boccacio's *Theseida* by the poet Anne de Graville (d. c.1540) is, unlike the works just discussed, neither personal nor familial, but much in her biography and the history of her library is relevant to this study. The Arsenal manuscript, presumed to be the royal presentation copy, is only one among several manuscript copies to have a dedication miniature and to be illustrated.[27] Anne, dame du Bois de Malesherbes (Loiret), wife of Pierre de Balsac, was one of Claude's ladies-in-waiting at a court that, in the early 1520s, included the young Anne Boleyn and Marguerite d'Angoulême, later de Navarre.[28] The Boccaccio was translated at Queen Claude's demand between 1521 and 1524.[29] Anne's own copy, more modest, must be BNF, MS fr. 25441, since it was used as a *livre de raison* by her daughter Jeanne.[30] Anne's translation was not published until the critical edition of 1965.

Anne was the daughter of the bibliophile Louis Malet de Graville, admiral of France (d. 1516). He angrily disinherited her over her clandestine marriage to her maternal uncle, Pierre de Balsac, in 1506. After a legal struggle—aspects of which continued for over a decade after Louis's death—Anne triumphantly inherited her father's library in 1518. In that same year her husband presented her with a newly translated manuscript of Berosus' *Chaldean Histories*, titled *Le Livre d'amour*, where Anne is pictured as the dedicatee, seated among her lady companions, receiving the book from a disembodied hand (London, BL, Phillipps MS 127, loan 36/1).[31] Anne continued to acquire manuscripts, notably in Rouen, in 1521.[32] Her family link to Catherine d'Amboise has been mentioned above. Anne's important library was inherited by her daughter Jeanne de Balsac (d. 1542), and then by Jeanne's husband Claude d'Urfé. It constituted the bulk of his well-studied collection.[33] Covering a wide range from classics to romances, most of the known works are in French translation; besides the 153 manuscripts counted by Vernet, about 15 printed books can be traced to Anne's library, and her son-in-law added some 30 more. It is obvious that Anne used her library frequently as the basis for her own writings, in which we find nothing of the personal tone of Catherine's work. Besides the Boccaccio translation only one other manuscript of Anne's poetry is known, a collection of rondeaux based on Alain Chartier's *La Belle Dame sans mercy*, probably dating from about 1524. It would seem that her reputation as a poet was considerable, to judge by Geofroy Tory's praise in his *Champfleury*, published in Paris in 1529 but largely written in 1525(NS)-26.[34]

There are some general points to be extracted from these three case histories. Private publication through manuscripts, in the case of these moneyed women writers, was probably directed at family members. The giving of books as significant gifts responds to a strong tradition both within families, as here, or among scholars. Whatever the sociological reasons that may have held these women back from print publication, we should keep in mind that even well into the sixteenth century, a text presented in manuscript form was highly valued.

Books of Hours and Prayerbooks

These devotional books had been a prized possession of aristocratic women since at least the fourteenth century.[35] By the sixteenth century the Parisian presses were turning out Books of Hours in unbelievable numbers. However, the moneyed aristocracy preferred manuscripts. The examples mentioned here make a point not just about female ownership—hardly an exception for this sort of book—but about the occasion they commemorated as gifts or, in the complicated case of Catherine de Médicis, how the book evolved and was handed down.

Hours of Françoise de Brinon (The Hague, Museum Meermanno-Westreenianum, MS 10 F 33).[36] This Book of Hours is a rare dated (1524) example of a manuscript that belonged to the lesser Parisian nobility in court service. My recent research has uncovered its family origins. Exceptionally the scribe was also the donor and a royal functionary, Jean du Luc, knight of Fontenay and Marcilly.[37] His wife, for whom he wrote and to whom he presented this Book of Hours, was Françoise de Brinon, one of a many-branched family of Parisian parlementary officials. She was the daughter of Yves, lord of Cire and Guyencourt, President of the Parlement of Paris (d. by 1530) and Gillette Picard. In 1538-40 Jean du Luc was procurator in Parlement and charged with the affairs of the *dauphin et dauphine*—the future King Henri II and Catherine de Médicis.[38] He served as solicitor and procurator general for Catherine when she was queen, until he was dropped from the accounts in 1564.[39] By 1571, Françoise was widowed, living in Paris, and mentioned as deceased in 1587.[40] Her niece, Jeanne, married Jean du Tillet, chief clerk of the Parlement of Paris and author of a number of important manuscripts concerning the French monarchy.[41] The final miniature, of the patrons presented by their patron saints (fol. 117v), is unfortunately very summary in style, however useful (and exceptional) it is in establishing the manuscript historically. While this otherwise beautifully illuminated manuscript is not documented as a wedding gift, Françoise's death, probably in the early 1580s, indicates that in 1524 she was very young and most probably newly wed.

Hours of Marie Chantault, Use of Chartres (BNF, MS Smith-Lesouéf 39).[42] This Book of Hours is another example of a personal gift by a husband and scribe within the circle of royal court appointees. Is this evidence of a fashion? Girard Acarie, lord of Fontenay-sur-Oise (d. 1557), is first mentioned in the royal accounts in 1512 as *aumônier* to the dauphin François.[43] By 1515, he was listed with the new king's *valets de chambre*, secretaries, and notaries.[44] The Book of Hours was copied by Acarie for his wife, Marie Chantault, dame de Carouges, Tesnière et le Rochoy (d. 1570). The couple are depicted four times in miniatures by a Rouen artist whom Acarie often used and who is named for him.[45] Acarie's appointment as *controlleur* for Normandy in 1524 may indicate a date for the manuscript.[46] Oddly, since it is stated unequivocally that the Hours are for Marie, the prayers are written in the masculine. Unlike the Brinon Hours, this one cannot have been for their marriage, since by 1525 the couple had four living children.[47]

Prayerbook of Marie de Gaignon (Paris, École Nationale Supérieure des Beaux-Arts, MS Masson 20).[48] Marie de Gaignon (1520-65) received this prayer book at the time of (or shortly after) her marriage in 1559 to Claude Gouffier (c.1500-70), lord of Bonnivet and Master of the Horse at the royal court.[49] Gouffier's second wife, Françoise de Brosse, had died in childbirth in 1558, leaving precious little time to fill an order for a new manuscript. Marie's arms on the opening folio and on several frames attest to her ownership; the Almanac, beginning with 1560, confirms the dating; and finally the love verse (fol. 179) makes sense in the marriage context.

With this manuscript we enter into a later period when not just art but devotional attitudes had become far more complex. By coincidence or design, the text of Marie de Gaignon's manuscript is as heterogeneous as the *Hours of Catherine de Médicis and Charles IX* at The Hague (Royal Library, MS 74. G. 39)[50] and the even more (and differently) complicated *Hours of Catherine de Médicis* that will be discussed next (Paris, BNF, MS nouv. acq. lat. 82). All are written in a similar italic script and are close in size.[51] Although both the title page and the rubric of the Gaignon manuscript proclaim it to be a Book of Hours for the Use of Rome, there is no trace of the text of the Hours of the Virgin which may have been lost in a rebinding, or never copied. The Gaignon artist also provided some miniatures for the *Hours of Catherine de Médicis* in The Hague, mentioned above. Another closely allied artist, more careful and precise, who had worked on a Gouffier illuminated printed Hours of 1558,[52] illuminated another manuscript Hours, dated 1561, also thought to be for Catherine de Médicis (Rome, Vatican Library, MS Vat. lat. 14936).[53] These interconnections emphasize that the popularity of manuscript Hours had not diminished, but that there were a decreasing number of artists available to produce them.

Prayers for Marguerite de France, duchesse de Savoie (Turin, Biblioteca Reale, MS var. 84), 1559.[54] This personalized prayerbook was offered to Marguerite de France (1523-74), the youngest daughter of François I, late King of France, as a wedding gift from Christoforo Duc (his name, not his title, also spelled Duch) di Moncalieri (d. 1563), long in the service of the dukes of Savoy. Her marriage to Emmanuel Philibert, duc de Savoie (1528-80), was part of the peace of Cateau-Cambrésis (April 1559) and was carried out on the eve of the death of her brother, King Henri II, who died on 10 July 1559. Marguerite took several specially dedicated books (both printed and manuscript) with her to Turin, but only one other manuscript was surely a wedding gift: La *Sphinge*, an illustrated poem by Valerio Saluzzo della Manta (Turin, Bibl. Reale, MS var. 266 bis), which turns on the symbolism of the pearl, or *margarita*.

While still on the subject of Books of Hours it should be noted that by 1540-50 we are faced with an odd (and contradictory) phenomenon. The number of editions of printed Books of Hours diminished dramatically around 1540—a conclusion easily checked by counting editions in any of the standard bibliographies.[55] Very grand manuscripts were, however, commissioned at court, and all of these were commissioned by men for themselves: the Hours *of King Henri* II, c.1543-47 (BNF, MS lat. 1429), originally commissioned by the Dinteville family and then given to the new king; the Hours *of Dinteville*, c.1550-54 (BNF, MS lat. 10558); the Hours *of the Constable Anne de Montmorency*, C.1549-53 (Chantilly, Musée Condé, MS 1479 [1943]); and the Hours *of Claude Gouffier*, c 1550-55 (New York, Pierpont Morgan Library MS M.538).[56] This sudden reflorescence had nothing to do with family and everything to do with a combination of newly revived orthodox Roman Catholic devotion, politics, and status.

Hours of Catherine de Médicis (Paris, BNF, MS nouv. acq. lat. 82).[57] This manuscript is principally famous for containing portraits of the sixteenth-century Valois monarchs and later descendants in the Lorraine line. There is no other illustration. Although I have studied it at length for the *Survey* catalogue, here I will limit the discussion to family matters. The primary association of the manuscript with the dowager Queen Catherine de Médicis (widowed in 1559, d. January 1589) is doubtless correct, keeping in mind that what belonged to a queen mother also belonged to her children, three of whom were kings of France (François II, Charles IX, Henri III). Indeed, the few personalized prayers the manuscript contains are for a king, not for Catherine. The manuscript passed down through the female line of the Lorraine branch, rather than through any of Catherine's own children (only Marguerite de Valois survived her).

Datable to 1573, the original set of thirty-four portraits on nineteen folios (including three repeats) would have been ordered by Catherine expressly for the manuscript, which I have shown did not originate from the time of François I, as has been universally supposed.[58] The portraits represent all of her and Henri II's children, including those that died in infancy, and the family of François I, Henri's father. There is no precedent for decorating a Book of Hours exclusively with family portraits, but the second half of the century in France saw a tremendous vogue of collecting independent portraits in albums of drawings, in tightly packed portrait galleries of paintings, and in jewelled lockets.[59] The dating of the original portrait set is based on the representation of Henri III as king of Poland, rather than king of France: he was offered the Polish crown in August 1573 and became king of France the next year. He married Louise de Lorraine in 1575. All of the couples represented in the original set of portraits were married by 1572, the memorable year of the Massacre of Saint Bartholomew (in August): this, the bloodiest event in the French Wars of Religion, interrupted the marriage festivites of Henri de Bourbon and Marguerite de Valois. Thus in its first state the manuscript served as an elaborate illustrated dynastic *livre de raison* for the sixteenth-century Valois monarchy. It is a kind of hand-held version of the huge Valois rotunda designed for Saint-Denis, but never finished and subsequently demolished.[60] Instead of monumental carved tombs there are tiny portraits.

The fate of the Hours after Catherine's death in January 1589 is unclear but important. Her postmortem inventory of 1589 (where the Book of Hours does not appear) lists many framed portraits in her Parisian hôtel.[61] The Hours does not appear in her library inventories either.[62] Perhaps it was hiding in her jewels. After all, its extravagant binding sets it in that realm. She had portraits set in lockets; for example, in a gathering of *devises*, poems, and designs there is her own handwritten list of small circular portraits of the royal family to be made to hang around her neck.[63] It may also be that the manuscript was given by Catherine to Louise as a wedding gift in 1575, which would explain why it does not appear in any of Catherine's inventories. This would also explain why all of the miniatures from the reign of Henri III (except the one of him as king of Poland) are pasted in, including those of Louise de Lorraine (d. 1601). The assassination of Henri III in August of 1589 was followed by political chaos; the Orléans-Valois line died with him. There is no mention of the manuscript in Louise's postmortem inventories.[64] Next, the manuscript belonged to Louise's niece Françoise de Lorraine (d. 1669), or at least we presume it did because of the large number of later Lorraine portraits added to the already bound volume. Philippe-Emmanuel de Lorraine, Louise's half-brother, had arranged Françoise's marriage in 1609 to César de Vendôme, the natural child of King Henri IV and Gabrielle d'Estrées, legitimized in 1595. The latest portraits added to the Hours are those of the grand-daughters of Françoise de Lorraine, but since one married into the Savoy family and lived in Turin, and the other was queen of Portugal, it seems unlikely that either of them owned it. Françoise outlived all her children except Louis (d. 1670).

The manuscript reappeared in the possession of the Bourbons after their restoration in the early nineteenth century. The duchesse de Berry, Marie-Caroline-Ferdinande-Louise de Bourbon-Sicile (1798-1870), wife of King Charles X (d. 1820) took Catherine's Hours with her into Italian exile, but had to sell her manuscripts at the death of her second husband, the marquis Lucchesi-Palli. The manuscript's price equalled almost two-thirds of the total sale in 1864, when it was purchased for the Musée des Souverains.[65]

Catherine was generous with the female members of the Lorraine family. She clearly prized family drawings. She gave a large lot of these, a *"cassette carée contenante 551 portraits de divers nobilité"* to her grand-daughter Christine de Lorraine, grand duchess of Tuscany (d. 1637), whose collections were dispersed in Florence from 1738 onwards. Scholars have suggested that it is not coincidental that the Chantilly drawings of the Valois family were acquired by an English collector in Florence c.1738-58.[66] Catherine, who willed much else to Christine, gave her the monumental set of Valois tapestries that she took with her to Florence in the spring of 1589.[67] To state the obvious, Catherine's dynastic importance was vastly greater than that of the women who owned the other Books of Hours discussed here, yet the Queen's very personal Hours and other favored possessions seem to have been hers to pass along to favored women relatives. The sum of the varied documentation presented here should alert us to examine family history more carefully for significant dates and family relationships for both usual and unusual events and links.

Boston, Massachusetts

NOTES

1. Natalie Zemon Davis, "Beyond the Market: Books as Gifts in Sixteenth-Century France," Prothero Lecture, *Transactions of the Royal Historical Society* 33 (1983): 69-88. Davis' new publication does not emphasize books, but is nevertheless important: *The Gift in Sixteenth-Century France* (Madison, WI: University of Wisconsin Press, 2000).
2. Myra Dickman Orth, *Survey of French Renaissance Illuminated Manuscripts* (London: Harvey Miller Publishers/Brepols, forthcoming); idem, "Dedicating Women: Manuscript Culture in the French Renaissance—The Cases of Catherine d'Amboise and Anne de Graville," *Journal of the Early Book Society* 1 (1997): 17-47.
3. Robert Marichal, ed., *Marguerite de Navarre: La Coche* (Geneva and Paris: Droz and Minard, 1971); on the artist, see Myra Dickman Orth,"The Master of François de Rohan: A Familiar French Renaissance Miniaturist with a New Name," in *Illuminating*

the Book—Makers and Interpreters: Essays in Honour of Janet Backhouse, ed. Michelle Brown and Scot McKendrick (London: British Library, 1998), 71-72, 85, fig. 38; Jacques P. Meurgey, Les Principaux Manuscrits à peintures du Musée Condé à Chantilly (Paris: Société Française de Réproductions de Manuscrits à Peintures, 1930), 199-200, pl. 133 a, b.
4. Marichal, Marguerite, 76-77; see also Antoine-Jean-Victor Le Roux de Lincy, L'Heptaméron des nouvelles de très illustre princesse Marguerite d'Angoulême reine de Navarre soeur unique de François I (Paris: A. Eudes, 1880) 1: 191-92; and for the Oxford manuscript, Otto Pächt and J. J. G. Alexander, Illuminated Manuscripts in the Bodleian Library, Oxford: German, Dutch, Flemish, French, and Spanish Schools (Oxford: Oxford University Press, 1966), 1: 66, no. 850.
5. Paris, Bibl. de l'Arsenal, MS 5112, fols. 51-79, cited by Le Roux de Lincy, L'Heptaméron, 1: 188-91, and Marichal, Marguerite, 62-64; Berne, Bürgerbibliothek MS A65, illustrated in Robert Marichal, "Texte ou image?" in Mise en page et mise en texte du livre manuscrit, ed. Henri-Jean Martin and Jean Vezin (Paris: Promodis, 1990), figs. 419, 421; Marichal, Marguerite, 77-78; BNF, MS fr. 12485, fols. 52-75, Marichal, Marguerite, 64-70. Another manuscript is presumed lost: La Vallière collection sale, Paris, 1784, vol. 2, no. 3068, cited by Marichal, Marguerite, 78-79.
6. Lyon: de Tournes, 1547. Significantly it lacks the scene of presentation to the duchess. Described and illustrated in Ruth Mortimer, comp., Catalogue of Books and Manuscripts, Harvard College Library, Department of Printing and Graphic Arts: Part 1, French Sixteenth Century Books (Cambridge, MA: Belknap Press, 1964) 2: 463-64, no. 365.
7. Marichal, Marguerite, 135-36; S. Lefèvre, "L'Heptaméron entre éditions et manuscrits," in Marguerite de Navarre, 1492-1992, ed. Nicole Cazauran and James Dauphiné, Actes du colloque international de Pau, 1992 (Mont-de-Marsan: Éditions InterUniversitaires, 1995), 445-47. However, Marguerite's Miroir de l'ame pecheresse (Alençon: Simon du Bois, 1531) was the first publication in 16th-century France of a work by a living woman author: William Kemp, "Textes composés ou traduits par des femmes et imprimés en France avant 1550: Bibliographie des imprimés féminins (1488-1549)," Littératures 18, L'Écriture des femmes à la Renaissance française (1998): 151-220; idem, "Marguerite of Navarre, Clément Marot, and the 1533 Augereau Editions of the Miroir de l'âme pécheresse (Paris, 1533)," Journal of the Early Book Society 2 (1999): 113-56.
8. Robert Cottrell, "Figures emblématiques dans La Coche de Marguerite de Navarre," in Marguerite de Navarre 1492-1992, ed. Nicole Cazauran and James Dauphiné, Actes du colloque international de Pau, 1992 (Mont-de-Marsan: Éditions InterUniversitaires, 1995), 309-25; Marie-Madeleine Fontaine, "Les Deux Amours, ou l'arithmétique de Marguerite de Navarre, La Coche," in ibid., 327-49.
9. For historical background see Robert Knecht, Francis I (Cambridge: Cambridge University Press, 1982), 299-301.
10. For an analysis of the heraldry and the family members involved, see Marichal, Marguerite, 72-74. Family data in this and following notes is taken from père Anselme de la Vierge Marie [Pierre Guibours], Histoire généalogique et chronologique de la maison royale de France: des pairs, grands officiers de la couronne & de la maison du roy: & des anciens

barons du royaume: avec les qualitez, l'origine, le progrès & les armes de leurs familles; ensemble les statuts & le catalogue des chevaliers, commandeurs, & officiers de l'ordre de S. Esprit, 3d ed., ed. Honoré Caille Dufourny and les pères Ange de Sainte-Rosalie and Simplicien (Paris: La Compagnie des Libraires, 1726-1733) 1: 467-69. Charlotte died in 1604.

11. Marichal, *Marguerite*, 76. Guy I died in 1544, but Louise was still alive in 1602.

12. Jacqueline Sclafer, ed., *Manuscrits du Moyen Âge et de la Renaissance: Enrichissements du Département des manuscrits*, 1983-1992 (Paris: Bibliothèque Nationale de France, 1994), 104-6, illustrating fol. 8 (note that the correct page dimensions are 200 x 140 mm.); Orth, "Dedicating Women," 20-22, figs. 1, 2. I attribute the miniatures to the Paris Entry Master.

13. One is on deposit at the BNF by the Société des Manuscrits des Assureurs Français (SMAF MS 79-7) and the other is in a private collection, described by Peter Kidd in Sam Fogg, *Rare Books and Manuscripts*, Catalogue 1999 (exh. Blumka Gallery, New York, 1999), 128-31, no. 33; and in Orth, "Dedicating Women," 21-22. After seeing Jennifer Britnell's slides of Gabrielle de Bourbon's *Le Voyage spirituel entrepris par l'ame devote* (Paris, Bibl. Mazarine, MS 978), I tentatively link Catherine's copies of the *La Dame pasmée* to the same scriptorium, and I suspect (pending a more careful look) that the artists of Gabrielle's manuscript and the ex-Sam Fogg manuscript are the same.

14. Geneviève Souchal, "Le Mécénat de la famille d'Amboise," *Bulletin de la Société des antiquaires de l'Ouest et des Musées de Poitiers* 3 (1976): 485-526; 4 (1976): 567-612; see 4: 598-99 for Catherine.

15. BNF SMAF MS 79-7 and the manuscript listed by Fogg, *Rare Books*, contain this information, fols 4-5 and 4-5v, respectively. For more detail see Orth, "Dedicating Women," 21, 30, nn. 25-29.

16. The will is discussed in Marc Venard, "Le Testament du cardinal d'Amboise," in *De l'histoire de la Brie à l'histoire des Réformes: Mélanges offerts au chanoine Michel Veissière*, ed. Michel Bardon, Études et documents de la Fédération des sociétés historiques et archéologiques de Paris et de l'Iâle-de-France 2 (Paris, 1993) 15-28; Orth, "Dedicating Women," 19-20.

17. Michel d'Amboise, *Complaintes de l'esclave fortuné* (Paris, J. Saint-Denis, 1529), styles him as her secretary: see Richard Cooper, "Le Thème de la Fortune dans la poésie de Michel d'Amboise (c.1505-47)," in *Il tema della Fortuna nella letteratura francese e italiana del Rinascimento: Studi in memoria di Enzo Guidici*, ed. G. A. Brunelli et al. (Florence: L. S. Olschki, 1990), 107-22; idem, "Michel d'Amboise, poète maudit?" in *La Génération Marot: Poètes français et néo-latins, 1515-1550*, ed. Gérard Defaux, Actes du colloque international de Baltimore, 1996 (Paris: H. Champion, 1997), 445-70; on Fortune, see William Kemp and Fabrizio Frigerio, "The Evangelical 'Fortuna' Device of the Parisian Bookseller Jérôme Denis (1529)," *Trivium* 31 (1999): 117-130.

18. Souchal, "Le Mécénat," 599. See Anselme, *Histoire*, 7: 125-26.

19. Anselme, Histoire, 6: 61-70; cf. Orth, "Dedicating Women," 31 n. 31.

20. Kemp, "Textes composés."

21. Cited in Evelyne Berriot-Salvadore, *Les Femmes dans la société française de la*

Renaissance, Histoire des idées et critique littéraire, vol. 285 (Geneva: Droz, 1990), 418.
22. Illustrated in Orth, "Dedicating Women," fig. 6; the connection of Boethius with the *La Dame pasmée* was noted by Henri Omont, *Bulletin de la Société Nationale des Antiquaires de France* (1891): 154.
23. Jean-Jacques Bourassé, *Les Dévotes Epistres de Katharine d'Amboise publiées pour la première fois* (Tours: Mame, 1861); Orth, "Dedicating Women,", 22-23, fig. 3; Camille Couderc, *Bibliothèque nationale: Album des portraits d'après les collections du Département des manuscrits* (Paris: Berthaud, [1908]), pl. 149, 2.
24. BNF, MS fr. 2282, fols. 5v, 6v, 12v, and 18.
25. Souchal, "Le Mécénat," 599. Catherine Müller, currently studying this manuscript, believes that the second kneeling figure is also Catherine in a construct (or de-construct) that my literal mind doesn't quite grasp, although I am grateful to her for sharing her opinion.
26. Yves Le Hir, ed., *Anne de Graville:, Le Beau romant des deux amans Palamon et Arcita et de la belle et saige Emilia* (Paris: Presses Universitaries Françaises, 1965); Orth, "Dedicating Women," 23-25, figs. 4, 5. I attribute the frontispiece to the Master of Anne de Graville, and the narrative miniatures to a close associate of Étienne Collault.
27. There are five other known copies: Chantilly, Musée Condé, MS 1570 [513], with the arms of Claude de France; BNF, MS fr. 1397; BNF, MS fr. 25441 (Anne de Graville's copy); BNF, MS nouv. acq. fr. 719 (paper); BNF, MS nouv. acq. fr. 6513 (paper; fragmentary). The Chantilly copy is headed by an elaborate, but puzzling, armorial page with a large monogram G (=Graville) enclosing Claude's crowned arms. The G is formed by black and silver ermine brushes on which ermines climb and from which hangs a cordelière (both Claude's emblems); this is set on a pale purple ground strewn with smaller gold G's and ermine brushes; the whole is surrounded by a complicated knotted and twined cordelière with a few snakes. The facing dedication is the same as the Arsenal copy which states unequivocally that the text was composed by Anne at Queen Claude's demand.
28. Maxime de Montmorand, *Une Femme Poète du XVIe siècle, Anne de Graville: Sa famille, sa vie, son oeuvre, sa postérité* (Paris: Picard, 1917).
29. The dedication mentions the June 1520 Field of the Cloth of Gold at Ardres, where Henry VIII met with François I attended by the entire court, including Anne and Claude; Claude's death in 1524 provides the ending date.
30. O. Reure, "Fragment de généalogie de la Maison d'Urfé," *Bulletin de la Diana* 7 (1893-94): 316-21.
31. Paul Durrieu, "Les Manuscrits à peintures de la bibliothèque de Sir Thomas Phillipps à Cheltenham," *Bibliothèque de l'École des Chartes* 50 (1889): 381-432, esp. 428-31. The frontispiece is the only miniature, but the text is splendidly decorated. The anonymous author makes clear that *amour* (her husband) allowed this translation to be made for Anne (fols. 4, 31v). The original paste-down, with the date 1518, is inscribed *vrs bon cousin et amy c'est moy*, presumably by her husband.
32. On the date of inheritance and the Rouen purchases, partially documented

through inscriptions in certain of her manuscripts, see Montmorand, *Femme Poète*, 274-78.

33. Claude Longeon, "Catalogue des livres de la bibliothèque de la Maison d'Urfé," in *Documents sur la vie intellectuelle en Forez au XVIe siècle* (n.p., 1973), 143-56: André Vernet, "Les Manuscrits de Claude d'Urfé (1501-1558) au château de La Bastie," *Comptes Rendus de l'Académie des Inscriptions et Belles-lettres* (1976): 81-97. Further see Vernet, "La Bibliothèque de Claude d'Urfé," in *Claude d'Urfé et la Bâtie. L'univers d'un gentilhomme de la Renaissance* (Montbrison: Conseil Général de La Loire, 1990), 183-203. Further documentation may be found in Pierre Gasnault, "Charles-Henri de Clermont-Tonnerre et la bibliothèque des Minimes de Tonnerre," in *Du copiste au collectionneur: Mélanges d'histoire des textes et des bibliothèques en l'honneur d'André Vernet*, ed. Donatella Nebbiai-Dalla Guarda and Jean-François Genest (Turnhout: Brepols, 1998), 585-614. Anne's holdings are listed by Montmorand, "Femme Poète," 273-85, but an updated study remains to be made.

34. The rondeaux are in BNF, MS fr. 2253. See Montmorand, "Femmes Poètes," 281. They were published by Carl Wahlund, *La Belle dame sans mercy. En Fransk dikt författad* (Uppsala: Almquist and Wiksells, 1897). See Edward J. Hoffman, *Alain Chartier, His Work and Reputation* (New York: Wittes Press, 1942), 52, 82, 239. Tory's remarks in *Champfleury* (fol. 4, where he cites her rondeau with the refrain of "Pour le meilleur") were noted by Mawy Bouchard, "Anne de Graville (1492-1544) et la tradition épique au XVIe siècle," *Littératures* 18, *L'Écriture des femmes à la Renaissance française* (1998): 35. Tory's privilege dates from 1526, but he states that he began writing in January 1525 (NS, fol. 1). See Mortimer, *Catalogues* 2: 641-43. The long-running dispute as to whether or not Anne was "*La Dame sans sy*" is discussed in Henri Lamarque, "Autour d'Anne de Graville: Le débat de la 'Dame sans sy' et l'épitaphe de la poétesse," in *Mélanges sur la littérature de la Renaissance à la mémoire de V.-L. Saulnier* (Geneva: Droz, 1984), 603-11.

35. Most recently, see Roger S. Wieck, *Painted Prayers. The Book of Hours in Medieval and Renaissance Art*, exh. cat., Pierpont Morgan Library, New York City (New York: Braziller, 1997).

36. Also called the *Hours of Jean du Luc*, 1524; Museum Meermanno-Westreenianum, *Verlucte Handscriften uit eigen bezit 1300-1500*, exh. cat. (The Hague, 1979) 22, no. 39; 60, ill.

37. The inscription on fol. 117v documents this: "Ces heures furent escriptes l'an mil cinq cens vingt et quatre par noble homme Jean de luc Escuyer Sr. de Fontenay et Marcilly secretaire du roy et appartient a Demoiselle Francoys de Brinnon sa femme."

38. Institut de France, Académie des Sciences Morales et Politiques, *Catalogue des actes de François I*, Collection des Ordonnances des rois de France (Paris: Imprimerie Nationale, 1887-1908) 7: 569, no. 27024; Elizabeth A. R. Brown, "Royal Bodies, Effigies, Funeral Meals, and Office in Sixteenth-Century France," *Micrologus* 7, *Natura, scienze et società medievali: Il cadavere* (1999): 455.

39. Catherine de Médicis, *Lettres de Catherine de Médicis*, vols. 1-5 ed. Hector de la Ferrière; vols. 6-10 ed. Gustave Baguenault de Puchesse (Paris: Imprimerie Nationale, 1880-1909) 10: 524.
40. BNF, MS Carrés d'Hozier, vol. 134, fols. 326, 330, 332.
41. On one of these (BNF, MS fr. 2848) and further bibliography of Du Tillet, see Elizabeth A. R. Brown and Myra Dickman Orth, "Jean du Tillet et les illustrations du grand *Recueil des roys*," *Revue de l'Art* 115 (1997): 7-24.
42. Victor Leroquais, *Les Livres d'heures manuscrits de la Bibliothèque nationale, Supplément* (Mâcon: Protat, 1943), 34, no. 21, pls. 35-50.
43. BNF, MS fr. 7853, fol. 326v.
44. Margareta Friesen, commentary on facsimile of *Der Rosenroman für François I: New York, Pierpont Morgan Library*, M. 948, in *Codices Selecti*, 97 (Graz: Akademische Druck- und Verlaganstalt, 1993), 27; also n. 45 for Marie's genealogy.
45. On the Master of Girard Acarie see Friesen, Commentary, 137. The couple appear on fols. 1v, 24, 111v, and 112v. Friesen affirms (p. 29) that Acarie was sometimes a scribe.
46. Inscribed on fol. 114, the former paste-down, "Ces heures appartiennent a la contrerouleure generalle de normandie Marie chantault." Of course, this could have been added to an already finished book.
47. Friesen, commentary, 27.
48. Myra Dickman Orth, introduction to *Livres d'heures royaux. La peinture de manuscrits à la cour de France au temps de Henri II*, catalogue by Thierry Crépin-Leblond, exh. cat., Musée National de la Renaissance, Château d'Écouen (Paris: Réunion des Musées Nationaux, 1993), 61, no. 26. I attribute the miniatures to the Master of Marie de Gaignon.
49. On Gouffier, see Thierry Crépin-Leblond et al, *Les Trésors du Grand Ecuyer: Claude Gouffier, collectionneur et mécène à la Renaissance*, exh. cat., Musée National de la Renaissance, Château d'Écouen (Paris: Réunion des Musées Nationaux, 1994).
50. Dating from c.1560-74; The Hague, Museum Meermanno-Westreenianum, *Schatten van de Koninklijke Bibliotheek, acht eeuwen verlucte handschriften*, exh. cat. (The Hague, 1980), no. 92, ill. p. 222; Alexander Byvanck, *Les Principaux Manuscrits à peintures de la Bibliothèque Royale des Pays-Bas et du Musée Meermanno-Westreenianum à la Haye* (Paris: Société Française de Réproductions de Manuscrits à Peintures, 1924), 91-2, no. 32, pl. 40,2.
51. Gaignon, 97 x 60 mm; The Hague, 103 x 68 mm; Paris, 90 x 61 mm.
52. Hours for the Use of Rome (Paris: Vascosan, 1558), BNF, rés. vélins 1581. See Crépin-Leblond, *Livres d'heures royaux*, 60, no. 25; id., *Les Trésors*, 104.
53. Crépin-Leblond, *Livres d'heures royaux*, 55, no. 20; Giovanni Morello, *Die Schönsten Stundenbücher aus der Biblioteca Apostolica Vaticana* (Zürich: Belser, 1988), 18, pl. 24, figs. 45, 105, 120.
54. Sheila Edmunds, ed., *Les Manuscrits enluminés des comtes et ducs de Savoie* (Turin: Umberto Allemandi, 1990), 205, no. 77; Mauro della Valle, "Le Cod. Varia 84 de la

Bibliothèque royale de Turin," in ibid, 171-76, pls. 56-58.

55. Paul Lacombe, *Livres d'heures imprimés au XVe et au XVIe siècle conservés dans le bibliothèques publiques de Paris* (Paris: Imprimerie Nationale, 1907).

56. On all of these see Crépin-Leblond, *Livres d'heures royaux*, nos. 4, 14, 15, and 23.

57. Victor Leroquais, *Les Livres d'heures manuscrits de la Bibliothèque nationale* (Mâcon: Protat, 1927), 2: 230-34, no. 270; 3: pl. 123. The question of attribution is complex— most of the original set of family portraits are after drawings by François Clouet..

58. Orth, *Survey*, no. 100.

59. Louis Dimier, *Histoire de la peinture de portrait en France au XVIe siècle: accompagnée d'un catalogue de tous les ouvrages subsistant en ce genre, de crayon, de peinture à l'huile, de miniature, d'émail, de tapisserie, et de cire en médaillons* (Paris: Van Ouest, 1924-27), 1: 131-33.

60. André Chastel, *French Art: The Renaissance, 1430-1620*, ed. Christine Schulz-Touge with Camille Cloutier; trans. Deke Dusinberre (New York: Flammarion, 1995), 214-16.

61. Édmond Bonnaffé, *Inventaire des meubles de Catherine de Médicis en 1589* (Paris: Auguste Aubry, 1874), 134-43, no. 656-724.

62. Inventory of 1589 (BNF, MS fr. 14359) in Henri Omont, *Anciens Inventaires et catalogues de la Bibliothèque Nationale* (Paris: Imprimerie Nationale, 1908-21), 1: 438-75; see also Bonnaffé, *Inventaire*, 84-85 and 168-211. Another inventory, of 1597, with different books, is in Antoine-Jean-Victor Le Roux de Lincy, *Notice sur la bibliothèque de Catherine de Médicis et des extraits de l'inventaire de cette bibliothèque* (Paris: Techener, 1859), 17-32 (this remains to be researched, containing as it does a number of manuscripts that had belonged to Louise de Savoie).

63. . . . ."'pour la royne sa pinture pour pendre au coul," BNF, MS fr. 894, fol. 71, and in a different hand, fol. 77; see Yvonne Hackenbroch, "Catherine de'Medici and Her Court Jeweller François Dujardin," *Connoisseur* 163 (1966): 28-33; Michelle Bimbenet-Privat, "Dessins inédits de François Dujardin, orfèvre de Catherine de Médicis," *Gazette des Beaux-Arts* 109 (1987) 195; Centre Culturel du Panthéon, Paris, *Orfèvrerie parisienne de la Renaissance*, exh. cat., idem et al., (Paris: Ville de Paris, 1995), 125, no. 3.

64. Louise's inventory: Francoys Fromont, *Inventaire des meubles, bijoux et livres estant à Chenonceaux le huit janvier MDCIII, précédé d'une histoire sommaire de la vie de Louise de Lorraine, reine de France, suivi d'une notice sur le château de Chenonceaux* (Paris: Techener, 1856).

65. Anthony Hobson, *French and Italian Collectors and Their Bindings: Illustrated from Examples in the Library of J. R. Abbey* (Oxford: Roxburghe Club, 1953), 105.

66. Raoul de Broglie, "Les Clouet de Chantilly: Catalogue illustré," *Gazette des Beaux-Arts* 77 (1971): 266; Dana Bentley-Cranch, "L'Iconographie de Marguerite de Savoie (1523-1574)," in *Culture et pouvoir au temps de l'humanisme et de la Renaissance*, ed. Louis Terreaux; Actes du congrès Marguerite de Savoie, Annecy, Chambéry, Turin, 1974 (Geneva and Paris, Slatkine and H. Champion, 1978), 249.

67. For the items willed to Christine, see Bonnaffé, *Inventaire*, 24, 55. For the tapestries, now in the Uffizi, see Frances Yates, *The Valois Tapestries*, 2d ed. (London: Routledge and Kegan Paul, 1975), 120-29, with documentation.

WORKS CITED

Anselme de la Vierge Marie, père [Pierre Guibours]. *Histoire généalogique et chronologique de la maison royale de France: des pairs, grands officiers de la couronne & de la maison du roy: & des anciens barons du royaume: avec les qualitez, l'origine, le progrès & les armes de leurs familles; ensemble les statuts & le catalogue des chevaliers, commandeurs, & officiers de l'ordre de S. Esprit*, 3rd ed., ed. Honoré Caille Dufourny and les pères Ange de Sainte-Rosalie and Simplicien (Paris: La Compagnie des Libraires, 1726-1733). 9 vols. Paris: La Compagnie des Libraires, 1726-33.

Bentley-Cranch, Dana. "L'iconographie de Marguerite de Savoie (1523-1574)." In *Culture et pouvoir au temps de l'humanisme et de la Renaissance*, edited by Louis Terreaux, 243-56. Actes du congrès Marguerite de Savoie, Annecy, Chambéry, Turin, 29 Avril-4 Mai 1974. Geneva and Paris: Slatkine and Champion, 1978.

Berriot-Salvadore, Evelyne. *Les Femmes dans la société française de la Renaissance*. Histoire des idées et critique littéraire, vol. 285. Geneva: Droz, 1990.

Bimbenet-Privat, Michèle. "Dessins inédits de François Dujardin, orfèvre de Catherine de Médicis." *Gazette des Beaux-Arts* 109 (1987): 195.

———. *Les Orfèvres parisiens de la Renaissance (1506-1620)*. Paris: Commission des Travaux Historiques de la Ville de Paris, 1992.

Bimbenet-Privat, Michèle, et al. *Orfèvrerie parisienne de la Renaissance*. Exhibition catalogue, Centre Culturel du Panthéon. Paris: Ville de Paris, 1995.

Bonnaffé, Édmond. *Inventaire des meubles de Catherine de Médicis en 1589*. Paris: Auguste Aubry, 1874.

Bouchard, Mawy. "Anne de Graville (1492-1544) et la tradition épique au XVIe siècle." *Littératures* 18, *L'Écriture des femmes à la Renaissance française* (1998): 31-63.

Bourassé, Jean-Jacques. *Les Dévotes Epistres de Katharine d'Amboise publiées pour la première fois*. Tours: Mame, 1861.

Broglie, Raoul de. "Les Clouet de Chantilly: Catalogue illustré." *Gazette des Beaux-Arts* 77 (1971): 261-336.

Brown, Elizabeth A. R. "Royal Bodies, Effigies, Funeral Meals, and Office in Sixteenth-Century France." *Micrologus* 7, *Natura, scienze et società medievali. Il cadavere* (1999): 407-508.

———., and Myra Dickman Orth. "Jean du Tillet et les illustrations du grand *Recueil des roys*." *Revue de l'Art* 115 (1997): 7-24.

Byvanck, Alexander Willem. *Les Principaux Manuscrits à peintures de la Bibliothèque royale des Pays-Bas et du musée Meermanno-Westreenianum à la Haye*. Paris: Société Française de Reproductions de Manuscrits à Peintures, 1924.

Catherine de Médicis. *Lettres de Catherine de Médicis.* 10 vols. Vols. 1-5 edited by Hector de La Ferrière-Percy; vols. 6-10 edited by Gustave Baguenault de Puchesse. Paris: Imprimerie Nationale, 1880-1909.

Chastel, André. *French Art. The Renaissance, 1430-1620.* Edited by Christine Schulz-Touge with Camille Cloutier. Translated by Deke Dusinberre. New York: Flammarion, 1995.

Cooper, Richard. "Michel d'Amboise, poète maudit?" In *La Génération Marot. Poètes français et néo-latins (1515-1550),* edited by Gérard Defaux, 445-70. Actes du colloque international de Baltimore, 1996. Paris: H. Champion, 1997.

———. "Le Thème de la Fortune dans la poésie de Michel d'Amboise (c.1505-1547)." In *Il tema della Fortuna nella letteratura francese e italiana del Rinascimento: Studi in memoria di Enzo Guidici,* edited by G. A. Brunelli et al., 107-22. Florence: L. S. Olschki, 1990.

Cottrell, Robert. "Figures emblématiques dans *La Coche* de Marguerite de Navarre." In *Marguerite de Navarre 1492-1992,* edited by Nicole Cazauran and James Dauphiné, 309-25. Actes du colloque international de Pau, 1992. Mont-de-Marsan: Éditions InterUniversitaires, 1995.

Couderc, Camille. *Bibliothèque nationale: Album des portraits d'après les collections du département des manuscrits.* Paris: Berthaud, [1908].

Crépin-Leblond, Thierry, catalogue; Myra Dickman Orth, introduction. *Livres d'heures royaux. La peinture de manuscrits à la cour de France au temps de Henri II.* Exhibition Catalogue, Musée National de la Renaissance, Château d'Écouen. Paris: Réunion des Musées Nationaux, 1993.

Crépin-Leblond, Thierry, et al. *Les Trésors du Grand Ecuyer: Claude Gouffier, collectionneur et mécène à la Renaissance.* Exhibition Catalogue, Musée National de la Renaissance, Château d'Écouen. Paris: Réunion des Musées Nationaux, 1994.

Davis, Natalie Zemon. *The Gift in Sixteenth-Century France.* Madison, WI: University of Wisconsin Press, 2000.

———. "Beyond the Market: Books as Gifts in Sixteenth-Century France." Prothero Lecture. *Transactions of the Royal Historical Society* 33 (1983): 69-88.

Della Valle, Mauro. "Le Cod. Varia 84 de la bibliothèque royale de Turin." In *Les Manuscrits enluminés des comtes et ducs de Savoie,* edited by Sheila Edmunds, 170-76. Turin: Umberto Allemandi, 1990.

Dimier, Louis. *Histoire de la peinture de portrait en France au XVIe siècle: accompagnée d'un catalogue de tous les ouvrages subsistant en ce genre, de crayon, de peinture à l'huile, de miniature, d'émail, de tapisserie, et de cire en médaillons.* 3 vols. Paris: G. Van Oest, 1924-27.

Durrieu, Paul. "Les Manuscrits à peintures de la bibliothèque de Sir Thomas Phillipps à Cheltenham." *Bibliothèque de l'École des Chartes* 50 (1889): 381-432.

Edmunds, Sheila, ed. *Les Manuscrits enluminés des comtes et ducs de Savoie*. Turin: Umberto Allemandi, 1990.
Fogg, Sam. *Rare Books and Manuscripts, Catalogue 1999*. Exhibition catalogue, Blumka Gallery, New York. London and New York, 1999.
Fontaine, Marie-Madeleine. "Les Deux Amours, ou l'arithmétique de Marguerite de Navarre, *La Coche*." In *Marguerite de Navarre 1492-1992*, edited by Nicole Cazauran and James Dauphiné, 327-49. Actes du colloque international de Pau, 1992. Mont-de-Marsan: Éditions InterUniversitaires, 1995.
Friesen, Margareta, commentary on facsimile of *Der Rosenroman für François I*. New York, Pierpont Morgan Library, M. 948. In *Codices Selecti*, 97. Graz, Austria: Akademische Druck- und Verlaganstalt, 1993.
Fromont, Francoys. *Inventaire des meubles, bijoux et livres estant à Chenonceaux le huit janvier MDCIII, précédé d'une histoire sommaire de la vie de Louise de Lorraine, reine de France, suivi d'une notice sur le château de Chenonceaux*. Paris: Techener, 1856.
Gasnault, Pierre. "Charles-Henri de Clermont-Tonnerre et la bibliothèque des Minimes de Tonnerre." In *Du copiste au collectionneur: Mélanges d'histoire des textes et des bibliothèques en l'honneur d'André Vernet*, edited by Donatella Nebbiai-Dalla Guarda and Jean-François Genest, 585-614. Turnhout: Brepols, 1998.
Hackenbroch, Yvonne. "Catherine de'Medici and Her Court Jeweller François Dujardin." *Connoisseur* 163 (1966): 28-33.
Hobson, Anthony. *French and Italian Collectors and Their Bindings. Illustrated from Examples in the Library of J. R. Abbey*. Oxford: Roxburghe Club, 1953.
Hoffman, Edward J. *Alain Chartier, His Work and Reputation*. New York: Wittes Press, 1942.
Institut de France, Académie des Sciences Morales et Politiques. *Catalogue des actes de François I*. 10 vols. Collection des ordonnances des rois de France. Paris: Imprimerie Nationale, 1887-1908.
Kemp, William. "Textes composés ou traduits par des femmes et imprimés en France avant 1550: Bibliographie des imprimés féminins (1488-1549)." *Littératures* 18. *L'Écriture des femmes à la Renaissance française* (1998): 151-220.
———. "Marguerite of Navarre, Clément Marot, and the 1533 Augereau Editions of the *Miroir de l'âme pécheresse* (Paris, 1533)." *Journal of the Early Book Society* 2 (1999): 113-56.
Kemp, William and Fabrizio Frigerio, "The Evangelical 'Fortuna' Device of the Parisian Bookseller Jérôme Denis (1529)." *Trivium* 31 (1999): 117-30.
Knecht, Robert J. *Francis I*. Cambridge: Cambridge University Press, 1982.
Lacombe, Paul. *Livres d'heures imprimés au XVe et au XVIe siècle conservés dans le bibliothèques publiques de Paris*. Paris: Imprimerie Nationale, 1907.

Lamarque, Henri. "Autour d'Anne de Graville: Le débat de la 'Dame sans sy' et l'épitaphe de la poétesse." in *Mélanges sur la littérature de la Renaissance à la mémoire de V.-L. Saulnier*, 603-11. Geneva: Droz, 1984.

Lefèvre, S. "L'Heptaméron entre éditions et manuscrits." In *Marguerite de Navarre 1492-1992*, edited by Nicole Cazauran and James Dauphiné, 445-47. Actes du colloque international de Pau, 1992. Mont-de-Marsan: Éditions InterUniversitaires, 1995.

Le Hir, Yves, ed. *Anne de Graville: Le beau romant des deux amans Palamon et Arcita et de la belle et saige Emilia*. Paris: Presses Universitaires Françaises, 1965.

Leroquais, Victor. *Les Livres d'heures manuscrits de la Bibliothèque nationale*. 3 vols. Mâcon: Protat, 1927.

———. *Les Livres d d'heures manuscrits de la Bibliothèque nationale, Supplément*. Mâcon: Protat, 1943.

Le Roux de Lincy, Antoine-Jean-Victor. *L'Heptaméron des nouvelles de très illustre princesse Marguerite d'Angoulême reine de Navarre soeur unique de François I*. 3 vols. Paris: A. Eudes, 1880.

———. *Notice sur la bibliothèque de Catherine de Médicis et des extraits de l'inventaire de cette bibliothèque*. Paris: Techener, 1859.

Longeon, Claude. "Catalogue des livres de la bibliothèque de la Maison d'Urfé." In *Documents sur la vie intellectuelle en Forez au XVIe siècle*, 143-56. n.p. 1973.

Marichal, Robert, ed. *Marguerite de Navarre. La coche*. Textes littéraires français. vol. 173. Geneva and Paris: Droz and Minard, 1971.

———. "Texte ou image?" In *Mise en page et mise en texte du livre manuscrit*, edited by Henri-Jean Martin and Jean Vezin, 426-34. Paris: Promodis, 1990.

Meurgey, Jacques P. *Les Principaux Manuscrits à peintures du Musée Condé à Chantilly*. Paris: Société Française de Reproductions de Manuscrits à Peintures, 1930.

Montmorand, Maxime de. *Une Femme Poète du XVIe siècle, Anne de Graville. Sa famille, sa vie, son oeuvre, sa postérité*. Paris: A. Picard, 1917.

Morello, Giovanni. *Die Schönsten Stundenbücher aus der Bibliotheca Apostolica Vaticana*. Zürich: Belser, 1988.

Mortimer, Ruth, comp. *Catalogue of Books and Manuscripts, Harvard College Library,. Department of Printing and Graphic Arts: Part 1, French Sixteenth Century Books*. 2 vols. Cambridge, Mass: Belknap Press, 1964.

Museum Meermanno-Westreenianum. *Verlucte Handscriften uit eigen bezit, 1300-1500*. Exhibition catalogue. The Hague, 1979.

Museum Meermanno Westreenianum and Koninklijke Bibliotheek. *Schatten van de Koninklijke Bibliotheek: Acht eeuwen verluchte Handscriften: Tentoonstelling in het Rijksmuseum Meermanno-Westreenianum/Museum van het Boek*. Exhibition catalogue. The Hague, 1980.

Omont, Henri. *Anciens Inventaires et catalogues de la Bibliothèque Nationale*. 5 vols. Paris, Imprimerie Nationale, 1908-21.

———. [note], *Bulletin de la Société Nationale des Antiquaires de France* (1891): 154.
Orth, Myra Dickman. "Dedicating Women: Manuscript Culture in the French Renaissance. The Cases of Catherine d'Amboise and Anne de Graville." *Journal of the Early Book Society* 1 (1997): 17-47.
———. "The Master of François de Rohan: A Familiar French Renaissance Miniaturist with a New Name." In *Illuminating the Book—Makers and Interpreters: Essays in Honour of Janet Backhouse*, edited by Michelle Brown and Scot McKendrick, 69-91. London: British Library, 1998..
———. *Survey of French Renaissance Illuminated Manuscriptsts*. London: Harvey Miller/Brepols, forthcoming.
Pächt, Otto, and J. J. G. Alexander. *Illuminated Manuscripts in the Bodleian Library, Oxford: German, Dutch, Flemish, French, and Spanish Schools*. Vol. 1. Oxford: Oxford University Press, 1966.
Reure, O. "Fragment de généalogie de la Maison d'Urfé." *Bulletin de la Diana* 7 (1893-94): 316-21.
Sclafer, Jacqueline. *Manuscrits du Moyen Âge et de la Renaissance: Enrichissements du Département des manuscrits, 1983-1992*. Paris: Bibliothèque Nationale de France, 1994.
Souchal, Geneviève. "Le Mécénat de la famille d'Amboise." *Bulletin de la Société des antiquaires de l'Ouest et des Musées de Poitiers*, 3 (1976): 485-525; 4 (1976): 567-612.
Venard, Marc. "Le Testament du cardinal d'Amboise." In *De l'histoire de la Brie à l'histoire des Réformes: Mélanges offerts au chanoine Michel Veissière*, edited by Michel Bardon, 15-28. Études et documents de la Fédération des sociétés historiques et archéologiques de Paris et de l'Iâle-de-France, 2. Paris, 1993.
Vernet, André. "Les Manuscrits de Claude d'Urfé (1501-1558) au château de La Bastie." *Comptes Rendus de l'Académie des Inscriptions et Belles-lettres* (1976): 81-97.
———. "La bibliothèque de Claude d'Urfé." In *Claude d'Urfé et la Bâtie: L'univers d'un gentilhomme de la Renaissance*, 183-203. Exhibition Catalogue. Montbrison: Conseil Général de la Loire, 1990.
Wahlund, Carl. *La Belle Dame sans mercy. En Fransk dikt författad*. Uppsala: Almquist and Wiksells, 1897.
Wieck, Roger S. *Painted Prayers: The Book of Hours in Medieval and Renaissance Art*. Exhibition catalogue, Pierpont Morgan Library, New York City. New York: Braziller, 1997.
Yates, Frances. *The Valois Tapestries*. 2d ed. London: Routledge and Kegan Paul, 1975.

List of Manuscripts Cited in the Text, by City, Library, and Shelf Number

Berne, Bürgerbibliothek, MS A65, Marguerite de Navarre, La Coche, c.1543
Chantilly, Musée Condé, MS 522 [1848], Marguerite de Navarre, La Coche, 1542
Chantilly, Musée Condé, MS 1479 [1943], Hours of the Constable Anne de Montmorency, c.1549-53
Chantilly, Musée Condé, MS 1570 [513], Anne de Graville, Roman de Palamon et Arcita, 1521-24
Hague, Museum Meermanno-Westreenianum, MS 10 F 33, Hours of Françoise de Brinon (also called the Hours of Jean du Luc), 1524
Hague, Royal Library, MS 74 G 39, Hours of Catherine de Médicis and Charles IX, c.1560-74
London, BL, Phillipps MS 127, loan 36/1, Le Livre d'amour (translation of Berosus, Chaldean Histories), 1518
New York, Pierpont Morgan Library, MS M.538, Hours of Claude Gouffier, c.1550-55
Oxford, Bodl. MS Douce 91, Marguerite de Navarre, La Coche, 1542
Paris, Bibl. de l'Arsenal, MS 2037, Catherine d'Amboise, Livre des prudens et imprudens des siecles passés, 1509
Paris, Bibl. de l'Arsenal, MS 5112, Marguerite de Navarre, La Coche, c.1543
Paris, Bibl. de l'Arsenal, MS 5116, Anne de Graville, Roman de Palamon et Arcita, 1521-24
Paris, Ecole Nationale Supérieure des Beaux-Arts, MS Masson 20. Prayerbook for Marie de Gaignon, 1559-60
Paris, BNF, MS fr. 894, Designs for jewelry for Catherine de Médicis
Paris, BNF, MS fr. 1397, Anne de Graville, Roman de Palamon et Arcita
Paris BNF, MS fr. 2253, Anne de Graville, Rondeaux, c.1524
Paris, BNF, MS fr. 2282, Catherine d'Amboise, Dévotes Epistres, c.1525-30
Paris, BNF, MS fr. 2848, Jean du Tillet, Le Grand recueil des roys de France, 1566
Paris, BNF, MS fr. 7853, royal household accounts (copy)
Paris, BNF, MS fr. 12485, Marguerite de Navarre, La Coche, c.1543
Paris, BNF, MS fr. 14359, Inventory of Library of Catherine de Médicis, 1589
Paris, BNF, MS fr. 25441, Anne de Graville's copy of her Roman de Palamon et Arcita, c.1524
Paris, BNF, MS nouv. acq. fr. 719, (paper) Anne de Graville, Roman de Palamon et Arcita
Paris, BNF, MS nouv. acq. fr. 6513, (paper, fragmentary) Anne de Graville, Roman de Palamon et Arcita
Paris, BNF, MS nouv. acq. fr. 19738, Catherine d'Amboise, La Complainte de la Dame pasmée contre fortune, c.1525
Paris, BNF, MS lat. 1429, Hours of Dinteville/Henri II, c.1543-47

Paris, BNF, MS lat. 10558, Hours of Dinteville, c.1550-54
Paris, BNF, MS nouv. acq. lat. 82, Hours of Catherine de Médicis, 1573-74
Paris, BNF, MS Smith-Lesouëf 39, Hours of Marie Chantault, c.1525
Paris, BNF, Carrés d'Hozier, vol. 134, Genealogies and documents
Paris, BNF, MS deposit, Société des Manuscrits des Assureurs Français MS SMAF MS 79-7, Catherine d'Amboise, La Complainte de la Dame pasmée contre fortune, c.1525
Rome, MS Vat. lat. 14936, Hours of Catherine de Médicis, 1561
Turin, Bibl. Reale, MS var. 84, Prayerbook of Marguerite de France, 1559
Turin, Bibl. Reale, MS var. 266 bis, Valerio Saluzzo della Manta, La Sphinge, 1559
Location unknown, **private collection**, Catherine d'Amboise, La Complainte de la Dame pasmée contre fortune, c.1525

List of Sixteenth-Century Printed Editions Cited in the Text

Amboise, Michel de. *Complaintes de l'esclave fortuné*. Paris: J. Saint-Denis, 1529
Hours for the Use of Rome. Paris: Vascosan, 1558. BNF, rés. vélins 1581
Marguerite de Navarre, *Miroir de l'ame pecheresse*, Alençon: Simon du Bois, 1531
———. *Suyte des Marguerites de la Marguerite des princesses*. Lyon: de Tournes, 1547
Tory, Geofroy. *Champfleury*. Paris: G. Tory, 1529

Christine de Pizan and the Book: Programs and Modes of Reading, Strategies for Publication
JACQUELINE CERQUIGLINI-TOULET

Unlike some scholars, Christine de Pizan cannot say, like Guillaume de Machaut, "Je, qui ai esté a l'escole,"[1] or, like Eustache Deschamps, evoke, indirectly, her universities.[2] However, Christine's graphic culture is important. She spent her childhood in a cultured environment, close to both a father who read and had a library, and to a king who loved and fostered books, by his commissions and his politics of translation. Christine in fact evokes this atmosphere of feverish composition in the *Livre des fais et bonnes meurs du sage roy Charles* V, speaking of "des livres de gramaire ou d'autre science, que on escript tous les jours."[3] What does the book represent for her, in its double mode of apprehension: reading and writing?

In fact, for Christine, everything begins with writing—historically in her biography, chronologically in the history of the composition of her texts, or more exactly, in both cases, in their *mise-en-scène*. For her, the figure of the father is sketched behind the book. She explains in L'*Advision*[4] how, after the deaths of the king, of her father, and of her husband, and after having settled pressing material matters—juridical proceedings and lack of money—she began to write: "et vous happay ces beaulx livres et volumes et dis que aucune chose recouvreroi de mes pertes passees" (A*dvision*, part 3, ch. 10, p. 110). And these "losses," surely, are everything that she did not learn during her childhood, either through levity, childishness, or lack of encouragement, but they are also of those figures of educated men who had surrounded her and whom the books bring back. The use of the verb *happer*, a violent verb—death is said to "happe," to

CHRISTINE DE PIZAN AND THE BOOK 113

seize—expresses Christine's compulsion, her desire. But if Christine reads to the point of surfeit, she also constructs a program of apprenticeship that is reasoned and progressive: "comme l'enfant que au premier on met a l'a.b.c., me pris aux histoires anciennes des commencemens du monde; [...] Puis me pris aux livres des pouetes" (ibid.).

A liberally chosen path, which allows Christine to avoid the pitfalls into which, despite themselves, young scholars had fallen. In fact, the latter suckle antifeminism along with the milk of grammar that they learn in Ovid's *Remedia amoris*, or in the manuals composed by teachers preaching the "blaming" of women, such as those evoked by Christine in L'*Espitre au dieu d'amours*:[5]

> Dittiez en font, rimes, proses et vers,
> En diffamant leurs meurs par moz divers;
> Si les baillent en matiere aux premiers
> A leurs nouveaulx et jeunes escolliers
> En maniere d'example et de dottrine. (ll. 261-65)

And as for the *Remedia amoris*:

> Si ont les clers apris trés leur enfance
> Cellui livret en premiere science
> De gramaire. (ll. 291-93)

Stressing the fact that she had not had any scholastic apprenticeship in composition (" Car le ditter je n'ay mie henté "),[6] Christine de Pizan emphasizes her existential relationship to this activity and her "election": she is a writer who has received a gift from God and from Nature—she is an inspired writer. She affirms this in her dedication to Queen Isabeau de Bavière when she presents her with the book that is the British Library Ms Harley 4431.[7] The book, she says, is

> Pris ou stile que je detiens
> Du seul sentement que retiens
> Des dons de Dieu et de nature. (ll. 20-22)

The same formula is present at the beginning of the *Livre des fais et bonnes meurs*: "mais douée de don de Dieu et nature" (vol.1, p. 5).

Such an attitude has two consequences. Christine shows no anxiety about running out of material. In some way, her election and her sex would bring about a new way of looking at both aspects of the production and distribution of her books. The feminine point of view is from the start a new look at the questions that one may be led to address. Christine de Pizan expresses this principle forcefully in L'E*pistre au dieu d'amours*, where the very syntax strikes one as a provocation, where an inversion forces the reader to pause at the formula ". . .les livres ne firent/ Pas les femmes" (ll. 409-10). The sentence is repeated by Droiture in L*e Livre de la cité des dames*:[8] "Et te promet que les livres qui ce dient, les femmes ne les firent mie"(bk 2, ch. 13, pp. 252-254). Likewise, concerning its dissemination, the book composed "de sentement de femme" enjoys success as a curiosity (A*vision*, part 3, ch. 12, p. 113).

Christine de Pizan and the Materiality of the Book

Christine de Pizan was part of a movement among fourteenth-century poets to become more and more involved in the material production of their works. The case of Guillaume de Machaut is typical. The poet keeps a journal of his writing in the *Livre du voir dit*, in which he notes points such as the length of the book: "et tenra environ XII coiers de XL poins" (Letter 45, p. 770). Christine does likewise in the A*vision*, for all of the works she has written up to this point: "compillés en ce tendis XV volumes principaux sans les autres particuliers petis dictiez, lesquelz tout ensemble contiennent environ LXX quaiers de grant volume" (part 3, ch. 10, p. 111). This remark shows that Christine, like Guillaume de Machaut, kept a register of her complete works.

But we can go more deeply into Christine's studio, and grasp what for her, in its material aspect, constituted a beautiful book. The ideal image is contained in the bull left to her by the goddess Loyalty in D*it de la rose*:[9]

> Le parchemin de fin or yere
> Et les lettres furent escriptes
> De fin azur, non trop petites
> Ne trop grans, mais si bien formées
> Que mieulx ne peust.

Admittedly the manuscripts that Christine had executed for her patrons are not on gold parchment, but the care with which they were confected attests to this taste for beautiful objects and to the price attached to them. Thus we read in the dedication to Queen Isabeau:

> Si l'ay fait, ma dame, ordener
> Depuis que je sceus qu'assener
> Le devoye a vous, si qu'ay sceu
> Tout au mieulx et le parfiner
> D'escripre et bien enluminer
> Dès que vo command en receu. (ll. 49-54)

The rondeau that closes L'*Epistre à la reine*[10] in the manuscript BNF, f.fr. 580 attests to Christine's care for the calligraphy of her works, when they were to be presented as gifts:

> Prenez en gré, s'il vous plaist, cest escript
> De ma main fait apres mienuit une heure.
>
> Noble seigneur, pour qui je l'ay escript
> Prenez en gré.
>
> Quand vous plaira, mieulz vous sera rescript,
> Mais n'avoye nul autre clerc à l'eure.
>
> Prenez en gré, s'il v...

Likewise, we have her testimony about the illumination of her works. In *Le Livre de la cité des dames*, she lauds the works of Anastaise, "experte et apprise a faire vigneteures d'enlumineure en livres et champaignes d'istoires," "fleureteure," and she adds: "Et ce scay je par experience, car pour moy mesmes a ouvré d'aucunes choses qui sont tenues singulieres entre les vignetes des autres grans ouvriers"(bk 1, ch. 41, p. 192).

This knowledge of the art of illumination surfaces in her writing, giving rise to images from that art. She speaks in these terms of the composition of the *Livre des fais et bonnes meurs*:

> tout ainssi comme une pierre precieuse, digne et fine et de grant chierté on envelope en or, en esmail ou drap de soye et souefves odours, est bien raison que la juste veritable narracion de ses dignes meurs soit fleurettée de memoires proffitables et de digne efficace. (vol. 1, bk 1, ch. 3, pp. 9-10).

Christine de Pizan and the Composition of the Book

The dedication of the Harley manuscript to Queen Isabeau de Bavière shows Christine's literary awareness. She is aware of the obligatory terms of a prologue, and like Chrétien de Troyes, attests to having put her *peine* into the work: "mon labour et lonc travail" (l. 73) as well as her *entencion*: "en benigne devocion/Vous plaise mon entencion/Prendre en gré" (ll. 88-90). We are struck by the great richness of the technical vocabulary. Christine makes a distinction between the book, an object presented as a gift ("Pour ce livre cy que je tiens/Vous presenter" [ll. 16-17], the "livre que mes en vo bail" [l. 74]), and books in the sense of works contained in the book-object (*livre*) or volume ("Et sont ou volume compris/Plusieurs livres" [ll. 25-26]). She also uses the word *euvre* to designate the content of the manuscript: "Que mon euvre estre presentée/Vous doye"(ll. 63-64); "Du livre [...]/Qui contient grant euvre et penible" (ll. 74-75). This awareness and interest can be found in all of Christine's work. They can be seen most markedly in her use of the expression "il n'est si beaulx mestiers" (l. 46), an expression that we find also in Watriquet de Couvin's[11] praise of the good minstrel: "ceuls qui font le biau mestier " (v. 103), or in Jean Froissart, when he evokes literary activity, and more particularly amorous writings, in terms of the "gai mestier" in *La prison amoureuse*[12] or the "mestier gens" in the *Joli Buisson de jonece*.[13]

Just as she had commented on the materiality of the act of writing, Christine describes the composition of her works. For example, she points out her passage from verse to prose in her letter to Guillaume de Tignonville:[14]

> Aussi, chier seigneur, ne vous soit a merveille, pour ce que mes autres dictiéz ay acoustuméz a rimoyer, cestui estre en prose. Car comme la matiere ne le requiere autressy, est droit que je suive le stille de mes assaillans. (Letter 2, p. 8)

Likewise in the *Livre des fais et bonnes meurs du sage roy Charles V*: "emprens nouvelle compilacion menée en stille prosal et hors le commun ordre de mes autres choses passées" (vol. 1, part 1, prologue, p. 5).

She gives an account of her process of writing by explaining the reasons—"une fievre soubdaine" (l. 8733)- that led her to pass from verse to prose in the writing of the chapter on the Jews in *La mutacion de Fortune*:[15]

> Mais, pour mon ouvrage haster,
> Mettray la prose en la maniere
> Que mot a mot l'escri plainiere.

She points out the plans that she adopts: "Ainsi sera mon dit volume contenu en .III. parties, qui toutes s'assembleront à une seule chose, c'est assavoir: [...] le sage roy Charles"(*Livre des fais et bonnes meurs*, vol. 1, part 1, prologue, p. 6).

She comments on her versification. This metatextual distancing allows her a perspective on the material that she is dealing with when the latter is amorous. This is the case in the *Livre du duc des vrais amans*,[16] where, after a preliminary *explicit* we read:

> A tous ditteurs, qui savoir
> Ont en eulx, celle savoir
> Fait, qui ce dittié ditta,
> Qu'en trestous les vers dit a

> Rime leonime ou livre,
> Et tel tout au long le livre. (ll. 3557-562)

She stresses the figures of style that she uses: metaphor and antiphrase, which she notes the most often. Thus she speaks of "metaphore" in *Le Livre de la mutacion de Fortune*:[16]

> Attroppos a nom la portiere,
> A parler selon la maniere
> Qui a methafore compete,
> Ainsi l'appella le poete. (vol. 1, ll. 2819-822)

As for the antiphrase, she speaks humorously of merchants in the same work: "Mais ceulx la vi je en cellui estre / Par antifrasim, loyaulx estre" (vol. 2, ll. 6365-366). In *La Cité des dames*, Reason makes the antiphrase into a necessary figure if women are to read antifeminist writings. She teaches Christine:

> Et des poetes dont tu parles, ne scez tu pas bien que ilz ont parlé en plusieurs choses en maniere de fable et se veulent aucunefois entendre au contraire de ce que leurs diz demonstrent? Et les peut on prendre par une figure de grammaire qui se nomme antifrasis qui s'entent, si comme tu scez, si comme on diroit tel est mauvais, c'est a dire que il est bon, aussi a l'opposite. Si te conseille que tu faces ton prouffit de leurs dis et que l'entendes ainsi, quelque fust leur entente es lieux ou ilz blasment les femmes. (Part 1, ch. 2, p. 48)

This is very audacious advice. Just as one can read pagan authors while moralizing them—i.e. while converting their text, linguistically and ideologically, as in *L'Ovide moralisé*—likewise, one can read antifeminist writings while converting them through the figure of the antiphrase. Feminist reading is a "moralized" reading. It has morality's force and finality.

Christine has the feeling that she is constructing a work, in the modern sense—a total work—and she communicates this sentiment to the reader by incessant repetitions. Each new book is put into perspective in relation to the preceding ones. She harks back, in the *Livre de la Cité des dames* to the *Epistre au dieu d'amours* ("Et de ce as tu souffisamment parlé en ton *Epistre du Dieu d'Amours*" [*Cité des dames*, bk. 2, ch. 47, p. 336]); to the *Epistres sur le "Roman de la rose"* ("car toy mesmes as assez souffisamment traictié la matiere tant contre cellui Ovide, comme contre autres, en ton *Epistre du dieu d'amours* et es *Epistres sus le 'Rommant de la Rose'*" [ibid., bk. 2, ch.54, p. 376]); and to the *Livre de Othea* ("si que toy meimes as touchié en ton *Livre de Othea*" [ibid., bk. 1, ch.36, p. 176]). The *Livre des fais et bonnes meurs* is mentioned in the *Livre du corps de policie*,[17] in *Le Livre de la paix*,[18] and so on. There are multiple examples like this. The reader is even invited to skip certain passages if he or she has already read them in an earlier work. A striking example of this is Sibylle de Monthault's letter, which appears in *Le Livre du duc des vrais amans* (pp. 162-71) and is repeated in *Le Livre des trois vertus*,[19] with this observation:

> Pour ce que l'espistre qui est contenue ou *Livre du Duc des Vrais Amans*, ou il est mis que Sebile de la Tour l'envoia a la duchece, puet servir au propos que ou chapitre cy aprés ensuit, sera de rechief recordee. Si la puet passer oultre qui veult, se au lire lui anuye ou se autre foiz l'a veue. (p. 109)

This idea of the reader's choice, which presupposes an individual reading, can be found already in Guillaume de Machaut, concerning the letters inserted in the *Voir dit*: "Et briément la response orrés, / Si la lirés quant vous volrés" (ll. 6261-262) and in Oton de Grandson's *Livre messire Ode*,[20] concerning a complaint in the form of a dialogue between his body and his heart: "Et s'ennuyer ne vous vouloit, / Voir la pourrés ycy endroit" (ll. 1524-525). Christine de Pizan takes up this process in the idea that she has of her work as a whole. Her formulation can be compared to that of George Chastelain, fifty years later, in his *Chronique*.[21] He never repeats information that he has already provided, and alerts the reader to this in the following terms:

> "pour cause que la mesme response en forme a esté récitée icydevant, là où elle servoit, n'est pas besoing pour tant de la renouveler droitcy, puisque elle peut gésir sainement en la memoire des lisans" (vol. 3, bk 4, ch. 42, p. 205).

Christine de Pizan repeated, leaving it up to the reader to read or not read, while George Chastelain put his trust in the reader's memory.

Reading, Writing

Where does the book spring from? From books. The *mise-en-scène* of Christine's writing is often anchored in a scene of reading. Voluntary reading is entertainment, as is the case in *Le Livre de la cité des dames*, where Christine describes herself as "auques traveillié de recueillir la pesanteur des sentences de divers aucteurs"(p. 40). Reading can also be consolation, as in the *Livre du chemin de long estude*,[22] where the poetess presents herself as "cerchant [i.e. *skimming*] un livre ou deux" (l. 177) but not finding therein the expected comfort, which she will finally find with Boethius. The entry into writing is determined by particular circumstances of place ("une estude petite" [*Chemin*, l. 173]) ; of time, like the night ("Et ja estoit nuit serree"[ibid., l. 196]) ; of being shut-in ("Ainsi fus la enserre" [ibid., l. 195]). It's as though writing can only be born when one is cut off from the world - an isolation such as a molting bird must undergo in order to sing. We see this image, furthermore, in the beginning of the *Livre des trois vertus*, where the "cité des dames" is the cage where young women "le doulz chant apprengnent de celles qui desja y sont hebergees"(part 1, ch. 1, p. 9). Writing is born from an intermediary state, a state of fatigue, of depression, which, as with the mystics, brings vision. Thus, she writes at the beginning of the *Livre des trois vertus*: "je, comme personne traveillie de si grant labour avoir accompli et mis sus, mes membres et mon corps lasséz pour cause du long et continuel excercite"(p. 7), and at the beginning of the third part of the *Fais d'armes et de chevallerie*:[23] "mon entendement, aucques lassé de la pesanteur de la matere el labour des precedens parties, adonc surprise de somme en mon lit, couchiee, m'apparut en dormant par semblance une creature" (part 3, ch. 1). The reading referred to is of a book -Boethius in the case of the *Chemin de long estude*, and Matheolus in *La Cité des dames*—but it could also be the reading of a work of art, like the paintings of the Château de Fortune in *La Mutacion*.[24] The world is for reading, and for being transcribed. The work grows out of what could be called exhibited writings. This is the case for Chaoz who, at the beginning of *L'Advision*, bears the five letters of his name inscribed upon his forehead. This is also the image of Sapience in *Le Livre du chemin de long estude*:

> En sa bouche un escript tenoit,
> Dont la lettre ainsi contenoit:
> M'engendra et fist grant usage
> M'enfanta Memoire, la sage. (ll. 5399-402)

The word must be written, and in a monumental fashion.

In fact, Christine has an architectural conception of writing. The work is an edifice. It is so by the very technique of its writing, by its compilation. Christine extracts stones from the careers of others "tout ainsi comme l'ovrier de architecture ou maçonnage n'a mie fait les pierres et les estoffes, dont il bastist et ediffie le chastel ou maison"(*Le Livre des fais et bonnes meurs*, vol. 1, part 2, ch. 21, p. 191). The writing, born from the author's retreat from the world, circumscribes an entrenched territory. The parallel between writing a book and constructing an edifice is constantly and explicitly drawn, from *La Cité des dames* to the *Livre des fais d'armes et de chevallerie*, for example. In the latter, Honoré Bovet, the author of *L'arbre des batailles* addresses the sleeping poetess:

> Et pour bastir ediffice partinant aux diz de Vegece et des autres dont jusques ycy t'es aydee, te convient retrenchier les branches d'icelluy arbre, prendre le meilleur et sur celluy merrien fonder partie de ton dit ediffice (part 3, ch. 1).

The relationship is implied in the link established by Christine between Charles V the reader and Charles V the builder, whom she praises in Le Livre des fais et bonnes meurs. Here we read in book 3, "Cy dit comment le roy Charles estoit droit artiste et apris es sciences, et des beaulx maçonnages, qu'il fist faire" (ch. 11), and "Cy dit comment le roy Charles amoit livres |et des belles translacions, qu'il fist faire|" (ch. 12). Christine returns to this parallel movement in Le Livre de la paix: "Ains fait à considerer comment en ou meismes temps se faisoit les devant dis ediffices, les translacions des livres cy devant nomméz, et autres plusieurs cousteux ouvrages sans avoir faulte de paiement nulle part" (part 3, ch. 28, p. 158). To edify -in the sense of both to educate and to construct an edifice- is the role that Christine assigns herself, since the book has both a market value and a moral value.

The Book and Its Exchange Value

In L'Advision, Christine retraces the success of her works. Members of the nobility "les virent voulentiers et receurent a joie [...]. Et ainsi furent en pou d'eure ventillez et portez mes dis livres en plusieurs pars et pays divers" (part 3, ch. 11, p. 111). The book becomes token money for exchange. It is because the earl of Salisbury is fond of the "dictiez"and is himself a "gracieux dicteur" that, after having seen ("veu") Christine's "dictiez," he attaches her son to his household. Note that the verb used to designate the relationship between high-ranking nobility and the book is always "voir" (to see), and not "lire"(to read). For identical reasons, after the death of the earl of Salisbury, Henry of Lancaster took an interest in the poetess's son: "Le roy Henri [...] vid desdits livres et dictiez" (ibid., p. 112), and it is once again thanks to her books that Christine can bring her son back to France: "Et a brief parler, tant fis a grant peine et par le moien de mes livres que congié ot mon dit filz de me venir querir par de ça pour mener la, qui encore n'y vois"(ibid., p. 113). Likewise, Christine attracts the attention of the duke of Milan "par les dessertes de mes livres," as she tells us in L'Advision (part 3, ch. 12, p. 114). The book gives Christine a name, a renown: "comme ja m'eussent donné nom mes ditz volumes" (ibid., p. 113). Her books bring her love: "Phelippes, duc de Bourgongne, [...] m'ot par l'acointance de mes dis livres et volumes prise a amour" (ibid., ch. 13, p. 114).

The Book and Its Moral Value

Books have a price, known to princes, and they have a value. It is interesting to see Gerson, in the debate over the *Roman de la rose*, contrast the moral value and the market value of the book—in Latin in the epistle *Talia de me*,[25] and in French in his sermon of December 24, 1402, *Poenitemini*: "se je avoie ung *Roumant de la Rose* qui fust seul et vaulsist mil livres, je l'ardroie plus tost que je le vendisse pour publier, ainsi comme il est" (ibid., p. 182). Christine shares Gerson's view. The book should be useful and its primary usefulness, besides providing comfort, is to drive away ignorance, as she affirms in her dedication to Queen Isabeau de Bavière:[26]

> Car, si que les sages tesmoignent
> En leurs escrips, les gens qui songnent
> De lire en livres voulentiers,
> Ne peut qu'aucunement n'eslongnent
> Ygnorence.

There is a generosity in the book that Christine makes resonate, thanks to the rich rhyme: *livre* (*liber*) and *livre* (present of the verb *livrer*). Thus she speaks about Valerius: "Dit Valerius en son livre/Cinquiesme, qui maint bon dit livre." (*Le Livre du chemin de long estude*, ll. 5525-526). From this spring the many injunctions that punctuate Christine's works, attesting to her culture and to her mode of writing. "Lis les histoires des empereurs," says Droiture to Christine in *Le Livre de la cité des dames* (bk. 2, ch. 49, p. 342); "Ne fault que lire en leurs gestes et croniques" says the same character about popes and members of the clergy; "Ne t'esteut que regarder ou *Miroir histoirial*," advises Justice (bk. 3, ch. 9, p. 460). In fact, everything points toward reading. The same is true of the word itself. We have seen the speech of an allegory transformed into a monumental writing. Likewise, for Christine, the interior word is to be read. The lover in the *Livre du duc des vrais amans* introduces one of his *rondeaux* with these words: "Et ces paroles disoye/Qu'en ma pensée lisoye" (ll. 823-24). Likewise Chevalerie, in the *Livre du chemin de long estude*, answers Raison in this manner: "Adont celle commence a lire/Voire ou secret de sa pensee [...]/Si dist" (ll. 3166-168 and 3170). As she recalls in the beginning of *L'Epistre de la Prison de Vie Humaine*,[27] Christine does her "devoir par moien d'escripture" (p. 18, ll.50-51). This is her mission, just as she sets herself the task of "multiplying" books. She expresses this forcefully at the end of the *Livre des trois vertus*: "me pensay que ceste noble oeuvre multiplieroye par le monde en pluseurs copies, quel qu'en fust le coust" (part 3, *Fin et conclusion de cest present livre*, p. 225). She no longer answers her patrons' orders, but disseminates her work. The beginnings of this were apparent in her *Epistre a*

Eustace Mourel,[28] where she proposed to the poet that if he had the " apetis " to look over her "dittiez" she should send him whatever he wanted (ll.33-38). In her letter to Jean de Montreuil in the *Débat sur le "Roman de la rose,"* she affirmed, "vueil dire, divulguer et soustenir manifestement" (p. 12). This concerted politics of publishing is especially marked by the use of the verb *ventiler*. *Divulguer* and *ventiler* were both neologisms in Christine's day. Both the word and the thing were new. The work must be "ventilee, espandue et publiee en tous païs", it must "s'estendre et estre veue"(*Le Livre des trois vertus*, p. 225). Two wills come together in this desire—the will to be useful and the will to survive: "ne demourra pas pour tant vague et non utile nostre dicte oeuvre, qui durera au siecle sanz decheement par diverses copies"(ibid.). For inscription in a single book is not enough; this inscription must be multiplied to assure its ongoing survival. Christine suggested this in *Le Livre des fais et bonnes meurs*, by establishing a discreet parallel between Ovid and herself: "mais, comme dit Ovide en la fin de son livre *Methamorphoseos*: 'Je ay fait une oeuvre, laquelle par feu ne fer ne peut estre destruitte,' comme livres qui tost sont ventillés en plusieurs pars par diverses copies n'en puist estre destruitte la matiere"(vol. II, part 3, ch. 49, pp. 131-32). She says it forcefully in the *Livre des fais d'armes et de chevallerie*, justifying her borrowings, not only toVegetius, but to the teaching of "saiges chevaliers":

> Par quoy, s'il est ainsi que par aucun qui lire pourra en cest endroit ou l'ouir, ait autresfoiz ceste belle ordenance qui s'ensuit, veue par escript ou ouÿ dire de bouche, ne vueille pour tant avoir en despris ains en estre content, pensant que dommaige seroit que la foiblesce d'un pou de papier qui se pourrist en petit de temps eust la memoire anientie de sy nottable ordonnance, qui bien est digne qu'enregistree soit afin qu'estre puist secourable meesme en ce royaume se le cas escheoit es temps advenir. (Part 2, ch. 20)

Christine situates her works with an eye on the future, if not on eternity. The frequency with which she uses the expression "le temps a venir" is significant. It's as though, pushing to the extreme the parallel she has suggested between herself and the Sibyl, she prophesied the survival of her work and her recognition. Dame Opinion tells Christine at the end of the second part of *L'Advision*: "Et si te prophetise que ceste lecture sera de plusieurs tesmoingnee diversement. [...] Et le temps a venir plus en sera parlé qu'a ton vivant" (ch. 22, p. 89).

In his sermon at the end of the *Roman de la rose*, the character Génius enjoined his audience to turn to natural generation to combat death. Christine combats death through the book. For her books are her children.

The use of the metaphor of childbirth is striking. Nature addresses the poetess in these terms in L'*Advision*: "Or vueil que de toy naissent nouveaulx volumes, lesquelz les temps a venir et perpetuelment au monde presenteront ta memoire devant les princes et par l'univers en toutes places, lesquelz en joie et delit tu enfanteras de ta memoire" (part 3, ch. 10, p. 110). But by an impossible twist that belongs to the Christian mystery, the book that is a son to Christine is also her father. Christine gives birth to book, and she is also born from her books. As we have seen, it is her books that give her her name—a name that, as the Cumean Sibyl affirms in Le Livre du chemin de long estude, "sera reluisant/[...] par longue memoire" (ll. 496-97).

Mother and daughter of her books, Christine is a new figure of the Virgin. The scene of the Annunciation at the beginning of the Livre de la cité des dames is proof of this.[29] Just as the Virgin, by giving birth to Christ, overcame death, so Christine overcomes death and oblivion through the book.

Maurice Blanchot wrote in L'*Espace littéraire*:[30] "Voir comme il faut, c'est essentiellement mourir, c'est introduire dans la vue ce retournement qu'est l'extase et qu'est la mort" (p. 156).

Christine de Pizan was able to achieve this reversal. She sees and she writes.

> Université de Paris-Sorbonne
> translated by Roxanne Lapidus

NOTES

1. Guillaume de Machaut, Le Livre du voir dit, ed. Paul Imbs and Jacqueline Cerquiglini-Toulet, l. 8553, Le Livre de Poche, Lettres gothiques, no. 4557. (Paris: Librairie Générale Française, 1999).
2. Eustache Deschamps does it in the nostalgic mode, regretting his "vit d'Orleans" (ballad 1480, in vol. 6 of Œuvres complètes, ed. Queux de Saint-Hilaire and Gaston Raynaud, 11 vols. [Paris: Firmin Didot, 1878-1903]) or by evoking the student *mores* of his son in ballads 1433 and 1480, (vol. 8).
3. Ed. Suzanne Solente, 2 vols. (Paris: Champion, 1936 and 1940), (1:190).
4. Christine de Pizan, L'*Advision Cristine*, ed. Christine Reno and Liliane Dulac (Paris: Champion, 2001).
5. Œuvres poétiques de Christine de Pisan, ed. Maurice Roy, vol. 2 (Paris: Firmin Didot, 1891).
6. First ballad (l. 26) of the Cent Ballades, in Œuvres poétiques, ed. Maurice Roy (Paris: Firmin Didot, 1886).
7. In ibid. 1, xiv-xvii.
8. Christine de Pizan, Le Livre de la Cité des dames/La Città delle Dame, ed. Earl Jeffrey Richards, Italian trans. Patrizia Caraffi, 2^d ed. (Milan: Luni Editrice, 1998).
9. In Œuvres poétiques, ed. Maurice Roy, vol. 2, ll. 573-77.
10. Ed. Angus J. Kennedy, Revue des Langues Romanes, 92, (1988) : 253-64.

11. Li Dis du fol menestrel, in Dits de Watriquet de Couvin, ed. Auguste Scheler (Brussells: Devaux, 1868).
12. Jean Froissart, La Prison amoureuse, ed. Anthime Fourrier (Paris: Klincksieck, 1974), l. 288.
13. Jean Froissart, Le Joli Buisson de jonece, ed. Anthime Fourrier (Geneva: Droz, 1975), l.162.
14. Christine de Pizan, Le Débat sur le "Roman de la rose", ed. Eric Hicks (Paris: Champion, 1977).
15. Le Livre de la mutacion de Fortune, ed. Suzanne Solente, 4 vols. (Paris: Picard, 1959-66), 2, ll. 8736-738.
16. In Œuvres poétiques, ed. Maurice Roy, vol. 3.
17. Christine de Pizan, Le Livre du Corps de Policie, ed. Angus J. Kennedy. (Paris: Champion, 1998), part I, ch. 6, p. 8.
18. Ed. Charity Cannon Willard (The Hague: Mouton, 1958), part 3, ch. 30, p. 162.
19. Ed. Charity Cannon Willard and Eric Hicks (Paris: Champion, 1989), p. 109.
20. In Oton de Grandson, sa vie et ses poésies, ed. Arthur Piaget (Lausanne: Payot, 1941).
21. In Œuvres, ed. Kervyn de Lettenhove, 8 vol. (Brussells, 1863-66).
22. Ed. Andrea Tarnowski, Le Livre de Poche, Lettres gothiques, no. 4558 (Paris: Librairie Générale Française, 2000).
23. Ed. Christine Moneera Laennec, in " Christine 'antygrafe' : Authorship and self in the prose works of Christine de Pizan with an edition of B.N. Ms 603, Le Livre des fais d'armes et de chevallerie" (Thesis, Yale University, 1980), abstract in dissertation Abstracts, 50, (1989-1990) : 3581 A.
24. Jacqueline Cerquiglini-Toulet, "D'une mise en scène du texte littéraire à la fin du Moyen Age: sa naissance dans l'oeuvre d'art," in Actes du XIVe Congrès international de l'Association Guillaume Budé, Limoges 25-28 août 1998 (Paris: Les Belles Lettres, forthcoming), pp. 531-540.
25. In Christine de Pizan, Le Débat, p. 173.
26. In Œuvres poétiques, ed. Maurice Roy, vol. 1, p. XV, ll. 37-41.
27. Ed. Angus J. Kennedy (University of Glasgow, 1984).
28. In Œuvres poétiques, ed. Maurice Roy, vol. 2, ll. 33-38.
29. Jacqueline Cerquiglini-Toulet, "Fondements et fondations de l'écriture chez Christine de Pizan. Scènes de lecture et scènes d'incarnation," in The City of Scholars: New Approaches to Christine de Pizan, ed. Margarete Zimmerman and Dina De Rentiis (Berlin and New York: Walter de Gruyter, 1994), pp. 79-96.
30. (Paris: Gallimard, 1955), p. 156.

WORKS CITED

Blanchot, Maurice. L'Espace littéraire. Paris: Gallimard, 1955.
Cerquiglini-Toulet, Jacqueline. "Fondements et fondations de l'écriture chez Christine de Pizan. Scènes de lecture et scènes d'incarnation" In The City of Scholars: New Approaches to Christine de Pizan. Edited by Margarete

Zimmerman and Dina De Rentiis, 79-96. Berlin and New York: Walter de Gruyter, 1994.

———. "D'une mise en scène du texte littéraire à la fin du Moyen Age: Sa naissance dans l'oeuvre d'art." In *Actes du XIVe Congrès international de l'Association Guillaume Budé, Limoges 25-28 août 1998*, 531-40. Paris: Les Belles Lettres, forthcoming.

Chastellain, George. *Œuvres*, 8 vols. Edited by Kervyn de Lettenhove. Brussells, 1863-66.

Christine de Pizan. *L'Advision Cristine*. Edited by Christine Reno and Liliane Dulac. Paris: Champion, 2001.

———. *Le Chemin de longue étude*. Edited by Andrea Tarnowski. Le Livre de poche, Lettres gothiques, no. 4558. Paris: Librairie Générale Française, 2000.

———. *Le Débat sur le Roman de la Rose*. Edited by Eric Hicks. Paris: Champion, 1977.

———. *Epistre à la reine*. Edited by Angus J. Kennedy. *Revue des Langues Romanes*, 92, (1988) : 253-64.

———. *Epistre de la Prison de Vie Humaine*. Edited by Angus J. Kennedy. Glasgow: University of Glasgow, 1984.

———. *Le Livre de la cité des dames/La città delle dame*. Edited by Earl Jeffrey Richards. Italian translation by Patrizia Caraffi. 2^d ed. Milan: Luni Editrice, 1998.

———. *Le Livre de la Mutacion de Fortune*. 4 vols. Edited by Suzanne Solente. Paris: Picard, 1959-66.

———. *Le Livre de la Paix*. Edited by Charity Cannon Willard. The Hague: Mouton, 1958.

———. *Le Livre des fais d'armes et de chevallerie*. Edited by Christine Moneera Laennec. In idem, "Christine 'antygrafe': Authorship and Self in the Prose Works of Christine de Pizan with and Edition of B.N. Ms 603 *Le Livre des fais d'armes et de chevallerie*." Thesis, Yale University, 1988 . Abstract in *Dissertation Abstracts*, 50, (1989-90) : 3581 A.

———. *Le Livre des Fais et Bonnes Meurs du Sage Roy Charles V*. 2 vols. Edited by Suzanne Solente. Paris: Champion, 1936 and 1940.

———. *Le Livre des trois vertus*. Edited by Charity Cannon Willard and Eric Hicks. Paris: Champion, 1989.

———. *Le Livre du chemin de long estude/Le Chemin de longue étude*. Edited by Andrea Tarnowski. Le Livre de Poche, Lettres gothiques, no. 4558. Paris: Librairie Générale Française, 2000.

———. *Le Livre du corps de policie*. Edited by Angus J. Kennedy, Paris: Champion, 1998.

———. *Œuvres poétiques*. 3 vols. Edited by Maurice Roy, Paris: Firmin Didot, 1886-96.

Deschamps, Eustache. *Oeuvres complètes*. 11 vols. Edited by Queux de Saint-Hilaire and Gaston Raynaud. Paris: Firmin Didot, 1878-1903.
Froissart, Jean. *La Prison amoureuse*. Edited by Anthime Fourrier. Paris: Klincksieck, 1974.
——. *Le Joli Buisson de jonece*. Edited by Anthime Fourrier. Geneva: Droz, 1975.
Guillaume de Machaut. *Le Livre du voir dit*. Edited by Paul Imbs and Jacqueline Cerquiglini-Toulet. Le Livre de Poche, Lettres gothiques, no. 4557. Paris: Librairie Générale Française, 1999.
Piaget, Arthur. *Oton de Grandson*, sa vie et ses poésies. Lausanne: Payot, 1941.
Watriquet de Couvin. *Dits de Watriquet de Couvin*. Edited by Auguste Scheler. Brussells: Devaux, 1868.

The Patroness and the Poet: The Religious Allegories of Gabrielle de Bourbon and Jean Bouchet

JENNIFER BRITNELL

In this paper I compare the religious writing of the Bourbon princess Gabrielle de Bourbon (c.1465–1516) with that of the poet and historian Jean Bouchet (1476–c.1558), who worked for her between about 1510 and 1516. The focus is on two narrative allegories depicting a pilgrimage of the soul, Gabrielle's *Voyage espirituel entreprins par l'ame devote pour parvenir en la cité de bon repoux* (c.1510?)[1] and Bouchet's *Les Triumphes de la noble et amoureuse dame* (1530).[2] At first sight the comparison may seem grotesque. Gabrielle's text survives in a single manuscript copy of only twenty-nine leaves; the first edition of Bouchet's work has some 180 closely printed folio leaves, and there were at least fourteen further editions. Nevertheless, given that Bouchet knew and frequently praised his patroness's devotional writing, we can be sure that his choice of a pilgrimage allegory for the *Triumphes* was not uninfluenced by Gabrielle's *Voyage*. A comparison of the two works illuminates the transition in religious writing for the laity, and particularly for women, from the situation before the Reformation to an era when the new factor of "heresy" had to be taken into account.

Gabrielle was the daughter of Louis de Bourbon, comte de Montpensier, and Gabrielle de La Tour.[3] In 1484 she married Louis de La Trémoille, a marriage arranged by Anne de Beaujeu. We know nothing about her education, but it is tempting to suppose that as a girl she may have spent some time in a convent. Jean Henry, a Sorbonne theologian, dedicated a devotional book to her before her marriage; he dedicated works to other Bourbon ladies, and also to nuns at Fontevrault, with which the Bourbons had strong connections. In the work dedicated to Gabrielle he notes that she cannot embrace poverty as she might wish, because of her duty to her father.[4] This might reflect her personal wish to be a nun or it may be no more than a convention of the genre, an issue we shall explore later.

Bouchet worked for Gabrielle and her family, not primarily as the equivalent of a court poet, but in the lowlier role of *procureur*, a solicitor or notary who carried out routine legal transactions.[5] He was working for them by 1510 and continued to do so all his life, being succeeded eventually by his probably significantly named eldest son, Gabriel. His connection with Gabrielle was severed by her death in 1516, precipitated, it seems, by grief at the loss of her only child, Charles, prince de Talmont, at the battle of Marignano. Bouchet in his writings makes it clear that both Gabrielle and her son came to value him for his literary as well as his professional ability. Charles presented some of Bouchet's work at the court of Louis XII; Bouchet dedicated one of his volumes to Charles and made him the subject of an extensive memorial poem after his death.[6] Louis de La Trémoille, killed at Pavia, is also the subject of a memorial work; from this we draw most of our information about Gabrielle and Bouchet's relationship with her.[7] Bouchet presents her as the model pious great lady: a devoted wife and mother and careful administrator of the estates, but also a seriously devout woman who prized religious reading and contemplation—and who, more unusually, herself wrote devotional tracts. Bouchet presents these as having been intended for the instruction of the young women in her entourage. Later he uses her repeatedly as an exemplar for women reading and writing about religion.[8]

The inventory of the books Gabrielle possessed at her death has been analyzed by Berriot-Salvadore.[9] No woman of standing was without her Book of Hours; Gabrielle owned six. The rich vernacular literature of meditation is extremely well represented.[10] Such meditation was principally on the life of Christ and of the Virgin, imagining oneself at the scene—but with very special reference to the Passion of Christ. A contemporary text written by a nun for a laywoman assures her that nothing is more efficacious for salvation than thinking of Christ's Passion.[11] Although much religious literature composed in French during the fifteenth century was aimed at nuns, Jean Gerson, the chancellor of the University of Paris at the beginning of the fifteenth century, was deeply concerned with spreading instruction down to the less educated and wrote for his sisters, laywomen, as well as for fellow religious; many writers imitated him, like Jean Henry.[12] That a layman could compose such pious texts is shown at the highest level by René of Anjou and his *Mortifiement de Vaine Plaisance*,[13] but there is little doubt that most were generated by members of the clergy, and that Gabrielle and Bouchet were both rather unusual in their authorship.

Three texts by Gabrielle survive. Bouchet mentions them all, as well as a fourth now lost.[14] Only one manuscript of each is known, although to judge from the inventory made after her death more copies were originally made. The surviving manuscripts are fair copies on vellum, illuminated with miniatures carefully designed to go with the text. In these Bouchet had some hand, although he does not tell us so himself; an account shows a payment to him for arranging to have books of Gabrielle's illuminated.[15] The three texts, recently edited by Evelyne Berriot-Salvadore, represent three different types of allegory, but with a connecting link of character and narrative. The first is a *Petit Traicté sur les doulleurs de la passion du doulx Jesus et de sa benoiste mere, pour lesquelles voir et santir le.* ♥ *. contemplatif amene avecques soy l'Ame Devote.*[16] In this meditation on the Passion, the Cueur Contemplatif invites the Ame Devote to follow the events of Holy Week in the role of handmaiden to the Virgin Mary. The two voices tend to take on the characteristics of a hectoring male teacher and a passive female pupil—not quite up to the flights of contemplation required.[17] Interestingly the Ame Devote rebels at the end of these meditations and requests a more joyful theme. The Cueur Contemplatif obliges, rather patronizingly, and shows her the joys of Mary, from the Annunciation, Visitation, and Nativity through to the Dormition, Assumption, and Coronation as Queen of Heaven. Thus the final vision is of heaven itself, a subject found in other literature for the laity, notably in Gerson's *De la mendicité spirituelle.*[18] The Ame Devote is left longing both to renew the vision and to make it a reality. The second text, the *Voyage*, carries on from this idea; the narrator is summoned by a much more confident Ame Devote to write the account of how the Ame reached heaven, figured as the "Cité de Bon Repoux." The Soul has good cause to be confident, because she is speaking from the Cité; at the end of the narrative we see her reception in heaven and her many rewards. In this allegorical pilgrimage of seven days, the Soul and her companions encounter and defeat a succession of vices. The last work of the three, *Le Fort Chasteau pour la retraicte de toutes bonnes ames fait par le commandement du glorieux Sainct Esperit*,[19] is a building allegory, describing a castle constructed by the Holy Spirit as a haven for devout souls. Ames Devotes are now pluralized and, particularly in conjunction with the illustrations, become reminiscent of nice little girls at a convent boarding school.[20]

There is every reason to suppose that Bouchet's contact with Gabrielle influenced his later role as a religious writer; it is far from clear, however, what influence, if any, he had on her. The assumption often made, that he assisted her in writing or functioned in some way as her spiritual adviser, seems to me quite unnecessary and unfounded.[21] Why should a great lady accept advice on such matters from her lay attorney when she had chaplains whom she could choose for herself? No doubt she discussed religious matters with Bouchet, but she had no reason to depend on him. It was moreover after Gabrielle's death that Bouchet became known as a religious writer. As we shall see, the gulf between them in terms of quantity of theological content is massive, and their aims are different. It seems more likely that influence was mainly in the other direction, alerting Bouchet to the attraction of religious allegory for female readers.

Bouchet began writing religious texts from the time of his employment by Gabrielle. First of all, in the E*pistres familieres*, not printed until 1545, there are three *epistres* addressed to her. As two of these reflect themes from Gabrielle's works, they are probably a complimentary response to her texts.[22] In 1517 came the deceptively titled H*istoire et cronicque de Clotaire*,[23] which is as much hagiography as chronicle, being a life of King Clotaire's fourth wife, Saint Radegonde. Gabrielle had a role in the book's genesis; it is dedicated to Queen Claude, but Bouchet states that it had originally been commissioned by Charles VIII, and that Claude's mother, Anne of Brittany, had asked him to revise it, as had Gabrielle who had introduced him to the queen's notice.[24] His next religious text remained in manuscript except for a small part; this is the *Cantiques et oraisons contemplatives de l'ame penitente traversant les voies perilleuses*, a collection of verse prayers, closely influenced by the Book of Hours and the liturgy of the Mass.[25] It was dedicated to another aristocratic woman, Hélène de Hangest, the widow of Artus Gouffier, *grand-maître* of France (d. 1519). She and Marguerite de Navarre are both addressed in dedicatory letters in the L*abirynthe de Fortune* of 1522; in part a memorial to Gouffier, it also has, with its reflection on the meaning of fortune and the primacy of God's providence, a considerable theological component.[26] Bouchet's major religious work was to come in 1530, after he had become disturbed by the spread of Lutheranism. Dedicated to the new queen of France, Eleanor, the T*riumphes de la noble et amoureuse dame* is an extended pilgrimage allegory and also a very substantial manual of theological instruction.

One obvious question when comparing the two writers is the extent to which Bouchet's response reflects the changes in religious climate in the years following Gabrielle's death. Gabrielle died before the Reformation had begun, but the 1520s were deeply marked by the spread of Lutheranism and reactions against it. Three strands of development need to be considered here. The first is a movement, going back at least to Gerson and his imitators but made more feasible by printing, to provide more religious books in the vernacular. This movement, encouraged by bishops concerned with the quality of lay piety, was greatly impeded in the 1520s because of fears of heresy. The second strand is the influence of Erasmus and evangelically minded Catholics, who promoted lay Bible reading and questioned excessive reliance on mechanistic good works and on merit. The third is the spread of Lutheranism and the fear of heresy. It is clear that Bouchet was very much committed to making more material available in the vernacular to lay readers, so he can certainly be counted within the first strand. The spread of Lutheranism makes him more not less determined to do so; in this he reacts quite differently from the theologians of the Sorbonne, and is thus one of very few writers between 1525 and 1540 who sought to counter heresy by providing orthodox instruction in vernacular books.[27] The response to Erasmus and evangelical writers is more complicated to tease out. Bouchet warmly defends some features of devotional practice that they attack, such as prayer to saints. In the preface to the *Triumphes* he cites unglossed translations of the Bible among the dangerous books women are reading: this must be a reference to the translation of Jacques Lefèvre d'Étaples. But on the other hand, the conviction that lay people need more instruction chimes with the spirit of Erasmus' *Enchiridion militis christiani*, and Bouchet quotes from that work at the beginning of the *Triumphes*, although without acknowledging that he is doing so.[28] In the preface to the *Cantiques* he argues that French men and women who know no Latin would benefit from having their prayers in French; Erasmus argued against the Sorbonne that people should understand their prayers.[29] Another issue on which Bouchet was listening to Erasmus and the evangelicals was the role of merit and good works, a theological topic providing one of the most striking contrasts between Bouchet's allegory and that of Gabrielle.

A first area of comparison concerns the voices that are speaking to us in these texts, their target audiences, and the authorial commentaries on the purpose of the enterprise. Bouchet represents Gabrielle's aims in writing as follows:

> Et si estoit son esprit ennobly et enrichy de tant bonnes sciences, qu'elle emploioit une partie des jours à composer petiz traictez à l'honneur de dieu, de la vierge Marie, et à l'instruction de ses damoiselles.[30]

Gabrielle herself claims a less defined audience of "gens simples." The interplay of allegorical voices in her texts is complex, but there is a female authorial first-person voice that appears at the beginning and end of the two parts of the *Petit Traicté* and of the *Voyage*, and that is present throughout the *Fort Chasteau*; this voice, referred to as "L'acteur" in the *Voyage*, is identified with Gabrielle at the beginning of the *Petit Traicté* in the first illustration: a noblewoman writes at a desk before a large cross to which the Bourbon-Montpensier and La Trémoille arms are affixed.[31] The voice claims variously that she writes "pour tousjours esmouvoir les cueurs à devotion [...] ainsi que le Cueur contemplatif m'enseigne"; and "en ay fait ce petit traicté qui pourra à gens simples, qui n'entendent la saincte escripture en plus que moy, valloir pour eulx mectre en la bonne voye."[32] In spite of several perfunctory *clausulae humilitatis*,[33] the voice is surprisingly upbeat and confident: in particular, the narrator says of the Holy Spirit:

> et aux simples personnages et femmenins entendemens, leur fait ceste grand grace de leur donner sçavoir et pouvoir d'escrire quelques petites contemplations, qui seront plus plaisantes à ouyr à pauvres femmeletes et simples gens que les haultes et profundes escriptures des saincts docteurs.[34]

This suggests a listening audience of possibly illiterate people; elsewhere, however, reading is specified in an equally confident assertion:

> Toutesfoys ma fiance est si grande en celuy par le commandement duquel je l'ay escript [that is, the Holy Spirit] que, par sa bonté, il permectra que ceulx ou celles qui le liront et bien le gousteront, suys certaine qu'ilz y profiteront.[35]

Bouchet's description of Gabrielle's tastes confirms the bent away from theology and towards contemplation:

> Elle se delectoit sur toutes choses à ouyr parler de la saincte escripture, sans trop avant s'enquerir des secretz de theologie. Plus amoit le moral et les choses contemplatives que les argumens et subtilitez escorchees de la lettre, par lesquelles le vray sens est souvent perverty.[36]

While this conforms to a stereotype of female piety, it is confirmed in Gabrielle's texts, the first of which begins, "Pour tousjours esmouvoir les cueurs à devotion," stressing emotional religious feeling rather than instruction. The *Petit Traicté* is of course designed as affective meditation on the Passion and the joys of the Virgin, but the *Voyage* and the *Fort Chasteau* have only the simplest instructional content, mostly about virtues and vices. Her texts, then, are intended to delight and to feed the religious sentiment of readers and listeners cut off from more intellectual exposition, the value of which is treated rather dismissively. While the limited circulation of Gabrielle's texts suggests that, whether male or female, these readers were of elevated social class, and probably mostly her "damoiselles," as Bouchet implies, the readers invoked are not exclusively female; they conform to the established target of vernacular religious texts, the "simples gens" in general.[37] But the authorial voice speaking to them is unequivocally female and not particularly apologetically so.

Bouchet by contrast writes as an established male author, a poet and moralist with an increasing reputation as a historian; he can defend and explain his enterprise in authorial prefaces in his own voice. He is, however, a layman, and certainly received some criticism for the subjects he dared to tackle in the *Triumphes*.[38] His defense is the authorities he has relied on—"il n'y a rien du mien, fors l'invencion," he claims[39]—for, of course, his qualification for writing to instruct relies on his Latin-based learning. Women certainly form a large part of his intended audience. As we have seen, every single one of his religious works is dedicated to a woman, in each case to a royal or aristocratic woman. On several occasions Bouchet defends the concept of women reading. He first raises the subject when depicting how Saint Radegonde spent her time. He argues that the reading of moral works and history is a suitable pastime for noblewomen, who have no need to labor in order to earn their living. Not only will it offer suitable examples of virtue, but it will also obviate the perils of idleness.[40] Bouchet then tackles the problem of whether women can understand theology:

> Et pour respondre à ceulx qui dient que l'esprit d'une femme n'est disposé ne capable pour recevoir et comprendre une bonne proposition concernant nostre foy, je ne dy pas aussi qu'elles doibvent estudier en la theologie ne se mectre si avant en argumentations theologalles, mais en choses moralles et instructives de meurs et vertuz. Combien que qui vouldroit rememorer combien il y a eu de femmes fermes en la foy catholicque et qui l'ont soustenue par argumentations et martires, comme saincte Catherine et saincte Barbe, on trouveroit qu'elles ont triumphé contre les infidelles aussi bien que les hommes.[41]

This ambiguous statement—typical of Bouchet's regular manner of argument—first appears to accept the conventional wisdom that women should be concerned with moral rather than theological instruction, but then undermines it with the example of triumphant female martyrs indulging in argumentation. Except in a context where women are the central focus, however, Bouchet normally bundles up women in the conventional way with other "simple" people: the crucial issue is explicitly ignorance of Latin. Thus in the *Triumphes*, written after heresy had become a problem, women are not the first target group mentioned: Bouchet is concerned with the instruction

> de mes enfans, et de ceulx qui n'entendent les lectres latines, ou n'ont le povoyr d'avoir tous les livres de la saincte escripture, ou ne veulent prendre le labeur de les lire pour la multitude d'iceulx.[42]

Women come in for particular mention in relation to reading heretical books:

> Et encores plus pour distraire femmes et filles de plus lire la translacion en françoys du vieil et nouveau testament, qui est chose dangereuse à lire en plusieurs passaiges scelon la seulle lectre, et certains petiz traictez d'aucuns Alemans heretiques traduictz de latin en françoys, esquelz soubz la doulceur de la doctrine evangelique sont plusieurs erreurs interposees trop scandaleuses et pernicieuses en la crestienté.[43]

Elsewhere he describes the bare letter of scripture as dangerous to "femmes et simples gens non letrez."[44] His defense of translations other than biblical ones in the preface to a book of church history in 1544 implies both male and female readers.[45] Thus level of education is the key. He dedicates his works to the great ladies whose patronage he would like to cultivate, the most distinguished among his readers, but his actual target audience is considerably wider and not limited to women. The frequent reprinting of his text and the shift from folio to cheaper octavo format meant that his book reached a wide audience and no doubt played its part in countering reformist propaganda for both male and female readers. But although he does not have an exclusively female agenda, it is significant that he represents women, of whose taste for devotional reading he was well aware, as particularly at risk from evangelical and Protestant publications. This perhaps explains his choice for the *Triumphes* of religious allegory, a type of text he knew from observation of Gabrielle to be attractive to women.

Unlike Gabrielle, Bouchet concentrates in his religious writing on instruction rather than devotion and meditation. This is not simply a reaction to the threat of heresy; even his earlier saint's life and collection of prayers reveal a quite unusual concern with the provision of accurate information. The life of Saint Radegonde has a title that turns it into national history, and throughout the book Bouchet is identifying and assessing his sources. In other words, he is attempting to bring standards of historical accuracy to the hagiographic tradition, which, in its more popular forms at least, so signally lacked such standards. The very perception that truthfulness and accuracy are important criteria in hagiography, and that they should override the concerns of pious edification, marks a step towards new standards of historiography which will be applied increasingly in the sixteenth century. The prayers in the *Cantiques* are predictable derivatives of the tradition established by Books of Hours, but they reveal a concern, particularly in those for use during the Mass, that the person using the prayers should understand some of what is happening at the altar and should not be divorced from it in parallel meditation. The *Triumphes* itself offers detailed explanations of issues like the priest's power of the keys, transubstantiation, and predestination and free will; there is a real effort to make available in the vernacular the sort of instruction that those with some knowledge of Latin could have. In comparison, the tradition of meditation on the life of Christ and the Virgin, which loomed so large in Gabrielle's devotional practices, plays a very restricted role in Bouchet's output. One of the early *epistres* dedicated to Gabrielle herself is in the voice of the Virgin Mary addressing humanity on the subject of her sorrows, and part of the prayers for the Mass in the *Cantiques* are structured on the Mysteries of the Passion.[46] But, in general, Bouchet is much more concerned with imparting information than with the meditation that was central to Gabrielle's religious reading.

Although the extensive instruction turns the *Triumphes* into something very different from Gabrielle's *Voyage*, we can continue to make useful comparisons by considering the level of the story line, the adventures that befall the Soul and her companions. Here the effects of changing emphases provoked by evangelical and reformist challenges are particularly obvious. Perhaps the most significant difference between Bouchet's allegory and that of Gabrielle is that Bouchet depicts his Soul in the process of falling into mortal sin and being saved by divine grace, whereas Gabrielle's Soul is sorely tempted but never falls.

Throughout her writing Gabrielle's theological point of view is an encouraging one and tends towards the cheerful. The Soul in contemplation in the *Petit Traicté* is weak but willing, particularly if offered joyful subjects. In the *Voyage* she has the cheering companionship of Goodwill, Fortitude and Hope, not to mention her guardian angel. Although she takes the wrong path and has to fight off a series of vices, she always wins; finally she attains heaven. The little souls in the *Fort Chasteau* are securely guarded; refusal to remain in the castle, although possible, is almost inconceivable:

> Et si ne fault pas dire que ce lieu soit comme ung lieu de prison, car nous avons nostre liberal arbitre de en sortir quant il nous plaira. Mais tant y a que mauldit sera celuy qui n'y vouldra faire sa demeure, tant qu'il sera en ceste vallee de misere, car mieulx ne sçauroit estre ne en meilleurté.[47]

Lifting the soul in meditation of the life of Christ is a delight, a Mount Pleasant in this vale of tears; indeed, none of the temptations of World, Flesh, or Devil seem very tempting in Gabrielle's writing. They are distressing; a haven from them is what all her texts seek. As a result, the *Voyage* is, as I have argued elsewhere, a virtually sin-free zone.[48] Gabrielle never depicts the process of falling into mortal sin (which would be tantamount to leaving the castle in the *Fort Chasteau*). The Soul, with a new, confident voice unlike anything she has in the *Petit Traicté*, tells the narrator at the outset that she, the narrator, is to recount how the Soul reached the Cité de Bon Repoux. Thus we know already that the Ame Devote is saved. She sets out on her journey with three companions: Bon Vouloir, Force, and Esperance; Force is looking after the Soul's little bagful of good works. A further companion is visible in the pictures, the Cueur Contemplatif, perhaps to be equated with the Soul's guardian angel, who becomes visible at the end of her journey.[49] The Soul tells her companions that she has been given a white dress by Dame Confession—implying, then, that she has sinned in the past—and she must not get it dirty.[50] Never is it suggested that she stains this dress in the course of the journey, and when she finally arrives in heaven she receives an array of rewards that implies that we have been watching the progress of a very saintly Soul. The one thing that does go wrong, apart from the admittedly dangerous and distressing assaults of various vices duly repulsed, is that they take the wrong turning on the first day. They are misled into following a rocky path that leads into the lands of the World. This does not cause them to fall into any of the temptations offered, but it lays them open to attack from many tempters and makes their path harder than it would otherwise be.

Bouchet in the *Triumphes* also sends his Soul on a journey, but with a very different progress. In the course of its three parts we follow the Soul from birth to death. The Soul is betrothed to Christ at baptism, and the first part is concerned with her moral education as she passes from childhood to adolescence in the company of her three principal advisers, Entendement, Memoire, and Volunté; her chambermaid, Sensualité; and her governess, Raison. In the second book she progresses into the land of youth, and the assaults of her tempters begin; the Prince de Volupté woos her with love letters. The Soul, after some resistance, goes to the Palais de Volupté and is there seduced and ends up with all her companions (except Raison, who has been left behind) in the Brothel of Impenitence. She is saved by Grace Divine, led to the Fontaine de Penitence (where she will be washed and given new white clothes); the instruction shifts to a detailed account of the theology of sin, repentance, confession, and absolution. In the third book the Soul makes her way with all her companions to the land of Old Age, fighting three great battles against the World, the Flesh, and the Devil, and finally sails through the straits of death (le Pas de la Mort), leaving Théologie to tell the author what can be surmised about her hope of salvation.

The fall into mortal sin is plainly an important theological difference between the two texts. As well as being sin-free, Gabrielle's *Voyage* is nearly theology-free. Her story line, bereft as it is of any theological explanation, could obviously lend itself, especially for later readers, to the interpretation that the Soul, with her little bag of good works, is fighting her way through temptation by her own efforts. After a decade of arguments about justification by faith and the role of human merit, Bouchet avoids giving any such impression. Unlike Gabrielle, Bouchet constantly stresses the Soul's sinfulness and the boundless mercy of God. As well as depicting the Soul after her fall as helplessly bound in sin until rescued by Grace Divine, he also refrains from following the Soul after she has left her body and stays, in the persona of the *acteur*, being instructed on her probable fate by Theologie.

From a literary point of view, a significant difference is the metaphor Bouchet uses to suggest the fall into mortal sin, that of committing adultery. This metaphor depends on the common allegory, popularized by Saint Bernard in his sermons on the Song of Solomon, of the Soul as the bride of Christ. The metaphorical use of adultery has a biblical source in the figure of Israel as the faithless wife in the prophet Hosea. It does not, however, seem to be a very favorite metaphor in the sort of texts Gabrielle read. Rather, the bride of Christ allegory is used in the motif of Christ visiting the Soul in her chamber as a representation of contemplative prayer; this is exploited by Gerson in *De la mendicité spirituelle*.[51]

Gabrielle never employs the figure of adultery, and uses the Soul as the bride of Christ only as a minor motif. At the beginning of the *Voyage*, Esperance tells the Soul:

> Rejouys toy ma fille mamye, car je t'asseure pour verité que au parfaict de nostre voyage tu gaigneras ung espoux qui te couronnera de couronne royalle comme royne.[52]

The Soul is reminded of this by Bon Vouloir as they arrive in Heaven.[53] And God duly rewards her, in a scene reminiscent of the mystic marriage of Saint Catherine:

> Et sur cela il luy fist abiller siege royal, et là il la couronna de la couronne de gloire en la faisant royne et son espouse, luy mectant l'anneau au doy qui tant riche estoit, et s'appelloit ledit anneau Augmentation de Gloire.[54]

The motif reappears in *Le Fort Chasteau* when the good souls sweep and decorate their rooms in preparation for Christ:

> Et la cause pourquoy elles sont si ardantes de bien parer leursdictes petites chambretes, c'est que leur sainct desir et parfaicte intention est que leur amoureux Jhesus et tant leal espoux, à la requeste du Sainct Esperit, viendra les visiter. La chaisre paree de verité est aprestee pour luy. O quelle joye recepvra à l'heure la bonne ame.[55]

They also gather (allegorical) flowers in the enclosed garden of the castle:

> Après plusieurs parolles consolables dictes aux bonnes ames de par ladicte bonne dame [Perseverance], chescune en son endroit se retire en ses petites chambretes, toutes chargees de beaulx chappeaulx, couronnes, boucquetz, palmes et branches d'ollives pour les embellir, et aussi pour faire present à leur seigneur et amy qui souvant les visite et console.[56]

This, however, represents the full extent of the exploitation of the metaphor in Gabrielle's work; she is manipulating the notion of Christ the heavenly lover to some small degree, and that of sin as adultery not at all.

In Bouchet, by contrast, the motif is developed into a narrative of adultery from his very first use of such an allegory, in a text written for Gabrielle herself. An *epistre* for her is entitled *Epistre envoyée par l'acteur à ladicte Vicontesse de Thouars, en la personne de l'ame, qui rescrit à son amy par amours Jesus, par le bon ange.*[57] The sorrowful Soul addresses Christ. The allegory of the *Triumphes* is already here in embryo, but used in a somewhat different way involving two stages. The Soul's infidelity and descent into a brothel can be redeemed only by the sacrifice of Christ; it figures initially the fall and redemption of human nature generally. But that fall and redemption, after which the Soul is espoused to Christ, is followed by further infidelity, now figuring the post-baptismal sin of an individual.

Well established as this motif of adultery is in religious language, one can see that it could have certain disadvantages, particularly when accompanied by the notion of the attractiveness of temptation. In the *Triumphes* Bouchet develops this aspect extensively, and far from avoiding any dwelling on the literal level, he actually, when depicting the seduction of the Soul, draws from it practical lessons for young girls on the dangers of listening to men or getting into a position where they are alone with them. First Volunté is seduced by the flattering words of the Prince de la Chair:

> "...Bien est mon amour si grant et vehement que je vouldrois bien estre toujours avec vous, et non ailleurs, soit de jour ou de nuyt." En disant ces parolles, ou aultres semblables, approcha sa bouche de celle de Volunté, et après l'avoir baisée, commença taster son virginal tetin, ce qu'elle luy permist, luy defendant le demourant, qui estoit follie à elle, car à peine l'un est sans l'autre. Et voyla la forme et maniere comment les jeunes mondains deçoyvent plusieurs filles et femmes qui leur prestent les aureilles et donnent lieu à leurs deceptives parolles.[58]

Memoire is seduced by Monde; Entendement, a male personification, by the feminine Ambicion—here the moral advice is for both sexes:

> Luy estant en ceste perplexité, Ambicion retourna qui le vinst embrasser et baiser, et par ces amoureux actraictz fut par elle gaigné sans y pouoir donner resistence de luy mesme sans l'ayde de Dieu, duquel il ne demandoit le secours. C'est une chose tres-dangereuse que compaignie de jeune femme avec un homme en lieu suspect tant vertueux puisse estre, car c'est vouloir marcher à pié nud sur les ardens charbons sans se brusler, qui est presque impossible.[59]

So Bouchet by no means allows the reader to forget the physical reality which is being used to figure the spiritual fall. The sweetness of the temptation is of course countered by the sordidness of the fall: we are told that Sensualité is effortlessly seduced by Plaisir Charnel in the privy, and that the Soul is prostituted by the Prince de Volupté:

> Car le Prince de Volupté, nommé peché, après avoir fait à son plaisir de l'Ame incorporée, l'habandonna à tous ceulx de son Palais, et finablement aux pages et pallefreniers, c'est-à-dire à tous pechez. Et pour tout salaire elle, devestue de sa robbe d'ignoscence, fut mise et habandonnée au bourdeau de Obstinacion, toute souillée, pollue et macullée de sorte qu'elle sembloit estre lepreuse.[60]

Yet I think we can see that for a female writer, particularly one writing for young girls, this could be a difficult metaphor to deploy, both from an unwillingness to discuss sexual license, and, perhaps, from a reluctance to depict sexual activity as at all attractive. While Gabrielle is willing to express human weakness and distress, the possibility of falling into mortal sin seems unthinkable.[61] Had she wished to depict it, the various references to the Soul's white dress of innocence suggest that she might have employed staining the dress as a metaphor. It is difficult to imagine her invoking a sexual analogue. Not all female writers, of course, have this reluctance: Marguerite de Navarre later will employ the metaphor of adultery in the *Miroir de l'ame pecheresse*; for her the theological need to stress the sinfulness of the soul and the all-powerfulness of grace has become imperative.

Bouchet is also much readier than Gabrielle to exploit the theme of the Soul as the bride of Christ as a way of rendering more emotionally accessible the mutual love of Christ and the Soul. For Gabrielle the theme was restricted to the joyful motif of the little Souls decking their chambers in readiness for Christ's visiting them in prayer, and to the notion of reward in heaven. Bouchet actually depicts Christ visiting the Soul in her chamber, although his urge to instruct seriously dilutes any emotional force, since Christ proceeds to deliver a sermon on prayer. But Bouchet, unlike Gabrielle, employs verse as well as prose, and there he fuses the language of secular love poetry with the expression of the love of God. Already in the *Epistre* [. . .] *en la personne de l'ame*, written for Gabrielle, he sets up a comparison with secular love, and thereafter the sinful Soul writes as the repentant unfaithful lover.[62] The verse in the *Triumphes*, which includes a series of *epistres* exchanged by the Soul and Christ, was one of its most attractive features, so popular indeed that it was printed separately in a pirated edition.[63] The use of such language implies that the experience of earthly romantic or sexual love is a means to understanding divine love, as Marguerite de Navarre makes Parlamente state explicitly in the *Heptaméron*.[64] It is doubtful whether Gabrielle would altogether have agreed with them. Her very limited use of the metaphor of Christ the heavenly bridegroom perhaps suggests that it had no particular appeal for her.

Indeed, a further comparison to be made between the two writers has a bearing on the status to be accorded to earthly love, and that is the way they treat the theme of virginity. Gabrielle was a married woman (although she did not see much of her soldier husband).[65] The young girls of her household, the most obvious audience for her texts, could probably expect to marry. From a religious point of view at the time the prime determiner of a woman's status was whether she was a married woman, a widow, or a nun; Saint Jerome's assertion that the glory to be obtained in heaven is thirtyfold for the faithful married person, sixtyfold for the chaste widow, and one hundredfold for those who have vowed and kept virginity is often invoked.[66] It was difficult to conceive of a piety wholly divorced from that of a religious order. Writings for pious women tend to assume that they have only married out of obedience to their fathers. The *Petite Instruction et maniere de vivre pour une femme seculiere*, another text written by a woman for a woman, begins with an anecdote about a young married woman who tells a theologian that she has married out of obedience and is persuaded that it is in the interests of her salvation that she should follow the path of marriage; clearly, though, it does not correspond to her personal wishes, and she would not remarry.[67] Virginity is usually the principal virtue of female saints.[68] It is therefore perhaps unsurprising that in Gabrielle's *Voyage* there should be, or so it seems to me, an internal contradiction in the way the allegory can be read on this issue. On the one hand the Ame Devote and her companions are misled, take a wrong turning, and find themselves in the territory of the World; the temptations they encounter there are to worldly ambition, pleasure, riches, power. The advice of the Soul's companion virtues is that she must walk through the lands of the World without believing its false promises.[69] This then suggests the allegorizing of a secular life. On the fourth day of her journey, however, she meets Perseverance, who commends the Soul to the care of her daughter Virginity:

> Fille, prens ta seur l'Ame devote et la mayne en sa chambrete tant pure, tant necte, toute blanche, sans nulle tache.
> Là commencerent à deviser les deux vierges ensemble, de la gloire que auront ceulx qui seront en la cité de eternel repos et ont passé les desers du monde, combatu contre les aguillons de la chair, sans estre vaincues ny macullées
> O seur, se dist Virginité, ceste consideration nous devroit estre si plaisante que nulles peynes mondaines ne nous sauroient grever. Il n'est rien si plaisant à Dieu que virginité, comme le preuve la descendue qu'il luy pleut faire dedans le ventre virginal de sa sacrée mere, Marie, qui est vray exemplaire et la guyde de toutes celles qui veullent par ladicte voye aller.[70]

And indeed, no doubt encouraged by this cozy scene, the Soul wins in heaven the Palm of Virginity. I think there is a confusion in the text, and that even as Gabrielle writes for an audience of young women who are waiting to be married she cannot shake off the monastic ideal.[71] The *Fort Chasteau* is less problematic on this question; virginity, although praised, does not have to be read as something to which all the Souls aspire:

> Les unes prenoient des branches de ce bel arbre, nommé palme, duquel le fruict en est plaisant, et comment leur appartenoit en leurs mains comme vierges. Aultres, chappeaulx de cest tant odorant arbre, nommé laurier, mectoyent en leurs chiefz comme victoriennes contre les tentations. Aultres avoient de belles branches d'ollivier en signe de paix entre Dieu et elles.[72]

Bouchet is much clearer on this issue and while conceding the superiority of the monastic state, speaks less ambiguously to married women. Certainly the wedded life of Saint Radegonde presents no very encouraging model of happy marriage: Radegonde would much rather have been a nun and certainly does not enjoy sexual intercourse.[73] Yet the really interesting thing about the narrative is that Bouchet represents the saint as partaking in any sexual activity at all, however reluctantly. To do so he has energetically rejected a version popularized in some contemporary accounts of her life according to which, although married to Clotaire, she remained a virgin.[74] He does this primarily on historical grounds, and on the known character of Clotaire, for none of his older, more reliable sources suggest the marriage was not consummated. But it also allows him to make the point that Radegonde, married and then later a nun, can be a pattern for all women, whatever their status.

In the *Triumphes*, the Soul is explicitly not that of a monk or nun. After the Soul's fall and repentance, she comes to a crossroads that is a choice between the religious and the secular life; the advantages and disadvantages of both are explained at length. It is Grace Divine who makes the choice for the Soul and sends her down the secular road:

> L'Ame trouva Grace Divine, qui n'estoit loing de Foy, Esperance et Charité, et la pria en grant humilité l'adroisser à la voie meilleure pour elle. Grace Divine la mist au chemin de la grant religion chrestienne comme celle qui savoit laquelle des deux voyes luy estoit la plus aisée et asseurée. L'Ame se voulut enquerir avec elle pourquoy ne l'avoit adroissée à la voie de claustralle religion, actendu qu'elle estoit plus seure. Mais dame Foy l'empescha, luy disant, "Ne vous enquerez des secrectz jugemens de Dieu, mais croiez, puis que Grace Divine vous a mise en ce chemin, qu'il est plus utille pour vous, combien qu'il pourroit estre à ung aultre dangereux et damnable."[75]

Doubtless an answer often given to daughters who inconveniently did not wish to marry. The allegory does not in fact make explicit whether the owner of the Soul marries or not, but the moral instruction concerning marriage has already been supplied in the first part by the cardinal virtue Prudence. In two sections entitled "Comment et pourquoy on se doit marier" and "Comment mary et femme doyvent converser en leur lict de mariage" Bouchet draws on a sermon on marriage by Jean Raulin.[76] Thus, without accepting the Erasmian view that marriage is not necessarily a lower state than celibacy in a religious order, Bouchet takes much more seriously the teaching that it is the proper calling for many, and to that extent faces up rather more to the real state of married women. Indeed, it is no doubt only because he is writing religious texts, which normally assume the desirability of virginity, that his depiction of marriage is not more enthusiastic. The way he depicts the sweetness of married life with reference to his own experience in E*pistre familiere* 67 accords much better with his exploitation of the metaphor of marriage and of the language of love poetry.

Gabrielle warmly espoused a fifteenth-century tradition of affective meditation adapted for laywomen, and within that tradition worked with a certain feisty independence, choosing the themes that particularly inspired and moved her; these do not include the depiction of female allegorical heroines committing mortal sins. Her use of allegory appears to depend on her familiarity with allegorical texts and the motifs occurring in them; the underlying doctrines are not always clear or coherent. They did not, however, need to be; she does not write against a background of doctrinal dispute, and she seeks to move her readers rather than to instruct them. Bouchet is an important figure in vernacular French Catholic instruction in the first decades of the Reformation; he attacks Lutheranism but accepts criticism not only of abuses within the church but also of the way that some of the church's doctrines were customarily taught. Certainly as a male writer he may have been less drawn to the affective meditation that had so strongly characterized female piety,[77] but the demands of the historical moment are also important. Affective meditation perhaps no longer appeared a valid substitute for sound instruction.[78] Socially, Gabrielle was greatly Bouchet's superior; in learning he was greatly hers. But the example of this great lady's piety impressed him in an enduring way, and he was sufficiently impressed by her little pilgrimage text to use the concept for his own massive (and massively successful) manual of instruction.

NOTES

1. Gabrielle de Bourbon, Œuvres spirituelles 1510–1516, ed. Evelyne Berriot-Salvadore (Paris: Champion, 1999), 139–98.

2. Les Triumphes de la noble et amoureuse dame et l'art d'honnestement aymer, composé par le traverseur ses voyes perilleuses (Poitiers: J. Bouchet, 1530). There were many later editions, see Jennifer Britnell, Jean Bouchet (Edinburgh: Edinburgh University Press, 1986), 321–24.

3. On Gabrielle, see Berriot-Salvadore, introduction to Œuvres by Gabrielle de Bourbon; also idem, "Le Miroir des princesses: Un modèle de dévotion séculière au début du XVIe siècle," La Bible et ses raisons, ed. Gérard Gros (Saint-Étienne: Université de Saint-Étienne, 1996), 77–95.

4. Gabrielle de Bourbon, Œuvres, 32. Henry died in 1483. The work dedicated to Gabrielle was printed as Le Livre de meditation sur la reparation de nature humaine (Paris: J. Petit, n.d., c.1516); see Francis M. Higman, Piety and the People: Religious Printing in French, 1511-1551 (Aldershot and Vermont: Scolar Press, 1996), 245 (H5 and H7).

5. Auguste Hamon, Un Grand Rhétoriqueur poitevin, Jean Bouchet, 1476-1557? (Paris: H. Oudin, 1901; reprint, Geneva: Slatkine, 1970), 39 et seq. In the Epistres, Epistre familière IX, Bouchet thanks Gabrielle because "vous m'avez aux gages retenu/De vostre hostel, & assigné deniers."

6. Le Chappelet des princes (Paris: G. du Pré, 1517) and Le Temple de Bonne Renommée (Paris: G. du Pré, 1517); see Britnell, Jean Bouchet, 308–9; also Le Temple, ed. Giovanna Bellati (Milan: Università Cattolica, 1992).

7. Panegyric du Chevallier sans reproche (Poitiers: J. Bouchet, 1527).

8. As well as describing her in the Annales d'Acquitaine and the Panegyric, Bouchet includes her epitaph in Genealogies, effigies et epitaphes (Poitiers: J. Bouchet and J. and E. de Marnef, 1545), esp. 18. In the Jugement poetic de l'honneur femenin (Poitiers: J. and E. de Marnef, 1538) he cites her "'Contre ceulx qui veulent empecher les femmes de lire es livres françoys non prohibez par l'eglise': Feue madame Gabrielle de la maison de Bourbon, ayeule de monseigneur voustre espoux, ne doit estre mise en oubly: qui composa en langue vulgaire de France plusieurs livretz de devotion: et entre autres la louable conversation des dames et le temple du Sainct Esprit. Brief, si vouloys nommer toutes ses femmes de sçavoyr, qui ont esté par cy davant, seroyt chose trop

longue, et de parler de celles du temps present engendreroyt envie: mais suffise aux hommes mal parlans que les femmes ont esté, et sont capables des bonnes letres comme les hommes" (bb1ʳ–2ʳ).

9. Gabrielle de Bourbon, Œuvres, 19–23.

10. Ibid., 22–23; in particular, the Meditations sur la grant vie de Jhesu Crist are the extremely popular Meditations by Pseudo-Bonaventura.

11. See below, note 67.

12. For an overview of the careers of Gerson and Henry see the entries in the Dictionnaire de spiritualité, ed. M. Viller and others, 16 vols (Paris: Beauchesne, 1932–95); on Henry see also Geneviève Hasenohr, "Aspects de la littérature de spiritualité en langue française (1480–1520)," Revue d'Histoire de l'Église de France, 77 (1991): 29–45, esp. 37–38.

13. See Jennifer Britnell, "Gabrielle de Bourbon and the Not-So-Sinful Soul." In Women's Writing in the French Renaissance, eds Philip Ford and Gillian Jondorf (Cambridge: Cambridge French Colloquies, 1999), 1–26, esp. 9–10.

14. See Gabrielle de Bourbon, Œuvres, 8–9, 37.

15. Ibid., 37, 50; Hamon, Un Grand Rhétoriqueur, 58–59; L. Sandret, Louis II de La Trémoille (Paris: Société bibliographique, 1881), 93 n.

16. Gabrielle de Bourbon, Œuvres, 53–138.

17. On this relationship and on the cueur Contemplatif, see Britnell, "Gabrielle de Bourbon." On images of the soul, see Caroline Walker Bynum, "'. . . And Woman His Humanity": Female Imagery in the Religious Writing of the Later Middle Ages." In Gender and Religion: On the Complexity of Symbols, eds Caroline Walker Bynum, Stevan Harrell, and Paula Richman (Boston: Beacon Press, 1986), 257–88, esp. 268–73.

18. Gerson, Œuvres complètes, ed. P. Glorieux, vol. 7, bk. 1 (Paris: Desclée, 1966), 220–80; see esp. 249–51.

19. Gabrielle de Bourbon, Œuvres, 199–225. See David Cowling, Building the Text: Architecture as Metaphor in Late Medieval and Early Modern France (Oxford: Oxford University Press, 1998), 69–80.

20. See particularly Gabrielle de Bourbon, Œuvres, illustrations facing 208 and 220.

21. Berriot-Salvadore rightly stresses (ibid., 29–35) the influence of Henry and other devotional writers on Gabrielle long before Bouchet entered her service. I would, however, hesitate to ascribe as much influence to Bouchet even in the period 1510–16 as she does (35–37).

22. Epistres morales et familieres du traverseur (Poitiers: J. Bouchet and J. and E. de Marnef, 1545), Epistres familieres IX, X, and XI. It must be borne in mind that these poems had at some point been rewritten; Bouchet abandoned the lyric caesura by 1516, and when republishing his earlier works always corrected them in order to eliminate it (Britnell, Jean Bouchet, 27–29, 60 n. 47). We cannot know what other changes were made. It is a matter of opinion whether these poems respond in a complimentary way to Gabrielle's texts or whether they are a formative influence on them; I incline to the former view, and Berriot-Salvadore perhaps rather more to the latter (introduction to Œuvres, by Gabrielle de Bourbon, 35–37).

23. Poitiers: E. de Marnef, (n.d.; privilege dated January 27, 1517 [1518]). See Jennifer Britnell, *Jean Bouchet*, 132–36, 202–5, and Giovanna Bellati, "Entre hagiographie et historiographie: L'*Histoire et cronique de Clotaire ou vie Sainte Radegonde* de Jean Bouchet," *L'Analisi Linguistica e Letteraria* 1 (1998): 61–84.
24. *Histoire et cronicque de Clotaire*, aa1^{r-v}: "[. . .] par le commandement de feue de bonne memoire ma dame Anne [. . .] vostre mere, et à la requeste de feue madame Gabriele de Bourbon [. . .] par laquelle fuz adroissé à madicte dame vostre mere."
25. BN MS. n. a. f. 11555; see Jennifer Britnell, "Jean Bouchet's Prayers in French for the Laity," *Bibliothèque d'Humanisme et Renaissance* 38 (1976): 421–36.
26. Britnell, *Jean Bouchet*, 230–48.
27. Ibid., 194–202; Francis M. Higman, "Premières réponses catholiques aux écrits de la Réforme en France, 1525–c.1540." In *Le Livre dans l'Europe de la Renaissance*, Actes du XXVIIIe Colloque International d'Études Humanistes de Tours, ed. P. Aquilon, H.-J. Martin, and F. Dupuigrenet Desrousilles (Paris: Promodis, 1988), 361–77.
28. Britnell, *Jean Bouchet*, 233–4.
29. Ibid., 194, 208–9.
30. *Panegyric*, M1^r.
31. Gabrielle de Bourbon, *Œuvres*, 55.
32. Ibid., 198.
33. Ibid., 55: "combien que c'est une chose de quoy je me sçay tresmal aider que de mectre telle chose par escript"; 138, "non pas si bien que le Cueur m'a enseigné, mais au mieulx que j'ay peu. Suppliant à ceulx qui le liront n'avoir regard aux faultes mais seullement aux bons propoux, pour en faire leur proffit"; 198, "combien que je n'aye pas le sens ne le savoir pour avoir le tout bien reconnu"; 224–5, "duquel chasteau j'ay dit non pas le tout car, comme j'ay par cy davant dit, mon entendement n'est pas assez suffisant pour ce faire."
34. Ibid., 214.
35. Ibid., 225.
36. *Panegyric*, L8^v. He himself was commissioned to have her works checked by a theologian: *Annales d'Acquitaine* (Poitiers: E. de Marnef, 1557), fol. 203^r; *Panegyric*, M1^v.
37. Gerson explains in *La Montaigne de contemplation* why he writes in French and "aux simples gens," "à gens simples sans lettre"—but also "plus aux femmes que aux hommes." *Œuvres complètes*, vol. 7, bk 1, 16.
38. *Epistres*, *Epistre familiere* CIV.
39. *Triumphes*, +3^r.
40. *Histoire et cronicque de Clotaire*, f. x^r.
41. Ibid.
42. *Triumphes*, +2^v.
43. Ibid.
44. *Jugement poetic de l'honneur femenin*, bb2^v.
45. Liminary epistle in *L'Histoire de Theodorite evesque de Cyropolis*, trans. D. M. Mathee (Poitiers: J. and E. de Marnef, 1544), ã 6^v–7^r; see Britnell, *Jean Bouchet*, 201–2.

46. Britnell, "Jean Bouchet's Prayers," 432.
47. Gabrielle de Bourbon, Œuvres, 199.
48. Britnell, "Gabrielle de Bourbon," 13–21.
49. Ibid.,12–13; Gabrielle de Bourbon, Œuvres, 192.
50. Gabrielle de Bourbon, Œuvres, 145.
51. Œuvres, vol. 7, bk. 1: 277.
52. Gabrielle de Bourbon, Œuvres, 147.
53. Ibid., 195.
54. Ibid., 197.
55. Ibid., 211–2.
56. Ibid., 223.
57. Epistres, Epistre familiere X, ff. xi^v–xii^v.
58. Triumphes, f. lxvii^v.
59. Ibid.
60. Ibid., f. lxviii^r.
61. Cf. the Petite Instruction cited in note 67 below.
62. Epistres, Epistre familiere X, f. xii^{r-v}.
63. Britnell, Jean Bouchet, 330.
64. Ed. Renja Salminen (Geneva: Droz, 1999), 187.
65. According to Bouchet, "Elle estoit si magnanime que bien se contantoit estre la pluspart du temps privée des plaisirs et doulceurs de mariage, et dormir seule en ennuy et regret, à ce que son espoux en servant le roy et s'emploiant aux affaires du royaume et du bien public acquist honneur et louange" (Panegyric, M1^r).
66. Used for example by Robert Ciboule in Le Livre de meditation sur soy mesmes (Paris: S. Vostre, 1510), ff. lxxxi^v–lxxxii^r. The numbers are from the parable of the sower, Matt. 13: 23; see Saint Jerome's commentary on Matthew, PL 26, col. 89. On the dilemmas of pious married women see Dyan Elliott, Spiritual Marriage. Sexual Abstinence in Medieval Wedlock (Princeton: Princeton University Press, 1993).
67. Petite Instruction et maniere de vivre pour une femme seculiere, BL C.175.b.36, s.l., s.d., variously dated by the BL catalogues as [1505?] and [1520?]. A copy in Paris, BN Rés. D 17400(3), is dated by Higman, Piety and the People, 261–2 (155), to c. 1516. Other editions turn up in Books of Hours—a notoriously conservative form of publication — in the 1560s and 1570s, for example, BL C.47.c.16(2); C.30.1.4.(2); see also Paul Lacombe, Livres d'heures imprimés au XVe et au XVe siècle (Paris: Imprimerie nationale, 1907). See Alice A. Hentsch, De la littérature didactique du Moyen-Age s'adressant spécialement aux femmes (Cahors: A. Coueslant, 1903; reprint, Geneva: Slatkine, 1975), 223–6, and Geneviève Hasenohr, "La Vie quotidienne de la femme vue par l'Église: L'enseignement des 'Journées chrétiennes' de la fin du moyen-âge." In Frau und spätmittelalterlicher Alltag (Vienna: Österreichischen Akademie der Wissenschaften, 1986), 19–101, esp. 87–89. The writer is a nun; a date of composition at the beginning of the century is suggested by the recommendation that the recipient read a printed work by Olivier Maillard (B4^r).

68 The very popular life of Saint Margaret is an obvious example.
69. Gabrielle de Bourbon, Œuvres, 159–64.
70. Ibid., 178–9.
71. It is not, of course, impossible that Gabrielle is thinking of a spiritual virginity that has more to do with an attitude of mind and will than with an actual physical state, but she gives no pointers to such an interpretation.
72. Ibid., 222.
73. Histoire et cronicque de Clotaire, ff. xxv^v–xxvi^v.
74. See Britnell, Jean Bouchet, 202–4.
75. Triumphes, f. cxx^v.
76. Ibid., ff. vii^v–ix^r.
77. For an excellent study of many aspects of female piety, see Caroline Walker Bynum, Holy Feast and Holy Fast: The Religious Significance of Food to Medieval Women (Berkeley and Los Angeles: University of California Press, 1987).
78. In Piety and the People, 10–11, Higman notes that in terms of number of publications, meditation literature gave way to more instructional texts by the mid-sixteenth century.

WORKS CITED

Bellati, Giovanna. "Entre hagiographie et historiographie: L'Histoire et cronicque de Clotaire ou Vie Sainte Radegonde de Jean Bouchet." L'Analisi Linguistica e Letteraria, 1 (1998): 61–84.

Berriot-Salvadore, Évelyne. "Le Miroir des princesses: un modèle de dévotion séculière au début du XVIe siècle." In La Bible et ses raisons, edited by Gérard Gros, 77–95. Saint-Étienne: Université de Saint-Étienne, 1996.

Bouchet, Jean. Les Annales d'Acquitaine. Poitiers: E. de Marnef, 1557.

———. Les Cantiques et oraisons contemplatives de l'ame penitente traversant les voies perilleuses, Bibliothèque Nationale MS. n. a. f. 11555.

———. Le Chappelet des princes. Paris: G. du Pré, 1517.

———. Epistres morales et familieres du traverseur. Poitiers: J. Bouchet and J. and E. de Marnef, 1545.

———. Genealogies, effigies et epitaphes. Poitiers: J. Bouchet and J. and E. de Marnef, 1545.

———. L'Histoire et chronicque de Clotaire. Poitiers, E. de Marnef, n.d., privilege dated January 27, 1517 [1518].

———. Le Jugement poetic de l'honneur feminin. Poitiers: J. and E. de Marnef, 1538.

———. Labirynthe de Fortune. Paris and Poitiers: E. de Marnef and J. Bouchet, n.d. [1522].

———. Le Panegyric du Chevallier sans reproche. Poitiers: J. Bouchet, 1527.

———. Le Temple de bonne renommée. Paris: G. du Pré, 1517; edited by Giovanna Bellati. Milan: Università Cattolica, 1992.

———. *Les Triumphes de la noble et amoureuse dame et l'art d'honnestement aymer* [...] Poitiers: J. Bouchet, 1530.

———. Liminary epistle in *L'Histoire de Theodorite evesque de Cyropolis* translated by D. M. Mathee. Poitiers: J. and E. de Marnef, 1544.

Britnell, Jennifer. "Gabrielle de Bourbon and the Not-So-Sinful Soul." In *Women's Writing in the French Renaissance*, edited by Philip Ford and Gillian Jondorf, 1–26. Cambridge: Cambridge French Colloquies, 1999.

———. *Jean Bouchet*. Edinburgh: Edinburgh University Press, 1986.

———. "Jean Bouchet's Prayers in French for the Laity." *Bibliothèque d'Humanisme et Renaissance* 38 (1976): 421–36.

Bynum, Caroline Walker. "'... And Woman His Humanity': Female Imagery in the Religious Writing of the Later Middle Ages." In *Gender and Religion: On the Complexity of Symbols*, edited by Caroline Walker Bynum, Stevan Harrell, and Paula Richman, 257–88. Boston: Beacon Press, 1986.

———. *Holy Feast and Holy Fast: The Religious Significance of Food to Medieval Women*. Berkeley and Los Angeles: University of California Press, 1987.

Ciboule, Robert. *Le Livre de meditation sur soy mesmes*. Paris: S. Vostre, 1510.

Cowling, David. *Building the Text: Architecture as Metaphor in Late Medieval and Early Modern France*. Oxford: Oxford University Press, 1998.

Elliott, Dyan. *Spiritual Marriage. Sexual Abstinence in Medieval Wedlock*. Princeton: Princeton University Press, 1993.

Gabrielle de Bourbon. *Œuvres spirituelles, 1510–1516*, edited by Évelyne Berriot-Salvadore. Paris: Champion, 1999.

Gerson, Jean Charlier de. *Œuvres complètes*, edited by P. Glorieux, 10 vols in 11. Paris: Desclée, 1960–74.

Hamon, Auguste. *Un Grand Rhétoriqueur poitevin, Jean Bouchet, 1476–1557?*. Paris: H. Oudin, 1901. Reprint, Geneva: Slatkine, 1970.

Hasenohr, Geneviève. "Aspects de la littérature de spiritualité en langue française (1480–1520)." *Revue d'Histoire de l'Église de France* 77 (1991): 29–45.

———. "La Vie quotidienne de la femme vue par l'Église: L'Enseignement des 'Journées chrétiennes' de la fin du moyen-âge." In *Frau und spätmittelalterlicher Alltag*, 19–101. Vienna: Österreichischen Akademie der Wissenschaften, 1986.

Henry, Jean. *Le Livre de meditation sur la reparation de nature humaine*. Paris: Jean Petit, n.d., c.1516.

Hentsch, Alice A. *De la littérature didactique du Moyen-Age s'adressant spécialement aux femmes*. Cahors: A. Coueslant, 1903. Reprint, Geneva: Slatkine, 1975.

Higman, Francis M. *Piety and the People. Religious Printing in French, 1511–1551*. Aldershot and Vermont: Scolar Press, 1996.

———. "Premières réponses catholiques aux écrits de la Réforme en France, 1525–c.1540." In *Le Livre dans l'Europe de la Renaissance*, Actes du XXVIIIe

Colloque International d'Études Humanistes de Tours, edited by P. Aquilon, H.-J. Martin and F. Dupuigrenet Desrousilles, 361–77. Paris: Promodis, 1988.
Lacombe, Paul. *Livres d'heures imprimés au XVe et au XVe siècle.* Paris: Imprimerie Nationale, 1907.
Marguerite de Navarre. *Heptaméron* edited by Renja Salminen. Geneva: Droz, 1999.
Petite Instruction et maniere de vivre pour une femme seculiere. British Library C.175.b.36, s.l., n.d.
Sandret, L. *Louis II de La Trémoille [. . .].* Paris: Société bibliographique, 1881.
Viller, M., ed. *Dictionnaire de spiritualité.* 16 vols. Paris: Beauchesne, 1932–95.

Les Albums Poétiques De Marguerite D'Autriche: The Dynamics of an Early Renaissance Court

JANE H. M. TAYLOR

Marguerite d'Autriche was, of course, one of the most remarkable artistic patrons of early sixteenth-century Europe. She offered her protection to countless architects and artists and artisans for the elaboration of the magnificent church at Brou which was to be the mausoleum for herself and her husband Philibert of Savoie;[1] she collected a stable of musicians[2] and poets that included, notably, Jean Lemaire de Belges;[3] she assembled the luxuriant and tasteful and eclectic library described and catalogued in Marguerite Debae's magnificent recent study.[4] Given this wealth of possibilities, it may seem perverse to concentrate on a rather unspectacular little volume of verses, usually known as her *Album poétique*, but it will be my argument that this unassuming manuscript should be set alongside *loci classici* like Charles d'Orléans's personal manuscript (Bibliothèque Nationale Française, MS français 25458,)[5] Marie de Clèves's equivalent (Carpentras, Bibliothèque Municipale, MS 375,)[6] or the collection of *rondeaux* published by Raynaud from Bibliothèque Nationale Française, MS français 9223[7]—*loci classici* because, imaginatively interpreted, these côterie manuscripts seem to give us access to the dynamics of a cultured and creative court at the very end of the Middle Ages.

But first, the manuscript[8]—and a puzzle. Brussels, Bibliothèque Royale, MS 10572, consists very largely of rondeaux, despite the fact that the inventory of Marguerite's books drawn up in 1523-24[9] says that it *ce nomme* Plusieurs Balades.[10]

I have called it "unassuming": it has little decoration other than a few pen flourishes, and, with one notable exception to which I return later, it is all written in same neat hand. Each rondeau or ballade begins on a new page, and each has one peculiarity: in the margin to the left of virtually every lyric is a name, in an elementary code whereby the true name is discovered by reading each word backwards, and eliminating its first and last letters: thus ZNIDEZ, Edin, ETOCIPI, Picot, ZAMS HELLESIOMEDA ZICNALPO, Ma demoiselle Planci, GRUEINGISNOMO SEDZ TUSSUOBA, Monsignieur de Boussu. Now, as I show in detail below, it is possible to match virtually all of the names so inscribed with members of Marguerite's court—and hence the puzzle I mentioned at the beginning of this paragraph, which centers on the role that each of the persons named might have played in the confection of the anthology.

Marcel Françon, who has edited the poems in this collection, is remarkably—and, I would argue, unnecessarily—cautious:[11] he is, he says, wary of supposing that the names represent the authors of the pieces to which they are attached, and this on several grounds. First, the names are not those of professional poets: they are courtiers and councillors, diplomats and doctors. Second, he maintains, one cannot discern personalities: there is, he says, no tone or subject common to the different poems said to be written by the same poet. Third and finally, the poems, he says, all read rather the same: it is difficult, that is to say, to distinguish poet from poet. I shall address these reservations in reverse order. On the third point, that the poems read rather the same, I suggest that Françon's own reading may have been a little hasty; true enough, tone and style seem to differ very little, but on the other hand, as we know, this is unsurprising, in a period when the lyric possessed a standard lexicon and a set of more or less standard topoi. And within the tonal and stylistic homogeneity that this imposes, the rondeaux and ballades of this collection are on the contrary rather interestingly varied: true, regrets and laments predominate, but there are cheerfully cynical rondeaux whose theme is card games (e.g. xxxii), or "Plenty more women where she came from!" (e.g. ii, ix), or "Had enough of *her*!" (e.g. xix). The second point, that there is no consistency between the poems said to be by the same poet, I return to later: an essential plank in my argument in this paper will be that on the contrary, "personalities"—by which of course I mean no more than "poetic personae"—do emerge. But the first point, that these are not the names of professional poets, seems to me, frankly, slightly bizarre. Françon himself concedes (p. 56) that "il est vrai qu'il n'y avait pas besoin d'avoir beaucoup de talent ni de métier pour composer de telles œuvres;" but surely the supposition that only professional poets were capable of fashioning a neat rondeau or a competent ballade runs contrary to all that we know of poetic practice in the fifteenth and early sixteenth centuries? No one, after all, has disputed that the poems in Charles d'Orléans's personal manuscript are the work of those whose names are attached to them, and by far the majority, starting indeed with Charles himself, are not "professional poets:" they are people like his chamberlain Guyot Pot, his secretaries Étienne Le Gout and Hugues Le Voys, his squires Gilles des Ormes and François Faret, his *argentier* Benoît Damien, his doctor Jean Caillau,[12] and that is quite apart from the visitors and amateurs who, it seems, were drawn into the game: "Composer des poésies," says Pierre Champion, "c'était en quelque manière payer l'écot de l'hospitalité que la cour de Blois donnait à ses hôtes."[13] To turn a verse, witty or elegant or sighingly sentimental, was part of the stock-in-trade, the *habitus*,[14] of any young man (or woman) of comfortable rank or courtly ambition in the courts of the fifteenth century,[15] from Boucicaut, whose training included the art of composing *balades, rondiaulx, virelais, lays et complaintes d'amoureux sentement*,[16] to Margaret of Scotland, who "passait des nuits entières à composer des rondeaux,"[17] to the members of the early fifteenth-century cour *d'amour*—jurists and civil servants and aristocrats to a man—all of whom were to possess *experte congnoissance en la science de rethorique*.[18] Françon is, of course, principally a *seiziémiste* and not a medievalist: is he arguing backwards, then, from a Renaissance when indeed poetry was increasingly to become the preserve of professional poets? He is obliged to fall back on the hypothesis that each name might be that of the courtier who *inspired* the poem concerned, whereas the simplest solution, which Occam's razor would then seem to enjoin, is surely that by far the majority of the anagrams represent the poets (*rimeurs* might often be a better term) responsible for each individual poem: that Malines matched "le miracle du séjour de Blois qui mue un médecin, un comptable, un notaire en poète."[19] I am encouraged in this supposition by some interesting codicological *faits divers* which relate to a not especially distinguished little rondeau, "C'est pour jamés" (f. 21v; Françon, 131), entitled, according to the convention of this manuscript, *Chanson Faite Par Semadams* (Fig. 1). It is written in a rapid, angular hand (and in a black ink) quite different from the hand of the remainder of the manuscript, and scholars seem to agree that the hand is Marguerite's own, comparable with that in another note known to be holograph.[20] And not only that: the song also resurfaces in one of Marguerite's other albums (Brussels, Bibliothèque Royale, MS 228), this time set to music, Picker argues, by Pierre de la Rue, one of Marguerite's most favored musicians.[21] The pertinent point is that the folios on which it is written are splendidly illuminated (Fig. 2) with decorated initials and a floral border including daisies, "marguerites."[22] This point is interesting because although the manuscript was indeed richly illuminated on the opening folios, the illuminated borders continue only to 18r, then start again on ff. 50v-51v only for this rondeau, "C'est pour jamés," after which the decoration vanishes again apart from pen flourishes and grotesques. It is difficult to avoid the conclusion that such lavish and careful decoration is likely to have been conceived for a patroness's poem, rather than for some anonymous, nondescript rondeau.

If this is indeed so, if Marguerite's own poem, in her own hand, is labeled with one of the manuscript's characteristic anagrams, then this surely represents some sort of endorsement for the manuscript as a whole: why should this single poem from MS 10572 be by the poet whose name is anagrammatically attached to it, if the remainder of the poems are simply *inspired* by their signatures? For my own part, I shall risk accusations of scholarly recklessness by assuming that the poets are indeed those whose thinly disguised names appear alongside the poems, and it is in that light that I propose to analyse the dynamics of the manuscript—conceding of course that these operate irrespective of the authorship of each individual poem. My hypothesis will be, as I suggested earlier, that the manuscript does allow us fugitive glimpses of Marguerite's "cultured and creative" little court at Malines, and I shall draw analogies with two of the other côterie manuscripts that I mentioned earlier: Charles d'Orléans's personal manuscript, Bibliothèque Nationale Française, MS français 25458,[23] and another, MS français 9223,[24] which seems to emanate from the court of Savoie.[25]

But let me start, more mundanely, with the poets and with what we can know about each of them from manuscript and archive sources:[26]

1. Pierre Picot: this was Marguerite's doctor, who was being paid a salary of 4000 livres a year in 1515 or so.[27] His skills were obviously multiple, since he was also consulted on matters astrological: Gattinara (see no. 7 below) writes to Marguerite in February 1514 asking her to consult the doctor about what is presaged by the appearance of three moons and three suns together in the sky.[28] He had also attended Henri de Nassau (see below, no. 9).[29]

2. Edin: Jean d'Ostin, known as Hesdin, was Marguerite's *maître d'hôtel*.[30] Relations between him and his family, and Marguerite, were warm: Marguerite addresses his wife, in a letter of November 17, 1522, as "Tres chiere et bien amée."[31] He appears repeatedly in Marguerite's correspondance as a trusted adviser and emissary, "nostre amé et féal conseiller et maistre d'hostel,"[32] both for her and for her nephew Charles-Quint,[33] and she later appointed him governor of Béthune.[34]

3. Aubigny: Robert Stuart, seigneur d'Aubigny, later marshal of France, was present at Marguerite's *delivrance*—that is, at the signing of her marriage contract to the future Charles VIII of France—on May 16, 1483.[35] It would seem, however, rather unlikely that the "Aubigny" so summarily referred to in the *Album* could be anyone quite so exalted.

4. La Baume: There are three candidates, from a family all the members of which seem to have enjoyed Marguerite's confidence. The first is Gui de la Baume, comte de Montrevel, seigneur de la Roche et d'Irlens, who had come from the court of Savoie and was *chef* of Marguerite's *conseil privé* in Brussels;[36] he was later to be appointed *bailli d'Amont*.[37] His son, Claude, held much the same offices as his father, and a third possibility is Marc, who was Marguerite's *chevalier d'honneur* and whose daughter was one of her *demoiselles d'honneur*.[38]

5. Bouton: Again, there are two possible candidates. The first is Claude Bouton, seigneur de Courbaron, captain of Marguerite's guard[39] and later councillor and *maître d'hôtel* to Charles-Quint;[40] the second is Philippe Bouton, one of the gentlemen who accompanied Marguerite back from Spain in 1499.[41] But as Françon rightly points out (p. 54), the former is the more likely: Claude's motto was *Souvenir tue*, and one of the poems said to be by him, xxii, uses the tag as its opening words and refrain.

6. Poupet: Charles de Poupet, seigneur de la Chaulx, *bailli d'Aval* to Marguerite,[42] and another trusted emissary.[43] He was later to be Charles-Quint's "chier et feal chevalier et gentilhome de nostre chambre" and *second chambellans*.[44]

7. Président de Dôle: Mercurin de Gattinara, a jurist who entered Marguerite's service in 1502, became in 1504 *président du Conseil* of Bresse, and in 1508 *président du Parlement* of Dôle; he was chef of her *Conseil privé*, then in 1518 became Grand *chancelier du royaume de Castille* on behalf of Charles-Quint, and finally, in 1529, cardinal.[45] Marguerite, it seems, particularly appreciated his discretion[46] and his wit;[47] she addresses him, quite consistently, as "tres chier et feal."[48]

8. La Foy: I find only one possible candidate, "Jehanne de Foy, de la chambre," who was being paid a sizable annual salary of 49 *livres* in 1504.[49]

9. "Nansso": The name remains mysterious, but is it remotely possible that this is Henri, comte de Nassau (1483-1538), who was married to Françoise de Savoie? He was an influential member of Marguerite's court: she addresses him as "mon cousin,"[50] and was instrumental in his marriage to Françoise.[51] He appears repeatedly as one of Marguerite's correspondents and addresses her in affectionate terms,[52] and was later to be Charles-Quint's *grand chambellans*.[53] What would argue against this, perhaps, are two things: no other of Marguerite's more eminent "poets" is referred to quite so unceremoniously, and in all critical honesty, I find no other evidence of Henri de Nassau's ever being referred to simply as *Nassau*, let alone *Nansso*.

10. Monseigneur d'Uselle: Another mysterious name—and puzzlingly so, since he is titled *Monseigneur* and should therefore be identifiable. Is it remotely possible that this is Florent d'Egmont, seigneur d'*Ysselstein*? Florent figures everywhere in Marguerite's correspondance,[54] as one of her principal military advisers, and was to become Charles-Quint's general from 1506. She addresses him, like Henri de Nassau, as "mon cousin."[55] Again, I have to admit to having found no evidence for his being called *d'Uselle*— Marguerite always addresses him as Floris d'Isselstain—but is it conceivable that a Francophone scribe has failed to catch the name properly?

11. "Liquerque": This person remains unidentifiable.[56]

12. Seigneur de Boussu: A scion of the distinguished house of Hennin-Bossu, he was *prévôt-le-comte* at Valenciennes[57] and later one of the court of Charles-Quint.

13. Bâtard de Bourbon: Another distinguished member of Marguerite's court. He was appointed *gentilhomme* to the future Charles-Quint, on January 29, 1511,[58] and was highly regarded by Maximilian of Austria[59] and by Marguerite: there is a letter of October 14, 1514, from her to the duchess of Bourbon, announcing his death in warmly affectionate terms: "et vous asseure, Madame ma bonne tante, qu'il est dommage de sa mort car il estoit homme de bien."[60]

14. Sauvaige filz du president de Brabam: This is Jean le Sauvaige, seigneur d'Escanbeque et de Ligny, *chancelier* of Brabant et *président de Flandre*. He is mentioned by Erasmus as a patron of letters, and was designated by Maximilian to be part of Marguerite's household. He was later to become president of her privy council, and was often sent by her on confidential embassies.[61]

15. The demoiselles de Planci, de Huclam, de Baude, and de Vere: The identities of these ladies are, alas, undiscoverable: however, might Mademoiselle de Huclam, conceivably, be from a town in Flanders called Hueckelein?

16. "Beavoir": I find no trace of this name. There is a seigneur de Beau*fort*, who married one of Marguerite's *filles d'honneur*, the damoiselle de Hallewin, in 1524; Marguerite seems to have attended the marriage.[62] And there is also an Anne de Beau*mont*, another of her *demoiselles d'honneur*, whom Marguerite in 1512 appointed one of the *dames d'honneur* of Eleanor, Isabelle, and Marie d'Autriche,[63] and for whom, later that year, Marguerite was attempting to secure *la premiere commanderie de dames, vacante dans ledit ordre de Saint-Jacques*.[64]

One is, of course, forcibly reminded of what I alluded to, briefly, above: the côterie of poets surrounding Charles d'Orléans which included, as I said, his intimates and cronies and employees, his doctor, his *argentier*, and his visitors. The names attached to the poems are those of members of a similarly eclectic group, constituted not dissimilarly: jurists and diplomats, visiting notables, friends and intimates, who display an easy familiarity one with another just as do the poets who dialogue with each other, compete with each other, or—for instance—occasionally engage in teasing dialogues with Charles himself in the latter's personal manuscript.[65] I argue elsewhere[66] that the disposition of the pieces in Charles's manuscript, the interaction between poem and poem, gives us tempting and tantalizing glimpses of the closed and complicit circle that surrounded Charles, and allows us to guess at networks of cultural practice.[67] It is my contention that Marguerite's *Album*, like other côterie manuscripts, works in the same way: that it provides fugitive images of a cultured early Renaissance court at play and at leisure;[68] I shall try to substantiate this, briefly and selectively, in what follows.

Let me start —appropriately enough no doubt—with the relation of court and patron, and with a little rondeau which, labelled ZAMO TEMADI, is this time probably addressed to, rather than composed by, Marguerite.

> Fortune fortunoit fort une
> En heure si bien opportune
> Que point ne soit imfortunée
> Celle a qui dure destinée
> A livré fortune importune.
>
> Jamais ne luy face rancune
> Fortune monstrant face brune;
> Mais comme tresbien fortunée
> Fortune fortunoit [fort] une.
>
> La non pareille soubz la lune,
> Sans avoir paragunde aulcune,
> Plus que nulle, puis cent an née,
> Mieux digne d'estre coronnée.
> Dont en bien, par la voix commune,
> Fortune fortunoit fort une.   (vi, p. 111)

Now the key to this little poem is the fact that Marguerite's own *devise* was *Fortune infortune fort une*—and this poem plays, dizzyingly and flatteringly, with that very conceit. The unknown poet is a master of synonymy and near-

LES ALBUMS POÉTIQUES... 157

synonymy (*fortune, destinée, opportune*); of rich rhyme (*fort une/opportune/importune*); of ambiguity (does *heure* here mean "fortune," or "hour"?). I would not wish to claim, of course, that this is a masterpiece; it does, on the other hand, develop a phrase in ways that must have pleased Marguerite (this is a prime example of the rhetorical figure *traductio*) by juggling pleasingly with sound and meaning. And is it a coincidence that the poem which follows it, in the *Album*, is a rondeau addressed to PERTSONH KEMADO, Nostre Dame?

> Dames qu'estes de Dieu la fille [et mere],
> Qui conceustes vostre souverain pere
> Et l'anfantant demourastes pucelle,
> Conduisés moy a mener vie telle
> Que par pechier mon ame ne se altere.   (vii, p. 112)

Is this not particularly original little poem—the *fille/mere* paradox is a commonplace in late medieval Marian devotion[69]—another piece of indirect flattery: some courtier, in other words, devising a poem designed to cater to his patroness's well-documented personal piety? I am inclined to go further, and argue that the two poems interact thematically: in Marguerite's *infortune*, is not her best recourse reliance on the compassion of *Nostre Dame*? My argument here is, of course, that the architecture of the Album is no accident: that its juxtapositions are *sequences*[70] in which poem responds to poem.

Let me pursue this latter point by looking at another sequence of lyrics which constitutes a sustained dialogue between two of the stalwarts of the *Album*, "Edin" (Jean d'Ostin) and "Pirot" (sic: Pierre Picot), Marguerite's doctor. Jean d'Ostin is, it seems, responsible for the first of the poems—which is also, by coincidence, the first poem of the collection. His rondeau is melancholic—the characteristic lexicon, the characteristic topoi of the lachrymose lover:

> Las, quel regret, quelle melancolie,
> Las, quel soucy, quelle tristesse en l'ame
> Est d'ung amant qui a *perdu* sa dame
> Gracieuse, moult plaisante, jolye! (i, p. 91)

I italicize *perdu* here, because it is this lexeme, specifically, that will shape and structure the dialogue that follows; Picot seizes it and weaves it into a bracing, commonsensical response:

> C'est peu de fait, tant vous [François *vour*] fais asavoir
> Qu'avoir *perdu* l'amour d'une maistresse,

> Combien que fut bien belle et en jonnesse,
> Car l'on en peult assez telles avoir. (ii, p. 92)

Edin is unconvinced:

> Povre d'amours et riche de tristesse
> Est ung amant, cela j'ose bien dire,
> Qui a *perdu* sa dame, sa maistresse;
> son cueur gemit quant sa bouche on voit rire.
> Je croy qu'a part grandement en souspire
> Quant *perdu* a ung si bon personnaige
> Qu'avoit choisi ou n'avoir que redire.
> Telle *perte* doit plaindre ung homme saige. (iii, p. 93)

But Picot remains unrepentantly dismissive:

> L'on ne doit point mectre Son soing et cure
> A tant aimer fille, quoy que soit belle,
> Qu'on ne pensoit que ma dame Nature
> En a formé qu'on treuve plus ou telle;
> Et puis beaulté, tant d'aultre que de celle,
> Tost se passe comme beaulté de rose;
> Qui telle *pert*, choisisse une nouvelle;
> Ou recouvre a, *perdre* c'est peu de chose. (iv, p. 95)

I have quoted this exchange at such length because only so can one begin to see its dynamics. The verses, of course, are neither particularly ingenious nor particularly flashy: none of the rhymes is rich, there is a dismaying number of fillers ("tant vous fais asavoir," "plus ou telle,") and the refrains lack the punch with which the best poets of the period (Charles himself, Villon, Jean Lemaire) invest them. The poets are, on the other hand, adroit enough: even if the sentiments for which the poems are a vehicle are conventional, even if the lexicon is unremarkable, Jean d'Hesdin and Pierre Picot have managed to confect something stylish. And not only that: their tongue-in-cheek dialogue has a pointedness, a humor, to which it is difficult not to respond. Take, for instance, Jean d'Hesdin's ballade, which opens "Povre d'amours. . . ." Jean's tone is severe, admonitory: Picot, he seems to suggest, is either incurably frivolous and lightweight (an *homme saige* must surely mourn the loss of a virtuous lady), or else is concealing a heavy heart behind a mocking exterior: "son cueur gemit quant sa bouche on voit rire." Or take the final ballade of the series, Pierre Picot's, and its manipulation of what by the sixteenth century was a weary topos, the Horatian *carpe diem*,

LES ALBUMS POÉTIQUES... 159

"gather ye rosebuds:" Picot, unrepentant, rewrites the commonplace. Unlike Horace, unlike the latter's countless epigones, he uses the *rose* metaphor as a consolation: "beaulté...se passe comme beaulté de rose," so the lover would in any case soon have tired of an aging, fading *belle fille* and should simply, and without regret, move on. But what is most striking is the relish with which the two poets attack the key lexeme, inflecting the etymon *perdere* though its different forms, verbal and nominal (*traductio* again); these are knowing *reprises* which suggest that this complicit circle took a knowing and real pleasure in linguistic agility.

And, I suggest, a knowing pleasure in the playing out of consistent roles—how far they relate to the "real" poets is of course unknowable: "poetic personae" for the *poètes de circonstance* that the A*lbum* creates. Pierre Picot's consistent poetic stance, for instance, throughout the A*lbum*, is precisely the devil-may-care cynicism that the little exchange I have just quoted has crystallised: his is the rakish voice against which the more dutifully tearful of his colleagues are to be measured. A poet who is, for once, anonymous is sleepless:

> De quatre nuys les trois veillier
> Et la quatresme sommeillier
> En despitant ma vie toute
> Me fait celle qui passe route
> De cueur amoureux traveillier. (xii, p. 117)

Picot will have none of this mawkish sentimentality:

> De quatre nuys les trois que veille
> Et la quatresme ne sommeille,
> Il ne fault faire point de doubte
> Qu'il ne soit ung fol, somme toute,
> S'ainsi par amours se traveille. (xiii, p. 118)

On another occasion, Monseigneur de Poupet borrows a disillusioned lyric, handily, from the J*ardin de Plaisance* (f. 115v);[71]

> Au plus offrant ma dame est mise
> Et au dernier encherisseur.
> Je ne sçay se c'est par honneur
> Mais je n'en prise pas la guise. (lxxi, p. 178)

Picot devises a firm, and rather witty, response from *ma dame*, a response which picks up, ingeniously, precisely the same rhyme-scheme:

> Je ne suis pas en vente *mise*:
> Nul n'est qui soit de moy vendeur,
> Car, selon le bon entendeur,
> Ce n'est pas des dames la *guise*.   (lxxii, p. 179)

Picot's forte, in other words, is light-hearted, often sharp-witted, cynicism, and his is expedient verse, verse at the service of other members of the court, not the verse of conviction.

But not always: by contrast, another sequence of verses plays the political against the personal. The originator, rather disconcertingly given his usual poetic persona, is. . . . Pierre Picot, modulating from what looks like mere platitude into seriousness:

> Le temps est trouble, le temps se esclarcira;
> Apres la plue [sic] l'on atent le beau temps;
> Apres noises et grans divers contens
> Paix adviendra et maleur cessera.
>
> Mais entre deulx que[l] mal l'on souffrera! (xlvii, p. 154)

Picot's respondent, FELY STNEDISERPO ZEDO XELODZ, the président de Dôle, will have none of this qualified optimism: the future cardinal's is a dignified seriousness that befits the political and diplomatic status with which Marguerite had endowed him:

> Le tout va mal et sans loy est la terre,
> Ou puissance tient le lieu de justice
> Et ou le jour fait de la nuyt l'office
> Et le fuir tient lieu de bonne guerre. (xlviii, p. 155)

His measured rondeau drags the *Album* into a temporary solemnity from which it is distracted by a rondeau by "Beavoir," who seems to have seized upon the opening lexeme of Picot's rondeau, but converted its unexpected seriousness into amorous self-centeredness:

> Le *temps* m'est long et j'ay bien le pourquoy,
> Car ung jour m'est plus long que une sepmainne;
> Dont je prie Dieu que mon corps tost ramainne
> Ou est mon cueur qui n'est plus avec moy. (l, p. 157)

LAS PELLESIOMEDA SEDZ FEREVO, demoiselle de Vere—the kidnapper of "Beavoir"'s tragic heart?—is tartly unimpressed by these lachrymose phrases:

> Le *temps* vous dure, je le croy,
> Et a moy non, je vous assure. . . . (li, p. 158)

But just as the sequence seems to be veering towards the conventionally sentimental, the président de Dôle—and his poetic persona is, visibly, one of unshakeable solemnity—reverts to the refrain that he had embroidered earlier and tugs the *Album* back to the social and political:

> Le *tout va mal* par grant varieté
> Car ung est deulx, mal pour bon est admis,
> Et a present amis sont ennemis,
> Dont plus n'a lieu en terre pieté. (lii, p. 159)

What I am implying here is, of course, that just as Picot's voice is sharply characterized in this miscellany as cynical, insouciant, so Gattinara's, ponderous, substantial, comes to embody moral reflection: whatever their respective personalities—and nothing, of course, allows us to reconstruct them—their poetic personae have a certain depth and resonance, and their interactions, when examined closely, leap off the manuscript page.

I am tempted to pursue these points further—there are other poets in this collection who could be analyzed in the same way—but I am wary of exhausting the reader's patience; as I implied earlier, what I write here is an attempt towards a new project. What I am arguing is a case that I propose to extend to other côterie manuscripts: I am, for instance, inclined to believe that similar conclusions about the workings of a particular court society could be drawn not only for the courts of Orléans, Savoie, and Malines, but also of Bourbon[72]—and for other courts that I have not yet identified. Daniel Poirion talks of the poetic ferment of the court of Orléans—the metaphor he uses is *cristallisation poétique* or *littéraire*;[73] on a less ambitious and expert scale, ought we not to think of something rather similar elsewhere in the French-speaking world, and certainly, as I hope to have suggested here, in Malines?

St Hilda's College, Oxford

NOTES

1. On Marguerite's artistic patronage, see among others Francisque Thibaut, *Marguerite d'Autriche et Jehan Lemaire de Belges, ou, de la littérature et des arts aux Pays-Bas sous Marguerite d'Autriche* (Paris: E. Leroux, 1888; repr. Geneva: Slatkine, 1970), 65-101.
2. The best source of information here is Martin Picker: see his *The Chanson Albums of Marguerite of Austria* (Berkeley/Los Angeles: University of California Press, 1965), esp. 21-47; "A New Look at the 'Little' Chansonnier of Margaret of Austria," in *Muziek aan*

het Hof van Margaretha van Oostenrijk/Music at the Court of Marguerite of Austria. Jaarboek van het Vlaamse Centrum voor Oude Muziek 3 (1987): 27-31; "Three Unidentified Chansons by Pierre de la Rue in the Album de Marguerite d'Autriche," The Musical Quarterly 46 (1960): 329-43; "The Chanson Albums of Marguerite of Austria: MSS. 228 and 11239 of the Bibliothèque Royale de Belgique, Brussels," Annales Musicologiques 6 (1963), 145-285. Cf. also G. Cammaert, "De muziek aan het hof van Margareta van Oostenrijk," Handelingen van de Kon. Kring voor Oudheidkunde, Letteren en Kunst van Mechelen 84 (1980): 76-95.

3. See G. De Boom, Marguerite d'Autriche-Savoie et la Pré-Renaissance (Paris: E. Droz, 1935), and on Lemaire more specifically, F. Thibaut, Marguerite d'Autriche et Jean Lemaire.

4. La Bibliothèque de Marguerite d'Autriche: Essai de reconstitution d'après l'inventaire de 1523-1524 (Louvain and Paris: Peeters, 1995).

5. On which see principally Pierre Champion, Le Manuscrit autographe des poésies de Charles d'Orléans (Paris: H. Champion, 1907).

6. On which see Pierre Champion's introduction to his edition of Charles d'Orléans's Poésies, 2 vols., Classiques Français du Moyen Âge (Paris: H. Champion, 1923-24), 1: xvi-xviii.

7. Ed. Gaston Raynaud, Rondeaux et autres poésies du XVe siècle, Société des Anciens Textes Français (Paris: Firmin Didot, 1889); I return to this anthology below.

8. There is a full and excellent description in Debae, La Bibliothèque, 94-96.

9. Published by H. Michelant, "Inventaire des vaisselles, joyaux, tapisseries, peintures, manuscrits, etc. de Marguerite d'Autriche, régente et gouvernante des Pays-Bas, dressé en son palais de Malines le 9 juillet 1523," Bulletin de la Commission royale d'histoire, 3rd series, 12 (1871): 5-78, 83-136; M. Debae's study is based on this inventory. An earlier inventory, drawn up in 1516, is fragmentary; it is preserved in the Archives du Nord, in Lille, and was published by A. Le Glay, Correspondance de l'empereur Maximilien I et de Marguerite d'Autriche, sa fille, gouvernante des Pays-Bas de 1507 à 1519, publiée d'après les manuscrits originaux (Paris: J. Renouard, 1839), 2: 468-77.

10. The cataloguer is mistaken, but understandably so: on the first page of the MS appears what is presumably, anagrammatically, the title, VLEDNORA TRUOPA ZAMO HEMADY (= Rondel pour ma dame).

11. Albums poétiques de Marguerite d'Autriche (Cambridge Mass.: Harvard University Press/Paris: Droz, 1934), 53-58. His wary approach has been followed, I believe, by all later critics: see Debae, La Bibliothèque, 94, De Boom, Marguerite d'Autriche-Savoie, 222-3. Émile Gachet, in his Albums et œuvres poétiques de Marguerite d'Autriche, gouvernante des Pays-Bas, Publication 17 (Brussels: Société des Bibliophiles Belges, 1849), puts forward another, but not very convincing, argument: that the names are concealed, in this rather elementary way, because the rondeaux attached to each name are satirically intended, perhaps by Marguerite herself.

12. Pierre Champion gives a list: see his Vie de Charles d'Orléans, 1394-1465 (Paris: H. Champion, 1911), 595-608.

13. Ibid., 609.

14. The expression, meaning cultural capital to be deployed strategically, is Pierre Bourdieu's: see his "Champ de pouvoir, champ intellectuel et habitus de classe," *Scolies: Cahiers de recherche de l'École Normale Supérieure* 1 (1971): 7-26. Bourdieu envisages social space as a site of struggle and strategy within which the trump cards is *habitus*—that is, things such as elegance, beauty, ease of manner, language, which we possess or acquire, and use strategically for purposes of social inclusion or advancement.

15. It is almost otiose to footnote this point, but a prime study is of course Daniel Poirion's: *Le Poète et le prince: L'évolution du lyrisme courtois de Guillaume de Machaut à Charles d'Orléans* (Grenoble: Allier, 1965); see esp. chap. 4: "L'Activité des amateurs, des artistes et des serviteurs." 145-90.

16. *Le Livre des fais du bon messire Jehan le Maingre, dit Bouciquaut, mareschal de France et gouverneur de Jennes*, ed. Denis Lalande, Textes Littéraires Français (Geneva: Droz, 1985), 32.

17. According to G. de Beaucourt, *Histoire de Charles VII*, 6 vols. (Paris: Librairie de la Société Bibliographique A. Picard, 1881-91), 4: 309; alas, none seems to survive.

18. See Carla Bozzolo and Hélène Loyau, *La Cour amoureuse dite de Charles VI*, 2 vols. (Paris: Le Léopard d'Or, 1982-92), 1: 36.

19. Champion, *Vie de Charles d'Orléans*, 592.

20. The manuscript in question is reproduced by Debae (*La Bibliothèque*, plate 1b, p. 586) from Brussels, Bibliothèque Royale, MS 9503-04.

21. For the arguments, see Picker, "Three Unidentified Chansons;" what I say here echoes Picker's argument.

22. MS 228 is reproduced in facsimile, with an introduction by Picker: *Album de Marguerite d'Autriche*: Brussel, Koninklijke Bibliotheek MS. 228 (Peer: Alamire, 1986). That elaborate manuscript production, as well as highly complex musical settings, may be designed as a tribute to particular admired or generous patrons is suggested by Leeman L. Perkins, in his *Music in the Age of the Renaissance* (New York and London: W. W. Norton, 1999), 635-39.

23. Which, for the purposes of this particular paper, is best consulted in an edition more recent than Champion's (see note 6 above) and which transcribes the poems precisely as they follow one another in Bibliothèque Nationale Française, MS français 25458: Charles d'Orléans, *Ballades et rondeaux*, ed. Jean-Claude Mühlethaler, Lettres Gothiques (Paris: Le Livre de Poche, 1992).

24. Ed. Gaston Raynaud, *Rondeaux*. I am preparing a study of this manuscript as part of an ongoing project on the circulation of lyric poems at the end of the Middle Ages.

25. See Pierre Champion, "Remarques sur un recueil de poésies du milieu du XVe siècle (B.N. fr. 9223)," *Romania* 48 (1922): 106-14. Champion takes issue here with Raynaud, who edited the collection: the latter (*Rondeaux*, pp. v, xix-xxi) believes the whole manuscript to have been designed and excerpted for Jacques, bâtard de la Trémoïlle.

26. I use the following sources, abbreviated as follows in the footnotes: **Thibaut**: Francisque Thibaut, *Marguerite d'Autriche et Jehan Lemaire de Belges* (see note 1); **Le Glay**: A. Le Glay, *Correspondance de l'empereur Maximilien Ier et de Marguerite d'Autriche* (see note 9); **Van den Bergh**: L. Van den Bergh, *Correspondance de Marguerite d'Autriche, gouvernante des Pays-Bas. . . .*, 2 vols. (Leiden: S. and J. Luchtmans, 1845); **Itinéraire**: M. Bruchet and E. Lancien, *L'Itinéraire de Marguerite d'Autriche, gouvernante des Pays-Bas* (Lille: L. Danel, 1934); **Bruchet**: Max Bruchet, *Marguerite d'Autriche, duchesse de Savoie* (Lille: L. Danel, 1927); **De Boom**: G. De Boom, "Documents concernant les relations d'Antoine de Ligne avec Philippe le Beau, Marguerite d'Autriche, Charles-Quint, et Henri VIII, roi d'Angleterre," *Bulletin de la Commission Royale d'Histoire* 115 (1950): 383-426.

27. See Thibaut, 118-19.

28. Le Glay, 1: 437.

29. Van den Bergh, 2: no. 144, pp. 332-34.

30. See *Itinéraire*, 340-41.

31. Ibid., 385.

32. In a letter of December 25, 1518: see De Boom, 409.

33. See Van den Bergh, 1: nos. 62, 98, 99; Le Glay, 1: 71, 240-44, 298-99; 2: 164, 353-54.

34. Van den Bergh, 2: no. 265, pp. 194-97.

35. See Bruchet, 10, n. 5; the document is transcribed by him, 301-5. I am most grateful to Miss Godfrey, who reminded me of d'Aubigny's identity.

36. See Bruchet, 59.

37. See Le Glay, 1: 147. By *bailli* d'Amont is meant the officer in charge of one of the three bailliwicks of Burgundy. Besides Amont, which comprised Vesoul, Gray and Baumes-les-Nonnains, they were the bailliage de Dôle and the bailliage d'Aval, consisting of Montmorot, Salins, Pontarlier, Poligny, Arbois et Orgelet.

38. The name *Marc* derives from Le Glay, 2: 314, but there is no obvious authority for it: no Christian name is given in the document that he quotes.

39. His appointment to this office is made in a letter from Maximilian Ier to Marguerite, May 25 1509, in which Maximilian refers to him as "nostre amé et féal escuier:" see Le Glay, 1: 148.

40. *Itinéraire*, 379, and for Claude Bouton's position vis-à-vis Charles-Quint, cf. Van den Bergh, 3: nos. 277, pp. 217-20.

41. See Bruchet, 25, n. 5, and and Thibaut, 119-20.

42. *Itinéraire*, 354, and Le Glay, 2: 3, 5.

43. Ibid., 356.

44. See the document (1537) published by Bruchet, 436-37.

45. The best-documented by far of the poets; see especially Carlo Bornate, *Ricerche intorno alla vita di Mercurino Gattinara, gran cancelliere di Carlo 5* (Novara: Fratelli Miglio, 1899).

46. He was one of the delegation to the court of France (1515) sent to arrange the

marriage of Charles-Quint with Renée de France: see Théodore Juste, *Charles-Quint et Marguerite d'Autriche: Étude sur la minorité, l'émancipation et l'avènement de Charles-Quint à l'Empire*, Mémoires couronnés et autres mémoires publiés par l'Académie Royale de Belgique, 7 (Brussels: M. Hayez, 1858), 74-77. Gattinara was used constantly as a confidential emissary and adviser: one has only to consult the index to Le Glay.

47. See Thibaut, 39, and Bruchet, 46.
48. *Itinéraire*, 369
49. See Emmanuel, conte de Quinsonas, *Matériaux pour servir à l'histoire de Marguerite d'Autriche, duchesse de Savoie, régente des Pays-Bas*, 3 vols. (Paris: Delaroque Frères, 1860), 3: 152.
50. Cf. also in a letter published by Van den Bergh, *Correspondance*, 2: no. 154 (Oct. 1511), p. 355.
51. See Bruchet, 105, 383-84, 390-91.
52. Consult the indexes in Van den Bergh and Le Glay, under Nassau; Marguerite commanded him to be one of her train when she received the emperor in 1512 (see Van den Bergh, 3: no. 181, pp. 37-8), and she stood godmother to Henri's son (see ibid., 3: no. 239, p. 149). One letter thanks Marguerite for *l'affection* which she has shown in negotiating an accord with the duc de Savoie; see Van den Bergh, 2: no. 141, p. 327.
53. See Bruchet, 436-37.
54. Consult the index in Van den Bergh, under Egmond, and in Le Glay, under Isselstain.
55. Van den Bergh, 2: no. 97, p. 237.
56. Remote possibilities—and alas, not very convincing: either Charles Le Clerc (*receveur de Louvain*: see Le Glay, 2: 111), or Daniel Leclerc, Maximilian's "amé et féal secretaire," who visited Marguerite on at least one occasion on July 6, 1509 (see Le Glay, 1: 159).
57. His appointment is recorded with pleasure and thanks in a letter from Marguerite to Maximilian, Oct. 1511; see Van den Bergh, 2: no. 154, p. 357.
58. See Le Glay, 1: 480.
59. See Le Glay 1: 81-82: "vous requérons. . .que ayez ledit bastart en tous ses affaires singulièrement pour recommandé; et nous ferez chose fort agréable." (August 25, 1508)
60. *Itinéraire*, 368.
61. Ibid., 93, 94, 352
62. Ibid., 262.
63. Quinsonas, *Matériaux*, 3: 224.
64. Le Glay, 2: 113.
65. See for instance the rondeaux in Champion's edition (2: 163-64), in which Charles trades macaronic bawdy with "Fradet."
66. I address the issues I suggest here in a book, *The Poetry of François Villon: Text and Context*, Cambridge: Cambridge University Press, 2001.

67. I return here to Pierre Bourdieu: see an interesting study of his work in this light, Alena V. Ledeneva, "Language as an Instrument of Power in the Works of Pierre Bourdieu," Manchester University, Department of Sociology, Occasional Paper 41 (Manchester, 1994).
68. Richard F. Green suggests something not dissimilar for the English royal court in parts of his *Poets and Princepleasers: Literature and the English Court in the Late Middle Ages* (Toronto and London: University of Toronto Press, 1980).
69. For evidence of this, and most particularly in Northern France and in the Low Countries, see Gérard Gros, *Le Poème du Puy marial: Étude sur le serventois et le chant royal du XIVe siècle à la Renaissance* (Paris: Klincksieck, 1996), and *Le Poète, la vierge et le prince du puy: Étude sur les Puys marials de la France du Nord du XIVe siècle à la Renaissance* (Paris: Klincksieck, 1992).
70. Charles Heppleston is preparing under my direction a thesis on Machaut's *La Louange des dames*, which will develop the notion of *sequences* in interesting and sophisticated ways: he argues, convincingly, that the apparently seamless monotony of the *Louange* is actually a tissue of *sequences*, grouped thematically, prosodically, and phonetically at the service of *narrativités latentes* (on which term see Paul Zumthor, "Les Narrativités latentes dans le discours lyrique médiéval," in *The Nature of Medieval Narrative*, ed. by Minnette Grunmann-Gaudet and Robin F. Jones, French Forum Monographs, 22 (Lexington, KY, 1980), 39-55).
71. Not all the poems in the *Album* are original, even though, as here, they may be attributed to one of Marguerite's "poets": were one or two of the less adroit and creative participants at a loss, did they, despairingly, present an occasional borrowed lyric as their own? Marguerite, notably, did possess a copy of the *Jardin de Plaisance*, which was published in 1501, had gone through several editions, and circulated widely (see Debae, *La Bibliothèque*, 390). For a table of lyrics from the *Album* to be found in this and other miscellanies and anthologies, manuscript or printed, see Françon, 75-78. Analogies might be drawn between the *Album* and Bibliothèque Nationale Française, MS français 9223, as edited by Raynaud: as I shall hope to show in much more detail elsewhere, that collection opens with strings of lyrics largely deriving from other collections including Charles's, but as it progresses, more and more named poets, otherwise unknown in that capacity and presumably courtiers and friends of the manuscript's patrons, provide poems of their own.
72. I am thinking of the three MSS copied by Jean Robertet, Bibliothèque Nationale Française, MSS français 1716, 1717, 1721, of which Robertet himself says (MS 1717, f. 91v): "Ce livre, composé de toutes pieces pour donner plaisir, passetemps et recreacion à ceulx qui le liront, est à celluy qui l'a (par faulte d'autre meilleure occupacion) assemblé et redigé en ceste forme et maniere, ainsi que les oeuvres des singuliers facteurs en langage françois de son temps se sont à luy presentées pour estre enregistrées au cathalogue des excellens engins, qui pour les invencions subtilles et monumens de leur langue melliflue, ont merité user en la memoire de leur posterité jusques à present, esperant que les modernes studieux, ensuivans leurs vestiges,

n'auront leur temps en vain consummé, mais vivront semblablement par louange et recommandacion en memoire perpetuelle." See Robertet's Œuvres, ed. Margaret Zsuppán, Textes Littéraires Français (Geneva: Droz, 1970), and cf. Zsuppán, "Jean Robertet's Life and Career: A Reassessment," Bibliothèque d'Humanisme et Renaissance 31 (1969): 333-42.

73. Le Poète et le prince, 178: he refers to the way in which a concatenation of circumstances—patron, social and political parameters, presence of poets and poetasters—creates a vibrantly creative poetic circle.

WORKS CITED

Album de Marguerite d'Autriche: Brussel, Koninklijke Bibliotheek MS. 228. With an introduction by Martin Picker. Peer: Alamire, 1986.

Beaucourt, G. de. Histoire de Charles VII. 6 vols. Paris: Librairie de la Société Bibliographique A. Picard, 1881-91.

Bornate, Carlo. Ricerche intorno alla vita di Mercurino Gattinara, gran cancelliere di Carlo 5. Novara: Fratelli Miglio, 1899.

Bourdieu, Pierre. "Champ de pouvoir, champ intellectuel et habitus de classe." Scolies: Cahiers de Recherche de l'École Normale Supérieure 1 (1971): 7-26.

Bozzolo, Carla, and Hélène Loyau. La Cour amoureuse, dite de Charles VI. 2 vols. Paris: Le Léopard d'Or, 1982-92.

Bruchet, Max. Marguerite d'Autriche, duchesse de Savoie. Lille: L. Danel, 1927.

Bruchet, Max, and E. Lancien. L'Itinéraire de Marguerite d'Autriche, gouvernante des Pays-Bas. Lille: L. Danel, 1934.

Cammaert, G. "De muziek aan het hof van Margareta van Oostenrijk." Handelingen van de Kon. Kring voor Oudheidkunde, Letteren en Kunst van Mechelen 84 (1980): 76-95.

Champion, Pierre. Introduction to Poésies, by Charles d'Orléans. 2 vols., 1: xvi-xviii. Paris: H. Champion, 1923-24.

———. Le Manuscrit autographe des poésies de Charles d'Orléans. Paris: H. Champion, 1907.

———. "Remarques sur un recueil de poésies du milieu du XVe siècle (B.N. fr. 9223)." Romania 48 (1922): 106-14.

———. Vie de Charles d'Orléans, 1394-1465. Paris: H. Champion, 1911.

Charles d'Orléans. Ballades et rondeaux. Edited by Jean-Claude Mühlethaler. Lettres Gothiques. Paris: Le Livre de Poche, 1922.

———. Poésies. Edited by Pierre Champion. 2 vols. CFMA. Paris: H. Champion, 1923-24.

Debae, Marguerite. La Bibliothèque de Marguerite d'Autriche: Essai de reconstitution d'après l'inventaire de 1523-1524. Louvain and Paris: Peeters, 1995.

De Boom, G. "Documents concernant les relations d'Antoine de Ligne avec Philippe le Beau, Marguerite d'Autriche, Charles-Quint, et Henri VIII, roi d'Angleterre." *Bulletin de la Commission Royale d'Histoire* 115 (1950): 383-426.

———. *Marguerite d'Autriche-Savoie et la Pré-Renaissance*. Paris: E. Droz, 1935.

Françon, Marcel, ed. *Albums poétiques de Marguerite d'Autriche*. Cambridge, Mass.: Harvard University Press/Paris: E. Droz, 1934.

Gachet, Émile. *Albums et Œuvres poétiques de Marguerite d'Autriche, gouvernante des Pays-Bas*. Société des bibliophiles Belges, Publication 17. Brussels, 1849.

Green, Richard F. *Poets and Princepleasers: Literature and the English Court in the Late Middle Ages*. Toronto and London: University of Toronto Press, 1980.

Gros, Gérard. *Le Poème du Puy marial: Étude sur le serventois et le chant royal du XIVe siècle à la Renaissance*. Paris: Klincksieck, 1996.

———. *Le Poète, la vierge et le prince du puy: Étude sur les puys marials de la France du Nord du XIVe siècle à la Renaissance*. Paris: Klincksieck, 1992.

Heppleston, Charles. "Machaut's *La Louange des dames*." Thesis in preparation.

"Inventaire des vaisselles, joyaux, tapisseries, peintures, manuscrits, etc. de Marguerite d'Autriche, régente et gouvernante des Pays-Bas, dressé en son palais de Malines le 9 juillet 1523." *Bulletin de la Commission Royale d'Histoire*, 3d series, 12 (1871): 5-78, 83-136.

Juste, Théodore. *Charles-Quint et Marguerite d'Autriche: Étude sur la minorité, l'émancipation et l'avènement de Charles-Quint à l'Empire*. Mémoires couronnés et autres mémoires publiés par l'Académie royale de Belgique, 7. Brussels: M. Hayez, 1858.

Lalande, Denis, ed. *Le Livre des fais du bon messire Jehan le Maingre, dit Bouciquaut, mareschal de France et gouverneur de Jennes*. Geneva: Droz, 1985.

Ledeneva, Alena V. *Language as an Instrument of Power in the Works of Pierre Bourdieu*. Manchester University, Department of Sociology Occasional Paper 41. Manchester, 1994.

Le Glay, A. *Correspondance de l'empereur Maximilien Ier et de Marguerite d'Autriche, sa fille, gouvernante des Pays-Bas, de 1507 à 1519, publiée d'après les manuscrits originaux*. 2 vols. Paris: Jules Renouard, 1839.

Perkins, Leeman L. *Music in the Age of the Renaissance*. New York and London: W. W. Norton, 1999.

Picker, Martin. *The Chanson Albums of Marguerite of Austria, MSS. 228 and 11239 of the Bibliothèque Royale de Belgique, Brussels*. Berkeley and Los Angeles: University of California Press, Cambridge University Press, 1965.

———. "The Chanson Albums of Marguerite of Austria: MSS. 228 and 11239 of the Bibliothèque Royale de Belgique, Brussels." *Annales Musicologiques* 6 (1963): 145-285.

———. "A New Look at the `Little' Chansonnier of Margaret of Austria." *Muziek aan het Hof van Margaretha van Oostenrijk/Music at the Court of Marguerite of*

Austria, Jaarboek van het Vlaamse Centrum voor Oude Muziek 3 (1987): 27-31.

———. "Three Unidentified Chansons by Pierre de la Rue in the *Album de Marguerite d'Autriche*." *The Musical Quarterly* 46 (1960): 329-43.

Poirion, Daniel. *Le Poète et le prince: L'évolution du lyrisme courtois de Guillaume de Machaut à Charles d'Orléans*. Grenoble: Allier, 1965.

Quinsonas, Emmanuel, conte de. *Matériaux pour servir à l'histoire de Marguerite d'Autriche, duchesse de Savoie, régente des Pays-Bas*. 3 vols. Paris: Delaroque Frères, 1860.

Raynaud, Gaston, ed. *Rondeaux et autres poésies du XVe siècle*. Société des Anciens Textes Français. Paris: Firman Didot, 1889.

Robertet, Jean. *Œuvres*. Edited by Margaret Zsuppán. Geneva: Droz, 1970.

Taylor, Jane H. M. *The Poetry of François Villon: Text and Context*. Cambridge: Cambridge University Press, 2001.

Thibaut, Francisque. *Marguerite d'Autriche et Jean Lemaire de Belges, ou, de la littérature et des arts aux Pays-Bas sous Marguerite d'Autriche*. Paris: E. Leroux, 1888. Reprint Geneva: Slatkine, 1970.

Van den Bergh, L. *Correspondance de Marguerite d'Autriche, gouvernante des Pays-Bas*. 2 vols. Leiden: S. and J. Luchtmans, 1845.

Zsuppán, Margaret. "Jean Robertet's Life and Career: A Reassessment." *Bibliothèque d'Humanisme et Renaissance* 31 (1969): 333-42.

Zumthor, Paul. "Les Narrativités latentes dans le discours lyrique médiéval." In *The Nature of Medieval Narrative*, edited by Minnette Grunmann-Gaudet and Robin F. Jones, 39-55. French Forum Monographs, 22. Lexington, Ky., 1980.

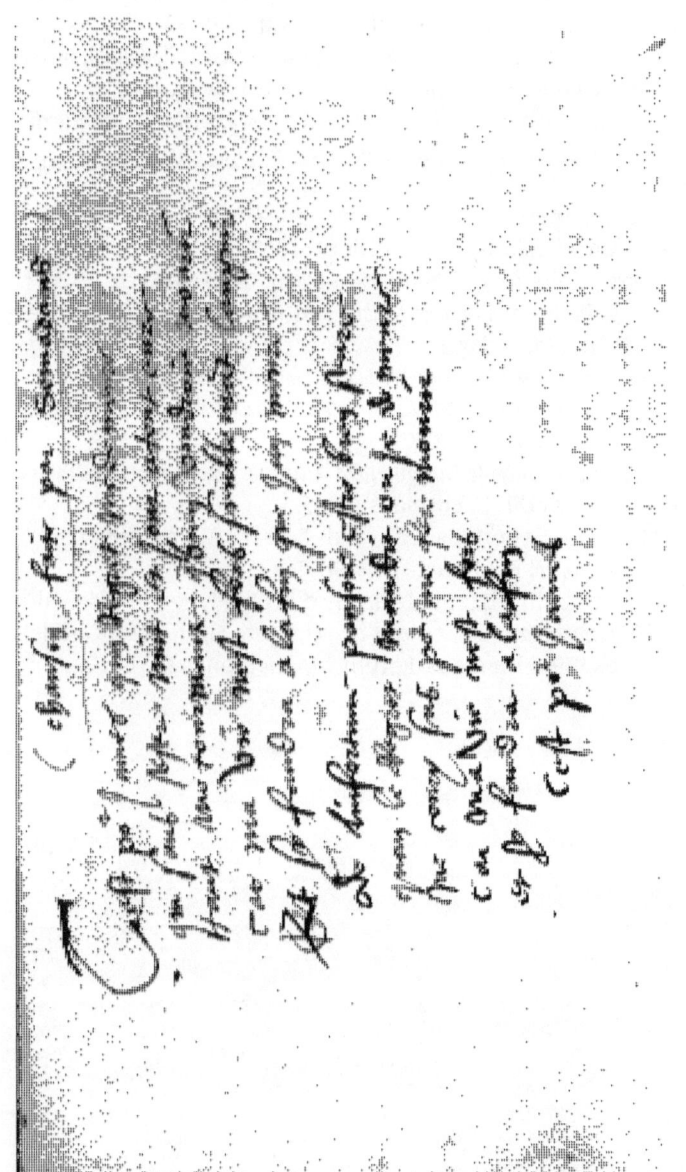

Fig. 1: Rondeau said to be written in Marguerite d'Autriche's own hand: Brussels, Bibliothèque Royale, MS 10572, f. 21v. Reproduced by kind permission of the Bibliothèque Royale.

LES ALBUMS POÉTIQUES... 171

Fig. 2: Brussels, Bibliothèque Royale, MS 228, f. 50v. Reproduced by kind permission of the Bibliothèque Royale.

Grief, Rape, and Suicide as Consolation for the Queen: Ambivalent Images of Female Rulers in the Books of Anne de Bretagne

CYNTHIA J. BROWN

Two stunning images of mourning decorate the dedication manuscript of the *Voyage de Gênes* (B.N. f.fr. 5091) offered to Queen Anne de Bretagne by the author Jean Marot about 1507.[1] The first presents a weeping female dressed in black and seated upon a throne in a room that is similarly draped in black; both her robe and the room's hangings are flecked with silver tears. Before her stand two men supporting a disconsolate woman (Fig. 1). The second image offers the reader an equally imposing scene, in which the same female mourner now lies on a bed inside a dark room draped in the same black pattern as in the previous illustration; she is surrounded by an old man and two grieving women (Fig. 2). These two miniatures initially seem out of place in a work that celebrates King Louis XII's victory over Genoa. And yet a closer examination of the miniatures and careful reading of the accompanying text confirm that the funereal drama played out in these images constitutes an allegorical staging of the defeat of the king's enemy, namely the city of Genoa herself (Gênes). The attempts of two of Genoa's sons, Marchandise (Merchant Class) and Peuple (the People), to console her are checked by Honte (Shame), thereby leading to her suicidal state. In a life-saving gesture, Raison intervenes, chasing off Rage, Douleur, and Désespoir. With her aid and enlightenment, Gênes enters the Chambre de Vraye Cognoissance (the Chamber of True Knowledge), where she finds peace, stability, and repose (Fig. 3).[2] In literal terms, Gênes ends her resistance to the foreign invader from France and succumbs to the domination of Louis XII—or, as Marot's partial interpretation would have the reader believe, Genoa, having finally come to her senses, gratefully accepts the judicious rule of the French victor. She has thus been converted to his ways. Metaphorically speaking, the nervous breakdown and near-suicide of a woman, translated visually and verbally into a scenario of grief and mourning, are transfigured into allegorical form so as to render all the more dramatic the king's triumphant expedition to Italy.

The 1,306 verses and 100 prose lines of the *Voyage de Gênes* recount in detail one of the most publicized events in the French king's reign up to that point: the revolt of Genoa against French rule in a popular uprising in 1506 and France's success in quelling the city's vigorous resistance through armed force, culminating in Louis XII's victorious entry into Genoa on April 29, 1507.[3] The majority of the eleven miniatures decorating B.N. MS 5091 depict these military skirmishes and triumphs (fols. 2v, 10v, 15v, 17v, 20v, 22v). By framing his chronicle, however, with an allegorical staging of Gênes admonishing her three children, Noblesse (Nobility), Marchandise, and Peuple, who are uncooperative in supporting her resistance to the French king (vs. 125–298), and her enlightened conversion to Raison following her defeat (ll. 39–100; vs. 861–1306), Marot embellished his eyewitness account of the king's victory over the Italian city to suit the taste of his dedicatee, Anne de Bretagne. He implies this in his prologue when he alludes to his effort to "faire chose plaisante à l'oeil, recreative à l'esperit, consolative au diuturnel travail de. . .[ma] maistresse [make something pleasing to the eye, agreeable to the mind, comforting to the daily trials of. . .my mistress]" (ll. 4–6). He declares his goal of making you forget "pour seullement par quelque bien petite espace d'heure les grandes cures et solicitudes de voz esperitz entreoublier. . .desirant par toutes voyes cercher moyens d'acomplir chose qui vous soit agréable [if only for a short time, the great cares and preoccupations of your mind. . .wishing to find the means to create something that will please you in every way possible]" (ll. 27–31). Four miniatures of this drama of personified figures present the artist's visual re-creation of Marot's allegorical narrative frame (fols. 6r, 27r, 34v, 37v).

This scenario from the *Voyage de Gênes* serves as my point of departure, because its images dramatically evoke certain ambiguities concerning the representation of late medieval women of power in French books written for and about them. Through an examination of the gender of mourning and of private and public activity, the manipulation of male and female grammatical genders, and the relationship between text and image, I propose to study the underlying sexual tensions in the depiction of females in this and one other illuminated manuscript text offered to Queen Anne de Bretagne: Fausto Andrelini's 1509 *Epistre. . .en laquelle Anne tresvertueuse royne de France, duchesse de Bretaigne, exhorte de son retour le trespuissant et invincible roy de France Loys dousiesme, son mary estant en Italie.*[4] Far from the source of delight or consolation that they are purported to be, these works served as "ideological carriers;"[5] that is, agents in the construction of the female gender that restricted women to interior spaces, mourning, and prayer.

Jean Marot's dedication of B.N. MS 5091, with its elaborately painted miniatures, to Anne de Bretagne was obviously intended to be a gesture of homage, as the opening miniature of the poet on his knees offering the book to his patroness confirms (Fig. 4). And yet despite this visual exaltation of the queen in her empowered state as a benefactor, an image corroborated by Marot's accompanying verbal self-deprecation,[6] considerable ambivalence about the role of women is transmitted by the manuscript book's author as well as its artist, Jean Bourdichon, the famous miniaturist of the *Heures d'Anne de Bretagne*.[7]

The images of Louis XII and his forces in B.N. MS 5091 are consistently spectacular and grandiose. Seated astride his horse outside the gates of Alexandria upon his departure from the city (fol. 15v), before his vast number of troops gathered on the outskirts of Genoa, as urban delegates request his clemency (fol. 20v),[8] and surrounded by his entourage as it escorts him through Genoa in his triumphant entry (Fig. 5), the French king figures at the center of military and political activity.[9] While it is not surprising that focus is placed on Anne de Bretagne's husband in a work that celebrates his "magnanime victoire [noble victory]" (l. 7), the staging of a female protagonist in countervailing images is unusual and stands in sharp contrast to the depictions of the king. This tension can be explained in historical terms by the fact that a foreign power was making his entrance into a reluctantly supportive city, but the details of the literary reconstruction of this event prove rather troubling.

Indeed, what is most visually striking throughout the queen's manuscript copy of the *Voyage de Gênes* is the conspicuous differentiation between the illustrations of the victorious battles and entries, which literally portray King Louis XII in very public spaces filled with crowds, and the miniatures depicting the allegorized tale of the domineering, then dolorous and depressed, and finally reborn figure of Gênes, all of which are located in increasingly constricted interior spaces, with a diminishing number of actors.[10] The scenes of Gênes move from semi-public council rooms, the first with windows (Fig. 6), the second without (Fig. 1), to her bedroom (Fig. 2), and finally to the private chapel presumably located next to her chambers (Fig. 3). This juxtaposition of manuscript illuminations of majestic exterior settings and of confining interior spaces ever so subtly explores the implication that the male king has successfully invaded the territory and space of the female, but this violation is made explicit in an extraordinary passage in one of Gênes's speeches in which she draws this very analogy in the most violent of terms, that of the rape of a virgin:[11]

> Ainsi vaincue, palle, blesme, adollée,
> De desespoir presque toute affollée,
> Contrainte fuz de luy ouvrir ma porte
> Et, neantmoins que jamais maculée
> N'avoyt esté, fut lors despucellée,
> Car jamais homme n'y entra de la sorte. (vs. 897–902)
>
> [Thus vanquished, pale, wan, afflicted,
> Almost completely diminished by despair,
> I was forced to open my door to him
> And, although I had never been
> Sullied, I lost my virginity then and there,
> For never had a man entered in that fashion.]

Alluding to the idea of constriction and constraint in both visual and verbal terms, and to the king's forced entry in textual terms alone, the manuscript book collocates literal imperialist tropes of the dominating French male who triumphs and allegorical renditions of the resistant female enemy who is sexually assaulted and battles depression and suicide before finding supposed consolation by capitulating to the foreign victor. The one image which can be construed as conjoining the allegorical world of the female ruler–victim with the literal space of invading male royal power is the Milan entry scene itself (Fig. 5), which presents adoring girls and admiring female spectators looking out windows along the entry route,[12] as Louis XII, clad in military attire, makes his way through the city streets.[13]

A rather shocking dimension of the manuscript book's entire staging,—at least for the postmodern reader—especially in light of the author's advertised aim of providing Anne de Bretagne with pleasant, entertaining, and comforting distraction from the daily demands of her life (ll. 4–6), is the expectation that Marot's female dedicatee will sympathize with and celebrate the violator, her husband. Such a contradiction between authorial intention and textual (and even visual) realities suggests that the *Voyage de Gênes* was really a book made by men for men—the author and artist were presumably "speaking" through the queen to the king—since the monarch's implicit comforting of the converted Gênes and the author's supposedly consoling words to Anne de Bretagne are seriously undermined by anti-feminine representations.

These underlying sexual tensions in the *Voyage de Gênes* manuscript are reinforced not only by the author's offhanded misogynistic remarks, whose conventional nature doubtless rendered them barely noticeable,[14] but also by a curious gender distortion. For Gênes's children and subjects, Noblesse, Marchandise, and Peuple, are all textually and visually depicted as males,[15] despite the fact that only one of the words used—Peuple—is of the masculine grammatical gender. Author and artist have colluded in depicting the agents of the aristocratic and bourgeois classes, Noblesse and Marchandise, as well as Peuple, in masculine and, we may suspect, more authoritative bodies. Only when they fail to stand up for her against the French king does Gênes reconfigure two of her children in feminine terms—but in derogatory fashion—as she labels her spineless sons, Marchandise and Peuple, effeminate: "O lasches cueurs, effeminez enffans [Oh cowardly hearts, effeminate children]" (v. 1008).[16]

By contrast, Gênes visually and textually retains the feminine grammatical form of her name, as she plays the role of the admonishing mother and enemy ruler. The pejoratively named Honte likewise maintains her feminine grammatical identity,[17] precipitating Gênes's depression through association with her two cowardly sons and sending her into a state of deep grief (Fig. 1). Both text and image recount how Gênes repeatedly breaks into tears and experiences fainting spells, laments her fate, and suffers fits of despair that lead her to near-suicide (vs. 182-83, 190-95; ll. 40-72; vv. 993–1001, 1058, 1068–82). As characters personified in female form in accordance with the grammatical gender of their names, Rage and Douleur too participate in this grieving (Fig. 2). The only male figure involved in this mourning process is the monstrous old man portraying Désespoir, whose association with suicide and insanity is verbally manifest, as the following terrifying description (terrifying at least for the author, who withdraws from the scene quaking in his boots) confirms:

> En ses douloureux et lamentables regrets, Genes, tout ainsi comme(e) desesperée, ne se povant plus soustenir à cause des terribles et merveilleux acces de dueil, se va jetter à l'envers sur ung lit, que Rage et Douleur luy avoyent acoustré dedens une chambre tenebreuse et obscure, tendue de tapiz noirs semez de lermes blanches. Pres de sa couche y avoit une chaire dedens laquelle estoit assiz ung viel homme ayant le regard espoventable à merveilles, la barbe longue, face et mains (et) velues, portant plus forme monstrueuse que humaine, vestu d'ung manteau en escharpe auquel estoyent despaints gens de diverses sortes, dont les ungs, ayans les bras croisez, avoyent cordeaulx autour de leurs coulz, les aultres tenoyent glaives dedens leur estomac, les aultres avoyent le chief enclin, eulx arrachans les cheveulx qui me fut, à verité dire, chose si espoventable à regarder que fremissant retir[ay] pié arriere en telle tremeur que je trembloye tout ainsi comme les fueilles font dedens les arbres. (ll. 55-71)

[With grievous and dolorous lamentations, Genoa, in complete despair, no longer able to sustain herself because of terrible and horrendous attacks of grief, threw herself across a bed, which Rage and Grief had prepared for her in a dark, gloomy chamber hung with drapes of black flecked with silver tears. Near her bed was a chair in which sat an old man with a terribly terrifying look, a long beard, and hairy face and hands, of a bearing more monstrous than human; he was clad in a tattered coat on which were depicted men of various sorts—some, with arms crossed, had cords around their necks, others had swords in their stomachs, still others had their heads inclined, and were tearing out their hair. This was in truth such a terrifying thing to witness that, shaking, I withdrew in such fear that I quaked like the leaves on a tree.]

Corroborating Paul Binski's assessment of lamentation in medieval art, namely that "gestures of despair" were considered to be female attributes[18] and that the "codification of grief" was usually "the special preserve of women" (51), one of the implicit ideological codes of this manuscript book is that mourning and depression are more appropriately associated with females.[19] On the surface at least, grieving assumes a negative valence in this particular work. whose aim is to justify and celebrate the French king's victorious assault on and entry into Genoa. Moreover, whereas it was men who had played the role of mourners in the historically anchored versions of Louis' entry into Genoa,[20] Jean Marot recasts this episode in almost exclusively feminine terms in his allegorical re-creation of the moment. With the exception of Désespoir, those forces resisting submission to French direction and guidance—Gênes, Honte, Rage, and Douleur—are depicted as female, whereas male enemy forces, Gênes's children, demonstrate less offensive behavior vis-à-vis the French, either by actually cooperating with the foreign ruler, such as Noblesse, who betraying his mother and brothers, was in fact an ally of the foreign ruler from the start (vs. 51–72, 133–64), or Marchandise and Peuple, who easily surrender to him (vs. 1017; 1928–37). Not only are gender lines readily crossed by collaborating author and artist for political expediency, but female figures in the Voyage de Gênes have essentially no redeeming value—until Raison makes her brief appearance at the end.

The final pose of Gênes on her knees before Raison in MS 5091 (Fig. 3), marking an end to her lamentations, is a resplendent miniature that contrasts with the two previous very somber scenes of "ceste hideuse et tenebreuse place [that dark, hideous place]" (l. 96). Moreover, it offers a spiritual dimension that is all but absent from Marot's text, for Raison visually resembles the Virgin Mary.[21] Attenuating the explicit violence of the textual metaphor of rape invoked earlier, this miniature, following Marot's allegorical protocol, situates the female protagonist in a less offensive and in fact quite familiar, controlled, and more acceptable posture, that of a woman praying alone within a private chapel. With the taming of Gênes as she progresses from her domineering position as an enthroned woman (Figs. 1 and 6) to one in mourning (Fig. 2) and then in enlightened prayer (Fig. 3)—a deceptive, but doubtless more palatable visual metaphor for her sexual and political submission to a male ruler—the *Voyage de Gênes* elucidates, consciously or unconsciously, late-medieval codes concerning the appropriate portrayal of (noble) women. In fact, the representation of Gênes ends up being all the more ambiguous, since the reader is uncertain whether she should actually sympathize with the female enemy figure during her psychological journey from ruler to ruled.[22] For in addition to the metaphor of rape,—a problematic image to promote in a work offered to the French queen—the literary construction of Gênes as a mourner inevitably recalls her allegorical ancestors such as France in Alain Chartier's *Quadrilogue invectif* (1422) or Dame Chrestienté in André de la Vigne's *Ressource de la Chrestienté* (1494), of which a magnificently illustrated copy figured in Anne's library (B.N. f.fr. MS 1687).[23] The grieving of Chartier's France and of La Vigne's Dame Chrestienté, who in a state of dishevelment and near-madness bemoan the divisive nature of their children's actions, was clearly designed to elicit audience sympathy. With such intertextual references in mind, Anne de Bretagne's loyalty to her husband and support of his violation of a woman must have been sorely tested—at least in literary terms—with this partially sympathetic portrayal of his female victim in the *Voyage de Gênes*.

Indeed, the similarity between the spaces inhabited by both Gênes and Anne de Bretagne in this and subsequent manuscript miniatures inextricably associates these two female figures with each other more than it does the queen with the king, whose alliance is the more expected one. Like Gênes, the queen appears in a semi-public interior space (Fig. 4), one seemingly more appropriate to women in B.N. MS 5091. Although Anne de Bretagne is textually revered and visually displayed in a position of power in this miniature, as she, like innumerable patrons of this period, receives the dedicated book from the author, she is nevertheless a rather passive agent here. One senses that the French queen too is being "kept in her place," all the more so since the position of her seat at floor level contrasts visually with that of Gênes whose throne is raised above her subjects in her initial presentation (Fig. 6), but who essentially "pays the price" in the end by being dethroned.[24] Anne's lower seated position in this and dedication miniatures associated with other works she was offered[25] thus distinguishes her from the "ruler image"[26] visually associated with Gênes in the *Voyage de Gênes* manuscript and with the queen's husband in an illuminated manuscript in which they share visual prominence.[27] B.N. MS 5091's promotion of the idea that enthroned women in action, like Gênes, end up being cast in less domineering, more interiorized roles as women grieving or submitting to a higher authority is all but confirmed verbally, for it is the French monarch's "ruler image" that replaces that of Gênes, who exclaims: "Et luy estant en siege magnifique/Me prononça nouvelles loix et drois [And from his magnificent seat/He pronounced new laws and decrees]" (vs. 917–18).[28]

The B.N. 5091 manuscript of the *Voyage de Gênes*, then, although written and decorated with the goal of pleasing and even comforting the French queen, offers a rather contradictory image of the very female to whom the work was dedicated. Superficially speaking, the image of Anne de Bretagne in Marot's dedication manuscript interfaces nicely with the glorified portrait of French royalty commonly celebrated by male writers and artists in historical and cultural documents of the period. But at a more subtle level, this miniature contests the very celebration of royal women through Anne's implicit affiliation with the female anti-protagonist. This and other examples of the potential conflict that surfaced in male-authored, male-illustrated works for and about noble females point to a deep-seated ambivalence concerning the representation of women of power in late medieval Europe,[29] corroborating Caviness's suggestion that images of women bookowners in earlier centuries were sometimes made "against" rather than "for" them (106).

Not only is there an unexpected, and perhaps unconscious, association between Gênes and Anne de Bretagne in Marot's dedication manuscript of the *Voyage de Gênes*, but other portrayals of Anne, most of which appear in the very books that figured in her library, echo the visual and verbal depictions of Gênes in grief and in prayer in enclosed spaces that punctuate B.N. MS 5091. The image of Gênes in bed mourning (Fig. 2), for example, could easily have illustrated Anne de Bretagne's own distress over the death of her child Charles-Orland in December 1495. Philippe de Commynes' description of this moment contrasts with the repeated verbal image of her husband, King Charles VIII, whose more "rational" form of mourning was quite limited:

> Ledit seigneur en eut deuil, comme la raison le veut, mais peu luy dura le deuil; et la royne de France, duchesse de Bretagne, appellée Anne, en mena le plus grand deuil qu'il est possible que femme pust faire, et longuement luy dura ce deuil: et croy que, outre le deuil naturel que les mères ont accoutumé d'avoir de la perte de leurs enfans, que le coeur luy jugeoit quelque grand dommage à venir; mais au roy son mary dura peu ce deuil, comme dit est, et la voulut réconforter de faire dancer devant elle.[30]

> [The lord grieved, as reason would have it, but his grief lasted a short time; and the queen of France, the duchess of Brittany,

named Anne, experienced the greatest grief that is possible for a woman to have, and her grief lasted a long time. And I believe that, beyond the natural grief that mothers usually display at the loss of their children, her heart condemned her to some great future loss. But the king's grief lasted a short time, as has been said, and he attempted to comfort her by having dancers brought before her.]

Charles' seemingly inappropriate attempts to comfort his wife[31] remind us of Jean Marot's ambiguous efforts to console Anne de Bretagne by dedicating to her his *Voyage de Gênes*, a work filled with images of lamentation, rape, and suicide. Accounts of the queen's reaction in 1498 to Charles VIII's death point to an equally emotional display of grief, making reference to her death wish, a common *topos* in lamentation descriptions:

> . . .dans les moments qui suivent le décès du mari, les chroniqueurs nous la présentent effondrée, prostrée pendant vingt-quatre heures dans un coin de sa chambre, dans la pénombre, refusant toute nourriture, se tordant les mains, "ne respondant autre chose à ceux qui parloient à elle, sinon qu'elle avoit résolu de suivre le chemin de son mary." "La royne continue toujours en son deuil, et l'on ne peut l'appaiser," écrit le 11 avril le seigneur du Bouchage.[32]

> [. . .in the moments following her husband's death the chroniclers present her collapsed, prostrate for twenty-four hours in a corner of her room, in the dark, refusing all food, wringing her hands, "responding to those speaking to her only by saying that she would follow the path of her husband." "The queen continues always in her grief, and she cannot be appeased," writes the lord of Bouchage on the 11th of April.]

Another dedication miniature offers a similarly ambivalent message when placed in the context of the volume in which it figures. Some four years before Marot's reverent submission of his *Voyage de Gênes* to Anne was illuminated in the opening illustration of B.N. MS 5091, Antoine Dufour's humble offering of his *Vies des femmes célèbres* to the queen was visually recorded.[33] Again, despite the ceremonial manifestation of submission of author to patron in terms of visual rhetoric, a condescending and superior attitude on the part of the male writer vis-à-vis his female patron repeatedly surfaces in the text of this dedication copy of the volume. Dufour's conflicting position as literary servant and moral instructor of the queen, as a Church representative writing about famous women, explains his numerous misogynistic slips throughout the work, whose conservatism is often visually promoted in miniatures by Jean Pichore.[34] The similarly ambiguous message in the *Voyage de Gênes*, transmitted consciously or unconsciously through the words and images of collaborating male artists, is even more provocative, given the text's explicit sexual metaphor that authorizes and celebrates the ravishment and appropriation of a female (space) by a male.

Although lacking a dedication miniature, Anne de Bretagne's manuscript of the fictional *Épîtres en vers françois* supposedly exchanged between the queen and Louis XII about 1509 provides strikingly similar dynamics to those found in the B.N. MS 5091 copy of the *Voyage de Gênes* manuscript. In the first work of this collection, *Epistre. . .en laquelle Anne tresvertueuse royne de France, duchesse de Bretaigne, exhorte de son retour le trespuissant et invincible roy de France Loys dousiesme, son mary estant en Italie*,[35] author (Fausto Andrelini), translator (Macé de Villebrême), and artist (Jean Bourdichon)[36] figure the French queen in a first-person voice as a woman mourning. Just like Gênes, Anne de Bretagne in the miniature associated with this work is dressed in black mourning clothes and located within the enclosed space of her bedchamber surrounded by women trying to console her.[37] Complementing the queen's visual portrayal are her verbal lamentations about her absent husband, whose departure for a military campaign in Italy has left her alone in France. Whereas the personified enemy had taken center stage as female griever in the *Voyage de Gênes*, it is the male-created voice of the historic figure of the queen who acts as female mourner in this *Epistre*, an association that reinforces the earlier alliance between both protagonists. As in Marot's account, masculine triumph is coupled with female grief in the opening verses, whose third-person introductory voice underscores the fictive nature of the queen's:

> La chere espouse ayant le cueur marry
> Pour le destour de son loyal mary,
> Joyeuse aussi pource que conquerir
> Va ses pars et triumphe acquerir,   4
> En contemplant neantmoingtz l'advanture
> De guerre extresme et doubteuse rupture
> Aussi qu'il est en estrangere voye,
> Ce triste escript luy transmet et envoye;   8
> Pource que tant une loyalle amante
> Penser doubteux fort opprime et tourmente,
> Quant en grief dueil de tristesse saisie
> De plaisirs deubz est toute dessaisie...   12 (fol. 2r)

[The cherished wife with heart saddened
Over her faithful husband's delay,
Joyous too because he sets out

> To conquer and gain victory,
> Concerned nonetheless by the prospect
> Of extreme war and fearful separation
> While he is abroad,
> Transmits and sends to him this sad letter;
> For fearful thoughts so strongly oppress
> And tourment this loyal lover,
> When in grievous mourning (she is) gripped by sadness
> And completely deprived of expected pleasures.]

The dramatic dissociation between male and female activity is rendered explicit in this passage through the juxtaposition of the king's victorious stance on the one hand (vs. 3–7) and Anne's mourning on the other (vs. 1, 8, 10–11). Although Anne's reaction here is not as excessive as the grief she displayed over the loss of her child or former husband, it is nonetheless remarkable not only that both author and artist have constructed her sadness upon the extended absence of her husband in terms of mourning, but also that the text repeatedly invokes these moments of "douleur tant melencolieuse [such grievous melancholy]" (fol. 5r), punctuating them with the conventional stance of a woman praying on bended knee before Notre Dame at the end of the E*pistre*, and thereby echoing once again Gênes's own psychological trajectory.[38] It is as if this extreme rhetorical and pictorial discourse was the only one authors and artists knew how to deploy in depicting female emotion. Even though the verse account of the E*pistre* actually places the queen's grief in the past tense, Anne's fictional voice reveals the news of her husband's Venetian victory in the final lines. Nonetheless, Bourdichon chose to depict the French queen in this past state of mourning rather than in a less grieving, optimistic posture that looked forward to Louis's return.

The significant differentiation between the marital status of Anne de Bretagne and Gênes allows the author of this E*pistre* to promote another conventionally limiting image of the female. Whereas the missing husband and father figure in the *Voyage de Gênes* reinforces the already precarious position of Gênes, behaving like an independent-minded single mother until submitting to the rule of the victorious foreign invader, who perhaps embodies an *ersatz* husband or father figure, Anne de Bretagne's ultimately different focus on her absent husband in the E*pistre* sets the stage for a network of references to the loyal wife. Allusions to Penelope (fol. 2r), the exemplum *par excellence* of marital fidelity, immediately shape and control the verbal and visual representation of Anne de Bretagne as mourner, but the queen's textual association with other past examples of faithful wives is carried even further as the author invokes analogies of female sacrifice, such as the self-imposed deaths of Iphias (the wife of Capaneus, one of the seven against Thebes, often called Evadne) and Portia, to render all the more dramatic the queen's thoughts of suicide, should her husband die in battle:

> Car si par sort de Fortune enragee
> Sa vie a mort la ce treuve changee,
> Par mort aussi bien tost je l'ensuyvray
> Si que long jours aprés luy ne vivray
> Comme Yphias quant elle vit ainsi
> Le sien mary par dure mort transi,
> En feu ardant pour son dueil terminer
> Elle se mist et sa vie finer.
> Porcye aussi sera de moy suivye,
> Qui pour Brutus voulut perdre la vie
> En retenant tous chaultz entre ses dens
> Force charbons enflammez et ardens....(fol. 5v)

> [For if by the fate of enraged Fortune
> His life is changed into death,
> By death I will follow him immediately,
> Such that I will not live long after him,
> Like Iphias, when she too saw
> Her husband changed by cruel death:
> Into the raging fire she threw herself
> To end her grief and terminate her life.
> Portia too will be followed by me,
> She who sought to end her life, on account of Brutus,
> By holding between her teeth
> Many extremely hot coals that were flaming and afire.]

The disturbing suggestion that female suicide was almost the natural extension of a woman's devotion and loyalty to her husband—and an implicitly admirable one at that—marks not only this work but pervades much late medieval, male-generated literature as well, more often than not through the examples of Lucretia or Dido. While Andrelini somewhat surprisingly puts suicidal ideas in the head of a Catholic queen in the E*pistre*, creating a close analogy between her and the two examples of devoted wives, and reinforcing the earlier association between Anne and Gênes,[39] Dufour in the V*ies des femmes célèbres*, although endorsing women's extreme loyalty toward their husbands during their lives and following their deaths, repeatedly reminds his dedicatee of the objectionable nature of suicide.[40] Curiously, if the reason that the artist of the V*ies des Femmes célèbres* manuscript depicted the scene leading to Lucretia's rape (fol. 31r) instead of her suicide was to avoid any Christian impropriety,[41] it is nonetheless an ambiguous gesture that places focus on the violation of a woman in a book offered to the queen.

What can we conclude about the relationship between Anne de Bretagne, her book and her bookmakers? At the very least, it was a tenuous and ambivalent one. The French queen's sociopolitical status presumably endowed her with exclusive power over the men who authored and illustrated the books dedicated to her. And yet Anne's bookmakers served, consciously or not, as ideological agents in the continued restriction of women's actions and powers. For it is not only that the male-endorsed associations between women and rape, suicide, and grief were so pervasive in the volumes examined here, but also that these images were repeatedly and even offensively presented as positive examples of female behavior. To complicate matters, these rhetorical and literary systems that essentially sought to control female comportment, which was more often than not contrasted with that of men, were translated through stunning miniatures whose beauty endorsed that message in resounding fashion. At once a superficially praiseworthy representation of female royalty and an insidious sanctioning of established cultural codes that kept women in their place, the verbal and pictorial discourse studied here made of Anne de Bretagne, in the final analysis, a victim as much as an honored recipient of the very books that were created in her name.

University of California, Santa Barbara

NOTES

1. The editor of the *Voyage de Gênes*, Giovanna Trisolini (Geneva: Droz, 1974), claims the work dates from 1507 (59). All references are taken from her edition. François Avril and Nicole Reynaud, *Les Manuscrits à peintures en France, 1440–1520* (Paris: Flammarion, 1995), date the work "vers 1508" (303).

2. This scene recalls the more complicated allegorical staging in Alain Chartier's *Traité de l'Espérance* (an unfinished work begun in 1428) in which Foy, Espérance, and Charité save the *acteur* from the depressive effects of Melencolie, Defiance, Indignation, and Désespérance.

3. For historical details, see John S. C. Bridge, *Reign of Louis XII 1498-1507*, vol. 3 of *A History of France from the Death of Louis XI* (Oxford: Oxford University Press, 1929), 252-94; Bernard Quilliet, *Louis XII* (Paris: Fayard, 1986), 377–83; and Frederic J. Baumgartner, *Louis XII* (New York: St. Martin's, 1994), 183–97. For a discussion of the cultural and artistic context of this event, see Robert W. Scheller, "Gallia Cisalpina: Louis XII and Italy, 1499–1508," *Simiolus* 15, no. 1 (1985): 37–42. For a discussion of the *Voyage de Gênes*, see Trisolini, Introduction, 25–33; Michael Sherman, "The Selling of Louis XII: Propaganda and Popular Culture in Renaissance France, 1498–1515"

(Ph.D. diss., University of Chicago, 1974), 120–25; and Cynthia J. Brown, *The Shaping of History and Poetry in Late Medieval France: Propaganda and Artistic Expression in the Works of the Rhétoriqueurs* (Birmingham: Summa, 1985), 47-51.

4. In Anne de Bretagne's manuscript of the fictional *Épîtres en vers françois* (St. Petersburg, State M. E. Saltykov-Shchedrin Public Library, MS Fr. F. v. XIV. 8), fols. 1r–9v. Andrelini's work, originally composed by the author in Latin, was translated into French by Macé de Villebrême, presumably for inclusion in the manuscript anthology of letters for the king and queen.

5. I borrow this term from Madeline H. Caviness, "Anchoress, Abbess, and Queen: Donors and Patrons or Intercessors and Matrons?" in *The Cultural Patronage of Medieval Women*, ed. June Hall McCash (Athens: University of Georgia Press, 1996), 142, who discusses female owners of books of piety in the 11th to the 14th centuries.

6. For example, Marot states (ll. 31–38): ". . .toutesfoys indigne et incapable de ce faire, je Jehan Des Marestz, vostre povre escripvain, serviteur treshumble des vostres treshumbles et tresobeyssans serviteurs, vous presente ce mien petit ouvrage à vous et non aultre voue et desdie, vous suppliant tant et si treshumblement comme faire le puys que à gré plaise, à l'humanité de vostre grace, ainsi que avez de l'heure de voz premieres intelligences jusques à ce jour continuellement fait, le recepvoir [in any case unworthy and incapable of doing this, I, Jean Marot, your poor writer, very humble servant of all your very humble and obedient servants, present and dedicate to you and none other this little work of mine, requesting you as humbly as I might that it please you and the humanity of your grace as you have continually done from the hour your were born to this day, to receive it]."

7. Although C. Coudrec, "Les Miniatures du *Voyage de Gênes* de Jean Marot," in *Les Trésors des bibliothèques de France* (Paris:Van Oest, 1927), 46–47; Scheller, "Gallia Cisalpina," 37; Trisolini, Introduction, 58–59, and others were more tentative about this attribution, François Avril, *La Passion des manuscrits enluminés: Bibliophiles français 1280–1580* (Paris: Bibliothèque Nationale, 1991), 104, clearly names Jean Bourdichon as the artist of these miniatures.

8. For black-and-white reproductions of these two scenes, see Coudrec, "Les Miniatures," Plates V and VII. See Avril and Reynaud, *Les Manuscrits à peintures*, Plate 167 (p. 304) for a color reproduction of fol. 15v.

9. This supports Luisa Giordano's claims about Louis XII's entries into Milanese territory about this time: "Toutes les entrées en Milanais eurent pour but de faire remarquer de façon éclatante qui était, désormais, le nouveau seigneur du domaine, et de lui signifier l'hommage et la fidélité de son peuple. Il s'agissait d'un grand rituel qui était une mise en évidence de l'état politique du moment et qui se faisait dans l'intérêt du roi comme des villes dominées [All the entries into the duchy of Milan had as a goal to make everyone notice in dazzling fashion who was henceforth the new lord of the domain and to offer him the homage and loyalty of his people. It was a question of a great ritual which was a staging of the political state of the moment and which was done in the interests of the king and of the conquered

cities.]" ("Les Entrées de Louis XII en Milanais," in *Passer les Monts: Français en Italie—l'Italie en France, 1494-1525*, ed. Jean Balsamo, Acts of Xe Colloque de la Société française d'étude du seizième siècle (Paris: Champion, 1998), 141–42. See also pages 144–48 for a discussion of the entry into Genoa. Quilliet, *Louis XII*, 381, goes further and states: "Si toutes ces scènes de grandeur et de majesté se ressemblent plus ou moins, il faut insister un peu plus sur celle-ci qui fut considérée par tous les témoins comme un des sommets du règne. . .|If all these scenes of grandeur and majesty more or less resembled each other, we must emphasize a little more that this particular entry was considered by all of the witnesses one of the highlights of (Louis XII's) reign]".

10. In *Images of Rape: The "Heroic" Tradition and Its Alternatives* (Cambridge: Cambridge University Press, 1999), 185–86, Diane Wolfthal confirms the existence of this paradigm in her discussion of the fact that women are generally associated with private, interior spaces in medieval art and literature, while men are associated with public, exterior spaces: ". . .both texts and images make clear that 'proper' women were to be enclosed in a private space" (186).

11. See Wolfthal, *Images of Rape*, 60–89, for an excellent discussion of images of rape in the context of war during the Middle Ages; such images, while usually sympathetic to the victim and critical of the assailant, could be quite ambivalent, since such sexual violation by soldiers was often considered legitimate. Wolfthal points out that women surviving rape were often expected to undergo a process similar to mourning (182), and that medieval images tended to offer a bleak aftermath to rape involving shame, suicide, and death (184), a particularly relevant observation for our analysis of Gênes in Marot's *Voyage de Gênes*. Note also the author's exploitation of the familiar metaphor of the "open door" for the "open body" of the woman.

12. See Scheller, "Gallia Cisalpino," 37, who interprets the presence of women in this way: ". . .the ladies of Genoa were expressly asked to show themselves at the windows lining the route, which was a useful ploy if one wanted to mollify a wrathful monarch. . . .the 'pentential choir' recalled the children who had greeted Cardinal d'Amboise at Milan in 1500. At Genoa it was girls and young women who, kneeling and waving olive branches, loudly cried out 'misericordia,' begging the king for compassion and forbearance."

13. See Jean d'Auton, *Chroniques de Louis XII* (Paris: Renouard, 1895), 4: 232, for a description of the armed monarch and his entourage. For a discussion of Louis in battle attire, see Giordano, "Les Entrées,"144–45. Scheller, "Gallia Cisalpina," 7–37, and Giordano, 139–46, offer details about the ceremonial nature of Louis XII's various entries into Italian cities during the first decade of the sixteenth century. Up until the entry into Genoa in 1507, Louis XII, like his predecessor Charles VIII during his campaign through Italy in 1494–95 to acquire the kingdom of Naples, had been willingly and cordially received at the time of his entries into Italian cities (Milan, 1499; Genoa, 1502), which had sought, for the most part, to ally themselves with the French monarch. But the Genoa entry of 1507 marked a change in this tradition, for

GRIEF, RAPE, AND SUICIDE AS CONSOLATION... 187

Louis entered as conqueror, as a martial albeit clement ruler entering a repentant city at the head of his army. This dynamic was symbolized by his armor and by the fact that, as Marot describes it, one of the French king's men followed the king carrying an unsheathed sword:

> Estant en armes, ainsi que conquereur,
> Avec partie de ses gens et puissance
> Entra à Genes en moult belle ordonnance...
> Jusqu'au palais soubz poille d'or exquiz,
> Que les quatre de la ville porterent,
> La teste nue ainsi que gens conquiz,
> Il fut conduyt. . . .
> Apres le poille fut monsieur le grant Maistre,
> Qui pour le roy en demonstrant victoire
> Portoit l'espée toute nue en main dextre,
> Faisant congnoistre à tous qu'il povoit mettre
> A feu et sang leur ville et possessoire.   (vs. 720–50)

> [Bearing arms, like a conqueror,
> With a party of his men and power
> He entered Genoa in a very beautiful formation...
> Up to the palace, under the canopy of exquisite gold
> That the four [representatives] of the city, with the bare heads
> Of conquered men, carried,
> He was led...
> Behind the canopy was the grand Master,
> Who carried for the king, as a sign of victory,
> His naked sword in his right hand,
> Signaling to all that he could reduce
> Their city and possessions to fire and blood.]

Jean d'Auton, *Chroniques*, 4:235, offers a similar account of Charles d'Amboise entering the city behind the king with unsheathed sword "comme capitaine, dompteur et vaincueur desdits Gennevoys, soubz la main du Roy [as captain, master, and conqueror of the people of Genoa, under the king's control]." According to an anonymous account, *La Conqueste de Gennes*, it was Louis XII himself who, having struck the city gates symbolically with his sword before passing through, held "his naked sword in his hand as a sign of victory," signaling both his entry as a conqueror rather than an invited guest and his intention of humiliating the Genoese (cited by Bonner Mitchell, *The Majesty of the State: Triumphal Progresses of Foreign Sovereigns in Renaissance Italy, 1494–1600* ([Florence: Olschki, 1986], 91). Quilliet, *Louis XII*, 382, quoting Jean d'Auton, alludes to this very humiliation in his description of the entry: "Au premier plan, face au roi, leurs longs cheveux blonds dénoués dans le dos, des jeunes filles en blanc tiennent des rameaux de paix, en signe de soumission. Si les louangeurs pensionnés ont surtout vu là gloire et magnificence, le public génois, finablement, fut surtout sensible à de telles humiliations. [In the foreground, across from the king, their long blond hair hanging untied down their backs, young girls in white hold branches of peace, as a sign of their submission. While the court propagandists saw in this glory and magnificence, the people of Genoa were in the end quite sensitive about such humiliations]." Bonner, 106, offers another example of a king's entry into a city as victor, this time François Ier's entry into the conquered Milan on October 11, 1515, with a man preceding the king carrying an unsheathed sword to symbolize conquest. The fact that the French king was armed at this time was consciously tempered by his less aggressive-looking costume.

14. See, for example, Marot's description of the women of Pavia:

> Mais de descrire me plaist bien les manieres
> Des nobles dames de beaulté si tresplaines
> Que bien sembloyent deesses souveraines.
> Mais avec ce, si bonne grace avoyent,
> Tant en regars comme en gestes humaines,
> Qu'on les jugeoit secondes Magdalaines,
> Qui des hommes les cueurs mortifioyent. (vs. 806–12)

> [But it pleases me to describe the manners
> Of the noble ladies of such utter beauty
> That they appeared to be sovereign goddesses.
> But besides this, they possessed such grace,
> As much in their looks as in their gestures,
> That one considered them second Madeleines
> Who made the hearts of men suffer.

Marot refers to the women of Milan as "si belle marchandise [such lovely merchandise]" (vs. 829).

15. The narrator refers to the three sons ("fils") of Gênes (vs. 114–15).

16. By comparison, André de La Vigne conscientiously maintains grammatical gender identity in his *Ressource de la Chrestienté* of 1494 (ed. Cynthia J. Brown [Montreal: CERES, 1989]). See the discussion of Alain Chartier's *mise en question* of the feminine gender in his *Quadrilog invectif* in Cynthia J. Brown, "Allegorical Design and Image-Making in Fifteenth-Century France: Alain Chartier's Joan of Arc," *French Studies* 53, no. 4 (October 1999): 385–404.

17. Honte is described in the following way: "Honte, ayant le chef courbe et enclin, ne jettant son torve regart fors en terre, comme une beste mue, laquelle si tost que iceulx enfans vouloyent à leur chetifve et dolente mere donner consolation pour aulcunement alleger sa douleur, retenoit leurs ditz en leur mettant les mains au devant de leur bouche, et tellement fist que ne peurent parler ne dire aulcune chose consolative à son triste pleur [et] lamentacion [Shame, with head bent over and inclined, looks only at the ground with a scowling look, like a dumb beast, and as soon as these children tried to console their poor grieving mother to somehow alle-

viate her pain, held back their words by putting her hands over their mouths in such a way that they could neither speak nor offer any consolation to her sad tears and lamentation|" (ll. 46–53).

18. See his *Medieval Death: Ritual and Representation* (Ithaca: Cornell University Press, 1996), 520.

19. See also *La Complainte de Gênes sur la mort de dame Thomassine Espinolle, Genevoise, dame entendyo du roy* (B.N. f.fr. 25419), attributed to Jean d'Auton, which recounts the death of an acquaintance of Louis XII from Genoa who, believing the French king had died in 1505, herself died. The city of Genoa accorded Thomassine a grand funeral. I am grateful to Myra Orth for calling my attention to this work.

20. The kneeling black-robed male mourners, urban representatives seeking the French king's clemency, who are depicted in the visual renditions of Louis XII's recapture of Genoa (fol. 20v) and who subsequently had to carry his canopy, constitute the literal version of Gênes's allegoricized funeral portrait. Marot includes women in his description of them:

> Et pour moustrer leur extresme douleur
> Hommes et femmes de drap noir se habilloyent.
> N'aultre couleur dessus eulx ne portoyent,
> Car entr'eulx fut conclud et ordonné
> Que icelluy deul jamais ne lesseroyent
> Tant que le crime que commis il|z| avoyent
> Leur fust du roy remiz et pardonné   (vs. 696–702

> |And to show their extreme grief,
> Men and women dressed in black,
> Wearing no other color,
> Because it was decided and ordered among them
> That they would never take off these mourning clothes
> Until the crime they admitted committing
> Was pardoned by the king.|

But D'Auton does not:

> Au devant de luy. . .vindrent trente cytadins gennevoys, des plus sollempnelz de la ville,. . .|avec| leurs chiefs descouvers, et tous robes noires, habillez en dueil, les testes raises et bien pesneuz. Lorsqu'ils arriverent en la presence du Roy, ils misrent les deux genoilz en terre, cryant misericorde. . .à quoy le Roy n'entendit, mais se mist en chemin. (233–34)

> |Before him. . .came thirty citizens of Genoa, the most solemn of the city, with their heads uncovered and all wearing black mourning clothes, their heads shaven and very saddened. When they arrived in the presence of the king, they knelt down on the ground

and cried for mercy, which the king ignored, but continued on his way].

21. Marot makes no mention whatsoever of the Virgin, although Raison makes an occasional reference to God in her speech—"Ne doubte pas que c'est Dieu qui te donne/Ces haultains biens [Do not doubt that it is God who gives you/These worthy goods" (vs. 1172–73)]; "Retourne à Dieu, soyes humble desormais [Return to God, be henceforth humble" (vs. 1197)]—as does Gênes (vs. 1215–19, 1302–06).

22. This suggests that the *voyage* of the title refers not only to the one traveled by Louis XII, but also that taken by Gênes.

23. For details, see André de la Vigne, *La Ressource de la Chrestienté*, 79–81.

24. Gênes herself proclaims: "Dame, j'estoyes, maintenant suys esclave;/Du solier suys descendue en la cave;/Jadiz batiz, maintenant suys batue (vs. 1102–4) [I was a lady; now I am a slave;/I have been kicked from solar to dungeon;/Once built up, I am now torn down]". See also vs. 959–61.

25. See, for example, the dedication miniature (fol. 1r) that introduces the manuscript copy of *Les Vies des femmes célèbres*, offered by Antoine Dufour to Anne de Bretagne, who had commissioned the work, about 1504. This dedication manuscript is currently housed in Nantes at the Musée Dobrée as MS XVII. For a reproduction of this particular illumination, see the frontispiece of G. Jeanneau's edition of the work (Geneva: Droz, 1970). For other similar examples of dedication scenes in which the queen's seat is at floor level, see the dedication miniature introducing the *Epistre de Saint Jhérôme* translated into French by Antoine Dufour (St. Petersburg, State M. E. Saltykov-Shchedrin Public Library, MS Fr. F. v. I. 3, fol. 1r) and the miniature introducing the *Epistre composee. . .par. . .Fauste Andrelin en laquelle Anne tresvertueuse Royne de France est courroucee que le trespuissant et invincible Roy Loys douziesme, son mary, soit de rechief contraingct guerre mouvoir contre les desloyaulx et rebelles Veniciens* (St. Petersburg, State M. E. Saltykov-Shchedrin Public Library, MS Fr. F. v. XIV. 8, fol. 40v), both of which are reproduced as Plates LVIII and LX respectively in A. de Laborde, *Les Principaux Manuscrits à peintures conservés dans l'ancienne Bibliothèque Impériale Publique de Saint-Pétersbourg* (Paris: Société Française de Reproductions de Manuscrits à Peintures, 1938). See also Tamara Voronova and Alexander Sterligov, *Western European Illuminated Manuscripts of the 8th to the 16th Centuries in the National Library of Russia, St. Petersburg* (Bournemouth: Parkstone Press, 1996), Figure 248.

26. John Lowden adopts this term in "The Royal/Imperial Book and the Image or Self-Image of the Medieval Ruler," in *Kings and Kingship in Medieval Europe*, ed. Anne J. Duggan (London: King's College, 1993), 215.

27. See Jean Lemaire's *L'epistre du Roy. . .a Hector*, St. Petersburg, State M. E. Saltykov-Shchedrin Public Library, MS Fr. F. v. XIV. 8, fol. 81v. For a reproduction of this scene of Louis XII seated on a raised throne, see Laborde, *Principaux Manuscrits*, Plate LXI, and Voronova and Sterligov, *Western European Illuminated Manuscripts*, Figure 205. Compare with the scene of Anne de Bretagne on fol 1v.

28. Mitchell, *The Majesty of the State*, 92, adds the following details about the French

king's entry into Genoa in 1507: "Louis, who seems to have had a keen sense of the dramatic and of the power of public spectacle, decided to hold a *siège royal*, or royal court of justice, in public view. A large platform was erected in the courtyard of the doges' palace, and on top of that construction a smaller platform was built to hold a throne. Both were draped with a rich cloth that was woven with fleurs-de-lys, and there was a *baldacchino* over the throne. . . . When Louis had taken his place, a *roy d'armes*, or master of ceremonies, cried 'De par le roy!'. . .to impose silence."

29. For a discussion of other manifestations of this ambivalence, see Cynthia J. Brown's "Textual and Iconographical Ambivalence in the Late Medieval Representation of Women," *Bulletin of the John Rylands University Library of Manchester* 81, no. 3 (Autumn 1999): 205–39, and "The 'Famous Women' *Topos* in Early Sixteenth-Century France: Echoes of Christine de Pizan," in *Mélanges Eric Hicks*, ed. Jean-Claude Mühlethaler et Denis Billotte (forthcoming).

30. Commynes, *Mémoires*, in *Historiens et chroniqueurs du Moyen Âge*, ed. A. Pauphilet (Paris: Gallimard, 1952), 1418–19. Leslie Abend Callahan offers a different interpretation in her "Signs of Sorrow: The Expression of Grief and the Representation of Mourning in Fifteenth-Century French Culture," PhD. diss., The City University of New York, 1996, 202-3.

31. Georges Minois, *Anne de Bretagne* (Paris: Fayard, 1999), 363, claims that doctors also encouraged this form of "traitement 'psychothérapique' pour chasser la mélancolie [psychotherapeutic treatment to drive out the melancholy]" of the queen. See *ibid.*, 374, for details of Anne's grief over the loss of five infants by the age of 21.

32. *Ibid.*, 377. Minois's strong reaction to Anne's apparent change of mood just two days after the king's death, which seemingly contradicts the lord of Bouchage's written account, is tinged with a misogynistic tone:

> Mais ce qui est surprenant, c'est que dès le lendemain, 9 avril, cette femme brisée, qui se disait prête à mourir, affirme sans faille son autorité de duchesse de Bretagne. Retrouvant brusquement son énergie, elle. . .affirme la plénitude de son pouvoir. . . . Sans aller jusqu'à parler de simulation, il faut sans doute attribuer ses marques excessives de chagrin à l'imitation des modes espagnoles qu'elle apprécie tant. Car une telle présence d'esprit, une telle activité et une telle clairvoyance sont peu compatibles avec l'état d'effondrement qu'elle affecte alors. (378–79)

> [But what is surprising is that the next day, April 9th, this broken woman, who claimed that she was near death, affirms without hesitation her authority as duchess of Brittany. Suddenly finding her energy again, she affirms. . .the plenitude of her powers. . . . Without going so far as to mention simulation, one must without doubt attribute her excessive manifestations of grief to an imitation of the Spanish manner which she so appreciates. For such a presence of mind, such activity, such clear-sightedness are hard-

ly compatible with the state of collapse she assumes at this time].

Jean Markale relates this moment in a much less judgmental way in his *Anne de Bretagne* (Paris: Hachette, 1980), 198: "On a dit qu'elle avait pleuré, s'était lamentée de son triste sort, veuve après avoir perdu cinq enfants. Peut-être, mais on ne sait rien...Son chagrin, si chagrin il y eut, nous ne le connaissons pas [It has been said that she cried, lamented her sad fortune, a widow after having lost five children. Perhaps, but it can't be confirmed.... Her grief, if there was grief, we cannot know.]"

33. Nantes, Musée Dobrée MS XVII, fol. 1r. See above, note 25, for details.
34. For further details, see Brown, "Textual and Iconographical Ambivalence," 219–25.
35. See above, note 4.
36. See Avril, *Passion*, 104, for attribution of the miniatures in this manuscript to Bourdichon.
37. For a reproduction of this miniature, see Avril and Reynaud, *Les Manuscrits*, Plate 168 (p. 305).
38. See her "Oraison à Nostre Dame" in this letter (fols. 5v–6r). This verbal image brings to mind the famous illumination of Anne de Bretagne from Bourdichon's *Heures d'Anne de Bretagne*.
39. See also Wolfthal, *Images of Rape*, 183.
40. Dufour suggests the following in relation to Dido (54): "Ceste hystoire me semble estre ung beau mirouer pour les chastes veufves chrétiennes. Je ne leur conseilleroye jamais de eulx tuer, mais chasteté et honnesteté à leur povoir garder [This story seems to be a good example for chaste Christian widows. I would never advise them to kill themselves, but (I would advise) chastity and honesty to protect themselves]." He comments about Lucretia in the following manner: "Saint Augustin dit que Lucresse ne fist fault sinon quant elle se tua [Saint Augustine says that Lucretia erred only in killing herself]" (66). All citations are taken from G. Jeanneau's edition of *Les Vies des femmes célèbres* (Geneva:Droz, 1970).
41. The miniature of this scene shows that Tarquin has entered Lucretia's room by a ladder through a window at the left. At the same time that his arms are holding the naked upper body of the victim in her bed, Lucretia makes a gesture with her right arm for him to stop. For a discussion of medieval images of Lucretia's rape and suicide, see Wolfthal, *Images of Rape*, 75–89. It is true that, by contrast, Dido's expression of marital fidelity through suicide by stabbing and subsequent self-immolation is graphically translated in the miniature that accompanies her biography in the *Vies des femmes célèbres* (fol. 25r).

WORKS CITED

MANUSCRIPTS

Andrelini, Fausto. *Epistre composee...par...Fauste Andrelin en laquelle Anne tresvertueuse Royne de France est courroucee que le trespuissant et invincible Roy Loys douziesme, son mary, soit de rechief contraingct guerre mouvoir contre les desloyaulx et rebelles Veniciens.* St. Petersburg, State M. E. Saltykov-Shchedrin Public Library, MS FR.F. v.XIV. 8, fols. 39v-50v.

———. *Epistre...en laquelle Anne tresvertueuse royne de France, duchesse de Bretaigne, exhorte de son retour le trespuissant et invincible roy de France Loys dousiesme, son mary estant en Italie.* St. Petersburg, State M. E. Saltykov-Shchedrin Public Library, MS FR.F. v.XIV. 8, fols. 1r-9v.

Auton, Jean d' (attributed). *La Complainte de Gênes sur la mort de dame Thomassine Espinolle Genevoise, dame entendyo du roy.* Paris, B.N. f.fr. 25419.

Dufour, Antoine. *Epistre de Saint Jhérôme.* St. Petersburg, State M. E. Saltykov-Shchedrin Public Library, MS Fr.F. v. I. 3, fols. 1r-63v.

———. *Les Vies des femmes celebres.* Nantes, Musée Dobrée, MS XVII.

Lemaire de Belges, Jean. *Epistre du Roy...a Hector.* St. Petersburg, State M. E. Saltykov-Shchedrin Public Library, MS FR.F. v.XIV. 8, fols. 82r-95v.

Marot, Jean. *Le Voyage de Gênes.* Paris, B.N. f.fr. 5091.

BOOKS

Auton, Jean d'. *Chroniques de Louis XII.* Edited by R. de Maulde La Clavière. Vol. 4. Paris: Renouard, 1895.

Avril, François. *La Passion des manuscrits enluminés: Bibliophiles français, 1280–1580.* Paris: Bibliothèque Nationale, 1991.

———. and Nicole Reynaud. *Les Manuscrits à peintures en France, 1440–1520.* Paris: Flammarion, 1995.

Baumgartner, Frederic J. *Louis XII.* New York: St. Martin's Press, 1994.

Binski, Paul. *Medieval Death: Ritual and Representation.* Ithaca: Cornell University Press, 1996.

Bridge, John S. C. *A History of France from the Death of Louis XI.* Vol. 3, *Reign of Louis XII, 1508–1514.* Oxford: Oxford University Press, 1929.

Brown, Cynthia J. "Allegorical Design and Image-Making in Fifteenth-Century France: Alain Chartier's Joan of Arc." *French Studies* 53, no. 4 (October 1999): 385–404.

———. "The 'Famous Women' *Topos* in Early Sixteenth-Century France: Echoes of Christine de Pizan." In *Mélanges Eric Hicks,* edited by Jean-Claude Mühlethaler et Denis Billotte (forthcoming).

———. "Textual and Iconographical Ambivalence in the Late Medieval Representation of Women." *Bulletin of the John Rylands University Library of Manchester* 81, no. 3 (Autumn 1999): 205–39.

———. *The Shaping of History and Poetry in Late Medieval France: Propaganda and Artistic Expression in the Works of the Rhétoriqueurs*. Birmingham: Summa, 1985.

Callahan, Leslie Abend. "Signs of Sorrow: The Expression of Grief and the Representation of Mourning in Fifteenth-Century French Culture." Ph.D. diss., The City University of New York, 1996.

Caviness, Madeline H. "Anchoress, Abbess, and Queen: Donors and Patrons or Intercessors and Matrons?" In *The Cultural Patronage of Medieval Women*, edited by June Hall McCash, 105–54. Athens: University of Georgia Press, 1996

Chartier, Alain. *Le Livre de l'Espérance*. Edited by François Rouy. Paris: Champion, 1989.

———. *Le Quadrilogue invectif*. Edited by E. Droz. Paris: Champion, 1910.

Commynes, Philippe de. *Mémoires*. In *Historiens et chroniqueurs du Moyen Âge*, edited by A. Pauphilet. Paris: Gallimard, 1952, 949–1448.

Coudrec, C. "Les Miniatures du *Voyage de Gênes* de Jean Marot." In *Les Trésors des bibliothèques de France*, 39–55. Paris: Van Oest, 1927.

Dufour, Antoine. *Les Vies des femmes célèbres*. Edited by G. Jeanneau. Geneva: Droz, 1970.

Giordano, Luisa. "Les Entrées de Louis XII en Milanais." In *Passer les Monts: Français en Italie—l'Italie en France, 1494–1525*, edited by Jean Balsamo, 139–48. Paris: Champion, 1998.

Laborde, A. de. *Les Principaux Manuscrits à peintures conservés dans l'ancienne Bibliothèque Impériale Publique de Saint-Pétersbourg*. Paris: Société Française de Reproductions de Manuscrits à Peintures, 1938.

La Vigne, André de. *La Ressource de la Chrestienté*. Edited by Cynthia J. Brown. Montreal: CERES, 1989.

Lowden, John. "The Royal/Imperial Book and the Image or Self-Image of the Medieval Ruler." In *Kings and Kingship in Medieval Europe*, edited by Anne J. Duggan. London: King's College, 1993, 213-41.

Markale, Jean. *Anne de Bretagne*. Paris: Hachette, 1980.

Marot, Jean. *Voyage de Gênes*. Edited by Giovanna Trisolini. Geneva: Droz, 1974.

Mitchell, Bonner. *The Majesty of the State: Triumphal Progresses of Foreign Sovereigns in Renaissance Italy, 1494–1600*. Florence: Olschki, 1986.

Minois, Georges. *Anne de Bretagne*. Paris: Fayard, 1999.

Quilliet, Bernard. *Louis XII*. Paris: Fayard, 1986.

Scheller, Robert W. "Gallia Cisalpina: Louis XII and Italy, 1499–1508." *Simiolus* 15, no. 1 (1985): 37–42.

Sherman, Michael. "The Selling of Louis XII: Propaganda and Popular Culture in Renaissance France, 1498–1515." Ph.D diss., University of Chicago, 1974.

Trisolini, Giovanna. Introduction to the *Voyage de Gênes* by Jean Marot. Geneva: Droz, 1974.

Voronova, Tamara and Alexander Sterligov. *Western European Illuminated Manuscripts of the 8th to the 16th Centuries in the National Library of Russia, St. Petersburg.* Bournemouth: Parkstone Press, 1996.

Wolfthal, Diane. *Images of Rape: The "Heroic" Tradition and Its Alternatives.* Cambridge: Cambridge University Press, 1999.

Figure 1: *Le Voyage de Gênes* (B.N. f.fr. MS 5091), fol. 27r: Gênes laments her fate before her sons, Marchandise and Peuple, whose attempts to console their mother are halted by Honte (cliché Bibliothèque nationale de France-Paris)

Figure 2: *Le Voyage de Gênes* (B.N. f.fr. MS 5091), fol. 34v: Gênes laments her fate before Rage, Douleur, and Désespoir, whom Raison comes to drive away (cliché Bibliothèque nationale de France-Paris)

Figure 3: Le Voyage de Gênes (B.N. f.fr. MS 5091), fol. 37v: Gênes kneels before Raison in thanks (cliché Bibliothèque nationale France-Paris)

GRIEF, RAPE, AND SUICIDE AS CONSOLATION... 199

Figure 4: Le Voyage de Gênes (B.N. f.fr. MS 5091), fol. 1r: Jean Marot dedicates his manuscript copy of the Voyage de Gênes to Queen Anne de Bretagne (cliché Bibliothèque nationale de France-Paris)

Figure 5: *Le Voyage de Gênes* (B.N. f.fr. MS 5091), fol. 22v: King Louis XII enters the city of Genoa (cliché Bibliothèque nationale de France-Paris)

GRIEF, RAPE, AND SUICIDE AS CONSOLATION... 201

Figure 6: *Le Voyage de Gênes* (B.N. f.fr. MS 5091), fol. 6r: Gênes speaks before her sons Noblesse, Marchandise, and Peuple (cliché Bibliothèque nationale de France-Paris)

Reinventing the *Roman de la Rose* for a Woman Reader: The Case of Ms. Douce 195[1]

DEBORAH MCGRADY

"...que fait a louer lecture qui n'osera estre leue ne parlee en propre forme a la table des roynes, des princesses et des vaillains preudefemmes—a qui convendroit couvrir la face de honte rougie?"
–Christine de Pizan, *Le Débat du "Roman de la rose"*

Early on in the *Roman de la rose* tradition, readers aggressively confronted the misogynous overtones of Jean de Meun's continuation of the romance. Soon after his addition, an extensive discourse grew around the work and assured that its shape and meaning would remain in constant flux. Its dual authorship and controversial stance on religion, love, women, and marriage provoked many readers to revise the work in consonance with their own beliefs or intentions. Already in 1290, the scribe Gui de Mori modified Jean de Meun's negative portrayal of marriage by adding his own commentary on jealousy. Also in the late thirteenth century, the redactor of B.N. MS f.fr. 25524 categorically removed anti-feminist passages from his version of the *Rose*. Many indeed are the manuscripts that record the audience's response to the *Rose*.[2]

In the early fifteenth century, the intense reactions of *Rose* readers reached a boiling point that resulted in a public *querelle* over the work's content and value. On August 25, 1401, Jean Gerson denounced the *Rose* during a public sermon. A year later, he returned to the subject in his *Vision*, in which he attacked, point by point, Jean de Meun's continuation. In 1402, Christine de Pizan, also a staunch detractor of the *Rose*, made public an epistolary debate that pitted her against Parisian literati who supported Jean de Meun. Copies of her compilation of select letters were offered to well-placed readers, in particular the queen of France, Isabeau de Bavière.³ As the epigraph to this paper makes apparent, Christine was distressed by the offensive nature of the text, especially for women. Her concern that women might read the text extended beyond the questionable morals it promoted to touch on the humiliation they would experience if subjected to such a deleterious portrait of their entire sex.

Yet Christine's claims that the romance could only bring horror to women's ears deterred neither men nor women from reading the popular work well into the sixteenth century.⁴ Like their earlier counterparts, late-medieval redactors continued to engage with the text by composing their own commentaries, excising offensive passages, and even rewriting the work to reflect Christian morality. Not only did the Roman de la rose undergo transformations at the hands of scribes; in addition, bookmakers and artists exploited the visual register as a means of revising the work.

Nowhere is the visual exploitation of the Roman de la rose more apparent than in Robinet Testard's late fifteenth-century copy, which was produced for the Cognac court of Charles d'Orléans and Louise de Savoie (Bodleian Library, Oxford, MS Douce 195).⁵ Testard's densely illustrated Rose copy (126 miniatures for 156 folios) has been largely ignored by both art historians and Rose specialists. Yet MS Douce 195 breaks with the traditional Rose iconography on multiple occasions and is enlightening for that very reason.

In particular, the insistent inclusion of spectators within the boundaries of miniatures draws attention to the audience's importance. Both men and women are found as spectators in Testard's copy, but in most cases the audience is represented as exclusively female. Such is the case on folio 108, where a two-column miniature at the bottom of the page offers the perplexing image of two women seated on the field of battle at the very moment that the God of Love seeks to penetrate the walls protecting the Rose (Fig. 1). The illumination stands out both as one of only seven miniatures spanning two columns in the manuscript and as a rare example in the collection of a continuous narration, as it includes multiple events within a single frame.⁶ The visual narrative begins on the left of the image, where the Lover is taken prisoner and beaten by Danger, Fear, and Shame. The action then spirals up and around the castle to the right, where the God of Love's army advances. In the foreground at the center of the image, the battle is underway. The tail end of the spiral leads us to two conspicuously placed aristocratic women seated on the battlefield. The unexpected presence of two women both at the heart of a battle and within the frame of a controversial work deemed inappropriate for women raises the question of their identity and purpose. Do they figure as the anticipated audience of MS

Douce 195? If the two women do indeed mirror the anticipated audience, did such an unlikely public influence other aspects of the copy? In short if, in this illumination, Testard took liberties in altering dramatically not only *Rose* iconography but *Rose* ideology to acknowledge women as readers and viewers of the romance, did he endeavor elsewhere to reinvent the *Rose* so as to accommodate women? Indeed, in certain cases, it appears that while the bookmaker and scribe, Jean Michel, chose to retain the very passages identified by Christine de Pizan as inappropriate for women's ears—namely the Friend's statements, including the Jealous Husband's tirade, and the Old Lady's advice to the Lover—Robinet Testard undertook to alter *Rose* iconography as a means of accommodating female spectators. Thus, although Jean de Meun's misogynous message remains intact in MS Douce 195, the illuminations, as supplementary material, both redefine the anticipated audience and model confrontational interpretative strategies that promote new readings of the text through the insertion of viewers engaging with events. Similar to the fictional audience in the miniatures, the real audience of MS Douce 195 is to engage with the text at key moments in the narrative to observe, evaluate, and discuss the events at hand.

MS Douce 195 lacks any dedication or inscription from which an owner could be identified. The opening historiated letter, however, presents the joined arms of Charles d'Orléans and his wife, Louise de Savoie. Furthermore, the inventory taken of the Cognac libraries following the sudden death of the count in 1494 allows us to date the manuscript as having been most likely produced between 1488, the year of the rather precipitate marriage of the count to Louise de Savoie, and the year of his demise.[7] Yet scholars do not agree about whether the count, the countess, or both were the intended recipient(s) of the work. Langlois identified MS Douce 195 as belonging to Charles d'Orléans. As for the historiated letter, Langlois speculates that it was added at a later date. Official documentation from the Bodleian Library concurs with Langlois, while the 1973 catalogue of the library holdings by Otto Pächt and Jonathan J. G. Alexander lists MS Douce 195 as having been owned by the countess, Louise de Savoie.

Affiliated with the Cognac court as early as 1473, Robinet Testard and Jean Michel produced a long line of deluxe manuscripts first for Charles d'Orléans, including *Les Heures de Charles d'Angoulême* (Paris, Bibliothèque Nationale Lat. 1173) and *Discours entre Entendement et Raison* (B.N. f.fr. 1191).[8] Following the count's marriage with Louise de Savoie, Testard and Michel produced additional manuscripts intended for the countess, including *Les Échecs amoureux* (B.N. f.fr. 143) and Ovid's *Héroïdes* (B.N. f.fr. 875). Both texts overtly acknowledge their female patron with extensive portraits of women and the inscription of the countess's initials and arms in window frames, on walls, and in surrounding marginalia.[9] If more subtle in its recognition of the countess, Testard's *Rose* nevertheless includes several imbedded visual allusions to a female audience.

We must proceed with caution in associating spectators with the real readers of Testard's *Rose*, since spectators represent a common theme in the illuminator's corpus. Frequently, his spectators observe events through windows. Sometimes they are on the interior looking out, as in the frontispiece to Charles de Coëtivy's *Discours entre Entendement et Raison*, where a man and woman look out of a castle window. Other times they are on the exterior looking in, as in *Les Heures de Charles d'Angoulême*, where a woman observes, through a window, a couple baking bread (fol. 6v) and a crowned man peers through a window at the enthroned Charles d'Angoulême (fol. 34v). Occasionally, spectators peer over barriers, also in the *Heures*, where Saint George's battle with the dragon is observed by a couple peeking over the wall (fol. 54v). Again, in *Les Échecs amoureux*, the lover and lady meeting in the foreground compete with two women conversing behind a wall in the background (fol. 165r).

This visual pun on the audience's presence outside the book in Testard's manuscripts is more pronounced in MS Douce 195, where a dozen miniatures depict observers peering through windows, peeking over fences, or in the case of folio 108, seated at the very center of the action. In only three cases are women not included as members of the inscribed audience in MS Douce 195. The first illumination to incorporate women as spectators comes at a key moment in the narrative, when the Lover enters the garden for the first time, as recounted in Guillaume de Lorris's half of the *Roman de la rose*. In *Rose* pictorial programs, the caroling scene is often privileged by a detailed visual rendition of the narrated events. In kind, Testard spotlights the event by painting a framed miniature that spans both columns (Fig. 2). The bottom portion of the image portrays the Lover standing on the sidelines with hat raised. Courtesy extends her hand as an invitation to join the dance. Faithful to the narrator's emphasis on the participants' dress, the illuminator takes great care in portraying the participants, dressing them in the finest of robes.

The caroling scene, as recounted by the Lover, lends itself to visual representation because of frequent mention of the pictorial richness of the scene. Aware of his inability to communicate a complete picture of the events unfolding before him, the Lover describes what the reader *would have seen* had he been present:

> **Lors veïssiez** bien caroller
> Et très moult prenrent aller
> Et faire mainte bele treche
> Et maint biau tor sor l'erbe freshe.

> Aussi y **veilles** fleuteors
> Et menestres et jugleurs. . . .
> (fol. 7v, column A; ll. 743–54; emphasis added).[10]

When Courtesy invites the Lover to join the dancers, the Lover willingly accepts because of the opportunity afforded to observe them more closely:

> Car sachiez que moult m'agria
> Dont cortoisie me pria
> Et me dist que je carollasse
> Car de curloler, se i osase,
> Estoye envieux et surpris.
> A **resgarder** lors ie me pris
> Les corps les façons et les chieres,
> Les semblances et les manieres
> Des genz qui il carollayent.
> Si vous dirai qui c'estoyent:
> Deduyt fu biaux et jeunes et drois
> Jamais a nul lieu ne viendroit
> Ou vos truissiez plus bel homme.
> (fol. 7v, column A; ll. 771–803; emphasis added)

Possibly responding to the narrator's emphasis on the visual richness of the scene, Testard enhances the image with a row of observers. In the top portion of the illumination, three female spectators and two male musicians, dressed in Burgundian fashion, observe the dance from the balcony. In particular, the woman at the center of the balcony directs the audience's attention to the dance below with her pointed finger. Thus, it appears likely that Testard's decision to adjust *Rose* iconography to make room for the audience was first inspired by the narrative itself. At the same time, the layout enhances a key passage in the text where the visual is promoted over the textual. Unable to express the richness he sees, the Lover longs for the reader to be present alongside him. Testard realizes the Lover's wish.

In addition to the caroling scene, numerous miniatures incorporating women as spectators punctuate MS Douce 195. In most instances, the inclusion of spectators, male or female, represents an extratextual addition by the workshop, as nothing in the text nor in traditional iconography warrants the presence of spectators.[11] Two of the miniatures decorating Ovidian material include allusions to the viewer. Both the scene of Dido's suicide (fol. 94v) and the scene of Jason before a dragon (fol. 95) situate women as observers. In the former, one female spectator raises her hands in shock upon viewing the brutal scene. An exclusively female audience also observes the God of Love embracing the Lover (fol. 15v),[12] the good shepherd tending his flock (fol. 144v), and Venus' final assault on the tower (fol. 147v). The battle between Fortitude and Fear places four women against a wall that divides the God of Love from the battle. Three of the women observe the events, while one turns her head to consider the God of Love (fol. 111v). In each case, the spectators are separated from the narrative by physical barriers in the form of walls and fences. Peering over these barriers or thresholds to witness events, the spectators in MS Douce 195 mirror the extratextual audience engaging with the volume.

The already discussed miniature on folio 108, where two women are seated on a battlefield, breaks from the pattern of physically separating the spectator from the action and instead encloses two women within a frame of narrative events. Eliminating barriers between the audience and the action, the image favors the audience's encounter with the text over the events detailed. The unconventional scene—both for *Rose* iconography and for Testard in general—displaces the reader, as she becomes the subject rather than the passive spectator. Furthermore, the body language of the two women suggests that they are in discussion, most likely about the events surrounding them, as the woman on the left in red casts her gaze on the battle unfolding before her, all the while placing her hand on the second lady's lap. In turn, the lady on the right appears to speak to the lady as she turns and slightly tilts her head toward her companion.

The decision to focus attention on the audience on folio 108 may have been directly inspired by the passage immediately following the image, for the narrator intervenes to address first the men and then the women in his audience. Turning to the "vaillanz fames" (l. 15195) who may read his work, the narrator assures them that no harm is intended by his harsh words regarding women:

> Si vous pri toutes, vaillans femmes,
> Soyent damoiselles ou dames,
> Amoureuses ou sans amys,
> Que ce mot i trouvez la mis
> Qui mordans semblent et chenins
> Encontre les meurs femenins,
> Que ne men vueillez pas blasmer
> Ne m'escripture diffamer,
> Qui toute est pour enseignement,
> Quonc ne dis riens certainement
> Ne volenté n'ay pas du dire,
> Ne par yvresse ne par ire,
> Par hayne ne par envie,
> Contre femme qui soit en vie. (fol. 112, column B; ll. 15195–208)

Indeed, the inclusion of the two women draws attention to the narrator's remarks on their role as readers. Yet why visually favor the address to women over the greeting to the men? If the presence of the two women on the battlefield serves as a visual cue for women to examine closely the passage in which they are directly addressed, then the illumination signals an explicit attempt to carve out space for women readers within the frame of a predominantly misogynist text.

By incorporating scenes of the audience engaging with the narrative, Testard inscribes a record of both the anticipated reading strategies of the audience and the makeup of the audience itself. As the fictive spectators lean over barriers to gaze at events or find themselves immersed in the narrative, so too the extratextual audience of MS Douce 195 would meditate on the illuminations that served as an intermediary between lay reader and text. The emphasis placed on the visual component of the manuscript as a tool for comprehending the text was a common theme in medieval works on reading.[13] As early as the twelfth century, Hugues of Fouilley had promoted reading images as a means of accessing works, and Jean Gerson continued in a similar vein by advising the illiterate to contemplate pictures in books as a substitute for reading. In addition, the multiple scenes of spectators in MS Douce 195 suggest that Testard intended his audience to adopt a certain type of reading, specifically group reading, since he typically favors a crowd of spectators over the single individual, and debate among the members of the audience, since he presents some spectators engaging with one another while observing events (e.g. fol. 94v and fol. 108).

MS Douce 195 not only records efforts to encourage discussion among the audience of the work but also inscribes the artist's own engagement with the text. If Jean Michel chose to provide a faithful copy of the *Rose* instead of adding his own commentary or excising passages according to his or his patron's taste, Robinet Testard unabashedly produced a miniature program that often enhanced the text, as in the case of the spectators, or undermined the text, as in the case of the seven miniatures decorating the Jealous Husband passage.[14] In the latter case, Testard uses the pictorial program to revisit a passage notorious for its harsh statements on women.

Traditionally, efforts to rehabilitate the *Roman de la rose* centered on revising the misogynous message communicated in Jean de Meun's continuation. In this vein, many commentaries on the Rose paid particular attention to the Jealous Husband diatribe recounted by Friend. The passage is a monologue of over 1,000 verses in which the Husband's complaint that his wife is coy, cunning, and deceptive takes center stage. Drawing on classical and Judeo-Christian literature, and on theological treatises, the Jealous Husband expounds on the deceptive nature of women. Spurred on by jealousy and escalating anger, he accuses his wife of adultery until his fury culminates in her violent beating.

In *Les Échecs amoureux*, an anonymous fourteenth-century commentary on the *Roman de la Rose*—a work produced for Louise de Savoie by Michel and Testard—the narrator deplores in particular the Jealous Husband's tirade, arguing that its only worth was the negative example it presented:

> Ce qui oncques ne fu mesmez ne qui ja ne sera adevine il et contreuve souvent par sa forsenerie, sy comme il est bien a plain contenu au Rommant de la Rose ou chapitre ou l'acteur parle de jalousie en la personne du jaloux courroucié qui lors dit ce qu'il ne scet mie; et pour ce ne doit nul arrester as paroles qui la sont contenues quant a ce que elle segnifient, maiz seulement en tant que elle nous ramentoivent comme le fol jaloux se tourmente et demainne desraisonablement quant il est esmeus et que elles nous enseignent son grant oultrage et sa grant vilenie et le peril aussi qui s'en peut enssuir. . . .[15]

While retaining the Jealous Husband passage in its entirety, MS Douce 195 echoes *Les Échecs amoureux* in its disapproval of the Jealous Husband passage in the accompanying miniatures. The pictorial program decorating the passage in Douce 195 is a particularly rich and dense example of the visual apparatus serving to revisit the romance's misogynous premise.

Pictorial series decorating the Jealous Husband monologue in medieval copies of the *Roman de la Rose* generally exhibit scarce iconographic variety. Though some illustrations accompany the passage in most illuminated *Rose* manuscripts, there are rarely more than three. The most commonly depicted segments are the opening scene in which Husband and Wife are described, the story of Lucretia, and the Husband's beating of the Wife (see Appendix for listing of select manuscripts). In contrast, MS Douce 195 contains seven miniatures for nine folios (recto/verso), making it possibly the most elaborately decorated Jealous Husband segment in the *Rose* tradition. The number of illuminations in MS Douce 195 and the originality they exhibit make it apparent that the passage held particular interest for Testard. Furthermore, the visual density of the passage would have certainly attracted the attention of the reader.

A close analysis of the cycle elucidates various strategies employed by Testard in his efforts to revise the work from the margins of the text. The first miniature in the narrative program decorates Friend's comparison of modern times to the Golden Age (ll. 8356–8456). Friend begins by contrasting men and women during the two periods. The accompanying miniature presents a seated couple dressed only in skimpy tunics, which are held together by ties on each side. A cherub-like figure gathers flowers before them while an older man picks apples. Sheep graze in the field surrounding the couple. In the background, yet again, a group of spectators dressed in late-medieval fashion peer over the hill, seemingly fascinated by the spectacle they behold (fol. 59v).

The second image in the Jealous Husband sequence contrasts sharply with the idyllic scene from the Golden Age (Fig. 3). The harmony of the first image is replaced by dissonance; open space gives way to the confines of a bare room. Introducing the Husband's monologue, the second image presents the principal actors of the drama: the Husband and the Wife. At the center of the image we discover, once again, a reference to the spectator in the young voyeur at the window who gazes at the couple. The young man may represent "Ce bachelier/Robichonet au vert chappel" (fol. 61, column A; l. 8529) whom the Jealous Husband identifies as his wife's lover (although he wears a red cap here). Regardless of the identity of the man in the window, the three characters form a troubling triangle. The young man closely observes the interaction between Husband and Wife. The Husband, to the left and in front of the young man, frowns in the direction of his young Wife. With one hand raised and the other holding a club, the Jealous Husband affects a domineering and unyielding stance. Clearly, the Jealous Husband exerts the type of authority that Friend critiqued earlier in his maxim:

> . . . ouncques amours et seigneure
> Ne firent ensemble compaignie
> Ne ne demourerent ensemble:
> Cil qui maistroye les dessemble. (fol. 60, column B; ll. 8451–54).

Wife sits before a burning fire with distaff and spindle. Busily engaged with her domestic activity, the Wife looks neither in the direction of the Husband nor of the lover, but rather appears to attach her gaze to the activity at hand.

Testard closely replicates the physical description of the husband in this second miniature of the pictorial program. The portrait of the Jealous Husband corresponds to assertions that he wears only clothing made of "buriaulx" (fol. 64v, column B; l. 9077), an inexpensive and rough fabric usually reserved for furniture in the Middle Ages. Testard even accentuates the shabbiness of the Jealous Husband's dress through realistic details of wear and tear: both his sleeves and his apron exhibit frayed edges. The portrait decidedly contradicts the Husband's own self-description as "debonnaire" (fol. 60v, column B; l. 8519), as it presents a grotesque and ridiculous man with unruly gray hair, a wide protruding nose, open mouth, and a scrawny mustache. The addition of the stick in his hand and the hammer at his belt alludes to the Husband's eventual beating of his Wife with his "petail" and his "haltre" (fol. 65v, column A; l. 9360). In addition to announcing the Husband's impending violence, these instruments point to the sexual anxiety developed throughout the passage. Michael Camille has already detailed the sexually charged nature of the chisel and hammer used in the Pygmalion miniature sequence of MS Douce 195.[16] As is the case in the Pygmalion images, the phallic quality of the club and sword functions as a pictorial leitmotif in the Jealous Husband cycle.

The angle of the hammer at the Husband's side directs our attention to the tip of the Wife's distaff. Unlike the Husband's portrait, the visual depiction of the wife draws little direct inspiration from the narrative. Whereas the Husband accuses her of adulterous behavior, Testard infuses the Wife's portrait with culturally charged symbols intended to arouse the audience's sympathies. The spindle and distaff held by the Wife are not mentioned in the text; instead, they are common symbols in medieval art intended to emphasize a woman's domesticity, chastity, and purity. The iconography of woman as spinner in medieval art and literature draws on Judeo-Christian and classical sources. In Proverbs, the description of the "virtuous woman" is defined as one who "layeth her hands to the spindle, and her hands hold the distaff" (31:19). As early as the second century, a legend surfaced claiming that Mary had been selected as one of the eight virgins to weave a new curtain for the temple. As a result, numerous art works throughout the Middle Ages portray Mary with spindle and distaff in hand as evidence of her honor and purity.[17] In classical literature, spinning and weaving are frequently associated with honorable wives. Livy stresses that Lucretia was spinning wool with her ladies when first observed by the king's son. Penelope uses the pretense of weaving an elaborate tapestry as a means of remaining faithful to her husband during his extensive absences. The inclusion of spindle and distaff in this pictorial preface to the Husband's tirade would very likely have inspired readers to associate the Wife with an established tradition of chaste women. The miniature thus encourages the viewer to look beyond the accusations lodged against the Wife and to consider her possible innocence.

Further evidence in the Jealous Husband pictorial program points to the artists' efforts to rehabilitate the Wife. First, the page layout of folio 60r spotlights the disjunction between text and image. Whereas the image portrays the Wife engaged in a respectable activity, the first line of text following the image expresses the Jealous Husband's seemingly misplaced claim that "...ele et nice et folle" (fol. 60, column A; l. 8459). Second, through the incorporation of the distaff and spindle, the portrait of the Husband and Wife elicits complex intertextual links with the text it introduces, for the Jealous Husband evokes as rare examples of chaste women the very names of Lucretia and Penelope. Although the Jealous Husband does not mention the spinning and weaving of the two heroines, a medieval reader might have easily fused the image of the wife spinning wool with the two exceptional women evoked by the Husband. Finally, the image of woman as spinner will reoccur in the final miniature of the Jealous Husband cycle. In the final illumination, which reintroduces Friend and his concluding remarks on ideal couples, the illuminator depicts yet another wife, also with distaff in hand (Fig.5). The repetition of women as spinners in the pictorial program, joined with allusions to women spinners in the text, serves to tie the segment together by means of the chaste women evoked, while drawing the medieval audience's attention to the clash between the narrative and its visual representation.[18]

A brief comparison with an illumination introducing the Jealous Husband's tirade in a later manuscript is enlightening. MS f.fr. 24392, now housed at the Bibliothèque Nationale in Paris, was owned by Anne of France in the late fifteenth century. Similar to MS Douce 195, MS 24392 presents a highly charged opening miniature to the Jealous Husband monologue. Here Husband, lover, and Wife are presented in a single frame. The Husband is poorly dressed and stands apart from the Wife and her lover, who, in contrast, are richly dressed in ermine-lined clothing. The Jealous Husband grabs the arm of his Wife in an obvious attempt to pull her away from her lover. While both miniatures present an uninspiring portrait of the Husband, their representation of the Wife differs dramatically. Whereas MS 24392 reinforces the accusations found in the text in the accompanying miniature, MS Douce 195 contradicts the Jealous Husband's character attacks on his Wife. The viewer of the MS Douce 195 portrait of Husband and Wife begins the passage with sympathies for the Wife, sympathies that will only be strengthened by the brute violence associated with the Husband throughout the passage.

Even before the beating scene, the Jealous Husband's penchant for violence is evoked in the pictorial program. As the Jealous Husband continues to rail at his Wife, he draws on various stories to reinforce his argument, of which three are illustrated in MS Douce 195. In each case, scenes of brutality are detailed for the audience. The first is the tale of Lucretia (Fig. 4). Within the text itself, the Jealous Husband develops the key points of her story, including her rape, her confession of the crime before her family, her subsequent suicide, and her dying request that her death be avenged. He uses Lucretia's story as an example to distinguish between the honorable women of yesteryear and their deceitful counterparts today.

A comparison of Testard's miniature depicting Lucretia with the iconographic tradition in *Rose* manuscripts reveals important shifts in MS Douce 195. As already briefly mentioned, *Rose* pictorial programs frequently include an illustration of Lucretia's story. A survey of twenty-three *Rose* miniature cycles in manuscripts from the late Middle Ages reveals that ten contain a miniature depicting Lucretia (Appendix). Nine of the ten miniatures portray Lucretia's suicide, typically before a male audience. MS Douce 195, however, differs dramatically, as the illumination depicts Tarquin preparing to rape Lucretia in her private chambers. If the conventional scene establishes the woman as the object of the voyeuristic gaze, Testard's vision directs the audience's gaze to the brutish actions of the violator. The sword that hangs from Tarquin's side in MS Douce 195—like the hammer on the Jealous Husband's belt in image two of the narrative cycle—insinuates further the similarity between Tarquin's aggression and the future violence of the Jealous Husband.

The theme of violence only escalates in the subsequent images. Two folios later, an illumination depicts the attack of Beauty and Ugliness on Chastity (fol. 63v). On folio 65v, yet another image presents Hercules' unsuccessful battle against a monster. While the Jealous Husband retells the story of Hercules to examine Deianira's perfidy, the miniature focuses on the battle itself. In a highly charged gesture, Hercules uses his sword to penetrate between the monster's legs. The miniature deflects the viewer's eye away from the woman to focus on male violence. The phallic instruments, wielded by both Beauty and Ugliness, and by Hercules, recall those possessed by the Jealous Husband on folio 60 of the cycle. Hercules' battle with the monster simultaneously recalls the rape of Lucretia, discussed earlier, in its suggestive penetration of the monster and announces the Jealous Husband's beating of his Wife to follow. The escalating violence eventually culminates on folio 66v.

As is typical of *Rose* iconography, Testard portrays the Jealous Husband pulling his wife by her hair across the floor (fol. 66v). Testard again links images in the pictorial program by way of a phallic sword at the husband's waist. The brutality of the scene is accentuated by the woman's exposed legs, which flail as she is dragged across the floor. Her mouth is twisted in an anguished grimace as she reaches back with one hand in an attempt to wrench her hair from her Husband's grasp. The miniature vividly captures the violence detailed by Friend:

> Lors la prent, tantost, de venue,
> Cil qui de mal talant tressue,
> Par les tresses, et saiche et tire,
> Rompt lien les cheveuls et descrir
> Li jalous, et seur li s'aourse,
> . . .
> Et par tout lostel la trayne
> Par courrouz et par atayne. . .
> Ains fiert et frappe et rolle et maille
> Et celle crye et brait et braille. . .(fol. 66v, columns A/B; ll. 9361–74)

If the image of the beating in MS Douce 195 offers a conventional depiction of events, it is unique in its inclusion in a series that spotlights violence.

The final image in the pictorial program accompanying the Jealous Husband passage announces a return to Friend, who glosses the Husband's tirade. The miniature portrays Friend's complaints regarding the negative impact of marriage on love: ". . .il couvient amours morir/Quant amant li veult seignorie" (ll. 9439–40). The last miniature places in the foreground a husband seated at one end of a table while at the other end, the wife sorts wool. Behind the table are two observers. Albeit to a lesser degree than the portrait of the Jealous Husband and his Wife on folio 60, the final image in the Jealous Husband cycle again presents a domineering husband (Fig.5). Common gestures of authority are used to express the husband's dominance. With legs crossed, hand on thigh, and his right hand raised with palm facing down, the husband adopts a position of command over his wife, whose inclined head indicates her submission.[19] The final miniature ensures that the audience also recognizes this couple as a negative model by way of the two spectators standing behind the husband. Unlike the other spectators examined earlier, these observers unabashedly direct the audience's reception of the passage. The observer in the background who looks directly out at the viewer stresses his disapproval of the scene through the charged image of his turned-down hand, which leads the viewer's gaze to the husband's hand. The inclusion of engaged spectators in the final image of the Jealous Husband pictorial program assures that the viewers of MS Douce 195 appreciate both the efforts to revise the passage through the visual addition and the attempt to promote the audience's critical engagement with the text. Indeed, the miniature echoes the reading suggestions offered by the narrator of *Les Échecs amoureux*, who suggests that we not understand the Jealous Husband's ranting as truth or his behavior as a model to imitate (cited above).

The Jealous Husband cycle in MS Douce 195 is a tightly orchestrated set of miniatures that are held together by the repetition of charged symbols that would have had a great effect on a medieval audience's reception of the passage. The distaff and spindle, and the phallic instruments (e.g., swords, sticks, and clubs) create visual links between the different components of the Husband's unruly discourse. Through the incorporation of phallic instruments, the sequence is bound together particularly by its concentration on aggression. The visual allusions to spinning simultaneously serve to undermine further the Jealous Husband's authority and violence through the association of the wife with a well-documented tradition of chaste women. The implementation of these symbols empowers the workshop to edit the Jealous Husband's tirade from the margins of the narrative.

Of the various points discussed in this study of the MS Douce 195 illumination program, three deserve to be stressed. First, there is substantial material evidence to suggest that Robinet Testard and, possibly, Jean Michel anticipated that women, specifically Louise de Savoie, would be the principal members of their audience. Second, the workshop responsible for MS Douce 195 used the pictorial program to inscribe at the very least models of female readers if not models of their reading strategies. The imagery clearly incites a new reading of the *Roman de la rose*, one that favors women and openly questions the misogynist and misogamous arguments found throughout the text. Indeed, the miniature cycle inscribes within the body of the text a model of confrontational interpretative methods. By revising at least one of the infamous misogynist and misogamous passages, the workshop responsible for MS Douce 195 revised the *Roman de la rose* through the eyes of its female readers. Thus, the pictorial program offers the radical example of a cycle in which a woman's anticipated gaze may have effected a new "reading" of the passage, thereby replacing the shame Christine de Pizan linked to the work's female audience with the sobering realization of the unjustified brutality inflicted on the female sex. Contrary to Michael Camille's recent claim that Testard's manuscript is typical in its identification of the woman as solely the object of the male gaze,[20] MS Douce 195 provided Louise de Savoie and other women with an extraordinarily innovative edition of the *Roman de la rose* in which women become the surveyors of events.

Finally, much of recent feminist scholarship in medieval studies seeks to unearth evidence of women's influence on culture and their contributions to the arts, with particular attention given to the relation between medieval women and books. Who among medieval women owned books?[21] How did women's involvement in the patronage system influence subject matter, decoration, and layout?[22] Were women intimately involved in book production?[23] What reading strategies did women employ?[24] These questions have revealed that women contributed in a variety of ways to the creation and promotion of manuscripts and incunabula. In view of such stimulating research, it is enlightening to consider MS Douce195 as having been produced for Louise de Savoie, whose commitment to the book industry following her husband's death has been well documented by Anne-Marie Lecoq and, more recently, Mary Beth Winn.[25] Their research reveals that Louise de Savoie consciously used the printing press to promote the political career of her son, the future François 1er. Scarce attention is given, however, to Louise de Savoie's earlier engagement with books. Yet the fruits of the countess's earlier patronage suggest an interest in promoting women through literature and the visual arts. In rewriting the history of medieval women, a return to the sources with an eye to revealing the traces of women's influence will undoubtedly unearth additional examples of female patrons who left evidence of their impact on literature in the works they commissioned and read.

    Tulane University

NOTES

1. I would like to thank the Medieval Institute at Western Michigan University for funding the initial stages of research for this project. I would especially like to express my appreciation to the faculty, staff, and graduate students at the institute for their insightful suggestions along the way.

2. Extensive liberties were taken with the *Rose*, as some excised offensive passages, while others retorted to the same passages in the margins. Still others rewrote or contradicted the misogynous sections by intercalating their own comments in future copies. Sylvia Huot examines the many variations in the *Rose* tradition in *The "Romance of the Rose" and Its Medieval Readers*; on Guillaume de Mori, see 103-04 and on the B manuscripts, see chapter 4. A systematic study of late medieval copies of the *Rose* has not been yet undertaken, as most scholars restrict their study to earlier versions of the text. In *"Le Roman de la rose" au XIVe siècle: Étude de la réception de l' œ uvre*, Pierre-Yves Badel provides an excellent study of later independant commentaries on the work, such as the anonymous *Échecs amoureux*.

3. See Hicks's introduction to his edition of Christine's *Débat* for an excellent presentation of the history of the querelle (ix – xxiii).

4. Langlois's *Les Manuscrits* lists eleven manuscripts that were owned by women.

5. The text is written on parchment measuring 342 mm by 231 mm. MS Douce 195 belongs to Langlois's second group of *Rose* manuscripts, as it shares many similarities with the grouping of MSS K, M, and N, including three substantial verse additions in the second half of the *Rose* (155). The addition of the Medusa passage (transcribed by Langlois, 453–54), the inclusion of the "Litany of love" (provided in Appendix C of Huot, *Medieval Readers*), and an expansion of the conclusion are all included in Douce 195. In addition, the scribe has "modernized" spelling and grammar to accommodate his late-medieval audience.

6. The scenes of the seven images spanning two columns are the following: 1. the frontispiece depicting the poet at work; 2. the caroling scene; 3. the God of Love seated; 4. Doux Regard and Bel Acceuil before the castle; 5. the battle before the castle; 6. the battle between Hardiesse and Peur; and 7. Venus attacking the castle.

7. On February 16, 1487, Charles d'Orléans, count of Angoulême, and Louise de Savoie were married at the Châtelet de Paris. Although the union of the 31-year-old count and the 12-year-old princess had been arranged by the former king, Louis XI, the sudden union caught many by surprise, including the spouses. The quick marriage was ordered by Anne de Beaujeu as ransom for Charles's freedom. Only days before, the count had been taken prisoner after a failed coup.

8. Recognized as one of the most accomplished illuminators of the late Middle Ages, Robinet Testard spent his entire adult life in the service of the house of Angoulême. Records of payment identify Testard as an *officier domestique* for the count as early as 1473. Presumably his artistic talents were in such demand by the count, a recognized bibliophile, that in 1487 records replace his title of *valet de chambre* with the title of *enlumineur*. Thus from 1487 onward, it appears that Testard's unique responsibility was to illuminate books. When the count of Angoulême died in 1494, Testard was retained as a private illuminator by the eighteen-year-old countess, Louise de Savoie. The last mention of Testard in the Angoulême books is in 1531, after Louise de Savoie's death, when her son, François Ier, allots a final payment of 80 livres to "le vieil Robinet, peintre." Works produced by Testard for the count and countess were vast and varied. His artistic output, primarily manuscripts but including some printed books, consists of historical, religious, and courtly works.

9. Some examples of Testard's incorporation of Louise de Savoie's initials and arms can be found in the window frames of BN f.fr. 875, fol. 5v, the garden wall in BN f.fr. 875, fol. 117v, and the framing marginalia in B.N. f.fr. 143, fol. 1 and fol. 198v.

10. All citations are quoted from MS Douce 195. The corresponding lines in Langlois' edition of the romance are given as well.

11. A later manuscript copy offered to Anne of France, BN f.fr. 24392, imitates MS Douce 195 in its incorporation of spectators. MS 24392 will be discussed later in this paper. Spectators are included in MS 24392 illuminations on the following folios: 84v, 86, 88, 97v, 123v, 124v, 125, 125v, 128v, 145v, 156v, 157, 157v, 166.

12. Image reproduced in Camille, *Medieval Love*, 139, fig.126.

13. Paul Saenger discusses the opinions of theologians on reading in *Spaces between Words*. See especially chapters 14 and 15.

14. This does not, however, preclude the possibility that Jean Michel played a role in determining the visual content of the manuscript. Michel may have specifically requested the incorporation of spectators.

15. Cited in Pierre-Yves Badel, *Réception de l'œuvre*, 303.

16. Camille, *Medieval Art of Love*, 149–51.

17. See Coatsworth, "Cloth-Making."

18. It should be noted, however, that woman as spinner was not universally associated with chastity and purity. Spinning also had an equally negative association. First, medieval art frequently represents Eve with distaff and spindle as representative of her punishment after the Fall. In addition, the spindle and distaff symbolized the disobedience of Noah's wife. Finally, medieval art and literature occasionally associated spinning with an excessive love for luxurious dress. The later association may suggest an opposing reading of the distaff and spindle in Testard's portrait of the Wife, since the Husband complains of his Wife's expensive taste for only the most costly fabric, that is red-dyed fabric, "escarlate" (ll. 9085 – 87). Indeed, she wears a red dress in the illumination. It is my contention that this reading does not hold up when the additional evidence discussed is taken into account. See

Biscoglio, "Unspun Heroes," for a discussion of the representation of Eve with distaff and spindle. Regarding the association of sorting wool with luxurious dress, see Coatsworth, "Cloth-Making," 27.

19. The husband's posture in Douce 195 imitates that of such royal figures as Jacob and David in medieval sculpture, which François Garnier discusses at length in his study of medieval gestures, *Langage de l'image*, pl.18 and 19.

20. Camille, *Medieval Art of Love*, 150.

21. On women patrons, see especially Mary Beth Winn, *Anthoine Vérard*, Susan Groag Bell, *Medieval Women Book Owners*, and June Hall McCash, *Cultural Patronage*.

22. On the influence of women's patronage of literature, see especially June Hall McCash, *Cultural Patronage*, Roberta Krueger, *Women Readers*, and Sylvia Huot, "A Book Made for a Queen." Regarding the specific case of Louise de Savoie, see Lecoq, *François 1ᵉʳ imaginaire*.

23. See especially Jane Taylor's edited collection for multiple examples. Much work has been done in Christine studies to show the extraordinary role that Christine de Pizan adopted in the production of her manuscripts. The reader is referred to the codicological studies of Charity Cannon Willard, Gilbert Ouy and Christine Reno, and Sandra Hindman.

24. In separate studies, Joan Holladay, "The Education of Jeanne d'Evreux" and Madeline H. Caviness, "Patron or Matron?" offer intriguing ideas about how Jeanne d'Evreux, as a woman, might have read the sexually charged and male-dominant illustrations decorating a book of hours offered to her by her husband, Charles V.

25. No one has better documented Louis de Savoie's commitment to and interest in books than Mary Beth Winn in her recent study of Vérard. Winn provides a detailed account of Louise de Savoie's transactions with Antoine Vérard, which date from as early as 1499, following the death of Charles d'Angoulême.

WORKS CITED

PRIMARY SOURCES

Christine de Pizan. *Le Débat sur "Le Roman de la rose"*. Edited by Eric Hicks. Geneva: Slatkine Reprints, 1996.

Lorris, Guillaume de, and Jean de Meun. *Le Roman de la rose*. Edited by Ernest Langlois. Paris: Firmin-Didot et Cie, 1914–24.

SECONDARY SOURCES

Alexander, Jonathan J. G. *Medieval Illuminators and Their Methods of Work*. New Haven, Conn.: Yale University Press, 1992.

Badel, Pierre-Yves. "*Le Roman de la rose*" au XIVᵉ siècle: *Étude de la réception de l' œuvre*. Geneva: Librairie Droz, 1980.

Bell, Susan Groag. "Medieval Women Book Owners: Arbiters of Lay Piety and Ambassadors of Culture." *Signs: Journal of Women in Culture and Society* 7, 4 (1982): 742–68.

Bentley, S. *Exerpta Historica or Illustrations of English History*. London, 1831.

Biscoglio, Frances M. "'Unspun' Heroes: Iconography of the Spinning Woman in the Middle Ages." *Journal of Medieval and Renaissance Studies* 25, 2 (Spring 1995): 163–84.

Blum and Lauer. *La Miniature française au XVe et XVIe siècle*. Paris, 1930.

Caviness, Madeline H. "Patron or Matron? A Capetian Bride and a Vade Mecum for Her Marriage Bed." *Speculum* 68 (1993): 333–61.

Camille, Michael. *The Medieval Art of Love: Objects and Subjects of Desire*. New York: Abrams, 1998.

Clanchy, M. T. *From Memory to Written Record: England 1066–1307*. Oxford: 1993.

Coatsworth, Elizabeth. "Cloth-Making and the Virgin Mary in Anglo-Saxon Literature and Art." In *Medieval Art. Recent Perspectives*, edited by Gale R. Owen-Crocker and Timothy Graham, 8–25, New York: St. Martin's Press, 1998.

Edmunds, Sheila. "Catalogue des manuscrits Savoyards." In *Les Manuscrits enluminés des comtes et ducs de Savoie*, edited by A. Paravicini Bagliani, 207–13. Turin: Umberto Allemandi & C., 1990.

Garnier, François. *Le Langage de l'image au Moyen Âge: Signification et symbolique*. Paris: Le Léopard d'Or, 1982.

Henry-Bordeaux, Paule. *Louise de Savoie: Roi de France*. Paris, 1954.

Hicks, Eric. Introduction to *Le Débat sur "le Roman de la rose,"* by Christine de Pizan. Geneva: Slatkine Reprints, 1996.

Hindman, Sandra. *Christine de Pizan's "Épistre Othéa": Painting and Politics at the Court of Charles VI*. Toronto: Pontifical Institute of Mediaeval Studies, 1986.

Holladay, Joan A. "The Education of Jeanne d'Evreux: Personal Piety and Dynastic Salvation in Her Book of Hours at the Cloisters." *Art History*, 17, 4 (December 1994): 585–611.

Hult, David F. *Self-Fulfilling Prophecies: Readership and Authority in the First "Roman de la Rose."* Cambridge: Cambridge University Press, 1986.

Huot, Sylvia. *The "Romance of the Rose" and Its Medieval Readers*. Cambridge: Cambridge University Press, 1993.

———. "A Book Made for a Queen: The Shaping of a Late Medieval Anthology Manuscript (B. N. fr. 24429)." In *The Whole Book: Cultural Perspectives on the Medieval Miscellany*, edited and with an introduction by Stephen G. Nichols and Siegfrie Wenzel, 123–44. Ann Arbor, Mich.: University of Michigan Press, 1996.

Kreuger, Roberta. *Women Readers and the Ideology of Gender in Old French Verse Romance*. New York: Cambridge University Press, 1993.

———. "Desire, Meaning, and the Female Reader: The Problem in Chretien's *Charrete*." In *Lancelot and Guinevere: A Casebook*, edited and with an introduction by Lori J. Walters, 229–45. New York: Garland, 1996.

Langlois, Ernest. *Les Manuscrits du "Roman de la rose": Description et classement*. Paris: Champion, 1910.

Lecoq, Anne-Marie. *François 1ᵉʳ imaginaire. Symbolique et politique à l'aube de la Renaissance française.*

Lefranc, Abel, and Jacques Boulenger. *Comptes de Louise de Savoie (1515, 1522) et de Marguerite d'Angoulême (1512, 1517, 1524, 1529, 1539).* Paris, 1905.

Legaré, A. M. *Le Livre des échecs amoureux.* Paris, 1991.

Mayer, Dorothy Moulton. *The Great Regent: Louise of Savoy, 1476–1531.* London, 1966.

Maulde la Clavière, René de. *Louise de Savoie et François 1ᵉʳ, trente ans de jeunesse, 1485–1515.* Paris: Perrin et cie, 1895.

McCartney, Elizabeth. "The King's Mother and Royal Prerogative in Early-Sixteenth-Century France." In *Medieval Queenship*, edited by John Carmi Parsons, 117–41. New York: St. Martin's Press, 1998.

McCash, June-Hall, ed. *The Cultural Patronage of Medieval Women.* Athens: University of Georgia Press, 1996.

Ouy, Gilbert, and Christie Reno. "Identification des autographes de Christine de Pizan," *Scriptorium* 34 (1980): 221–36.

Pächt, Otto, and Jonathan Alexander. *Illuminated Manuscripts in the Bodleian Library, Oxford.* Oxford: 1966–73.

Saenger, Paul. *Space between Words: The Origins of Silent Reading.* California: Stanford University Press, 1997.

Sénemaud, E. *La Bibliothèque de Charles d'Orléans, comte d'Angoulême au château de Cognac en 1496.* Paris: A. Claudin, 1861.

Taylor, Jane H. M., and Lesley Smith. *Women and the Book: Assessing the Visual Evidence.* London: The British Library and the University of Toronto Press, 1996.

Taylor, K., ed. *Gender Transgressions: Crossing the Normative Barrier in Old French Literature.* New York : Garland, 1998.

Tesnière, Marie-Hélène, and Prosser Gifford, ed. *Creating French Culture: Treasures from the Bibliothèque Nationale de France.* Introduction by Emmanuel Le Roy Ladurie. New Haven, Conn.: Yale University Press, 1995.

Walters, Lori. "A Parisian Manuscript of the *Romance of the Rose*." *Princeton University Library Chronicle* 51 (1989): 31–55.

———. "Illuminating the Rose: Gui de Mori and the Illustrations of MS 101 of the Municipal Library, Tournai." In *Rethinking the "Romance of the Rose": Text, Image, Reception*, edited by Kevin Brownlee and Sylvia Huot. Philadelphia: University Press of Pennsylvania, 1992: 166–95.

Willard, Charity Cannon. "An Autograph Manuscript of Christine de Pizan?" *Studi Francesi* 27 (1965): 452 – 57.

Winn, Mary Beth. *Anthoine Vérard: Parisian Publisher, 1485–1512—Prologues, Poems, and Presentations.* Geneva: Droz, 1997.

———. "Des Livres imprimés pour Louise de Savoie." In *Les Manuscrits enluminés des comtes et ducs de Savoie*, edited by A. Paravicini Bagliani, 136–46. Turin: Umberto Allemandi & C., 1990.
———. "Books for a Princess and Her Son: Louise de Savoie, François d'Angoulême, and the Parisian Libraire Antoine Vérard." *Bibliothèque d'Humanisme et Renaissance*, 46 (1984): 603–17.

APPENDIX

The following represents a brief and certainly incomplete listing of manuscripts that I have examined. Listed and described is the pictorial content of illuminations decorating the Jealous Husband passage, beginning with Friend's prefatory remarks (l. 8355) and ending with Friend's final comments on the subject of marriage (l. 9492). When possible, I have indicated number of illuminations or blank spaces in the entire manuscript.

	1. Idyllic lovers of the Golden Age, fol. 59v	2. Husband, Wife, and spectator (lover?), fol. 60	3. The rape of Lucretia, fol. 61v	4. Beauty and Ugliness assail Chastity, fol. 63v	5. Hercules fights a monster, fol. 65v	6. The Jealous Husband beats his Wife, fol. 66v	7. A husband and wife, fol. 67v.
1. B.M. MS Douce 195. 15th c. 126 min.							
2. B.N. f.fr. 12592. 14th c.		1. In margins, husband beating Wife, fol. 27v*				*	
3. B.N. f.fr. 24392. 15th c., 175 min.		1. Husband, Wife, and lover, fol. 69	2. Lucretia's suicide, fol. 70v			3. Husband beating Wife, fol. 76	
4. B.N. f.fr. 1560. 14th c.						1. Husband beating Wife, fol. 51v	
5. B.N. f.fr. 2195, 1361			1. Lucretia's suicide, fol. 58				
6. B.N. f.fr. 19153, 15th c., 33 min.	No decoration of passage						
7. B.N. f.fr. 24388, 14th c., 40 min.			1. Lucretia's suicide, fol. 60v			2. Husband beating Wife, fol. 65	
8. Morgan 324			1. Lucretia's suicide, fol. 59				
9. B.N. f.fr 1565, 1352			1. Lucretia's suicide, fol. 57			2. Husband beating Wife, fol. 62	

	1. Idyllic lovers of the Golden Age, fol. 59v	2. Husband, Wife, and spectator (lover?), fol. 60	3. The rape of Lucretia, fol. 61v	4. Beauty and Ugliness assail Chastity, fol. 63v	5. Hercules fights a monster, fol. 65v	6. The Jealous Husband beats his Wife, fol. 66v	7. A husband and wife, fol. 67v.
1. B.M. MS Douce 195. 15th c. 126 min.							
10. Garrett 126						1. Husband beating Wife, fol. 67	
11. B.N. f.fr 12595, 15th c., 80 min.		1. Husband and Wife, fol. 63v	2. Lucretia's suicide, fol. 64v			3. Husband beating Wife, fol. 69	
12. B.N. f.fr. 380, early 15th c., 47 min.		1. Husband and Wife, fol. 47				2. Husband beating Wife, fol. 62v	
13. B.N. f.fr 1567, 15th c., 79 min.		1. Husband beating Wife, fol. 61v*	2. Lucretia's suicide, fol. 63			*	3. Husband and wife, fol. 68v
14. Hof. Cod 2592, 13th c., 48 min.			1. Lucretia's suicide				
15. B.N. f.fr. 1570, 15th c, 78 min.			1. Lucretia's suicide, fol. 68v.				
16. B.N. f.fr. 1574, 13th c., blank spaces reserved		1. Blank space, fol. 63v				2. Blank space, fol. 69v	

	1. Idyllic lovers of the Golden Age, fol. 59v	2. Husband, Wife, and spectator (lover?), fol. 60	3. The rape of Lucretia, fol. 61v	4. Beauty and Ugliness assail Chastity, fol. 63v	5. Hercules fights a monster, fol. 65v	6. The Jealous Husband beats his Wife, fol. 66v	7. A husband and wife, fol. 67v
1. B.M. MS Douce 195, 15th c. 126 min.							
17. B.N. f.fr. 12587, 14th c., 70 min.	*No decoration of passage*						
18. B.N. f.fr 25526, 14th c., 48 min.						1. Husband beating Wife, fol. 71	
19. B.N. f.fr. 812, 15th c., 1 min. & 3 blank spaces	*No decoration of passage*						
20. B.N. f.fr. 1563, 15th c., 116 min.	*No decoration of passage*						
21. B.N. f.fr. 798, 15th c., 1 min. & 54 grisailles						1. Husband beating Wife, fol. 135	
22. B.N. f.fr. 1561, 15th c., 23 min.						1. Husband beating Wife, fol. 58	
23. B.N. f.fr. 805, 15th c., 19 min. & 5 blank spaces.						1. blank space, fol. 60	

* In both MS B.N. f.fr. 12592 and MS B.N. f.fr 1567, the opening miniature to the passage depicts the wife-beating scene typically placed immediately before the segment detailing the beating.

REINVENTING THE ROMAN DE LA ROSE 225

Fig. 1: Two women on a battlefield. Bodleian Library, University of Oxford, MS Douce 195, fol. 108.

Fig. 2: The caroling scene. Bodleian Library, University of Oxford, MS Douce 195, fol. 7.

Fig. 3: The Jealous Husband and his Wife. Bodleian Library, University of Oxford, MS Douce 195, fol. 60.

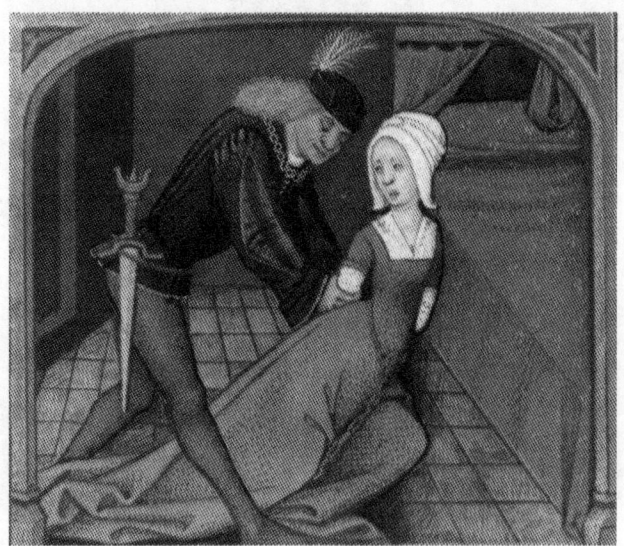

Fig. 4: The rape of Lucretia. Bodleian Library, University of Oxford, MS Douce 195, fol. 60.

Fig. 5: A domineering husband and his wife. Bodleian Library, University of Oxford, MS Douce 195, fol. 67v

Louise De Savoie, "Bibliophile"
MARY BETH WINN

Many scholars concerned with the subject of women and books will have perused the work of Quentin Bauchart entitled Les Femmes bibliophiles; and the focus of my research, Louise de Savoie, is in fact the first of the women he discusses in his book.[1] But Quentin Bauchart's very title raises a fundamental question, which launched my investigation: the idea of "bibliophile." While it has been applied to book collectors of all times, the French word itself originated only in 1740, during a period of such great bibliophiles as the duc de La Vallière. The English term dates from 1824, when the celebrated bibliographer T. F. Dibdin referred, significantly, to the "Society of Bibliophiles at Paris." By the nineteenth century, book collecting had flourished to such a degree that the seventh edition of the Dictionnaire de l'Académie française (1877) includes with its definition the following admonition: "Il est bon d'être bibliophile, mais il ne faut pas être bibliomane."

The Dictionnaire Robert currently defines the "bibliophile" as a "Personne qui aime, recherche et conserve avec soin et goût les livres rares, précieux."[2] The pitfalls for our period are readily apparent: how does one distinguish "rare" from "non-rare" at the dawn of printing, or determine what constitutes "conservation" or "goût?" Yet a recent publication by the Bibliothèque Nationale de France, La Passion des manuscrits enluminés: Bibliophiles français, 1280-1580, applies the term to medieval collectors; and although François Avril, in recognition of the anachronism, begins his introduction with the question "Peut-on parler de bibliophilie au Moyen Age?" he responds in the affirmative:

> Il me semble que. . .c'est le même double ressort fondamental qui aiguillonna les uns [collectionneurs médiévaux] et les autres [La Vallière, Yates Thompson, etc.]: plaisir égoiste et solitaire de manier en connaisseur, dans l'intimité de sa bibliothèque, de beaux livres, de

> goûter la qualité de leur calligraphie ou de leur typographie, de se laisser enchanter par leur illustration, de sentir sous le doigt la finesse du parchemin ou le velouté d'un papier rare, de caresser les reliures et d'en admirer le décor raffiné; mais, tout autant, plaisir social, émulation dans la recherche des belles pièces, rivalité dans le luxe de la présentation matérielle, joie de l'ostentation, désir, parfois, de laisser un souvenir à la postérité.[3]

My own question focuses not so much on the *existence* of bibliophiles among late medieval women as on the *recognition* of their bibliophilic interest by their contemporaries. Were medieval and Renaissance women (and indeed men) whom we now know as important patrons of the book renowned as such in their time? Was book collecting considered a noteworthy trait of these women? If so, where might one find indications to that effect? The obvious choices are prefaces by "makers" of books (authors, translators, publishers, etc.), poems honoring the patron, and epitaphs—materials that, in the case of Louise de Savoie, happen to be plentiful, if not always readily accessible. To these might be added iconographical evidence, although miniatures of a patron receiving a book are so commonplace within the patronage system that they need to be examined with caution.

Before embarking on an examination of such texts and pictures, however, we should first recall some preliminary documents concerning Louise's book collecting. The first is her expense account which records various purchases made from book dealers in Angoulême and Tours as well as the payment made to the Parisian publisher Anthoine Vérard for books delivered to her late husband.[4] While it was probably the publisher who provided such a detailed account of the books for Charles d'Angoulême, it is significant nonetheless that Louise paid the bill and had it fully transcribed in her own expense account. Equally important is the inventory of the count's library which was made at Louise's request following her husband's sudden death on January 1, 1496. To inventory the *biens meubles* of the deceased was undoubtedly standard practice, particularly for the aristocracy, yet the document detailing the count's estate reflects Louise's concern not only for establishing what belonged to her and her children but also for asserting her position as their tutor: "comme par cy devant par le roy notre seigneur elle avoit été déclairée tutrice de mesd. s[rs] ses enffans et de leurs biens."[5] We should not forget that while the count was thirty-seven years old at his death, Louise was not yet twenty,[6] and that both her age and her gender weighed against her being appointed tutor of her children. Indeed, Louis d'Orléans, the future Louis XII, had insisted on sharing the duties, and he is called "tuteur honnoraire" in the inventory. The document, dated November 20, 1496, states that the "grans affaires" that had befallen her at her husband's death had prevented her from attending to the inventory, which she was eager to complete: "elle n'avoit encore peu faire vacquer à l'inventaire des biens meubles appartenant à elle et mesd. s^{rs} ses enffans, ce qu'elle désiroit très fort de faire." The first items in the list are those located in the count's "chambre de librayrie," where seventy-five volumes are identified by their title and notable features: language, binding, illustration, support (paper or parchment), and technique (print or manuscript).

In her journal entry concerning her son's coronation in 1515, Louise refers to "toutes les adversités et inconveniens qui [lui] estoient advenues en [ses] premiers ans et en la fleur de [sa] jeunesse," but considers herself "amplement recompensée" by his accession to the throne.[7] She also notes that Humilité had accompanied her and Patience never abandoned her, identifying herself with the virtues long associated with her by her contemporaries. It is worth noting that one of the mottos attributed to Louise is "Libris et liberis,"[8] the validity of which is amply underscored by the number and types of books known to have been commissioned by her or prepared for her.[9] In a penetrating analysis of Louise and "le pouvoir du livre," Myra Orth has recently explored Louise's use of the book both to prepare her son for the throne and to assert his position as "dauphin."[10] Anne-Marie Lecoq's exhaustive study, François Ier imaginaire,[11] has demonstrated the symbolism pervading Louise's manuscripts in terms of text and image. While benefitting enormously from these studies, I am concerned with contemporary appreciation of Louise de Savoie as book patron, and my immediate focus is on the word livre (and what I will call its correlatives, clergie, sçavoir, escripture, etc.). I have explored a great number and variety of texts pertaining to Louise, but not all of them, and although I have tried to take into consideration their chronology as well as their genre and purpose, my investigation is on-going and my conclusions hypothetical at best. I have divided my sources into three large categories: dedications, poems in praise of Louise, and epitaphs, and I shall begin with the last.

Although never queen of France, Louise played a highly significant role in French politics as regent during the absence of her son, François I, first in 1516-17 for his Italian campaigns, and then in 1524-26 during his captivity. She was instrumental in achieving the Treaty of Cambrai, labeled the Paix des Dames because it was negotiated with her childhood friend and sister-in-law, Marguerite d'Autriche. It is not surprising, therefore, that her death in September 1531 was mourned as a national loss. Her son the king organized a funeral fit for a queen, and the official royal printer, Geoffroy Tory, published on the day of her funeral (October 17, 1531) a collection of twenty epitaphs by renowned court poets, in Latin and French.[12] Just nine days later, on October 26, Tory issued a second edition augmented by eleven pieces, using only the French title: Epitaphes a la louenge de ma Dame

Mere du Roy, faictz par plusieurs recommendables Autheurs.¹³ Among the poets who penned the epitaphs were Mellin de Saint-Gelais, Victor Brodeau, Antoine Héroët, Germain Brice, Antoine Macault, and other noted humanists. The collection opens with texts in Latin, and the first French epitaph is atttributed to "L.R"—that is "le Roy" François I himself.

Besides these two collections, however, her death inspired at least six other works:

1. Clément Marot, *Eglogue sur le trespas de ma dame Loyse de Savoye, mere du roy Françoys, Premier de ce nom.*

2. Jean Bouchet, *Jugement poetic de l'honneur feminin et sejour des illustres claires & honnestes Dames* (Poitiers: De Marnef, 1538 [but with a privilege dated 1536]).

3. Jean de Vauzelles, *Theatre de francoise desolation sur le trespas de la tres auguste Loyse* (Lyon: [Claude Nourry?] Nov [1531?]).

4. Jacques de la Hogue, *Le Livre de Facet: Comploration sur le trespas de deffuncte ma Dame la Regente, Mere du Roy Françoys Premier* (Paris: Pierre Vidoue pour Galliot Du Pré, 1535).

5. Scaliger, Giulio Bordone Della Scala, dit Jules-César, *Nouorum Epigrammatum Liber unicus. . .Hymni duo. . .Diua Ludouica Sabaudia* (Paris: Michel de Vascosan, 1533).¹⁴

6. Nicolas Bourbon, *Nugae* (Paris: Michel de Vascosan, 1533).¹⁵

The epitaphs in the Tory volume all celebrate Louise as peacemaker, and if her intelligence is mentioned it is in relation to her ability to reconcile foes. Thus, Antoine Macault envisions Jupiter himself addressing her as "Fille tressaige" who by her "grant sens, vertu & bon sçavoir/[A] peu l'yre des Roys en terre a Paix mouvoir" (fol. B4v). Germain Brice asserts that Louise had "Justice & Force, Atrempance & Prudence," if any woman had. She was endowed moreover with "savoir/D'administrer, ordonner & prevoir/Affaires grans du publicque salut" (fol. C1v). In a second epitaph, Brice admires her "sens & Prudence" by which peace was achieved (fol. C2). These are the same virtues identified by her son as the source of her ability to defend France against her enemies. François speaks of her "invincible vertu," which no one will ever equal: "si le monde dure autant qu'il a duré, . . .point n'aura seconde/L'approchant de vertu en cestuy mortel monde" (fol. B1v).¹⁶ She achieved peace by her "grand-vertu et tressage conduite," and her abilities surpass those expected of her gender: "O cueur qui ne sentiez de femme que le nom" (fol. B1).

Antoine Héroët assumes the voice of Louise herself to assert: "Dieu m'envoya du ciel icy dedans/Pour le regir, gouverner et mouvoir" (fol. B2).¹⁷ He admires the way in which "en peu de temps à Femme feust possible/Rendre une fois Chrestienté paisible." In a second, shorter, epitaph, Héroët reflects the current debate over the superiority of men, suggesting that, in the case of Louise, Nature had erred. Although Nature always preferred to create a man rather than a woman, the example of Louise, "tant noble creature," demonstrates either that the writings about the superiority of men are false, or that nature has "myeulx faict que pensé" (fol. B4).

Adrien de l'Aunay, secretary of Marguerite de Navarre, enumerates the virtues of Louise: three Christian (faith, hope, charity) and four cardinal (fortitude, prudence, temperance, justice). He also praises her "sçavoir" and her patience, and ends his lengthy encomium with two rather uninspiring stanzas constructed on her initial and emblem *L/aile*: "Car ung Oyseau sans L. a peine peult voler" (fol. C4).

All these texts emphasize Louise's political success at achieving peace, her ability to surpass the limits of her gender, and the immortality of her soul as opposed to the mortal limits of her body. While insisting that Louise's loss surpasses all expression, they also emphasize the inappropriateness of mourning one whose spirit had surely reunited with God and who had therefore achieved eternal life:

> Puis que la vie honneste & memorable
> Sert aprés Mort d'epitaphe honnorable,
> Puis que le dueil semble envieuse chose
> Quant il est faict pour l'esprit qui repose,
> Je doibz laisser triste Elegie escripre
> De vous ma Dame.[18]

When all the epitaphs are appraised, finally, it is evident that Louise was not remembered or eulogized as a bibliophile.

In contrast, one might look at the epitaph for her husband, written by Octovien de Saint-Gelais.[19] The very first line invokes writing implements: "Ha, plume et encre, a quoy ores t'amuses?" and line 4 notes that all "parchemincs" have not yet been used. The text proceeds with a panegyric on the power of Death which overpowers all, regardless of wealth, power, age, or station. Charles died suddenly at age thirty-seven, young for a nobleman, even for that time, whereas his widow lived to be fifty-four, which explains why there are no references to her dying before her time. Charles lived a very retiring life, far from battlefields and court intrigues, despite his high rank, so there is little to praise in terms of action. Saint-Gelais emphasizes instead his character, but there is nothing particularly distinctive in the long list of qualities he enumerates: *Prudence, Honneur, Loyaulté, Justice, Bonté, Doulceur, Grace* and *Pitié*. The count's "Sobre Parolle et Constante Maniere" are perhaps less conventional than his "Beaulté Parfaicte et Force Corporelle," but it is difficult to measure his "Prompte Justice et Grant

LOUISE DE SAVOIE, "BIBLIOPHILE" 233

Auctorité" or his "Misericorde meslee de Verité, Avec splendeur de la Foy Catholique." In several verses, however, Saint-Gelais emphasizes his "hault sçavoir qui le monde environne," a wisdom which, along with "vraye vertu," every prince should possess. He even addresses Louise as the "Heritiere de son loué sçavoir," saying "Demeuree estes de ses vertus aprinse." The most interesting passage, however, relates specifically to his learning and to his books:

> De tous les artz se voulut enquerir
> Pour acquerir tiltre de sapience;
> Les faictz antiques sceut si tresbien querir
> Et requerir qu'il en peust acquerir
> Ains que mourir certayne cognoissance.
> Experience eut de toute science
> Par diligence et eut livres si beaulx
> Que honnorés sont fleurs de liz et lambeaulx. (lines 666-73)

These references to books may arise in part from the count's distinguished ancestry (his father, Jean, brother of the poet Charles d'Orléans, was a known bibliophile), in part from a lack of more striking military or political activities, but the difference from the descriptions of Louise is remarkable nonetheless.

Another epitaph for Louise, the *Comploration* by Jacques de la Hogue,[20] reiterates the political and moral attributes already noted in the Tory collection. Atropos himself recounts Louise's merits to the French:

> "Ceste princesse, honnorable & begnine
> Onc ne cessa de vous monstrer le signe
> De vraye amour, employant sa puissance
> A vous garder de perte & de nuysance; (lines 81-84)
> . . .
> Incessamment pour vous a batraillé
> Tant nuyct que jour, couru & travaillé
> Pour mectre paix, & de sy bon accord
> Qu'en voz pays n'y a plus nul discord.
> Le roy son filz, surprins des ennemys,
> Par son bon sens a en France remys;
> Ses deux enfans qui tenoient ostage
> Vous a renduz, qui est tresroyal gaige.
> Que voulez vous que plus elle vous fasse?" (lines 91-99)

Louise should not be mourned, for she has been removed from the "monde miserable" to enjoy eternal happines. The author then has a vision of Louise's apotheosis. A chariot, called "Sapience", with Justice, Temperance, Fortitude, and Prudence as its wheels and Faith, Hope, and Charity as its horses, bears the soul of Louise heavenward, in the company of Eve, Sarah, and all the other noble ladies of the Old Testament. Pallas drives the chariot, guided by Saint Helen, and when Louise's soul arrives in heaven, all the martyrs, virgins, and widows welcome it, as the moon, sun, planets, comets, and all the elements pull the chariot up to the heavenly throne. Considering her "bonnes meurs," the author is convinced that she will have eternal life: "elle estoit des esleues/A posseder es cieulx joye eternelle."

Jacques de la Hogue's specific reference to comets recalls the event recorded by the Bourgeois de Paris:

> Audict an [1530], jeudy, vingtiesme jour de janvier, jour de Sainct Sebastien, au soir entre neuf et dix heures, il apparut sur ceste ville de Paris une grande comette au ciel, dont, à cause de ce, il sembloit que le ciel fut entreouvert de grande clarté et sembloit que le tout fut en feu et estoit de figure d'un dragon ou d'un serpent flamboyant en feu, qui estoit moult grand et long, aiant grande queue à merveilles. Et alla cheoir ce jour sur les fossez de la ville de Sainct Denis en France.[21]

The comet was interpreted as a premonition of the death of a great prince, but Louise considered it as foretelling her own,[22] and various poets agreed. In the rondeau "de la comette veue avant le trespas de feu Madame en l'an 1531," Victor Brodeau assures Louise that "il n'est aujourdhuy vivant homme,/Y fust Cesar tryumphant en sa Rome,/Qui tant soit peu approche votre gloire." The heavenly sign only underscored Louise's importance in the political realm:

> Si la comette au monde signifie
> La briefve fin d'un grant prince ou monarcque,
> J'e paeur que Mort, Madame, vous desfie
> Et qu'elle ait ja contre vous levé marque,
> Car voz faiz excellants je remarque.[23]

Although not published as epitaphs, two other works honor Louise after her death. Jean Du Pré published his *Palais des nobles Dames* in 1534 and dedicated it to Marguerite de Navarre.[24] Not surprisingly, he included in the text a lengthy encomium of her mother. Calling her an "Isis ou seconde Cybele," he admires Louise as a "femme saige, liberalle, prudente; et au prouffit du commun entendente" (lines 5431-32). He praises her as "moderatrice/du beau royaulme" and asserts that her "gestes precieux" are great and worthy of honor. Although he does not specifically mention her love of books, he states that she was "en jeune eage si droictement instruicte/ Qu'on la tenoit des pucelles l'eslite" (lines 5463-64). With "meurs nompareilles," she was justly renowned for her virtue, but Du Pré also praises her "cueur chevaleureux et tresconstant," especially during the captivity of her son, when she so ably governed France. For her "faictz illustres et haultaine regence, Dame Loyse, de clere refulgence" deserves first place among meritorious women.

In the "Apologie" addressed to Anne de Laval in the printed edition of Le Jugement poetic de l'honneur femenin, Jean Bouchet states that he had long ago presented this work to the king and had composed it "a l'honneur principallement de feue tresillustre & tresnoble dame, Madame Loyse de Savoye, sa mere."[25] Bouchet develops a lengthy apology of Louise's qualities, not only her physical beauty ("membres sains en leur proportion") but her moral virtues. Nature speaks of her "beaulté corporelle"; Fortune of her "grans biens temporelz," which enabled her to govern prudently; Grace of her "louables meurs & vertuz." Nowhere is she described as a bibliophile, and the only book mentioned is that of her accomplishments, when Fortune says: "de tous ses faictz & gestes le livre ay." Nevertheless, Grace asserts that "Par son sçavoir aultres dames deffaict" and notes that she surrounded her son with "gens lectrez" in order to assure his good education. Honor gives rather backhanded praise of her learning: "Elle sceut tout sans estre grand clergesse," but her "saige conduicte" and "courtoys entretien" are admired. Fortune describes her, once again, as earning masculine honors: "Je l'ay faicte aux honneurs parvenir/Non seulement femenins, mais virilles. . . ." Louise surpassed her gender: "Elle passa de son sexe la force/Et prinst le coeur & couraige mavorce. . ." (D4v). Although she is compared to other famous women, her accomplishments rival those of men: "A surmonté par paix plus d'ennemys/Que par combatz ne feit oncques Pompee. . . ."

Bouchet makes one final reference to a book which he describes as being "en belle impression": it is none other than Tory's volume of epitaphs for Louise. Bouchet names all those who contributed to the collection and mentions as well the "traicté pastoral" of Clément Marot.

Marot's eclogue innovates in its use of pastoral form to eulogize Louise, but it offers her rather ambiguous praise. One section is important, nonetheless, in our context. Louise is described as an educator, but in a moral rather than intellectual sphere: "Son beau mesnage en bon sens conduysoit."[26] She urged the young ladies in her charge to avoid vice and idleness by pursuing useful work, which in the pastoral setting included gardening and needlework.

Jean de Vauzelles addressed his *Theatre de francoise desolation sur le trespas de la tres auguste Loyse* to Marguerite de Navarre as consolation at the death of her mother.[27] Like many other texts, the poem of 256 lines characterizes Louise as prudent and wise: "Virille en sens, et pitié plus que femme,/Noble de cueur, religieuse en l'ame. . . ." Vauzelles admires her political skill, claiming that by achieveing peace she has earned the name "Auguste," and he employs an extraordinary oxymoron, "pudicque audace," to describe her ability to "tout gouverner," even the king himself, for

> . . . . ou est l'homme en France
> Qui vers le roy aye telle audience
> Ne qui osa si virillement dire
> Tout ce qu'au roy pouvoit ayder ou nuyre. (lines 187-90)

Vauzelles notes that the "trinité"—king, mother, and sister—will be shattered by Louise's death and, like Jacques de la Hogue, he considers the comet (lines 93-98) to forewarn of her death, for "sa grand noblesse/Meritoit bien ung signe au ciel avoir/Fort flamboyant. . . ." He concludes with the image of her tomb, where the hearts of all French people will be "conjoinctz par grans douleurs." This image corresponds, in fact, to the full-page woodcut on the verso of the title page, which depicts a tomb bearing the cross of Savoy, surmounted by a crowned L and the inscription "ENCOR LUMBRE." At the base of the monument is a series of small hearts each with the letter L in the center.

Vauzelles praises Louise and mourns her, but nowhere does he mention her reading or her desire for books. That he considers Louise to exhibit both "masculine" and "feminine" traits underscores contemporary attitudes toward gender and corroborates other writers' observation that Louise surpasses the expectations of her gender. In this light, it is significant that she is compared not only to female heroines and goddesses (Judith, Esther, Pallas, Isis) but also to male rulers and warriors: Augustus (by Vauzelles), Caesar (Brodeau), Pompey (Bouchet). It is apparent from all the epitaphs that Louise is remembered primarily as regent, mother to the king, and peacemaker. It is her virtue that is emphasized along with her "manly" accomplishments as ruler, and whatever aspects of her intelligence or learning may be mentioned, they are more allied to moral conduct than to book collecting.

If we consider now the texts composed for Louise while she was alive, we can distinguish two groups: a large corpus of dedications to her, in verse or prose, and a smaller corpus of poems about her. Most important among the latter is a celebrated manuscript now in Ecouen, containing a series of rondeaux on the seven virtues, each illustrated by a miniature.[28] One leaf is missing, so that only six of the seven texts are extant, but the seventh poem is found in several other sources. All the rondeaux are constructed on the acrostic of Louise's name, the thirteen letters LOISE DE SAVOIE corresponding perfectly to the *rondeau cinquain* form. Moreover, as the author specifies in the brief introduction to the collection, the rondeaux can be read both forward and backward, that is beginning with either the first line or the last: "pourrez relire lesditz rondeaux au rebours, commençant du bas en hault." The rondeaux are addressed to Louise in the second person singular ("toy") by the first-person author. Given the focus on virtues, it is not surprising that Louise is praised for her moral character, and there is no mention of books. In championing *liberalité* over avarice, however, the author remarks that Louise has always preferred acquiring knowledge above wealth:

> Incessamment as acquis du sçavoir
> Sans amasser or, argent, ny avoir,
> En desprisant tous tresors de pecune.

In describing her patience, he states: "Impossible est t'eslongner de raison," an idea he reiterates in two other rondeaux: on chastity, where he describes her as "Suyvant raison," and on sobriety, where he asserts: "Invincible as le cuer qui raison ayme." In the latter poem he admires both her morals and her mind: "Exquise en meurs et parfaicte en espris,/Sans point mentir, tu es de corps et de ame."

Two other poems about Louise are known. A rondeau, again constructed on the acrostic of her name, proclaims: "Saige en toulx faitz vous estes estimee."[29] A cabalistic interpretation of the letter S of her name is offered in the form of a rondeau beginning "Mirouer de lyeS" in L'*Introduction en la Cabale* by Jean Thenaud (Geneva, BPU MS 167). The author admires Louise's "magnanime haultesse/Bonté, prudence, & saigesse" and compares her to Juno and Pallas:

> Car Juno en sa richesse
> Et Pallas en sa prouesse
> Precellez par raison ample
> Dont le guydon & exemple
> Estez du feminin sexe.

The idea of Louise as "standard" or "guydon" can be related to the many texts where she acts as "compass," as in the well-known manuscript of *Le Compas du daulphin* (BNF MS fr. 2285), although, as we shall see, in the latter example she guides her son rather than the entire female population. In all, then, neither the epitaphs nor the poems in her honor recognize Louise as a patron or book collector, even though they praise in a very general way her wisdom of conduct and, occasionally, her learning.

    Not surprisingly, the dedications to Louise, found in numerous works prepared for her, offer a stronger impression of her patronage, but one must be wary of the self-serving nature of such texts. The "humble servant" praising his patroness seeks to maintain his position, and the superlatives used for his sponsor are as commonplace as the depreciation of his own authorial skills. Yet beneath the clichés are indications of Louise's patronage which shed light on her interest in books. Two writers in particular are known to have composed works for Louise, sometimes at her command—Jean Thenaud and François Demoulins. There are also, however, several anonymous texts with dedications to Louise, as well as works by Symphorien Champier, Etienne Le Blanc, Jean de Bourdigné, and by the Parisian bookseller Anthoine Vérard, all of which merit consideration. In addition to their revelations about Louise as bibliophile, these prefaces offer evidence for contemporary conceptions of the "book."

    Jean Thenaud dedicated several works to Louise and continued to praise her in those which he offered to her son. In the *Vie de Saint Jerome* (Paris, BNF MS fr. 421), composed while François was still only dauphin, Thenaud considers Louise to be "du nombre des tresillustres et tresnobles dames qui des vostre enfance avez toujours aimé vertuz." He offers her "ce petit livret"[30] knowing that by her "bonté and bienveuillance inestimable" she will appreciate the gift of her humble servant even if his style is neither "polly ne bien aorné." Her reception of the work will resemble that of God "qui des humains mieulx estime la bonne voulunté que l'oeuvre et effect, quant le povoir y deffault."

    In the *Epître en vers de Charles VIII à François I*, called the "traité de Clyo" and attributed to Jean Thenaud (BNF MS fr. 2286), the author remarks that Louise and her son willingly receive literary works of varying degrees of quality:

> la debonnaireté du Roy tresbenyn et vostre clemence ineffable si gracieusement recueillent tous ouvrages et dons de litterature qui vous sont presentez, qu'en acceptant en bonne extime les consummez et bien agencez euvres des souverains ouvriers au moindres donnés acueil gracieux et atraict favorable.

In the dedication of his *Triumphe de Prudence* to Louise, Thenaud praises the "purité, excellence et abismale sagesse de [son] heroïque esprit" and says that he has undertaken this work *at her command*, to provide a "passetemps" which is nonetheless profitable. He calls it "ung livre du Triumphe des Vertuz, et le recueil des Vertueux," and its very subject justifies the offering to Louise, paragon of all virtues. He asserts that she desires to surround herself only with virtuous books and people:

> autre chose ne desirez veoir, ouyr et avoir jouxte vous, fors livres, sieurs, dames et toutes gens d'honneur et vertuz, qui sont trop plus felices et heurez de veoir et ouyr vostre trescorruscante sapience que onques ne fut la royne Saba ny les domestiques de Salomon pour ouyr sa prudence et sagesse.[31]

Thenaud is not the only writer to acknowledge Louise's command for new works. François Demoulins begins his *Vie de la Magdalène* (BNF MS fr. 24955) with the following words:

> Madame, il vous a pleu de voustre grace me commander que misse en histoire la vie de la belle & clere Magdalene, ce que j'ay entrepris par grand desir de vous faire service, combien que me santisse indigne de vous servir et oncquorez plus de parler & tenir propoz d'une si saincte dame.

Like Thenaud, he also trusts in Louise's goodwill to accept works whose quality might not equal the author's good intentions. In the concluding ballade by which Demoulins presents to Louise his *Dialogue sur la folie du jeu* (BNF MS fr.1863), the author offers testimony to her gracious reception of works, as well as to her "sagesse":

> Si le bien fait estoit extimé
> Comme choses qui sont materielles,
> Par quantité je seroye estonné
> Et mes plumes a escripre rebelles,
> Mais je suys seur que selon bon vouloir
> Les petiz dons vous ay veu recepvoir
> A grant plaisir, magnificque princesse;
> Cela me fait comprandre hardiesse
> De vous bailler mon oeuvre mal ornee:
> Si non sçavoir par paresse la blesse,
> L'intencion veult estre regardee.
>
> Dame d'honneur, maistresse de sagesse,
> Laissez a part l'inutille simplesse
> De ma l(iv)re rudement composee,
> En regrectant du parler la rudesse
> L'intencion doit estre regardee. (fol. 14v)

Painted to the right of this text is a small miniature, in the form of a circle, depicting the kneeling author presenting his book to Louise, seated on a gold chair (Fig. 1).

Etienne Le Blanc also mentions Louise's command in the dedication of his *Genealogie de la maison de Bourbon* (BNF MS fr. 5719) to "Treshaulte, trespuissante, tresexcellente, magnanime et tresdebonnaire princesse. . ., mere tresbenigne et tressaige du treschrestien Roy de France." For her he has undertaken the research and writing of this work:

> Desirant comme vostre treshumble et tresobeissant serviteur et subject accomplir ce que de vostre benigne grace il vous a pleu me commander, j'ay depuis ung mois en ça serché, tant au tresor des chartres du Roy, en la chambre de ses comptes que aux anciennes hystoires de France, tout ce qui faict mention de Bourbon, d'Auvergne, de Clermont. . .et ce que en ay trouvé l'ay mis et redigé par escript en ce petit abregié.

Le Blanc also composed for Louise *Les Gestes de Blanche de Castille* (BNF MS fr. 5715), establishing a parallel between his patroness and Blanche, mother of Saint Louis, who "par sa prudence vertueusement" served as regent during her son's minority, "a laquelle regence a par sa grande prudence et vertu succedé treshaulte, trespuissante et tresexcellente princesse et ma tresredoubtee dame, Madame Loyse, mere du treschrestien Roy de France." Le Blanc asserts that Louise resembles two other heroines who saved their people, Judith and Esther: "Et vous madame, mere de sçavoir, par vostre grande providence avez jusques cy gardé et deffendu le peuple de France."

Louise's resemblance to Judith and Esther is depicted visually in a full-page illustration made especially for another work: Jean de Bourdigné's *Hystoire agregative des annalles et cronicques d'Anjou*, published in 1529.[32] Louise is seated on a throne in center-page, her left hand raised with pointed index finger, her right lowered to receive the book from the kneeling author (Fig. 2). Groups of courtiers and churchmen are seated below her on either side, and the two Old Testament heroines stand above them, Judith on the left, identified as "patrie liberatrix," and Esther on the right, "salvatrix populi." Each stands on a square dais, at Louise's shoulder level, inscribed with a Latin verse: Proverbs 8, "Per me principes imperant" for Judith and Proverbs 13, "Sapiens mulier edificat domum suam" for Esther. Both heroines are turned toward Louise, each holding a characteristic symbol: the one, the head of Holofernes on an upright sword, and the other, a document with official seals suspended from its lower edge. The three female figures form an inverted triangle with Louise at its focal point, equally liberator and savior of her people. The author, kneeling in the foreground, holds forth a large volume bearing the inscription DIVE SABAUDIENSI PALADI SICATUS LABOR.

In his dedication to Louise, the author notes that man's reason enables him to learn from past events to judge those to come, and that his own desire to "proffiter et donner recreation a tous nobles et vertueux espritz" has led him to undertake this work, despite the "debilité, rudesse et insuffisance de [son] entendement." His fears of inadequacy are vainquished by "l'amour de [son] pays et verité hystorialle," so that he can offer his work first to "treshaulte, tresvertueuse et tresnoble princesse, Madame Loyse, mere du Roy, duchesse d'Anjou et d'Angoulmoys, contesse du Meine et de Gyan. Et par apres a tous prelatz et nobles barons, chevaliers et escuyers, dames et damoyselles du pays d'Anjou."

A similar work, *Les Grandes Chroniques de Savoie*, had been dedicated to Louise a decade earlier, in an edition of 1516.[33] The author, Symphorien Champier, appeals to her "tant benigne supportacion" to excuse his authorial inadequacies, and although he makes no specific reference to Louise's bibliophilic interests, he does mention the renowned exemplar of libraries: to compose the chronicles well, he writes, would require "la bibliotheque de Ptolomee Philadelphe." Of all the dedications to Louise, Champier's is the only one to mention a collection of books.

Champier addressed a second work to Louise, this one a manuscript: *Le Doctrinal du jeune prince* (BNF MS fr. 1959). As the title indicates, the work concerns the education of a ruler, and it is dedicated to Louise in recognition of her role, for one must not neglect the "regime et gouvernement en jeunesse a ceulx qui ont la charge [des princes]." In offering her "ce petit labeur," Champier praises her as a "princesse pacificque, qui [est] une autre Pallas et tressaige Mynerve."

Louise's role as guide to the future king is also proclaimed, both visually and verbally, in the *Compas du daulphin* (BNF MS fr. 2285), as noted earlier. In the opening miniature, the mother stands behind her young son, clasping his left hand in hers. She holds forth in her right hand a large compass toward which François extends his arm, above the head of an oversized, upright dolphin positioned beside him.[34] The dedicatory *chant royal* praises Louise as a noble princess "de science garnye" and admonishes her to protect and instruct her royal son:

> Gardez le bien soubz vostre elle [i.e., *aile*] cherie,
> Car vous estes le compas & mesure
> Du daulphin a qui Dieu doint bonne vie.

Louise's love of Christ and her concern "pour le bien publicque de conduire salutairement monsieur vostre filz" have also inspired an anonymous author to compose for her the *Dicts sybillins* (BNF MS fr. 2362), which he terms a "doctrine vive et de soy salutaire." Like Le Blanc, he equates Louise with Queen Blanche and other "saintes meres" renowned for the care of their sons, the mothers of Saints Remy, Augustine, Bernard.

The anonymous author of the *Exhortacion sur un passage de l'Evangile* (BNF MS fr. 2449) selects Louise to receive his work "tant pour l'excellant don d'intelligence que Dieu vous a donné pour comprendre les grans misteres de sa loy, tant aussi pour ce que vous estes mere du Roy trescrestien." Considering Louise to be the intermediary between author and king, he offers her "ce petit livre ou est contenu le mistere du baptesme affin que par vostre bon moyen le Roy vostre filz le puisse veoir et oyr lire." The ultimate purpose extends, however, even beyond the realm of France, for just as the king will learn to act like a good Christian, so his subjects will do likewise, and "tellement que a nostre exemple tout le demourant du monde se puisse reduire et convertir au Roy des Roys Jhesucrist."

The idea of Louise as intercessor with her son is yet more strongly expressed in another religious text entitled *Le Zèle des princes pour l'Eglise* (BNF MS fr. 950). In his dedication to Louise, the author states that since the "monarchie inferieure et terrestre des François" should imitate as much as possible the "monarchie celeste," so Louise, as mother of the king, should imitate the Virgin Mary, "nostre bonne et treschere advocate envers Dieu." He admonishes her thus to assume a public role:

> Vous, ma dame, que [sic] estes mere du Roy, a l'exemple de la glorieuse et tresdigne mere du roy des roys, devez prendre et accepter envers le Roy, vostre trescher et tresaymé filz, mon souverain seigneur, l'estat et office d'advocate de ses subgectz pour luy remonstrer les choses concernans le bien et utilité de sa couronne et chose publicque et soulaigement de sesdictz subgectz.

The author presents her with "ce petit traictie" so that she might know that the "salut du prince" and of his people depends upon the "bonne disposition et reformation de l'estat de l'eglise et de religion."

That Louise actively sought to encourage her son's religious devotion is evident in another manuscript, composed by François Demoulins at her command: BNF MS fr. 2088, the *Interprétation du Psaume XXVI*. The introduction on fol. 1 explains the origin of the text as well as Louise's role:

> Le xiiie jour de fevrier mil cinq cens et seze a Horiol sur la ryviere de Drome, Madame fut spirituellement admounestee de faire parler son humilité a l'obeissance du Roy son filz, et le supplier que pour oraison devote il prinst le pseaulme xxvie, lequel est convenable pour luy, selon veritable narration suyvant la declaration de son adventure. Et moult luy profitera si a la requeste de la dame qu'il ayme tant il veult chanter et dire comme David, "Dominus illuminatio mea et salus mea, quem timebo?"

Illustrated by Godefroy Le Batave with a series of astonishing images of mother and son in place of David, this emblematic manuscript[35] underscores Louise's importance as spiritual counselor. On fol. 4, for example, the Psalm verse receives an extraordinary interpretation:

> Le Roy congnoissant la bonne inclinacion de sa pure, nete, honneste, et sage mere, pour la resjouir luy prant la main, et luy dyt en parlant d'elle mesmez: "Madame entre toutez les femmez du monde, j'en ay demanday une a Dieu; Et luy en feray requeste, affin que je habite en sa maison tous les jours de ma vie."

The manuscript concludes with an image of "LUDOVICA MATER" handing the cross to "FRANCISCUS FILIUS" as the text explains:

> Madame aymant myeulx l'ame spirituelle du Roy son filz que le corps materiel, luy presente la Croix et luy dyt: Monseigneur mon defenseur, mon repoux, mon desir, mon maistre, mon filz et mon amy, *festina lente*. Attends Dieu ton liberateur. Faictz virilement. Fortifie ton cueur. Et soutiens noustre Seigneur.

This spiritual role of Louise and particularly her resemblance, as mother of the French king, to Mary, mother of Christ, are also evident in the celebrated manuscript of poems from the puys d'Amiens (BNF MS fr. 145) offered to Louise shortly after her visit to Amiens in 1517. Like the poems themselves, all celebrating the Virgin Mary, the dedication assumes the form of a *chant royal*. It describes Louise as a "dame scientificque" as well as a "princesse pacifique" whose importance is underscored by the refrain: "Mere humble et franche au grant espoir de France."[36]

The analogy between the royal and the celestial mothers, the "mère du Roy" and the "mère du Christ," is also implicit in another well-known manuscript dedicated to Louise, on which I would like now to focus. BNF MS fr. 985 bears the title "La Vie Nostre Dame en rithme," written in brown ink on the paste-down of the front cover, next to the number "195" in Arabic numerals, indicating its presence in the personal library of François I. Consisting of 138 vellum leaves (276 x 166 mm), the manuscript is written in fairly large bastarda script, 24 lines to the page (justification 195 x 94 mm). Its text, which until now has been considered anonymous, is organized into quatrains of octosyllabic French verse, with paragraph markings indicating the beginning of most quatrains. In addition to painted line endings, there are three full-page miniatures (fols. 2v, 3, 102) and ninety-six smaller miniatures, painted two per page and separated by several lines of Latin text. On fols. 1v-2 is a dedication to a "princesse" who, although unnamed, is identifiable from references in the text and from the first full-page miniature (fol. 2v). Louise de Savoie, in a purple gown and black head-dress, is depicted seated beside her young son, her hands outstretched to receive the book from a kneeling donor (Fig. 3). On the facing page, another full-page miniature portrays the Virgin and Child surrounded by angels and seated below the Holy Trinity. A four-verse French prayer is inscribed beneath the angels. Viewed together, the two miniatures create a visual equation, Louise being aligned diagonally with the Virgin, her son with Christ, especially since François holds a baton pointing up toward the Virgin but, significantly, *through* the bookseller. Anne-Marie Lecoq saw in these miniatures evidence for the analogy between Louise and Mary,[37] and I myself used the miniature of Louise and François to corroborate the identification of the lady and son depicted in a group of books published by Anthoine Vérard.[38] What I had failed to notice, however, was the similarity between the manuscript's dedication to Louise and one of Verard's *printed* prologues. The two texts are so similar in form and expression that their relationship cannot be doubted,[39] and this relationship raises new questions about the origins of the manuscript and its connection with the Parisian publisher. It also, however, may help identify the intended recipient of one printed presentation copy.

The dedication to Louise takes the form of a ballade with *envoi*, although Lecoq erroneously refers to it as a *chant royal*, the form regularly used for poems to the Virgin and employed, as noted above, in the manuscript of the puys d'Amiens of 1517. The three stanzas and *envoi* share a refrain that, though varying slightly in each use, contains the key word *lire*. The three stanzas of the ballade contain twelve decasyllabic lines each, rhyming *ababbccddede*, with the *envoi* consisting of six lines, *fdedde*. It should be noted that although the dedication leaf shares the same justification as the rest of the manuscript, the text is written in a different script. Moreover, since the decasyllabic lines of the dedication are longer than the octosyllabic lines of the poem, the dedication lines extend noticeably beyond the outer line of the justification. That this leaf was added later seems highly probable.

In the first stanza, the dedication addresses the "princesse haultaine" destined for royal lineage:

> Tenant du liz la branche souveraine
> Pour parvenir au hault tiltre royal
> En augmentant le siege imperial.

She takes pleasure in her son without neglecting the necessary substance ("plaisance/substance"), and the author offers this little book for her recreation, claiming to have made it in his own study:

> Je vous ay fait en ma simple orature
> Ung petit livre pour prendre recreance
> Que vous lyrez tandiz que le temps dure.

In the second stanza, the poet suggests that it is human nature to find comfort in "plaisant diz," but that doing good works ("bonnes euvres") is essential to achieving final joy. The model to follow is the Virgin Mary, who is described in the third stanza as the fountain of virtue, mother of all, path to divine forgiveness. The poet alters the refrain to emphasize the value of knowing her life and therefore of reading the book he offers: "Lisez sa vie, tandiz que le temps dure." The envoi, addressed to the lady in a line which rhymes with no other, concludes with a summary of the book's subject and relevance:

> Treshaulte dame exellante,
> Prenez en gré par vostre bien vueillance
> Ce livre cy ou n'a pas grant facture;
> C'est la vie, la louenge et usance
> De Nostre Dame ou vous prendrez plaisance,
> Que vous lyrez tandiz que le temps dure.

If the dedicatory ballade is specifically geared both to the manuscript text and to the patron, the emphasis on approaching death, signaled by the refrain's "tandiz que le temps dure," strikes a somewhat incongruous note, especially when compared to the opening anticipation of the royal throne. It makes sense, however, when its origins are uncovered. The ballade in fact was first used as a prologue to the *Vigiles des mors*, a text consisting of the nine lessons of the Office of the Dead derived from the book of Job, which Vérard published sometime between 1496 and 1498. The ballade was originally addressed to Charles VIII, and as evident from the parallel texts, the form, rhyme scheme, and much of the vocabulary was maintained even when the patron changed gender and identity. As the dedication moved from one work to the next, the prefatory remarks in the third stanza changed from a focus on the masculine God viewed through Job to the feminine Virgin, with a corresponding alteration in gender-specific nouns (*roy, Dieu* to *Dame, mere*).

Vérard's edition, like Louise's manuscript, is undated, but typographical elements as well as the dedication to Charles VIII, who died on April 7, 1498, permit dating within a two-year period, 1496-98. The *Vigiles des mors* edition was, ironically, the last of the many books Vérard prepared for the king who had been his primary patron since acceding to the throne in 1483. The vellum presentation copies, however, have remained puzzling. The copy in the BNF, which belonged to the royal library, is illuminated in a rather inferior style and lacks the prologue to Charles VIII. In contrast, the copy at the Musée Condé in Chantilly contains the prologue and is beautifully illuminated by the Master of Jacques de Besançon, one of Vérard's chief illuminators. The full-page miniature depicts the publisher offering a crimson-covered book to a nobleman wearing a black hat and a floor-length gold robe trimmed in ermine who stands at the left in a small chapel with vaulted panels.[40] In a nimbus above them appear God, the Virgin Mary, and two angels holding a nude figure representing the soul. A corpse lies on the green patterned floor below. In a related scene painted to the left of the text, Death appears as a skeleton bearing two arrows and a scythe, while across the bottom of the page, below the text, skulls and bones on a green field further illustrate the subject. While the dedication would suggest that the nobleman is Charles VIII, the absence of crown, throne, fleurs-de-lis, or other signs of royalty typically employed by Vérard's artists led me to question this identification. The figure closely resembles the nobleman depicted in a vellum copy of *Tristan*, BNF Rés. Vélins 623, belonging to Louise's husband, Charles d'Angoulême,[41] and I believe that this copy of the *Vigiles* was probably prepared for the count. The use of the prologue in Louise's manuscript adds support to this hypothesis. Since the count died, however, in 1496, Vérard's edition must pre-date this event, even if the illuminated copy may not have been finished in time for presentation before his death. One other intriguing detail comes from Louise's account book: she purchased, unfortunately at an unspecified date, from Victor Cochon, libraire de Tours, "unes Vigilles en françoys, en parchemin, toutes ystoriees."

Vérard's connections with Louise's manscript can be further developed by looking at both the miniatures and the text. Louise and her son are portrayed in the first full-page miniature in a style already familiar to us from similar scenes.[42] The donor, however, resembles less the author than the young bookseller as he appears in several miniatures painted in Vérard's printed books of ca. 1500.[43] His youth is worth emphasizing in light of what we have discovered about the text: the *Vie Nostre Dame*, as found in Louise's manuscript (BNF MS fr. 985), is none other than the *Matines de la Vierge*, composed by Martial d'Auvergne. Born ca. 1430-35, Martial lived until 1508 but would have been an elderly figure at the time this manuscript was written. It is difficult to imagine him as the youthful donor depicted in the miniature, even if he was responsible for preparing the manuscript. It seems unlikely, however, that he had any part in its execution. Not only is his name absent from the text, but his poem has been re-edited for this manuscript by deleting all references to the original form, which followed the lessons, psalms, antiphons, and versicles of the hour of Matins from the Office of the Virgin. The history of the text is too complex to discuss fully here, and the recent edition by Yves Le Hir[44] unfortunately relies on an incomplete set of sources, failing to note all the known printed editions and manuscripts, including this one. Part of the problem, to be sure, is the variation in title and form. Early editions published the work as the *Louenges de la Vierge* and did not always distinguish the liturgical forms.[45] Excerpts were issued under the title *Le Trepassement et l'assumption Nostre Dame*.[46] Some manuscript copies are described as "Heures en français,"[47] and of course Louise's manuscript bears the title "La Vie Nostre Dame." One other set of sources must also be noted: several editions of Hours published by Simon Vostre and by Chappiel/Hardouyn, from ca. 1502-08, print portions of Martial d'Auvergne's text in the borders. And their model may have been a manuscript prepared by Vérard: the celebrated book of Hours which he prepared for Charles VIII (Madrid BN MS Vit. 24-1) includes many verses of Martial's text in its borders.[48]

We know from all these elements that Vérard had access to the *Matines de la Vierge*. We also know that he prepared at least one other manuscript for Louise, the Passion poem (BNF MS fr. 1686) for which he likewise edited a text.[49] We have discovered that he adapted a prologue composed for Charles VIII for use as a dedication to Louise in the manuscript *Vie Nostre Dame*. Is it unlikely therefore that the entire manuscript was planned and executed by Vérard for presentation to his favorite female patron, Louise de Savoie? The content of the manuscript, the dedication poem, and indeed the presentation miniature suggest that this is so.

In the way of conclusion, I would like to return to my original question: whether the bibliophilic interests of late medieval patrons were recognized by their contemporaries and recorded as noteworthy. As corollaries to that question, were women less likely than men to be described with respect to books, and do descriptions differ according to the gender of the patron? To what extent do references to book patronage reflect the interests of the "book-maker" rather than the patron?

My examination of texts for and about Louise de Savoie indicates that though Louise is now recognized as a "femme bibliophile," her contemporaries viewed her first and foremost as the influential mother of the king. Astute regent of France during his absence, champion of peace, she was praised both for "sens" and for "prudence," masculine and feminine qualities which prompted comparisons with heroes and heroines alike. Venerable widow, she was lauded as a model of virtue, but her highest calling was that of "compas" to the dauphin who would be king, another "sainte mere" who resembled the most venerable of all, the Virgin Mary. Unlike her husband, whose epitaph clearly records his possession of "livres si beaulx," Louise is not eulogized as a bibliophile, but her interest in books is amply attested nonetheless both in the number of volumes prepared for her and in the dedications themselves. Numerous manuscripts and printed books addressed to her, or bearing her portrait or arms, reflect her particular interests: treatises (moral, religious, political) to educate her son, histories of hereditary relevance (the chronicles of Savoy or Bourbon, the "gestes" of queen Blanche), and lives of special saints (Anne, the Magdalene, Jerome). At least three authors, Jean Thenaud, François Demoulins, and Etienne Le Blanc, refer explicitly to her desire and command for books, and so does the publisher Anthoine Vérard.

Vérard surely operated as much from self-interest as from a desire to flatter his patron, but the consistency with which he referred to her reading and her interest in books, in the four prologues he was known to have addressed to her,[30] resonated in a fifth, the prologue to the manuscript of La Vie Nostre Dame. The words "lire" and "livre" expose a connection with one of Vérard's printed prologues, which in turn reveals a web of relationships: between manuscripts and printed copies, books of Hours and the Vigiles des mors, Charles VIII and the Angoulême family, the life of the Virgin and the mother of the king. At their point of intersection stands the publisher-donor-manuscript-maker, Anthoine Vérard, who saw in Louise de Savoie the patron-bibliophile.

State University of New York at Albany

NOTES

1. Ernest Quentin Bauchart, Les Femmes bibliophiles de France (Paris, 1886; reprint, Geneva: Slatkine, 1993).
2. Dictionnaire alphabétique et analogique de la langue française (Paris: Robert, 1958), 1:464.
3. La Passion des manuscrits enluminés: Bibliophiles français, 1280-1580 (Paris: Bibliothèque Nationale, 1991), 9.
4. Her account, found in Paris, BNF MS fr. 8815, is cited in my Anthoine Vérard, Parisian Publisher, 1485-1512: Prologues, Poems, and Presentations (Geneva: Droz, 1997), 168, 471-73.
5. E. Sénemaud, La Bibliothèque de Charles d'Orléans Comte d'Angoulême au château de Cognac en 1496 (Paris: A. Claudin, 1861), 17.
6. Born September 11, 1476, she married Charles at age 10 on February 16, 1487; she gave birth at age 15 to Marguerite on April 11, 1492 and to François on September 12, 1494, the day after her 18th birthday.
7. "Journal de Louise de Savoye, duchesse d'Angoulesme. . ." in vol. 16 of Collection complète de mémoires relatifs à l'histoire de France, ed. Claude B. Petitot (Paris: Foucault, 1820), 397. In her article "Francis Du Moulin and the Journal of Louise of Savoy," The Sixteenth Century Journal 13, 1 (Spring 1982): 55-66, Myra Orth has convincingly proposed Du Moulin (Demoulins) as the "ghost-writer" of the journal, even though it is penned in the first-person voice of Louise.

8. Jean Michel Massing claims it for Louise, unfortunately without citing a source, in his introduction to *Erasmian Wit and Proverbial Wisdom: An Illustrated Moral Compendium for François I* (London: The Warburg Institute, 1995), 38. Anne-Marie Lecoq, *François Ier imaginaire* (Paris: Macula, 1987) does not discuss the motto.

9. Various lists of manuscripts belonging to Louise have been published: Léopold Delisle, *Le Cabinet des manuscrits de la Bibliothèque impériale* (Paris: 1868-81), 1:185; Quentin Bauchart, 13-23; Sheila Edmunds, "Manuscrits liés à d'autres membres de la maison de Savoie," in *Les Manuscrits enluminés des comtes et ducs de Savoie*, ed. A. Paravicini Bagliani (Turin: Umberto Allemandi & C., 1990), 207-13. For additional references and information about the manuscripts, see especially Lecoq and Orth. To the manuscripts must be added a number of printed books, many of which are discussed hereafter.

10. Myra D. Orth, "Louise de Savoie et le pouvoir du livre," in *Royaume de Fémynie: Pouvoirs, contraintes, espaces de liberté des femmes, de la Renaissance à la fronde*, ed. Kathleen Wilson-Chevalier and Eliane Viennot (Paris: Champion, 1999), 71-90. I am very grateful to Myra Orth for sending me a copy of her article as well as for sharing many materials related to Louise.

11. Cf. n. 8.

12. *In Lodoicae Regis Matris mortem. Epitaphia Latina & Gallica. Epitaphes a la louenge de ma Dame Mere du Roy, faictz par plusieurs recommendables Autheurs.* I have consulted the copy in Paris, BNF Rothschild 2786 (IV.6.50). For other copies, see Brigitte Moreau, *Inventaire chronologique des éditions parisiennes du XVIe siècle* (Abbeville: F. Paillart, 1992), vol. 4 (1531-35): no. 142. I focus here only on the texts in French and have therefore also excluded from my discussion the publications by Nicolas Bourbon and Scaliger cited below.

13. The subtitle notes the additions: *Avec autres nouvellement adjouxtez. Et les tous corrigez & bien emendez.* I have consulted the copy in Paris, BNF Rothschild 2787 (IV.6.65). For other copies, see Moreau, *Inventaire*, 4: no. 143. All following citations of the epitaphs are taken from this volume. No modern edition has yet been made of the entire collection, but individual poems have appeared in various editions, as noted below.

14. I have consulted the copy in Paris, BNF Rés. Yc 7851. Louise's epitaphs are printed on fols. e2v-e4v.

15. I have consulted the copy in Paris, BNF Rés. Yc 13221. The epitaph to Louise "Francisci Regis matris" appears on fol. f1v.

16. The complete poem is published in François Ier, *Oeuvres poétiques*, ed. June E. Kane (Geneva: Slatkine, 1984), 183-84.

17. Antoine Héroët's two epitaphs are published in his *Oeuvres poétiques*, ed. F. Gohin (Paris: Droz, 1943), 109-14.

18. This anonymous poem is entitled "Dict adressé a madicte Dame par l'ung de ses Serviteurs" (edition of October 26, 1531, fols. C2-C2v).

19. Still unpublished, it is found in Paris, BNF MS nouv. acq. fr. 1158, fols. 119-37. I wish to thank Christine Scollen-Jimack for sending me her study, "Funereal Poetry in France: From Octovien de Saint-Gelais to Clément Marot," forthcoming in *Vernacular*

Literature and Current Affairs in France, England and Scotland, 1500-1530, ed. Richard Britnell and Jennifer J. Britnell (Abingdon: Ashgate, 2000).
20. I have used the copy in Paris, BNF Rothschild 2779.
21. *Journal d'un Bourgeois de Paris sous le règne de François Ier*, 1515-1536 (Paris: Picard, 1910), 336-37.
22. The celebrated memorialist Brantôme records (*Les Dames galantes*, ed. M. Rat [Paris: Garnier, 1960], cinquième discours, 282) that three days before her death, Louise saw a comet from her window and interpreted it as a sign:

> Et soudain, faisant ouvrir son rideau, elle vid une comette qui esclairoit ainsi droit sur son lit. "Ha! dit-elle, voilà un signe qui ne paroist pas pour personnes de basse qualité. Dieu le fait paroistre pour nous autres grands et grandes. Refermez la fenestre: c'est une comette qui m'annonce la mort; il se faut donc preparer." Et le lendemain au matin, ayant envoyé querir son confesseur, fit tout le devoir de bonne chrestienne, encore que les medecins l'asseurassent qu'elle n'estoit pas là. "Si je n'avois veu (dit-elle) le signe de ma mort, je le croirois, car je ne me sens point si bas"; et leur conta à tous l'apparition de sa comette. Et puis, au bout de trois jours, quittant les songes du monde, trespassa.

The editor notes that the time in question was three weeks rather than three days, the comet being visible only from August 6 to September 7, 1531, and Louise's death occurring on September 29.
23. Victor Brodeau, *Poésies*, ed. Hilary M. Tomlinson (Geneva: Droz, 1982), 103.
24. Brenda Dunn-Lardeau has just completed an edition of this text, now in press (Paris: Champion) in the series Textes de la Renaissance. I am grateful to her for supplying me with an edition of the passages relevant to Louise.
25. Adrian Armstrong is preparing a critical edition of this text, and I thank him for sending me his transcription of various passages. I am especially grateful to Jennifer Britnell for lending me a microfilm of the British Library copy of the 1538 edition.
26. Clément Marot, *Oeuvres poétiques*, ed. Gérard Defaux (Paris: Bordas, 1990), I:224-31. The eclogue was originally published in the *Adolescence Clémentine* of 1532.
27. Only one copy of the edition is known, now in Seville, Biblioteca Colombina. I thank William Kemp for providing me with a reproduction of this text.
28. Musée National de la Renaissance, MS 1815. The texts have been published in Madame de Saint-Surin, *L'Hôtel de Cluny au moyen-âge* (Paris: Techener, 1835), 155-68 and in Amédée Boinet, "Choix de miniatures détachées conservées au Musée de Cluny, à Paris," *Bulletin de la Société française de reproductions de manuscrits à peintures* 6 (1922): 18-23. For a recent study, see Joanne S. Norman, "Image-Making at the Court of Francis I: Rondeaux for Louise de Savoie," in *Proceedings of the Canadian Society for the Study of Rhetoric* 4 (1991-92), 117-36. The poems are found in several other sources and warrant a critical edition.

29. The rondeau, beginning "La plus du monde a tout prendre acomplye," is found in Paris, BNF MS fr. 19182, fol. 3v.
30. Consisting of 131 leaves (316 x 197 mm), ruled in red for 31 lines (196 x 108 mm), the manuscript can hardly be called "petit" in dimension, but the epithet reflects Thenaud's professional modesty as well perhaps as the subject matter.
31. Jean Thenaud, *Le Triumphe des Vertuz, Premier Traité: Le Triumphe de Prudence*, ed. Titia J. Schuurs-Janssen (Geneva: Droz, 1997), 4.
32. Paris: Anthoyne Couteau and Galliot Du Pré for Charles de Bougne and Clement Alexandre à Angiers, 1529. I have consulted two copies in Paris, BNF Rés. fol. LK2.113B (on paper) and Rés. Vélins 761 (on vellum, with the metalcut illuminated).
33. Paris: Jean de La Garde, 1516. I have used copies in Paris, BNF Rés. Vélins 1173 and Rés. fol. LK 2.1536. The title page is decorated with a large woodcut of the arms of Savoy.
34. Reproduced in Lecoq, fig. 21.
35. On this aspect, see J. M. Massing, "A New Work by François Du Moulin and the Problem of Pre-Emblematic Traditions," *Emblematica* 2 (1987): 249-71 (1988).
36. See the facsimile edition by G. Durand, *Tableaux et chants royaux de la confrérie du puy Notre Dame d'Amiens, reproduits en 1517 pour Louise de Savoie, Duchesse d'Angoulême* (Paris/Amiens, 1911).
37. Lecoq 335, and figs. 154-55.
38. Originally presented in my article "Books for a Princess and Her Son: Louise de Savoie, François d'Angoulême, and the Parisian Libraire Antoine Vérard," *Bibliothèque d'Humanisme et Renaissance*, 46 (1984), 603-17; these books are also discussed in *Anthoine Vérard*, 168-82, 376-409.
39. The texts are printed in parallel columns in the appendix on page 257.
40. The miniature is reproduced in my *Anthoine Vérard*, 456.
41. Reproduced *ibid.*, 164.
42. See for example the reproductions of miniatures from printed books in *Anthoine Vérard*, 172, 176-78, 382, 393, 403. Similar miniatures from manuscripts are reproduced in Lecoq, fig. 21 and *passim*.
43. See for example, *Anthoine Vérard*, 187, 188.
44. Martial d'Auvergne, (Geneva: Droz, 1970).
45. There are editions from Lyon, ca. 1492, and from Paris, 1492 (Pierre Le Rouge), 1492/93 (Jean Du Pré), 1494 (Baligault, Eustace, Vostre), 1498/99 (Trepperel), 1509 (Vostre).
46. Paris: Jean Du Pré, ca. 1488.
47. For example, BNF MSS fr. 19243, fr. 2332, fr. 1804. MS fr. 19243, in particular, requires further examination. Although smaller in format than Louise's MS fr. 985, it consists of 194 vellum leaves, with justification for 24 lines (126 x 78 mm) on pages measuring 205 x 125 mm. The text is written in a rather large bastarda script, with paragraph markings at the beginning of each quatrain.
48. The manuscript has recently been published in facsimile: *Libro de Horas de Carlos VIII Rey de Francia* (Barcelona: Biblioteca Nacional, 1995) with an introduction by Ana

Domínguez Rodríguez, who previously transcribed the border texts, alas with numerous errors, in *Libros de Horas del Siglo XV en la Biblioteca Nacional* (Madrid, 1979), 45-66.
49. See Sheila Edmunds and M. B. Winn, "Vérard, Meckenem, and Manuscript B.N. fr. 1686," *Romania* 430-431 (1987): 288-344.
50.These appear in one manuscript (BNF MS fr. 1686) containing a poem on the Passion of Christ, and three printed editions: *Le Jeu des eschez moralisé*, 6 IX 1504 (BNF Rés. Vélins 1018), *Le Passetemps de tout homme*, ca. 1505 (BNF Rés. Vélins 2249), *Les Epistres sainct Pol*, 17 I 1507/8 (BNF Rés. Vélins 124). The clearest expression of Louise's interest in books is found in the last of the four (lines 41-44), where Vérard explains why he has prepared the *Epistres* for her:

> Pource que sçay et bien congnois pour voir
> Que desirez de livres vous pourveoir
> Beaulx et devotz, comme de vostre grace
> M'avez escript. . . .

WORKS CITED

Avril, François. *La Passion des manuscrits enluminés: Bibliophiles français, 1280-1580*. Paris: Bibliothèque Nationale, 1991.
Bauchart, see Quentin Bauchart.
Brantôme. *Les Dames galantes*. Edited by Maurice Rat. Paris: Garnier, 1960.
Brodeau, Victor. *Poésies*. Edited by Hilary M. Tomlinson. Geneva: Droz, 1982.
Delisle, Léopold. *Le Cabinet des manuscrits de la Bibliothèque impériale*. Paris: 1868-81.
Dictionnaire alphabétique et analogique de la langue française. Paris: Robert, 1958.
Domínguez Rodríguez, Ana. *Libro de Horas de Carlos VIII Rey de Francia*. Barcelona: Biblioteca Nacional, 1995
———. *Libros de Horas del Siglo XV en la Biblioteca Nacional*. Madrid, 1979.
Du Pré, Jean. *Le Palais des nobles Dames*. Edited by Brenda Dunn-Lardeau. Paris: Champion, in press.
Durand, G. *Tableaux et chants royaux de la confrérie du puy Notre Dame d'Amiens, reproduits en 1517 pour Louise de Savoie, Duchesse d'Angoulême*. Paris/Amiens, 1911.
Edmunds, Sheila. "Manuscrits liés à d'autres membres de la maison de Savoie." In *Les Manuscrits enluminés des comtes et ducs de Savoie*, edited by A. Paravicini Bagliani, 207-13. Turin: Umberto Allemandi & C., 1990.
———. and Mary Beth Winn. "Vérard, Meckenem, and Manuscrit B.N. fr. 1686." *Romania* 430-31 (1987): 288-344.
Epitaphes a la louenge de ma Dame Mere du Roy, faictz par plusieurs recommendables Autheurs. Paris: Geoffroy Tory, October 26, 1531.
François Ier, *Oeuvres poétiques*. Edited by June E. Kane. Geneva: Slatkine, 1984.
Héroët, Antoine. *Oeuvres poétiques*. Edited by F. Gohin. Paris: Droz, 1943.
"Journal de Louise de Savoye, duchesse d'Angoulesme. . . ." In vol. 16 of

Collection complète de mémoires relatifs à l'histoire de France, 1st ser. Edited by Claude B. Petitot. Paris: Foucault, 1816-1826.

Journal d'un Bourgeois de Paris sous le règne de François Ier, 1515-1536. Paris: Picard, 1910.

Lecoq, Anne-Marie. *François Ier imaginaire*. Paris: Macula, 1987.

In Lodoicae Regis Matris mortem. Epitaphia Latina & Gallica. Epitaphes a la louenge de ma Dame Mere du Roy, faictz par plusieurs recommendables Autheurs. Paris: Geoffroy Tory, October 17, 1531.

Marot, Clément. *Oeuvres poétiques*. Edited by Gérard Defaux. Paris: Bordas, 1990.

Martial d'Auvergne. *Matines de la Vierge*. Edited by Yves Le Hir. Geneva: Droz, 1970.

Massing, J. M. "A New Work by François Du Moulin and the Problem of Pre-Emblematic Traditions." *Emblematica* 2 (1987): 249-71 (1988).

———. *Erasmian Wit and Proverbial Wisdom: An Illustrated Moral Compendium for François I*. London: The Warburg Institute, 1995.

Moreau, Brigitte. *Inventaire chronologique des éditions parisiennes du XVIe siècle*. Vol. 4 (1531-35). Abbeville: F. Paillart, 1992.

Norman, Joanne S. "Image-Making at the Court of Francis I: Rondeaux for Louise de Savoie." In *Proceedings of the Canadian Society for the Study of Rhetoric*. Edited by Albert W. Halsall. Ottawa, 1991-92.

Orth, Myra R. "Francis Du Moulin and the Journal of Louise of Savoy." *The Sixteenth Century Journal* 13, 1 (Spring 1982): 55-66.

———. "Louise de Savoie et le pouvoir du livre." In *Royaume de Fémynie: Pouvoirs, contraintes, espaces de liberté des femmes, de la Renaissance à la fronde*, edited by Kathleen Wilson-Chevalier and Eliane Viennot. Paris: Champion, 1999: 71-90.

Quentin Bauchart, Ernest. *Les Femmes bibliophiles de France*. Paris, 1886; reprint, Geneva: Slatkine, 1993.

Saint-Surin, Madame de. *L'Hôtel de Cluny au moyen-âge*. Paris: Techener, 1835.

Scollen-Jimack, Christine. "Funereal Poetry in France: From Octovien de Saint- Gelais to Clément Marot." In *Vernacular Literature and Current Affairs in France, England and Scotland, 1500-1530*. Edited by Richard Britnell and Jennifer J. Britnell. Abingdon: Ashgate, 2000.

Sénemaud, Ed. *La Bibliothèque de Charles d'Orléans Comte d'Angoulême au château de Cognac en 1496*. Paris: A. Claudin, 1861.

Thenaud, Jean. *Le Triumphe des Vertuz. Premier Traité: Le Triumphe de Prudence*. Edited by Titia J. Schuurs-Janssen. Geneva: Droz, 1997.

Winn, Mary Beth. "Books for a Princess and Her Son: Louise de Savoie, François d'Angoulême, and the Parisian Libraire Antoine Vérard." *Bibliothèque d'Humanisme et Renaissance* 46 (1984): 603-17.

———. *Anthoine Vérard, Parisian Publisher, 1485-1512: Prologues, Poems, and Presentations*. Geneva: Droz, 1997.

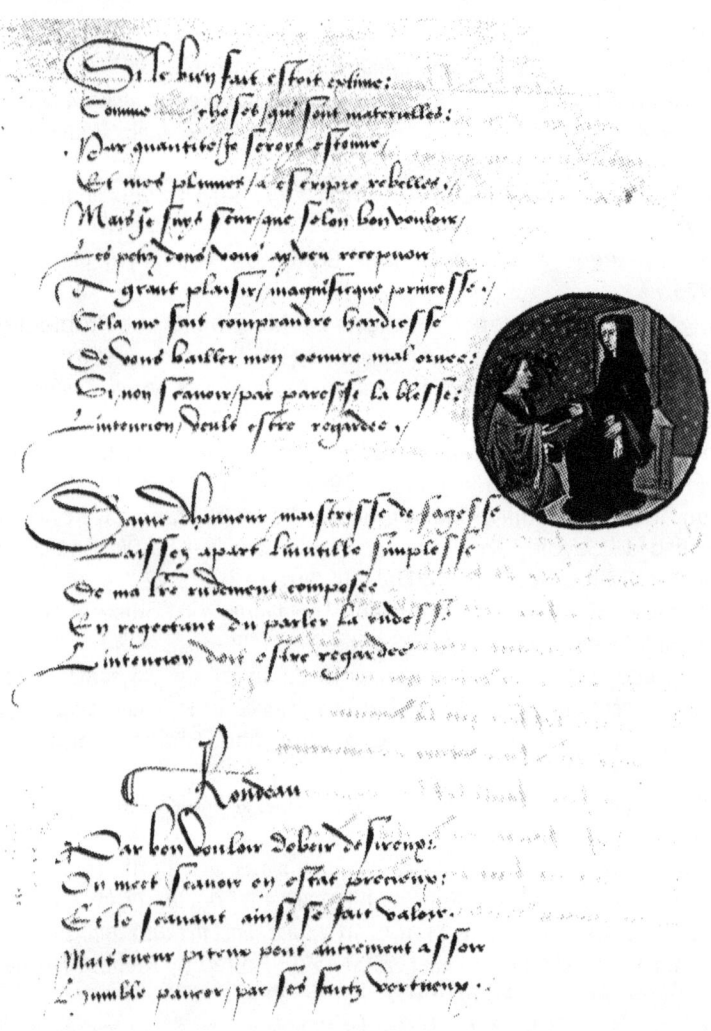

Fig. 1. François Demoulins, *Dialogue sur la folie du jeu*, BNF MS fr. 1863, fol. 14v. (cliché Bibliothèque Nationale de France, Paris)

LOUISE DE SAVOIE, "BIBLIOPHILE" 255

Fig. 2. Jean de Bourdigné, *Hystoire agregative des annalles et cronicques d'Anjou* (Paris: Anthoyne Couteau and Galliot Du Pré for Charles de Bougne and Clement Alexandre à Angiers, 1529), Paris, BNF Rés. fol. LK2.113, fol. 4v. (cliché Bibliothèque Nationale de France, Paris)

Fig. 3. *La Vie Nostre Dame*, BNF MS fr. 985, fol. 2v. (cliché Bibliothèque Nationale de France, Paris)

APPENDIX

Les Vigiles des mors Paris:
Anthoine Vérard, inter 7 V 1496 et 8 V 1498
Chantilly MC no. 1956, fols. a₁v.–a₂v.
(copy probably for Charles d'Angoulême)

La Vie Nostre Dame
[Martial d'Auvergne]/ Anthoine Vérard?
Paris, BNF MS fr. 985, fols. 1-1v.

Dedication to Charles VIII

Trosne d'honneur, couronne souveraine,
Tour de vertu, haulteur imperïal,
Liz reginal, crestïenté haultaine,
4 Tenant en main le hault tiltre royal,
Trescrestien Roy pour tiltre especïal
On vous clamë en singulier renon
Charles regnant huitiesme de ce nom.
8 Aprés tout dit et livres de plaisances,
Les diz de Job translatez en substance
Je vous ay fais en ma simple orature.
L'ame requiert plus que le corps sub-
stance,
12 Car le corps meurt et l'ame tousjours dure.

En plaisans diz souvent nature humaine
Prent reconfort, c'est proverbe rural;
En armes prent son plaisir capitaine,
16 De bonne foy aussi fait le vassal;
L'ame requiert le trosne magistral,
Le corps n'a point tel preminence, non.
De noz oeuvres la fin nous ordonnon
20 A bien mourir pour avoir jouïssance
Du bien parfont ou est nostre fïance,
Et tendre doit humaine creature;
Regardez y, souverain Roy de France,
24 Car le corps meurt et l'ame tousjours dure.

Souverain Roy, la plaisance mondaine
Ne fait pas tout; il fault, propos final,
Penser a Dieu, de vertu la fontaine.
28 C'est nostre roy et nostre capital.
Qui bien vivra ne finira point mal:
C'est nostre foy, ainsi le soustenon;
Job le monstra, aprés qui nous venon;
32 De bien vivre nous monstra la semblance.
Mourir convient, c'est commune ordon-
nance;
Si est saige qui au monde procure
Pour son ame de repos asseurance,
36 Car le corps meurt et l'ame tousjours dure.

Dedication to Louise de Savoie

La fleur d'honneur, princesse haultaine,
Fruit de vertu, prudence especial,
Tenant du liz la branche souveraine
Pour parvenir au hault tiltre royal
En augmentant le siege imperial,
Clamee vous estez en singulier non
Pour vostre filz qui est de grant renon
Ou vous prenez a present plaisance
Sans espargner en riens substance;
Je vous ay fait en ma simple orature
Ung petit livre pour prendre recreance,
Que vous lyrez tandiz que le temps dure.

En plaisant diz souvent nature humaine
Prent reconfort, c'est proverbe rural;
A bien faire chascun doit mettre paine,
Suivir les bons pour eviter tout mal,
Car l'ame pour brief propos final
Doit querir tel preminence non.
De bonnes euvres ainssy nous l'ordonnon
Affin qu'en fin a bien ait jouyssance
Du bien que fait ou est toute fiance
Et tendre y doit toute humaine creature.
Regardez, dame, sy vous plaist l'ordon-
nance
De ce livre tandiz que le temps dure.

C'est la vie qui est de grace plaine
De Nostre Dame qui n'a point son egal;
C'est la vertu, c'est la clere fontaine.
C'est nostre mere, nostre chef capital,
C'est la louenge du trosne magistral,
C'est nostre foy, ainssy le soustenon
C'est la dame en qui fiance avon.
De bien vivre nous monstre la semblance:
Ensuivans la sans aulcune muance,
Car envers Dieu pour nous tousjours pro-
cure.
C'est des pecheurs le chemin d'asseu-
rance;
Lisez sa vie, tandiz que le temps dure.

Prince royal ou gist toute puissance,
Prenez a gré par vostre bienvueillance
Ce que j'ay fait en ma povre facture;
40 L'ame paissez aprés resjouÿssance,
Car le corps meurt et l'ame tousjours dure.

Treshaulte dame exellante,
<u>Prenez</u> en <u>gré</u> <u>par</u> <u>vostre</u> <u>bien</u> <u>vueillance</u>
Ce livre cy ou n'a pas grant <u>facture</u>;
C'est la vie, la louenge et usance
De Nostre Dame ou vous prendrez plaisance,
Que vous lyrez tandiz que le temps <u>dure</u>.

(<u>underlined</u> words appear in same place as model)

(*italics* indicate words varying in placement or tense from model)

Nota Bene: Brief Notes on Manuscripts and Early Printed Books

Two Fragments of Lydgate's *Troy Book* in the Bodleian Library

LINNE R. MOONEY

Two manuscripts in the Bodleian Library preserve fragments of a single fifteenth-century manuscript of John Lydgate's *Troy Book*. The first is a quire of ten leaves, folios i to x, preserved in the front of MS Rawlinson Poet. 223, now separate from the main part of the manuscript which is written by another scribe, a copy of *The Canterbury Tales*. The second are two single leaves, now foliated 2 and 3, in MS Rawlinson D.913 (SC 13679), one of those volumes in the Rawlinson collection that bring together loose leaves and quires originally from many different manuscripts. The fragment in the latter manuscript has not been identified as a fragment of *Troy Book* in *The Index of Middle English Verse* or its *Supplement*.[1] The two fragments together are parts of a single 16-folio quire, the 4th through 13th leaves, the 14th and the 16th. While Kathleen L. Scott long ago noted that these were leaves of a single manuscript, some details of their relationship to one another and to the once-complete copy of the *Troy Book* of which they are the only surviving relics may be worth noting here.[2]

The first leaf of this quire must have been blank and unnumbered, since arabic foliation in the upper outer corners, recto, assign the numbers 3-12, 13 and 15 to the surviving folios in the two manuscripts. The second leaf of the quire, which must have been foliated '1', would probably not have been blank, or it would not have been given a number: perhaps it preserved a title or presentation illustration. The third leaf of the quire, numbered '2', must have been written with the first 79 lines of the Prologue, 39 or 40 lines on each side. The fourth through thirteenth leaves (that is, the center five bifolia) survive as a whole in Bodleian Library, Rawlinson Poet. 223, where they are preserved as a separate quire, now disbound from the rest of the volume, and foliated '3' to '12' by an older hand, and 'i' through 'x' by a modern hand as flyleaf folios in Rawlinson poet. 223. The fourteenth leaf is preserved as folio 3 of Bodleian, Rawlinson D.913; it also has the foliation number '13' to parallel the older foliation of the other fragment. The fifteenth leaf, which would have been foliated '14', is lost. The sixteenth leaf is preserved as folio 2 of Bodleian, Rawlinson D.913; it also has the foliation '15' to parallel the older foliation of the other fragment. It was clearly the last folio of a quire, since it has the catchword for the end of the quire at the bottom of its verso side. Of this original 16-leaf quire, then, the leaves have survived as follows: first three folios now lost, folios 4 through 13 preserved in Rawl. Poet. 223; 14 preserved as folio 3 in Rawl. D.913; 15 lost; 16 preserved as folio 2 in Rawl. D.913.

The now-lost third leaf of the original 16-folio quire, which would have been foliated '2' to parallel other foliation of the fragment, must have contained the first 79 lines of the Prologue to the *Troy Book*.[3] Folios 4 through 13 of the original quire, now in Rawlinson Poet. 223, preserve the text of *Troy Book* from the Prologue, line 80 through Book I, line 459. Folio 14 of the original quire, now numbered '3' in Rawlinson D.913, preserves Book I, lines 460-536 of the text; and folio 16 of the original quire, now numbered '2' in Rawlinson D.913, preserves Book I, lines 623-702 of the text. The missing 15th folio must have contained lines 537-622 of Book I. Both the expense of decoration (see below) and the catchword on the verso of the last folio suggest that these fragments represent the first quire of a once-complete copy of Lydgate's *Troy Book*.

The scribe of this copy of the *Troy Book* wrote in a loose secretary hand of the middle of the fifteenth century. The text is more formal, even tending toward horned letters in final 's' and 'e,' at the beginning of Book I (plate 2), but looser and less formal through most of the extant text (plates 1 and 3). The scribe writes the first word or words at the top of each page in large, bold script, as on documents of this period, with the initial larger still, shadowed in red and decorated in document style (plates 1 and 3). Sometimes other letters in the top line also have red shadowing (e.g. the "k" of "wrake" on plate 1). He sometimes exaggerates ascenders in the top line, and often exaggerates descenders in the bottom line, criss-crossing them in the usual document style (e.g. the "s" of "sawes" on plate 1).

This manuscript was also expensively illuminated and decorated, although it was not included in Lesley Lawton's descriptions of the illuminated and illustrated copies of Lydgate's *Troy Book*.[4] There are large illuminated initials on folios v recto of Rawlinson Poet. 223 (plate 2) and 2 of Rawlinson D.913. The seven-line initial in Rawlinson D.913 marks a break in the text of Book I, line 623, which Bergen in his edition marks with a large bold initial.[5] The initial, though large, is a simple solid gold 'T', without ground or sprays. The twelve-line initial on folio v of Rawlinson Poet. 223 (plate 2) marks the beginning of Book I. The solid gold initial is surrounded by a parti-colored blue and rose ground with white highlights, with sprays extending all along the left border, carrying green leaves, red berries and gold buds or balls. In the opposite (right) margin, in the same style and colors, similar sprays extend all along the margin from an illustration of two birds, an owl with another of unidentified species in flight attacking its back, the owl standing on a grassy plot. The style of this floral border and the owl grotesque mark these decorative elements as the work of two illuminators, one English, the other foreign and possibly Flemish, identified by Kathleen Scott in the article cited above.[6]

These fragments attest to the existence of another large and impressive copy of the Troy Book such as Lawton describes as having been prepared for noble or armigerous owners who would have purchased and displayed them as a matter of prestige.[7] It was of folio size, measuring 298 by 210 mm. in the Rawlinson Poet. 223 copy and 273 by 172 mm. in the more severely cropped Rawlinson D.913 copy. The illumination and decoration even on the surviving folios is impressive. It seems likely that this first quire was mutilated for its illumination and decoration: an illuminated initial and decorated border would have decorated the beginning of the Prologue on the missing third folio of the quire, parallel to or perhaps more fully decorated than the initial and borders at the beginning of Book I which survives on folio v recto of the Rawlinson Poet. 223 copy, judging from what may be generalized as the usual practice for illuminating and decorating initials of prologues and first books. The missing bifolium (second and fifteenth leaves of the original quire) may have contained a presentation miniature of Lydgate and Henry V on the first half, as at least six other extant illuminated copies of Troy Book did.[8] There must have been some writing or illustration on that folio to warrant its being included in the foliation of the second through sixteenth folios of the original quire; the first folio of the original quire apparently was not foliated, and so was probably blank. The 79 first lines of text accounted for by the missing third folio would fit the usual 38-40 lines per side of the other surviving folios, so there would be no room for a miniature on that folio, nor on the other hand any need to have the text begin on the preceding folio: it seems most likely, then, that the first half of the missing bifolium contained a miniature. Judging from the quality of the work of the foreign "owl artist" in other surviving examples of his workmanship, he would certainly have been capable of producing a very high quality miniature as a frontispiece on the first half of the missing bifolium. Kathleen Scott notes that he may be responsible for the seven historiated initials in British Library, Harley 2887,[9] and the two large historiated initials in Lambeth Palace MS 186.[10] On the other hand, the miniature could have been executed by a third artist, since at least four other artists/illustrators contributed elements to the other extant manuscripts partly decorated by the "owl artist" and his collaborator.[11]

Coats of Arms indicate noble and armigerous owners for several of the extant complete illuminated copies of the Troy Book.[12] British Library, Royal 18 D.II belonged first to Sir William Herbert, first earl of Pembroke and his wife Anne Devereux. British Library, Cotton Augustus A.IV belonged first to Sir Thomas Chaworth and his second wife, Isabella de Ailesbury. Cambridge, Trinity College O.5.2 belonged in the fifteenth century to various members of the Thwaites and Knevet families. Manchester, John Ryland's Library, English 1 belonged to a member or members of the Carent family: William Carent (1395-1476), his brother John Carent (d. 1478), or his son John Carent (1425-83). These are all revealed by coats of arms, which would usually appear on the first numbered folio of the volume, missing from these fragments. This clientele for Lydgate's *Troy Book* is of the same or higher class as that of the other manuscripts illuminated by the "owl artist" and his collaborator identified by Scott in her article. British Library, Harley 2887 was owned by members of the Gower family, stockfishmongers, of London, then by members of the Butler family, Earls of Ormond.[13] Oxford, Bodleian Library, Bodley 283 was owned by Thomas Kippyng of London, a prominent Draper.[14] Cambridge University Library MS Ee.4.36 may have been owned by a Thomas Swinborne, college chaplain at Oxford.[15]

The fact that the larger fragment of this copy of *Troy Book* was bound in with the Rawlinson Poet. 223 copy of Chaucer's *Canterbury Tales* might indicate that the *Troy Book* fragment came from the same collection as the Ra³ copy of *The Canterbury Tales*. It seems unlikely that the complete copy of the *Troy Book* of which these fragments are the only extant quire was bound at the front of the *Canterbury Tales* codex. As Manly and Rickert point out, given the quire signatures that survive in Ra³, there would have been only 14 or 15 quires and seven leaves of another preceding the current beginning (folio 6). This would give space enough for 11424 lines,[16] according to lineation of *The Canterbury Tales*, or between 17,290 and 18,250 if one follows the ca. 40 lines per side of the *Troy Book* fragments, still not enough to account for the more than 33,000 lines of *Troy Book*. On the other hand, Manly and Rickert suggest that Richard Rawlinson may have been responsible for binding the Rawlinson Poet. 223 fragment with *The Canterbury Tales*, when he had the *Canterbury Tales* rebound in the 18th century.[17]

Early ownership of Ra³ by John Aphowell, probably the John Aphowell who was steward of ten castles of the Duchy of Lancaster on the Welsh borders and was in 1486 associated with Jasper Earl of Pembroke and Duke of Bedford, and the noble ownership of the other *Canterbury Tales* manuscripts to which Ra³ is related, suggests no less than its expensive illumination and decoration that the *Troy Book* to which these fragments bear witness must have belonged to a member of the upper classes, probably one who moved in the same circles as the owners and associates of the related *Canterbury Tales* manuscripts: the Nevilles, Wydevilles, Buckinghams and Staffords.[18] Perhaps the missing second and third leaves of this first quire of the *Troy Book* would have revealed its early owner or owners.

NOTES

1. Carleton Brown and Rossell Hope Robbins, *The Index of Middle English Verse* (New York: Columbia UP, 1943) and Rossell Hope Robbins and John L. Cutler, *Supplement to the Index of Middle English Verse* (Lexington: University of Kentucky Press, 1965), no. 2516.
2. Kathleen L. Scott, "A Mid-fifteenth-century English Illuminating Shop and its Customers," *Journal of the Warburg and Courtauld Institutes* 31 (1968): p. 189, n. 119.
3. All line numbers refer to the edition of Henry Bergen, *Lydgate's Troy Book*, 4 vols., EETS e.s. 97, 103, 106 and 126 (1906, 1910, 1935).
4. Lesley Lawton, "The Illustration of Late Medieval Secular Texts, with Special Reference to Lydgate's 'Troy Book'," in *Manuscripts and Readers in Fifteenth-Century England: The Literary Implications of Manuscript Study* (Cambridge: D. S. Brewer, 1983), pp. 41-69.
5. See note 3 above: vol. 1 (EETS e.s. 97 (1906)), p. 29.
6. See note 2 above, esp. pp. 189-91.
7. Lawton, pp. 52-54.
8. British Library, Royal 18 D.II and Cotton, Augustus A.IV; Bodleian Library, Rawlinson C.446 and Digby 232; Cambridge, Trinity College O.5.2; and Manchester, John Ryland's Library, Eng. 1. New York, Pierpont Morgan Library M.876 contained a similar scheme of illustration but is missing its beginning; and Bristol, Public Library 8 apparently contained a similar scheme, including presentation miniature, but has been mutilated for its illustrations. See Lawton, pp. 54-55, 59-60 and Table 1 on pp. 56-8.
9. Scott, p. 172 and Figure 62b, illustrating folio 29.
10. Scott, p. 191 and Figures 66a and 66b, illustrating folios 1 and 109.
11. Scott, 195.
12. See Lawton, pp. 53-4, 66-68, a source for the information in this paragraph. Lawton cites D. A. Pearsall, "Notes on the Manuscript of *Generydes*," *The Library* 5th ser., 16 (1961), 205-9; J. C. Wedgewood and Anne Holt, *History of Parliament: Biographies of the Members of the House of Commons 1439-1509* (London, 1936), 520-1; and J. J. G. Alexander, "William Abell 'Lymnour' and Fifteenth Century English Illumination," in *Kunsthistorische Forschungen Otto Pächt zu seinem 70. Geburtstag*, ed. Artur Rosenauer and Gerold Weber (Salzburg, 1972), 166-72, esp. 169 n. 35.
13. Scott, 175-82.
14. Scott, 184-5.
15. Scott, 188-9.
16. John M. Manly and Edith Rickert, *The Text of The Canterbury Tales*, 8 vols (Chicago: Univ. of Illinois Press, 1940), 1.466.
17. See Manly and Rickert, 1.464.
18. See Manly and Rickert, 1.468-70.

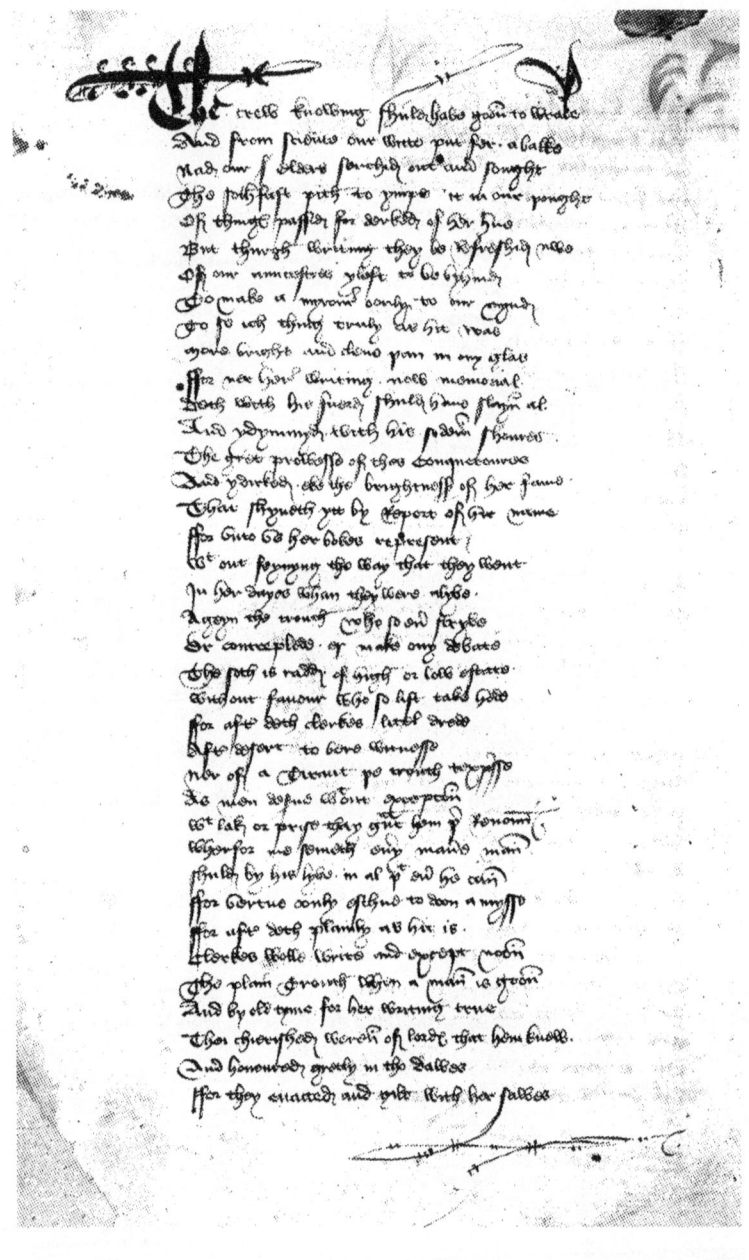

Plate 1. Oxford, Bodleian Library, Rawlinson Poet. 223, fol. ii (fourth of earlier foliation, fifth of original quire), recto. By permission of the Bodleian Library.

Plate 2. Oxford, Bodleian Library, Rawlinson Poet. 223, fol. v (seventh of earlier foliation, eighth of original quire), recto. By permission of the Bodleian Library.

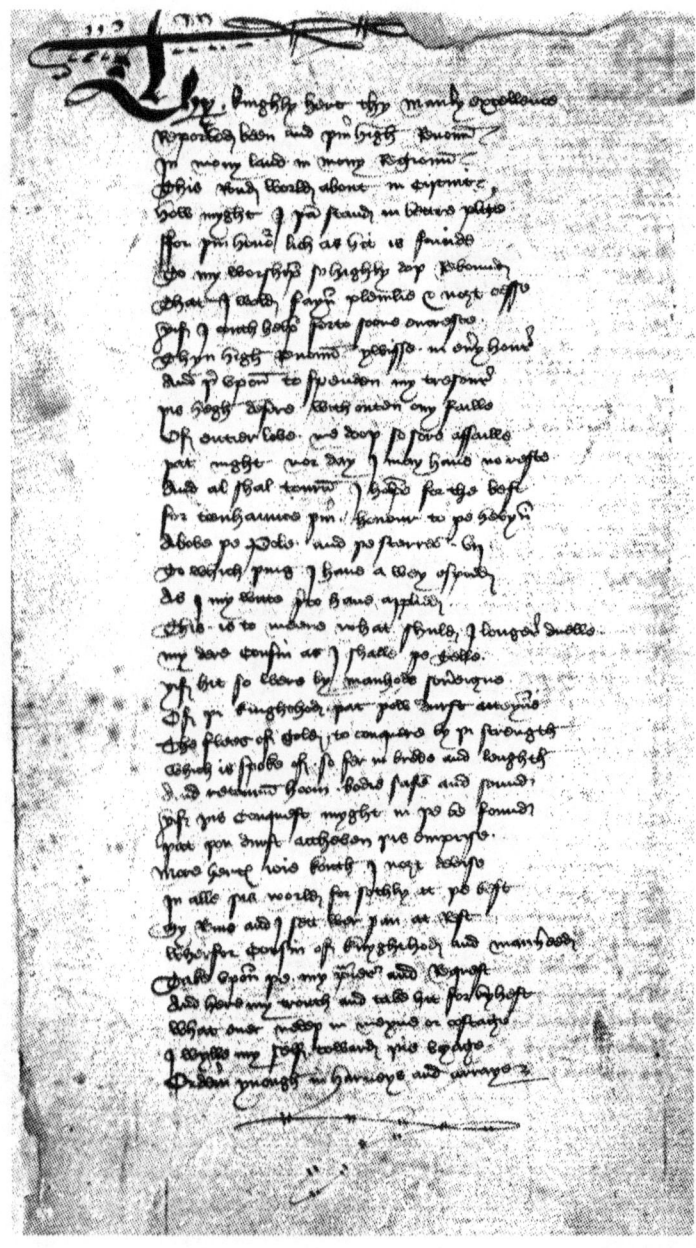

Plate 3. Oxford, Bodleian Library, Rawlinson D.913, fol. 3 (thirteenth of earlier foliation, fourteenth of original quire), recto. By permission of the Bodleian Library.

A New Manuscript Fragment of the Northern Homily Cycle

OLIVER PICKERING

In 1998 the John Goodchild Collection in Wakefield, West Yorkshire,[1] acquired a large collection of documents formerly belonging to the Radcliffe and Shaw families of Saddleworth, near Oldham, Lancashire,[2] among which was a sixteenth-century estate rental relating to land in north Derbyshire. This document was protected by a thick parchment wrapper consisting of leaves of Middle English poetry, which on investigation proved to be fragments of a manuscript of the collection of verse sermons on the Sunday gospels known as the *Northern Homily Cycle* (NHC).

These medieval leaves have now been detached from the rental, and are preserved separately. They comprise two bifolia—one of them with a page greatly darkened evidently as a result of having been an outer surface—and a single leaf formerly half of another bifolium and with a small triangular piece of its conjugate leaf still attached at the top. Still sewn in place down the innermost fold of the rental is a thin parchment strengthening strip, some 15 mm wide on either side of its own central fold. This strip bears the remains of Middle English verse apparently in the same hand as that of the Middle English leaves but not obviously from the same text.[3]

Examination shows that the medieval leaves had been folded for their protective purpose in the exact reverse of their original order, turning a sequence we may call A, B, C into C, B, A, as follows, C1^v being the now darkened page:

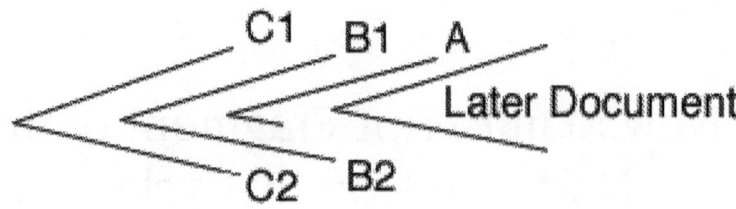

Reversed, this becomes:

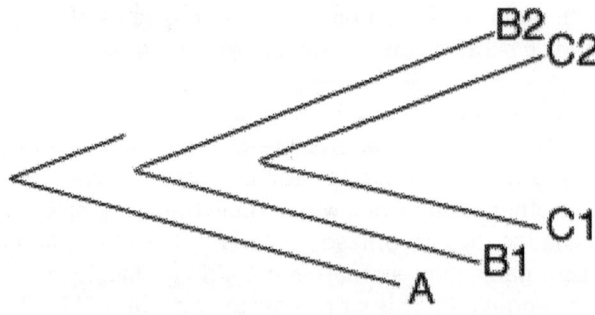

an arrangement that is confirmed, as will be seen, by textual evidence.
Evidence from the edges of A, B and C, in the form of further folds and the plentiful remains of threads and sewing holes, shows that the document cover was formed by laying what must have been three waste bifolia flat on top of one another, folding over between 10 and 20 mm of their edges on all four sides, and then sewing through these folded edges to hold them

securely together. The estate rental was then placed within the resulting 3-ply cover (6-ply at the edges), and the whole sewn together down a central vertical fold. The finished product was then folded vertically again, in legal fashion, to produce a document of tall, narrow format. Examination of the position of this fold in both the medieval leaves and the later rental shows that the parchment cover had been turned upside down before the rental was sewn into it. This brought C1^v to the front, the effect of the final fold being that this page ended up as the principal outer surface of the whole document:[4]

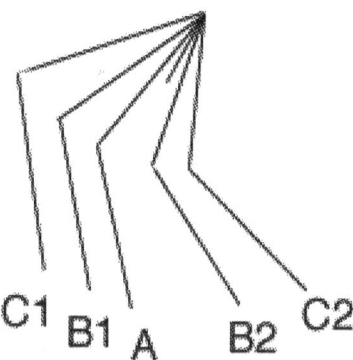

It is likely that A was also a complete bifolium at the time of the construction of the cover, and that one leaf was later roughly cut out, for an unknown reason.

The medieval leaves are approximately 305 mm tall x 215 mm wide, with the text of the NHC written in two frame-ruled columns of between 40 and 45 lines, within an overall writing area of, on average, 242 mm x 185 mm. Decoration, on these surviving leaves, is confined to the beginnings of new sections of text, which are marked by rubricated headings, red marginal pen-flourishing and two-line red initials.[5] The script used for the verse is a fluent, well-developed Secretary of the mid-fifteenth century or later, though with a small admixture of Anglicana forms. For the headings the scribe employed Textura quadrata. No signatures or catchwords are visible. The parchment is of no more than average quality, some slits having been repaired. A sizeable hole (c. 30 mm x 20 mm) now present in C1 has removed text in the second column of C1^r and the first of C1^v.

The extant leaves A, B1, C1, C2, B2 can be shown to be the remains of the three innermost bifolia of an originally eight-leaf quire. As will be set out below, the text runs continuously through these leaves, proving that C was a central bifolium. The only small doubt attaches to the position of the piece of conjugate leaf still attached to A, as it is just possible that this originally preceded that leaf, i.e. that Diagram 2 above should instead be expressed:

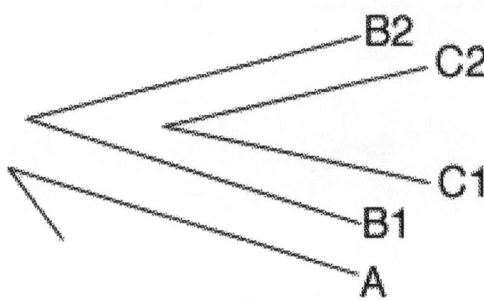

This, however, would mean that the manuscript was constructed, unusually, of 4-leaf instead of 8-leaf quires, and that the creator of the cover for the later rental took bifolia from more than one quire, a less likely procedure. Comparison of the few words still visible on the piece of parchment in question with the text that follows that of B2^v in a textually-similar manuscript, Cambridge University Library Dd.1.1 (fol. 197^{r-v}),[6] appears to confirm the hypothesis that A2, as it would have been, originally followed B2, as would be expected in an 8-leaf quire.[7]

With the proviso that C1^v is so darkened (through dirt, staining and rubbing) that it can no longer be read with the naked eye, it may be stated that the Goodchild fragment of the NHC contains 845 lines of text, running from the homily for the 15th Sunday after Trinity to that for the 19th, as follows. In all cases the homilies have the usual tripartite structure of gospel paraphrase, exposition, and illustrative *narracio*.

A^r
col.1: **15th Sunday after Trinity** (beginning imperfectly):[8] 41 lines
col.2: 44 lines
A^v
col.1: 10 lines to end of homily (i.e. the final 95 lines of the homily are present)
    Heading for **16th Sunday after Trinity**
    31 further lines

A NEW MANUSCRIPT FRAGMENT

col.2: 43 lines
B1ʳ
col.1: 40 lines
col.2: 43 lines
B1ᵛ
col.1: 43 lines
col.2: 40 lines to end of homily (i.e. the homily has 240 lines)
    Heading for **17th Sunday after Trinity**
    5 further lines
C1ʳ
col.1: 41 lines
col.2: 44 lines
C1ᵛ
cols 1 and 2: presumed total of 87 lines[9]
C2ʳ
col.1: 13 lines to end of homily (i.e. the homily has 190 lines)
    Heading for **18th Sunday after Trinity**
    26 further lines
col.2: 42 lines
C2ᵛ
col.1: 42 lines
col.2: 42 lines
B2ʳ
col.1: 41 lines
col.2: 23 lines to end of homily (i.e. the homily has 216 lines)
    Heading for **19th Sunday after Trinity**
    17 further lines
B2ᵛ
col.1: 44 lines
col.2: 43 lines (i.e. the homily ends imperfectly after 104 lines)[10]

    The text is that of the original, unexpanded, early-fourteenth-century version of the NHC, of which sixteen manuscripts were previously known.[11] In the absence of a critical edition of this version,[12] or a comprehensive published analysis of the textual differences between the manuscripts,[13] it is not at present possible to determine the position of the Goodchild fragment relative to the other witnesses. Some small comparison may however be made with T. J. Heffernan's important study of the choice of rubrics and Sunday gospel texts in the manuscripts of the NHC, a study that has led him to propose the Augustinian canons as the religious order most likely to have produced the collection.[14] The third of Heffernan's five 'cruces' is the choice of rubric to introduce the 18th Sunday after Trinity, one of the homilies preserved in the Goodchild fragment, which has the reading "Accesserunt ad ihesum pharasei" (C2ʳ). Of the seven NHC manuscripts that Heffernan records as containing this homily, only two (Lambeth Palace Library 260 and the Marquess of Bute manuscript) have this reading.[15] Seeing that Cambridge University Library Dd.1.1 has been used for comparison with Goodchild in the present paper, it may be noted that this manuscript, for some reason omitted from Heffernan's analysis, has the reading "Pharisei audientes" (fol. 194r), as in Cambridge University Library Gg.5.31.[16]

The language of the Goodchild manuscript is clearly northern, as is that of most other extant manuscripts of the NHC. The difficulty of localising northern manuscripts with any precision is discussed by the compilers of the *Linguistic Atlas of Late Mediaeval English* (LALME),[17] with the result that they felt themselves unable to localise several NHC manuscripts for which they nonetheless drew up linguistic profiles.[18] However, they included five NHC manuscripts on their maps, suggesting in each case the following locations:

– Bodleian Library, Selden Supra 52: West Riding of Yorkshire, near Huddersfield (LP 30, grid reference 417 412)
– British Library, Add. 30358: north of York (LP 190, grid reference 459 468)
– British Library, Harley 2391: Lincolnshire, near Brigg (LP 910, grid reference 496 408).
– CUL, Dd.1.1: Isle of Ely (LP 558, grid reference 543 288);
– Lambeth Palace Library 260: East Riding of Yorkshire, near Beverley (LP 361, grid reference 488 440)

In addition to the findings published in LALME, it has been suggested that the Bute manuscript may have been written in the general area of Newark on Trent;[19] that University of Minnesota, Z.822.N81, can be placed just north of Hull;[20] that the former Robartes fragment (now Bodleian Library, Latin misc. b.17) may have been written in southern Yorkshire;[21] that the former Porkington 10 (now National Library of Wales, Brogyntyn II.1) is possibly from the North-West Midlands;[22] and that the language of Huntington Library, HM 129, is that of an area immediately north of Dublin.[23]

For the purposes of the present article the language of the Goodchild manuscript has been analysed according to the principles of the LALME questionnaire, and the results submitted to Dr Margaret Laing of the Institute for Historical Dialectology at the University of Edinburgh. Her conclusion is that the manuscript "probably fits best in an area comprising the far north-east of Nottinghamshire and the far north-west of Lincolnshire and including the part of the West Riding of Yorkshire just north and west of that."[24] I print in the Appendix, below, the forms occurring in the

Goodchild manuscript for all the items in LALME for which dot or item maps are there provided. It may be noted that the scribe consistently uses the graph <y> rather than <þ> to render the sound /th/, a well-documented characteristic of northern scribes,[25] and in the Appendix below, I copy LALME in preserving this usage.

The consistency of the written language as revealed by the dialect analysis, the practised nature of the scribal hand, and the manuscript's layout, rubrication, and decoration, as noted above, could indicate that the Goodchild manuscript was produced in a scriptorium, although a certain untidiness and the fact that insufficient space is at times allotted to the rubricated headings may be evidence that the scribe was instead working without supervision. Thomas J. Heffernan argued strongly for the organised production of NHC manuscripts when describing the Bute manuscript, which was, he suggested, probably written both by and for a cleric, for the purposes of "oral reading to an assembled congregation."[26] The Goodchild manuscript, which at 305 x 215 mm is one of the largest extant NHC manuscripts, in fact has a considerably bigger page size than Bute (217 x 135 mm), making it in theory even more suitable for oral delivery.[27] If Heffernan is correct in his attribution of the composition and transmission of the NHC to the Augustinians, then a house of that order within the suggested area of linguistic origin of the Goodchild manuscript (for example Drax in the West Riding, or Thornholme in north Lincolnshire) might conceivably be its place of production.

The manuscript may not, however, have been written within the suggested linguistic area, which may simply be where its scribe originated or was trained. Evidence pointing instead to the far north of Derbyshire is provided by the contents of the later rental for which the discarded leaves of the NHC formed a cover. This rental, written in a professional hand of probably the earlier sixteenth century, is potentially of great importance in determining the Middle English manuscript's place of origin. The heading at the top of the first of its ten leaves, which appears to read "Tenentes ibidem secundum consuetudines manerii," i.e. "tenants in the same place according to the customs of the manor," shows that it is a manorial document, and the places given as headings within it (present-day Spinkhill, Ridgeway, Troway, Bramley, Mosborough, and Eckington) indeed all form part of the manor of Eckington, which is about five miles north-east of Chesterfield. This heading shows that what has survived is a continuation of what was presumably a rental for other parts of the manor, and it is not clear why these ten leaves should have been given their own cover. It is also noteworthy that a reference to John Earl of Shrewsbury under the Ridgeway entries shows that the document must be a copy of an earlier, fifteenth-century rental, since there was no John [Talbot] of this title between the death of the third fifteenth-century earl of this name in 1473 and the creation of the next Earl John in 1630.[28] Possibly the rental was specially copied when the manor changed hands, which it apparently did in 1540 when ownership passed from the Strangeways family (lords of the manor since the time of Henry V) to William Lord Dacre, cousin of the last Sir James Strangeways.[29]

The unbroken lay ownership of Eckington from the early fifteenth century onwards does not allow us to speculate, as it might have done if the manor had been in religious hands, that the waste Middle English leaves were fashioned into a rental cover by a new land-owner taking possession of religious property after the dissolution of the monasteries. The copy of the NHC to which they bear witness may still, however, have been produced in a neighbouring religious house, for example Beauchief (Premonstratensian) to the west or Worksop (Augustinian) to the east of Eckington, to which a scribe from further to the north-east had migrated.[30]

University of Leeds

APPENDIX

I give here the forms in the Goodchild manuscript for all items in LALME for which dot or item maps are there provided, preceded by the LALME questionnaire numbers.

(2) yes "these"
(4) sho "she"
(5) hir "her"
(7) yai ((ya)) "they"
(8) yam "them"
(9) yere "their"
(10) slyke, swylk, swylke, (such) "such"
(12) ilka, ilkone "each"
(13) many "many"
(14) man "man"
(16) mykyll "much"
(17) are, ar "are"
(18) ware "were"
(19) is "is"
(21) was "was"
(22) shall (sg. and pl.) "shall"
(23) shulde "should"
(24) will (pr.sg.) "will"
(25) wolde (pt. sg.), wold (pr. subj.) "would"
(26) till, tyll "to"
(28) fro "from"
(29) after "after"
(31) yan "than"
(33) iff "if"
(34) als, (as), ((alls)) "as"
(35) also...as "as...as"
(36) agayns "against"
(39) syne (conj.) "since"
(45) noʒt, noʒte, (not) "not"
(48) warld, (worlde) "world"
(49) yinke "think"
(50) wark, warke (sb.), wyrke (vb.) "work"
(51) yore "there"
(52) whar "where"

(54) yrughe "through"
(55) when "when"
(57) -and [present participle ending]
(65) abowte (prep. and adv.) "about"
(78) before (prep.) "before"
(85) both "both"
(87) broy*er*, brey*er* (pl.) "brother"
(90) besy "busy"
(91) but "but"
(92) by "by"
(93) call "call"
(98) kyrke "church"
(102) dede "death"
(107) erth "earth"
(116) far "far"
(125) fyrst "first"
(134) gar*re*, gar*e* (infin.) "gar"
(139) gude "good"
(160) knawe "know"
(164) law "law"
(169) lyffe "life"
(188) nay*er* ne "neither nor"
(202) awne "own"
(210) says "says"; sayd "said"
(211) seys "sees"; saw (sg. & pl.) "saw"
(213) sellffe "self"
(238) togeder "together"
(244) apon "upon"
(251) whey*er* "whether"

Note also the following, not included on LALME's dot or item maps but dialectally significant in the context of (169) above:

(171) liffe "live"
(173) luffe "love"

NOTES

1. The John Goodchild Collection, "an independent local history study centre for the central West Riding," is freely open to all researchers, by appointment. Its address is Below Central Library, Drury Lane, Wakefield, West Yorkshire, WF1 2DT, UK (telephone 01924 298929). Mr. Goodchild has arranged that the collection will eventually pass into the ownership of Wakefield Metropolitan District Council.
2. The family fortunes were established by the textile manufacturer John Radcliffe, who became one of the lords of the manor of Saddleworth and was much involved in local affairs. However, the document to be discussed here may have been acquired by his descendants, the Shaws, some of whom are known to have had antiquarian interests.
3. The strip preserves on the left, the endings, and on the right, the beginnings of verse lines, the former bracketed (as couplets) in red, and the initial letters of the latter picked out in red, neither of which practices is a feature of the main leaves. Whereas the text on this upper surface of the strip ends and begins on either side of its central fold, the text visible on the under side of the strip overlaps the fold, a lack of register that indicates that the strip must have been cut from the centre of a two-column leaf, and not from the centre of a bifolium (which would have produced identically-positioned space on upper and lower sides).
4. C2^r, though consequently folded in, remained vulnerable to wear and tear, and is also not easy to read.
5. On fol. B1^r a crudely drawn hand points to the beginning of a tale told by St. Gregory.
6. The text of the NHC in this manuscript, examined on microfilm, proved to be so similar to that of the Goodchild fragment in terms of extent and content, despite a missing leaf, that it has been used throughout this article for the purposes of comparison. Its corresponding text runs from fol. 188^v to fol. 197^r (fol. 196 is missing).
7. The recto of the surviving scrap of A2 bears the words "That/and ga (?)/For b (?)/he" (its verso is blank except for the extreme ends of verse lines.) These appear to correspond to the beginnings of the following lines in CUL Dd.1.1: [fol. 197r] "þat is to warne him of his synne/& makiþ him of his folys blynne/[fol. 197^v] for but if man sum tyme sike wore/he wold don synne ay mor & more."
8. The text begins: "Trowys in god in trinite/and haythyn folke does not so."
9. This figure has been arrived at as a result of comparing the text on C1^r col. 2 and C2^r col. 1 with CUL Dd.1.1.
10. The text ends: "Anoþer skyll is withowtyn lesse/Why gode castys man into seknes."
11. Convenient lists are provided in *The Northern Homily Cycle: The Expanded Version in MSS Harley 4196 and Cotton Tiberius E VII*, ed. by Saara Nevanlinna, 3 vols, Mémoires de la Société Néophilologique de Helsinki, 38, 41, 43 (Helsinki, 1972-85), I, p. 2; in James R. Sprouse, "The Textual Relationships of the Unexpanded Middle English *Northern Homily Cycle*," Manuscripta, 33 (1989), 92-108 (pp. 93-94); and in Thomas J.

Heffernan, "Orthodoxies' Redux: The Northern Homily Cycle in the Vernon Manuscript and its Textual Affiliations," in Studies in the Vernon Manuscript, ed. by Derek Pearsall (Cambridge: D.S. Brewer, 1990), pp. 75-87 (p. 81, n.8). There is great divergence between the manuscripts in terms of extent: as Nevanlinna notes, four are no more than short fragments, and three others contain narraciones only. The contents of all sixteen manuscripts are listed in Carleton Brown, A Register of Middle English Religious and Didactic Verse, 2 vols (Oxford, 1916-20).

12. The sole published edition of the unexpanded NHC remains English Metrical Homilies from Manuscripts of the Fourteenth Century, ed. by John Small (Edinburgh, 1862). This edition prints—without reference to other manuscripts—the text of Edinburgh, Royal College of Physicians (now MS. Anonima 11), which ends imperfectly during the homily for the Feast of the Purification. A substantial excerpt from the work's prologue, taken from the Edinburgh manuscript, is included in The Idea of the Vernacular: An Anthology of Middle English Literary Theory, 1280-1520, ed. by Jocelyn Wogan-Browne and others (Exeter, 1999), pp. 125-30.

13. For partial analyses see Gordon H. Gerould, The North-English Homily Collection: A Study of the Manuscript Relations and of the Sources of the Tales (Lancaster, PA, 1902), pp. 10-19; Maryann Corbett, "An East Midland Revision of the Northern Homily Cycle," Manuscripta, 26 (1982), 100-07; and Sprouse, "Textual Relationships." All analyse different homilies (none coinciding with those preserved in the Goodchild fragment) and a different range of manuscripts, and their findings in respect of manuscript groupings are partly contradictory. (Corbett identifies the Marquess of Bute manuscript and Bodleian Library, MS Selden Supra 52, as containing an East Midland revision of the text.) Heffernan, "Orthodoxies' Redux," pp. 83-87, provides some analysis of readings in unexpanded version manuscripts as compared to the expanded version preserved in the Vernon manuscript (Bodleian Library, MS Eng. poet. a.1).

14. Thomas J. Heffernan, "The Authorship of the Northern Homily Cycle: The Liturgical Affiliations of the Sunday Gospel Pericopes as a Test," Traditio, 41 (1985), 289-309.

15. Heffernan, "Authorship," p. 300. The Bute manuscript is now Cambridge University Library, MS. Add. 8335.

16. For the purposes of this paper the text of the homilies in the Goodchild manuscript has also been compared, in a general way, with the corresponding text in MSS Lambeth Palace 260 and CUL Gg.5.31. Both these manuscripts diverge considerably, in different ways, from the version of the homilies transmitted in Goodchild and CUL Dd.1.1.

17. Angus McIntosh, M. L. Samuels, and Michael Benskin, A Linguistic Atlas of Late Mediaeval English, 4 vols (Aberdeen, 1986), IV, p. x.

18. British Libary, Add. MS 38010 (LP 465, "possibly North Riding of Yorkshire"); CUL Gg. S.31 (LP 478, "northern Middle English"); Edinburgh, Royal College of Physicians (LP 375, "Yorkshire"); and University of Minnesota Z.822.N81 (LP 576, "East Riding of Yorkshire," but for the more precise localization of this manuscript see below and n. 20). In addition to these four manuscripts a further three were characterised as

northern but not given linguistic profiles: Bodleian Library, Ashmole 42 ("strongly northern"), and the two small Bodleian fragments Eng. poet. c.3 and Eng. poet. c.4 ("northern Middle English").

19. Thomas J. Heffernan, "The Rediscovery of the Bute Manuscript of the Northern Homily Cycle," *Scriptorium*, 36 (1982), 118-29, giving (p. 126) the opinion of Angus McIntosh, whom he had consulted. However, it has now been established that the Bute manuscript was owned during the medieval period by Denny Abbey, a Franciscan nunnery in Cambridgeshire; see *Catalogue of the Bute Collection of Forty-Two Illuminated Manuscripts and Miniatures*, Sotheby's sale, 13 June 1983 (London, 1983), Lot 7, pp. 36-38, where a page from the manuscript is reproduced, and where it is dated c. 1425-50 rather than the mid-fourteenth century proposed by Heffernan.

20. See J. Lawrence Mitchell, "A 'Nothern Homilies Cycle' Manuscript: Minnesota MS Z822 N81," *Scriptorium*, 35 (1981), 321-30, and subsequently Michael Benskin, "The 'Fit'-Technique Explained," in *Regionalism in Late Medieval Manuscripts and Texts: Essays Celebrating the Publication of* A *Linguistic Atlas of Late Mediaeval English*, ed. by Felicity Riddy (Cambridge: Brewer, 1991), pp. 9-26, where the Minnesota manuscript serves as Benskin's main example, his conclusion being that the origins of its dialect "appear to lie in the area between Beverley and York, towards Pocklington and Market Weighton" (p. 25).

21. Saara Nevanlinna, "A Note on the Robartes Manuscript of the *Northern Homily Collection*," *Neuphilologische Mitteilungen*, 67 (1966), 58-66.

22. Daniel Huws, "MS. Porkington 10 and its Scribes," in *Romance Reading on the Book: Essays on Medieval Narrative Presented to Maldwyn Mills*, ed. by Jennifer Fellows and others (Cardiff, 1996), pp. 188-207 (p. 205).

23. Angus McIntosh and Michael Benskin, "A Mediaeval English Manuscript of Irish Provenance," *Medium Aevum*, 41 (1972), 128-31.

24. Private communication. She continues: "Your linguistic profile has most in common (jointly) with LPs 514, 503, 507, 202 in Notts, LPs 588, 491, 45 in Lincs, and LPs 175, 240 and 473 in the West Riding."

25. See Micahel Benskin, "The Letters <ȝ> and <y> in Later Middle English, and Some Related Matters," *Journal of the Society of Archivists*, 7 (1982), 13-30.

26. Heffernan, "Rediscovery of the Bute Manuscript," p. 127.

27. The Goodchild manuscript also differs from Bute in having a two-column lay-out, as do two other NHC manuscripts of comparable size, Bodleian Library, Eng. poet. c.4 (347 x 217 mm), and Lambeth Palace 260 (277 x 210 mm).

28. I owe this observation to Professor David Smith of the Borthwick Institute of Historical Research of the University of York.

29. For the lords of the manor of Eckington, see H. J. H. Garratt, *Eckington: the Court Rolls*, Vol. III: 1506-89 (unpublished typescript, 1996, held at Derbyshire Record Office, Matlock), in part citing Joseph Tilley, *The Old Halls, Manors and Families of Derbyshire*, 4 vols (London, 1892-1902). For the Strangeways family, whose main seat was Harlsey Castle in Cleveland, see the genealogical table included in Joseph

Foster, *Pedigrees of the County Families of Yorkshire*, 2 vols (London, 1874), II.
30. In preparing this article I have benefited from the specialist help and advice of Sarah Costley, A. I. Doyle, Margaret Laing, David Smith, and the staff of Derbyshire Record Office. I should also like to thank John Goodchild for so readily granting me access to the manuscript.

Descriptive Reviews

MARIE AXTON AND JAMES P. CARLEY, eds.
'Triumphs of English': *Henry Parker, Lord Morley,*
Translator to the Tudor Court.
London: The British Library, 2000.

This volume of essays, dedicated to the late Jeremy Maule, explores a prominent figure of the Tudor court from the reign of Henry VII through to that of Mary Tudor. "Prominent," although accurate, is a somewhat misleading word, and David Starkey's introduction to the volume pertinently (in an always pertinent essay) quotes T.S. Eliot in comparing Henry Parker, Lord Morley (c 1481 - 1556), to J. Alfred Prufrock, "an attendant lord, one that will do/To swell a progress. . . . " Sadly (and not, I think, through any failure of the contributors), Morley is no better rounded a character at the end of the volume than at the beginning. The failure, one must conclude, is that of Morley himself.

My own interest in Morley developed when, working on Lady Margaret Beaufort, I read his encomium on the *Miracles of the Sacrament* (here printed as Appendix 7), offered as New Year gift to Mary Tudor on the first day of what was to be the last year of his life. My admiration for Morley was tempered in reading this volume, not because he proved to be a trimmer (because that is not, I think, what he is proved to be, although the word "ingratiating" is used of him [p. 53] and implied or expressed elsewhere), but simply because it is so hard to get a hold on a man who appears to maintain his own brand of integrity through four very different reigns with so little apparent (to us today, at any rate) effort. Morley's "continuities," as Starkey calls them (his anticlericalism, his religious conservatism, his trust in secular power, and his patriotism), appear to argue against his being a mere compromiser, but, instead of a hero of the old religion, he emerges as a rather dull man, appearing to offer little more than what Jeremy Maule calls "sheeplike charm."

In the section called "Writings," James Carley sets the context for the book by providing a thoroughly comprehensive bibliographical survey of "The Writings of Henry Parker, Lord Morley," in which he lists, dates (with important revisions to previous datings), and discusses Morley's works, principally, of course, those all-important New Year gifts which make up the major part of his output, six presented to Henry VIII and eight to his daughter, Mary. Julia Boffey and A.S.G. Edwards investigate "Books Connected with Henry Parker, Lord Morley, and his Family," seeking them through the St John family, into which Parker married, and identifying and contextualizing a list of twenty-two books recorded in a manuscript owned by the St Johns. Both essays are of fundamental value.

The next section, "Politics and Religion," deals with "Morley, Machiavelli, and the Pilgrimage of Grace" and "Morley and the Papacy: Rome, Regime, and Religion." In both Morley is credited with a more active deviousness than other contributors can find. K.R. Bartlett focuses on Morley's recommendation of Machiavelli to Thomas Cromwell (here printed as Appendix 2) as evidence of his distancing himself from his fellow Catholic peers during the Pilgrimage of Grace: "Morley had to prove his loyalty through the blood of others." Richard Rex looks at Morley's two most extensive pieces of original composition. In the anti-papal invective of *The Exposition and Declaration of the* Psalme, Deus Ultionum Dominus, dedicated to Henry VIII (here printed as Appendix 3), Rex, like Bartlett, sees a Morley "anxious to establish his credentials as a faithful subject." In the M*iracles of the Sacrament* offered to Mary, he sees Morley's true attitude towards the Catholic church (incidentally, much that of his former mistress, Lady Margaret Beaufort, whom he here eulogizes): a love of the Psalms, devotion to the Virgin Mary, and confidence in the sacrament of the altar. Rex's conclusion is that Morley was a religious conservative, forced to temporize and compromise, and fortunate that, having survived four reigns, he was not put to the test further under Elizabeth.

The emphasis so far, although always drawn from the evidence of Morley's writings (and, as Starkey points out, Morley is, at least, "an *articulate* attendant lord"), is biographical. The title of the volume, of course, suggests that Morley as English translator is the pre-eminent concern, and, indeed, the section on "Courtly Maker" provides the largest number of essays: "What did Morley give when he gave a 'Plutarch' Life," by Jeremy Maule; "Morley's Translations from Roman Philosophers and English Courtier Literature," by David R. Carlson; "The Sacrifice of Lady Rochford: Henry Parker, Lord Morley's Translation of *De claris mulieribus*," by James Simpson; "Lord Morley's *Tryumphes of Petrarcke*: Reading Spectacles," by Marie Axton; "Lord Morley's 'Ryding Ryme' and the Origins of Modern English Versification," by Susanne Woods. Maule's essay is sharp and clever and touches on numerous aspects of the writings, including the technical. Maule is unable to identify a highly political Morley, tackling James McConica's portrait of an "eminently Erasmian personality." Similarly for Carlson, Morley is a courtier-writer who offers no threat, whose writing proclaims his disengagement from politics. The fact that, only a year after the execution of his own daughter, Lady Rochford, Morley could offer as New Year gift the lives of forty-six good women from the *De claris mulieribus* is taken (and how else could it be taken?) by Simpson in the next essay as an explicit assurance to the King that the execution was justified. The final two essays in this section concentrate closely on the works themselves, rather than the man, Axton arguing for an earlier date for the *Tryumphes* than is usually propounded, and Woods arguing (unconvincingly, for this reader at least) for innovation in Morley's resurrection of the Lydgatian line.

The "Epilogue" to the volume is Richard Axton's account of "Lord Morley's Funeral," as chronicled in a previously unpublished (and unknown to the College of Arms) heraldic miscellany: "Everything about Morley's funeral tallies with what is otherwise known of him: it was doctrinally conservative and...modestly sumptuous." Like Rex, Axton reflects on the fortunate timing of Morley's death.

This admirable volume concludes with seven appendices offering transcriptions of the shorter unpublished texts. It is finely produced, well organized, with only a few (unfortunate) spelling errors (pp. 140, 141, 143). If, in the end, it offers less on Morley the translator and the "Triumphs of English" than on Morley the man, this is clearly because the mystery of Morley the man has so exercised each contributor. They all seem to have asked the questions formulated by Richard Rex in his essay: "Was he a Protestant who conformed under Mary only to save his skin? Was he a Catholic who conformed under Henry only to save his skin? Or was he a neutral, cynically writing to please whatever regime held the reigns of patronage? Or was he simply an obedient subject, dutifully informing his conscience according to that of his sovereign?" To me at least, the latter appears to be the case, and perhaps it is wrong for me to feel that Morley is diminished by it.

Susan Powell, University of Salford

ELIZABETH J. BRYAN
Collaborative Meaning in Medieval Scribal Culture: The Otho Lahamon.
Ann Arbor: The University of Michigan Press, 1999. 238 pp.

In 1992, at the first International Lahamon Conference, held at the University of Lausanne, I gave a paper on the Latin marginal glosses in the late thirteenth-century British Library Cotton Caligula Aix manuscript of Lahamon's *Brut*, attempting to identify their source and to focus, through them, on the early reception of the poem. In working on these marginal annotations, I was made aware of how little work had been done on including such marginalia as part of a wider, integrated approach towards the study of medieval texts. At the same conference, Elizabeth Bryan discussed the interpretive role of the proper nouns written in the margins of the lesser-studied British Library Cotton Otho c.xiii manuscript version of the poem. As she says in the preface to this book, it was the prioritization of the Caligula text over the Otho and the consequent devaluing of the latter as less authoritative in the Lahamon canon that led her, having examined the relationship between the two manuscripts in her Ph.D thesis, to question the traditional editorial approach which assigns textual authority to one version of a medieval text, even though the evidence for the privileging of one version over another is often lacking. This book posits an alternative editorial approach which gives equal attention and value to all manuscript texts by arguing for a less author-centered but more collaborative context for manuscript production and reception. Though directly relevant for those with a research interest in Lahamon's *Brut*, Dr Bryan justifies her extensive study of features of the Otho manuscript within an overall editorial approach to the study of medieval manuscripts. The main body of work is a detailed examination of several features of the Otho manuscript, building up a 'community of voices' in the production and interpretation of the Otho text, and this is clearly the central concern of the book. At the same time, however, the specific study is underpinned by a more theoretical approach to editorial theory in arguing for the viability of seeing texts in preprint scribal culture as collaboratively produced. As the author admits in her Preface, this agenda asks readers "to range widely among sections that embody different ways of approaching literature, from authorial and editorial theory to cultural criticism to formal analysis to detailed paleographic and bibliographic study," but she justifies this multifaceted content on the grounds of "how fruitful it can be for our understanding of medieval texts to make links among activities so often perceived of as disparate or even in opposition."

Part 1 of the book outlines the critical theory and methodology which will justify the approach taken to the Otho manuscript and is divided into two chapters: chapter 1 argues that a study of medieval secular texts such as Henry of Huntingdon's *Historia Anglorum* challenges the received conclusion that the terms *scribere* and *dictare* formed a binary opposition of meaning, and links this with the evidence from a selection of self-reflexive passages in early Middle English texts which "either obscure distinctions between copyists and composers or mete out the same reward to both" (p.34). Having identified medieval cultural attitudes which, Dr Bryan argues, favor a collaborative approach to the production of texts, she proposes in chapter 2 "a heuristic for reading texts that were produced by collaboration in medieval scribal culture" (p.47), and finds poststructuralism helpful in its movement away from the dominance of the author and its emphasis on social relations and process. The study of medieval texts becomes, thus, a study of the manuscripts rather than "the author-defined work" (p.55), and this confers validity and value to each medieval manuscript and all aspects of its make-up. Each medieval manuscript text presents "multiple voices" ranging from the scribe to the annotator, and these voices are all relevant, "revealing a wealth of meaning in the cultural accretions" that make up a manuscript text.

Part 2 of the book, the larger part and, to me, as a Lahamon enthusiast, of most direct interest, provides detailed and fascinating data of five "voices" from the Otho text, ranging chronologically from the markings of the Otho scribe to Elizabethan underlinings of particular words in the manuscript. Bryan brings to bear all the skills of the paleographer (and fiber optic backlighting and microscope) in her detailed and meticulous study of all 146 folios of the manuscript, teasing out words and letters not visible to the naked eye. In each of the five "case studies," as it were, of manuscript features, the detailed mapping of such features is accompanied by an extrapolation of a possible interpretative purpose. The first case-study (choosing one example for illustrative purposes), occupies pages 63 to 96 of the book, and takes as its subject the seventy-eight large decorated initials in the Otho text. The Otho scribe was responsible for directing the arrangement of the large initials, leaving large indented spaces ("guide letters are still visible in the scribe's ink and hand"), and Bryan follows in minute detail the presence of each through the text, noting in which part of the narrative each initial occurs. She compares the positioning of the decorated initials with the scribe's placing of paragraph marks through the manuscript, and comes up with the suggestion that the suppression of decorated initials in those portions of the narrative dealing with ancient Britain's struggles with Rome and the substitution of paragraph instructions for decorated initials in the Arthurian section of the poem mark the suppression of emphasis upon the Roman element in the poem, reflecting an awareness of doubts as to the historicity of Arthur's war with Rome which had already been expressed by readers of Geoffrey of Monmouth's Arthurian narrative within fifteen years of its appearance. Bryan recognizes that the Otho scribe may have been following the markings of the version he was working from, but this does not, in her eyes, invalidate the interpretation of the markings.

In a recent *Notes and Queries* article (n.s. 47), Carl Berkout examined the reading list for the history of the English language drawn up by the Elizabethan antiquary William Lambarde, and stated, in describing the final item, that "the B*rute* (B*rut*) here is surely the popular late-fourteenth-and fifteenth-century prose chronicle, not the early Middle English poem by Lahamon," adducing as evidence several notations in Lambarde's hand in a version of the prose chronicle in MS Harley 4627. Yet Bryan shows in the final chapter of her book that the Otho manuscript was consulted by at least one Elizabethan antiquary, as witnessed by twenty-two pen underlinings of words and passages which can be dated from this period and which correspond in the subject matter underlined to topics of interest to the Elizabethan College of Antiquaries. As a point of comparison, she examines a fourteenth-century Middle English prose translation of Wace's *Roman de Brut* owned and annotated by one of the members of the College, Joseph Holland, and finds some interesting correspondences in subject matter between the underlinings in the two texts. Furthermore, there are one or two corrections made to the prose text by Holland which suggest to Bryan that he had read the Otho text. This is, while interesting, pure speculation, and, as she acknowledges, the array of potential candidates for the LahBrut-Otho underliner(s) "is enormous" (p.142). What is more important, it seems to me, is the evidence for the continuing reception of the Lahamon text and the ways in which it could hold significance for later generations of readers.

Elizabeth Bryan has done a valuable service for Lahamon scholars by her pioneering work on the Otho manuscript which is now, with added material, available in print, and for medieval scholars in general by suggesting fruitful ways forward in an alternative (though I would add the *caveat* of not exclusive) approach to the study of medieval manuscripts. Though her interpretations of the Otho annotations may be open to argument, they are always interesting, while the detailed and solid scholarship on the manuscript text itself will be of lasting help to Lahamon studies. The book itself is well-produced and has been excellently proofread.

Carole Weinberg, University of Manchester

A.S.G. EDWARDS, VINCENT GILLESPIE,
AND RALPH HANNA, eds.
The English Medieval Book: Studies in Memory of Jeremy Griffiths.
The British Library Studies in the History of the Book. London:
British Library, 2000.

The death of Jeremy Griffiths in 1997, at the early age of 42, shocked and saddened all who knew him, even those, like myself, who knew him by sight and reputation rather than as a friend. Vincent Gillespie in the opening piece to this volume (which was delivered at Jeremy's memorial service) speaks eloquently and emotionally about Jeremy, the impact of the man, his life, and his death. The impact of the man and his life can be imagined very clearly from both this tribute and the next piece, "Travels with Jeremy" by the Serbian rare book collector Pedrag Milovanovic. The impact of his death is implicit throughout the volume in the several contributors who have been emboldened by the one shortcoming in Jeremy Griffiths (but not one which in any way overshadows his many qualities and diverse talents), his slowness to publish, to take up work they themselves have put to one side and failed to bring to perfection. These confessions of dilatoriness range from the minor (Christopher de Hamel's note on an unknown Bohun manuscript) to the major (Derek Pearsall's determination to produce the descriptive catalogue of Gower manuscripts embarked on twenty years ago with Jeremy and Kate Harris). In reading the volume, one is bound to reflect on the purgative nature of the (tragic) occasion, the consciences eased and the scholarship enhanced.

The volume begins with an Introduction by Ralph Hanna that gives context for the preceding tributes and subsequent essays. The first of these essays, "A New Bohun" by Christopher de Hamel, is an opportunity for de Hamel to write up his notes on an unnamed manuscript in "the private library of an English medieval castle" and to give one further clue: it left the Bohun castle at Pleshy in Essex but "it evidently did not move far." One part (ff. 3-111) is largely a Book of Hours with English work of around 1430; the first two folios, however, and the second part (ff. 112-93) are from a finer and earlier manuscript, with the arms of the Bohun family, illuminated by the same artist as the Bohun Psalter in Vienna. As such, this part of the manuscript is a new addition to an already known group of Bohun manuscripts; the fifteenth-century part bears the arms of the Baud family of Essex and Hertfordshire.

Ralph Hanna next provides a useful survey of "Augustinian Canons and Middle English Literature," intended to offset the last decades' concentration on what he calls "the posh and powerful," the Carthusians. That it does not topple the Carthusians is hardly Hanna's fault—it is a worthwhile piece of work. A.I. Doyle next undertakes to share research orginally intended to contribute to a project of Jeremy Griffiths and Angus McIntosh, a list of scribes whose hands are found in more than one manuscript. In "Ushaw College, Durham, MS 50: Fragments of the *Prick of Conscience*, by the same Scribe as Oxford, Corpus Christi College, MS 201, of the B Text of *Piers Plowman*," Doyle describes the only recorded copy of the *Prick of Conscience* with a pictorial illustration, written (but not illustrated) by the same scribe as the Corpus manuscript of *Piers Plowman*. "Minding the Gaps: Interpreting the Manuscript Evidence of the *Cook's Tale* and the *Squire's Tale*" is a rather different, and much lengthier, essay, in which Stephen Partridge looks closely at the manuscript context and the scribal treatment of these unfinished tales, arguing that gaps left after the tales "are a sign not only, or even primarily, of the scribes' indecision but rather of Chaucer's own uncertainty about how he would proceed."

Derek Pearsall next confesses to dilatoriness in relation to the "Descriptive Catalogue of the Manuscripts of the Works of John Gower" and offers as some satisfaction a description of "The Rede (Boarstall) Gower," London, British Library, MS Harley 3490, possibly, but not certainly, one of two Gowers bequeathed by Edmund Rede in 1489. A.S.G. Edwards, in the next essay, searches assiduously for evidence of "Fifteenth-Century Middle English Verse Author Collections." While finding some (for example, the English poems of Charles d'Orleans in London, British Library, MS Harley 682, or the carols and poems of James Ryman in Cambridge University Library, MS Ee.I.12), Edwards can find "only intermittently any coherent sense of the identity of the author and even more intermittently any inclination to signal that in distinctive ways." It is really only with the advent of the print culture that the author achieves prominence and recognition.

Linne R. Mooney's essay is a contribution to the clearing of Jeremy Griffiths' desk by publishing details of "A New Manuscript by the Hammond Scribe: Discovered by Jeremy Griffiths," London, British Library, Additional MS 29901. Mooney's meticulous detective work paves the way to finding further texts by the Hammond scribe and offers the possibility of his eventual identification. Julia Boffey in "Bodleian Library, MS Arch. Selden B.24 and Definitions of the 'Household Book'" takes her starting point from *Katherine Tollemache's Book of Secrets*, a household book edited by Jeremy for the Roxburghe Society. Boffey asks what makes up a household book: does it comprise texts of everyday usefulness, thereby excluding assemblages of literary material? She argues that a collection such as MS Arch. Selden B.24 (which she and Tony Edwards recently edited in facsimile) offers an instance where a household provenance might be ascribed to a compilation of non-practical literary texts, here supplied by the circulation of exemplars through Scottish family circles in such a way as to justify the term "household" for the compilation.

N. F. Blake next interrogates and modifies received opinion on "Caxton's Second Edition of the *Canterbury Tales*." Thomas Dunn's 1940 research on the edition established that Caxton's method of preparing the second edition was to write in on the current edition corrections from the new manuscript made available to him, working quickly and rather carelessly and not using the new manuscript as his copy-text. Blake's painstaking analysis gives an interestingly prominent role to Caxton's compositors, suggesting that Caxton made initial decisions but left detailed changes to the compositors who worked both from the annotated first edition and from the new manuscript. His conclusion is convincing and fully consonant with Blake's long-developed image of Caxton the businessman: "Caxton was interested in the broad sweep of the changes, but it is probable that the compositors introduced the more detailed changes."

Kathleen Scott takes up abandoned research between herself and Jeremy Griffiths on the Luton Guild Register. As Scott confesses, their delay has led to Richard Marks' publication on the Register ("Two Illuminated Guild Registers from Bedfordshire," in *Illuminating the Book: Makers and Interpreters*, edited by Michelle P. Brown and Scot McKendrick, reviewed in JEBS 3 [2000], 227-30). Scott concentrates on the imagery of the frontispiece painting, distinct from the other illustrations in the quality of its workmanship and in its intentions (to commemorate the founding of the Fraternity of the Holy Trinity). Her careful, comparative analysis of the frontispiece establishes it as Continental work with a lower register (Archbishop Rotherham and the royal family) compatible with traditional English pictorial usage but an upper register (the Trinity) in a "non-English world," where Scott is "less convinced that Rotherham gave precise instructions."

The next essay, by Vincent Gillespie, is on "The Book and the Brotherhood: Reflections on the Lost Library of Syon Abbey," of particular interest to this reviewer since it was through hearing Gillespie talk on the subject at Syon Abbey itself in 1994 that I came to investigate Syon preaching, as Gillespie's endnote 14 acknowledges. Gillespie here makes us privy to some of the fascinating insights revealed by his now nearly completed work on the Syon catalogue for the *Corpus of British Medieval Library Catalogues*. He sets in context the important role of books (at first manuscripts but then, with celerity, prints) at Syon, provides details of the libraries, their donors, and the books themselves, and describes the intricacies of the catalogue compiled by Thomas Betson in the first decade of the sixteenth century, with particularly interesting comments on what revisions and re-orderings evident from post-Benson annotations and re-read erasures tell us about deaccessioned and added volumes in the last two decades of Syon's existence. In general, it may be summed up as a comprehensive modernization of the library, taking full advantage of the print revolution, and resulting in the library described in 1527 by Gasparo Spinelli as "a mass of books such as I have never before seen assembled in one place." Of course, within a decade, that library was no more.

The final two essays are "Robert Hare's Books" by Andrew Watson and "Medieval Manuscripts at Longleat House" by Kate Harris. Watson investigates Hare and details the 46 manuscripts and 68 printed books he has tracked down, as well as those that are untraced. The main record of Hare's books is a list of volumes he gave to Trinity Hall, Cambridge, nearly all the manuscripts of which still survive there. The 1560s and 1570s appear to have been the main years of Hare's bookbuying. Sources of the manuscripts are hard to identify, but English abbeys supplied some (two from Syon, for example, "by means unknown," and two from the Royal Library, again, unfortunately, by means unknown). There is a little evidence of Continental bookbuying and very little of previous ownership. It may be that Hare's position as a recusant explains in some way the fact that he appears to have disposed of all his manuscripts before his death, so that his will refers only to printed books that should be sold and shared among his household servants. Finally Kate Harris, in her unique role as librarian to Longleat, discusses the library and writes with great interest, among other matters, on the relationship to the library of Humphrey Wanley and of John Urry. The volume closes with a list of the publications of Jeremy Griffiths.

It will be clear that this tribute to Jeremy is a fitting one. In almost every case, the contributions are geared to the contributor's own experience of Jeremy, and in every case, the essays would have been of interest to him. The generous contribution of Toshiyuki Takamiya has meant that the essays of de Hamel, Doyle, Partridge, and Scott are suitably, and helpfully, illustrated. There are almost no typos (but see pp. 107, 108, 128, and for "Henry VII" on p. 173 read "Henry VIII"). This is a volume of essays written with affection and scholarship by the leading names in manuscript studies today – it will enlarge souls as well as minds.

Susan Powell, University of Salford

SUSANNA FEIN, ED.
Studies in the Harley Manuscript: the Scribes, Contents, and Social Contexts of British Library MS Harley 2253.
Kalamazoo: Medieval Institute Publications, 2000.

British Library MS Harley 2253[1] has been largely appreciated by modern scholars for its importance as the repository of most of the Middle English secular lyrics that have survived from the early fourteenth century. A book of essays on the manuscript was promised by the late Rossell Hope Robbins around twenty years ago and has at last appeared, although in a different form than he might have imagined. One of the laudable features of this collection is the interest shown by many of its contributors in focusing attention on the lesser-known, or hitherto critically undervalued, texts in the manuscript. Another area of interest clearly centers on the vexed question of whether the manuscript is a miscellany of texts collected haphazardly or a planned anthology. In order to facilitate discussion here of the manner in which the essays in this collection variously deal with these concerns, I intend to concentrate on the two main, occasionally overlapping, thematic strands that stand out as the most important focus for critical discussion in the volume. These strands might be characterised as dealing with codicological and scribal issues, and generic and thematic concerns.

Generic and Thematic Studies

Many of the texts I have grouped under 'generic studies' offer an analysis of a text or texts of a particular type, often in the context of material from outside the manuscript. For example, Helen Phillips examines three texts of differing genres from Harley that all refer to dreams in some way; Richard Newhauser concentrates on a single complaint poem; and Karl Reichl analyses Harley's debate verse, discussing authorship and the question of defining the genre. Mary Dove examines another critically undervalued genre in Harley, the French verse, by an analysis of its formal characteristics. A similar line of interrogation is also followed by Elizabeth Solopova, who pays close attention to the layout, punctuation, and stanza form of the English poems, suggesting that the care and attention with which they are laid out and copied is attributable to the scribe rather than to his exemplars.

Of the generic essays, Michael Kuczynski's contribution on the religious texts is one of the few in the volume to take account of Harley 2253 as a whole. He includes references not only to the work of scribes A and B, but also to the flyleaves, which contain additional material. Critics have paid little attention to Harley's religious material in the past, and this essay is an attempt to redress the balance. John Scattergood relates Harley's political material to the historical events of the time, demonstrating that much of the political verse appeals to a sense of nationalism. Barbara Nolan draws attention to a group of texts (the fabliaux) that have been largely ignored. She argues that Harley is an anthology, preferring Carter Revard's model of juxtaposed texts.[2] Harley's fabliaux are analysed in relation to the contents of a block of quires that they inhabit. This anthologising strategy fits the Harley scribe's compilation methods since it looks at the manuscript in terms of its quires.

Codicological and Scribal Issues
Of the studies in this collection Carter Revard's is the only one that brings together all of the Harley scribe's known literary output.[3] The first part of his essay provides some extremely useful palaeographical information, concerning forty-one legal holographs in the Harley scribe's hand, enabling much of his work to be dated more accurately than had previously been the case. The holographs also provide us with over a hundred names with which the scribe may possibly have had connections. Of particular interest to scholars is a collection of twenty-seven monochrome plates, containing photographs of all the legal documents, and a calendar of all the deeds in appendix 2.

In the next section, Revard begins an analysis of the manuscripts in search of the scribe's training and interests, using several models of scribal employment. Examining the textual and codicological evidence from the scribe's three manuscripts in turn, he suggests a possible outline of his career as household chaplain and secretary. Also, by examining political texts in the light of the events of 1340-41, he builds an interesting case for patronage by Sir Laurence Ludlow of Stokesay. Some of the links between texts and patrons may seem rather tenuous, but this should not detract from an essay that is of great interest and practical use to the scholar, packed as it is with well-researched documentary, codicological, and palaeographical information.

Continuing on this theme, John Thompson is the only contributor to examine the work of Harley scribe A in any detail. He presents an analysis of this scribe's work as a 'mini-anthology' of French religious texts, in the light of other similar English productions. He also examines the biblical stories copied by the Harley scribe with reference to the *Vita Edward Secundi* and contemporary political and religious propaganda, arguing that the biblical narratives have been carefully shaped to provide a political and historical message.

Frances McSparran provides us with a thorough examination of the linguistic evidence concerning the various dialects of Harley's English poems. Considering the amount of codicological and textual studies, this approach is a welcome addition to the collection. She demonstrates that although the scribe's dialect is firmly located in the South West Midlands, he is heavily influenced by his exemplars, and includes many forms from outside his dialect area.

The next few essays all contribute in some way to the debate over the extent or presence of an organising principle behind the arrangement of texts in Harley. Theo Stemmler's argument focuses on an analysis of the items using a number of criteria, such as author, genre, content, language and form. By the end of the survey, the list of criteria has been narrowed down to verbal and phrasal links between texts for the most part, and while the author admits that any organising principle is not sustained throughout the manuscript, he stands behind the notion of Harley as an anthology. It is notable, however, that he ignores the work of scribe A completely, which leaves an intriguing question: how would Stemmler's theory work when applied to Harley in its entirety? Furthermore, how would it apply to the scribe's other known manuscripts, in the light of what we now know about the methodology he used when compiling them? Could the use of booklets as an organising principle in Royal 12 C. xii, for example, be a profitable avenue of research?[4]

David L. Jeffrey also argues that Harley is an anthology. His 'organising principle' relies on the Franciscan associations of a number of texts, and he tests this theory on models of patronage and provenance. He suggests possible patrons to be local Herefordshire families such as the Bohuns and Ludlows, as well as bishop Thomas de Charlton. He suggests parallels and a possible connection with the Irish BL MS Harley 913, positing a journey by the Harley scribe to Ireland between 1328-40.

Susanna Fein treads the middle path between Revard's juxtaposition theory (although she casts some doubts upon it due to the lack of marginalia and *incipits*), and Stemmler's verbal and phrasal link theory. Her essay is essentially in two parts. In the first, she examines the contents of Quire 7 as unified by the theme of the sexual appeal of women, focusing on the legend of Saint Marina. In the second, she discusses the manuscript's original purpose and audience, as well as the compiler's original plan for the book, raising a number of pertinent questions concerning patronage and audience.

Marilyn Corrie presents a comparative analysis of Harley and Oxford, Bodleian Library MS Digby 86. This is not the first such study, but it pays attention to underdeveloped areas, such as the Anglo-Norman texts, and divergences between the manuscripts. Her essay raises interesting questions regarding regional culture, the interaction of the vernaculars and book-production in pre-Chaucerian England.

The collection goes a long way to filling in the gaps left by previous scholarship, which has so often tended to concentrate solely on the secular English lyrics, or on Continental French writings. There is, however, a marked tendency here to consider Harley 2253 in the terms of Ker's 1964 facsimile, which for all its good points largely ignores the first section of the manuscript. There is hardly any mention of scribe C's work, and only one detailed analysis of scribe A's work in the collection. Furthermore, little attention has been paid to the scribe's other literary manuscripts, although this is perhaps to be expected in a volume which concentrates on a single book. These small objections aside, this volume will certainly reinvigorate the study of this interesting manuscript, and of the literary culture in which it was produced.

Jason O'Rourke, Queen's University, Belfast

NOTES

1. Hereafter referred to as 'Harley.' The compiler of the MS is referred to as the 'Harley scribe.'
2. Revard puts forward this argument in his article "*Gilote et Johane*: an Interlude in B. L. MS. Harley 2253," *Studies in Philology* 79 (1982): 122-46.
.3 The Harley scribe contributed to, and compiled, three manuscripts: British Library MSS Harley 273, Royal 12 C. xii and Harley 2253.
4. For the Harley scribe's methodology and use of booklets, see my article "British Library MS Royal 12 C. xii and the Problems of Patronage," JEBS 3 (2000): 216-26.

JEAN-FRANÇOIS GILMONT, ED.
The Reformation and the Book.
English edition and translation by Karin Maag.
Aldershot and Brookfield, Vermont: Ashgate, 1998. XXII + 498PP.
First published as *La Réforme et le livre: L'Europe de l'imprimé*
(1517-v.1570).
Paris: Editions du Cerf, 1990.

"Justification by Print Alone": A. G. Dickens's witty epigraph to the Reformation is almost as old as the Reformation itself. Martin Luther once called print "God's ultimate and greatest gift," although he added, with an apocalyptic sting in the tail, that it was "the last flicker of the flame which glows before the end of the world." Philip Melanchthon, too, judged printing an art communicated by God. In 1542, Johann Sleidan, in his *Address to the Estates of the Empire*, declared that the Gutenberg invention provided "proof that God has chosen us to accomplish a special mission," awakening in the German nation a zeal for new knowledge and amazement at its former blindness. Most famously, and at greatest length, John Foxe used print to explain the difference between the premature reformations of Jan Hus in Bohemia or the Lollards in England, and the successful revolution of Luther. Providence had granted the German a greater weapon than sword or spear against the bastions of Rome, so that "either the Pope must abolish knowledge & printyng, or printynge at length will roote him out."

It is the Luther affair that indeed has provided the archetype of the relationship between print and religious dissent, and also its best evidence. Although Luther's posting of the 95 Theses on the Wittenberg Schloßkirch door has assumed iconographic precedence, it has always been understood that the printed version had a radical effect in their dissemination. Copies of the Theses, printed in 1517 within weeks of their composition, survive from presses in Nuremberg, Leipzig and Basel. Luther's letters attest to at least one edition in a

German translation emanating from Nuremberg, and many other editions may have been made. Erasmus is among the multitude of readers who gained access to a copy in these early months, even before Luther put his hand to a serious academic edition, with copious annotations and a dedication to Leo X, in the summer of 1518. The story of the Theses has all the ingredients to justify its reputation as the first media sensation of the technological age. In the process, this transformed an obscure professor from an obscure German university into one of the most notorious figures in the Christian world in less than a year. Elizabeth Eisenstein is no doubt right in this connection to look to the diverse networks of printers, booksellers and other distributors as vital "agents of change."

In the grand narrative of European history, print and the Reformation have gone hand in hand. Indeed, at times it has seemed as if only an idea as big as the one could be sufficient to explain the other. Each topic has lent itself to the megalomaniac or monomaniac turn of phrase. In these more reticent historiographical times, perhaps it is not surprising that the more sensational pronouncements concerning cultural revolution have come to seem rather old-fashioned. This has had simultaneous effects on the study of the Reformation and of the early modern book. Eisenstein's *magnum opus* now represents the apogee in print studies of the philosophy of great cause for great effect, just as Dickens's work is now held up for respectful mockery of its enthusiasm in hailing the cultural inevitability of the German and English Reformations. Eisenstein's theory, produced with magnificent hindsight, that print would have produced enormous religious change "whether or not the Lutheran heresy spread, whether or not clerical abuses were reformed," now seems not so much a misjudged answer as a distinctly jejune and unanswerable question.

What is required, and what Eisenstein after all asked for, is a more sustained and substantial inquiry into the mingled worlds of books and of religion in the sixteenth century. *La Réforme et le livre: L'Europe de l'imprimé* was first published in Paris in 1990, the result of several years of collaboration between an international group of scholars under the aegis of Jean-François Gilmont. Gilmont's own work, which includes studies of both Jean Crespin and Jean Calvin, is an example of the prodigious efforts of inter-disciplinary research which are required to do this subject justice. It is a tribute to Gilmont's intellectual energy and his mastery of the field (in evidence here in the two pieces which enfold the book as a whole) that the resulting collaboration is so coherent and comprehensive. A feature of the book (in contrast to some multi-collaborator volumes) is the strictness of editorial brief as to the structure of essays, which all follow the three-part formula of printing and book-production, writing and authorship, and reading and reception. It is a tribute to the success of the original volume that it has now been published in English. Although much of the work under review is now over a decade old (many of the notes and bibliographies have been updated, but the texts are largely translated as written), it is still a book that belongs on the shelves of anybody who works in Reformation studies, and indeed in the reference stacks of any library of early printed books.

What gives this book its immediate distinction is its geographical range. Perhaps with its own sense of a reformed national hierarchy, it arises in Germany, floods out into France, the Low Countries, and England, takes a detour through the Inquisition in Spain and Italy, and then permeates through to Hungary, Bohemia and Moravia, Poland, Denmark and Norway, before finally silting up in Sweden and Finland. The importance of a geographical perspective is immediately felt in relation to Germany. If the Lutheran revolution is an archetype, it is also conspicuously a special case. The lack of a single dominant center of production—unlike Paris, Venice, Antwerp, or even London—allowed for the volatile and unpredictable dissemination of Luther's heresies, and inhibited effective ecclesiastical censorship. Indeed, John L. Flood argues that the new divisiveness of religion provided a commercial opportunity for new centers of production. Using Josef Benzing's bibliography of German printers, he shows that the first printing output in Ingolstadt, Sélestat, Halberstadt, Stuttgart, Coburg, Eilenburg, Grimma, Regensburg, Altenburg, Jena, Allstedt, Dresden, Königsberg, Wertheim, Halle, Luzern and Zwickau (just to take examples up to 1525) was of Lutheran, or just as significantly, anti-Lutheran material. Wittenberg's rise to become a major center of European literary culture was, of course, entirely due to Luther's personal output (although this resulted only from an uncharacteristic commercial blunder by Anton Koberger of Nuremberg, who was offered first refusal).

In terms of style and physical form, too, German book production was unusual. The pamphlet phenomena of unbound Flugschriften—of which the 95 Theses are an early example—seem to have been an invention of the German Reformation printers. It has been estimated that more than 3 million copies of these pamphlets were in circulation between 1518 and 1525, spread among a population of perhaps 13 million. This phenomenon was repeated later elsewhere only on a much smaller scale in special political circumstances such as in the French wars of religion or in England in the factional years leading to the fall of Thomas Cromwell. On the other hand, as Francis Higman remarks in his excellent chapter on French-speaking regions, the characteristic German quarto of eight or twelve leaves (Adam Petri's Basel imprint of the 95 Theses is again an early example) was never used in France. Here, an octavo of fifty or even a hundred pages was the dominant format for doctrinal and polemical treatises. While this partly reflects the sensibilities of Catholic small-book piety, it is likely that the main reason was ease of concealment. While the German product proclaimed its controversial status, the French book needed to be put away at speed, whether in delivery or in reading. The same trend is noticed in the brilliant chapter on Italy by Ugo Rozzo and Silvana Seidel Menchi, who also comment on the lack of illustrations in Italian Protestant or crypto-Protestant works—in marked contrast to the extraordinary visual impact of German books and pamphlets.

The importance of this culturally diverse approach to the field is shown most dramatically in the final sequence of chapters. The essays on Hungary, Bohemia and Moravia, and Poland, for instance, are written by eminent bibliographers from the National Libraries of Budapest, Prague and Warsaw respectively, who bring the benefit of their immense learning to a wider audience. This provides new insights to many areas, for instance to that most persistent of truisms about print and Protestantism, that the printed Luther succeeded whereas the printless Hus failed. Of the three authors in this book who cite Foxe's famous dictum, only Gilmont remarks that its source is the De typographiae inventione of Matthaeus Judex, published in Copenhagen in 1566. In fact, as Mirjam Bohatcová shows, the situation in Bohemia was much more complex and ambiguous. On the one hand, the circumstances of fifteenth-century religion in Bohemia show a heterodoxy quite at odds with the image of total suppression following Hus's condemnation at the Council of Constance in 1415. On the other hand, Hus himself was not widely reprinted in the 1520s, despite the new opportunities and his national fame. Bohemian religious culture (and, to some extent, Hungarian and Danish, too) worked in a quite different way from France or England or even Germany, because of competing political centers, and because of the different relationships between royalty and aristocratic power, and between the Court and the Bishops. This also enabled a different pattern in the production of books, with regional or princely patronage being of great importance.

From this broadened cultural map, Scotland is one important omission, made the more odd by the imprint of this new English edition in the series "St Andrews Studies in Reformation History." Also, although Basel is given a chapter to itself, and Geneva is given generous treatment within the French domain (and, rather less generously, Zurich among the Germans), the book might have benefited from a more sustained treatment of the different centers of the Swiss Reformations. It is only in Gilmont's conclusion that a remark is made on the different formats of production, and habits of reading, between Lutheran and Calvinist editions of the Bible. In 1974, Rolf Engelsing in Der Bürger als Leser dismissed as "a myth and a fable" the idea that Luther's Bible was ever an engine of popular reading. Other studies have shown that most printed German Bibles went to parish churches and clerical libraries, and were simply too expensive for widespread public purchase. On the other hand, Andrew G. Johnston here calculates that there was a Bible in circulation for every 25 Dutch speakers alive between 1520 and 1566. Although Catholic Bibles were produced in the Netherlands for priests and parishes, much of the Protestant production was not. Gilmont's suggestion that "the Calvinist Reformation preferred small formats, suggesting a more frequent private use" is left as a tantalizing thread for further comparative research. Similar arguments have been advanced for the use of the Geneva Bible in England, but unfortunately, David Loades's chapter ends in 1558. An inventory from 1569 of the Genevan bookseller Laurent de Normandie shows that the cost of production for a folio Bible was double that of a quarto, which was double in turn that of an octavo: such price differentials would increase in retail. It is an interesting case where economic, bibliographical and theological concerns are inseparable.

Famously, the Reformation was one of cities as much as nations, and this is reflected in a further editorial masterstroke in interpolating three chapters on individual cities into the middle of the volume. Just as traffic between cities altered the flow of ideas between different national confessions, so this triad of urban chapters alters the dynamics of the book. It is a simple but highly imaginative decision, and just as imaginative is the choice of the cities: Antwerp, Strasbourg and Basel. Strasbourg has the particular advantage of bringing the magnificent scholarship of Miriam Chrisman out of the footnotes and into the volume. Although Lyon or Nuremberg or Venice would have been equally instructive, the cities in question are characterized in a peculiarly significant way, as Gilmont argues, by their position on the borders, between northern and southern Renaissance humanism, between Germanic and romance languages, between Rome and its heretics. At these borderlines the printed book exercised its greatest, and most unpredictable, power. All three cities benefited as well as suffered by being caught in the nexus of religious conflict, and all three contributed commercially and ideologically to the volatile trade in ideas. In the literal sense, too, they were cities of the translation of books.

Antwerp rose with astonishing speed to become a true metropolis of the sixteenth century. Its fortunes coincided with, and followed, the vicissitudes of religious division. The cornerstone of the northern Habsburg empire, and the key to financial command of the North Sea, it became in this period for a while the trade capital of western Europe. It provided a unique meeting place between Spain and the Baltic, or between East Anglia and Lower Saxony. Entirely on this basis of cosmopolitan exchange (the city had neither Bishop nor university), Antwerp also became an intellectual capital. For a time its printing production rivalled that of Paris, although both were only distant poor relations of Venice. Its status as a free area allowed the printers to escape the traditional Catholic bias of the city authorities, and led to a plethora of religious books in a diaspora of languages, not only in Dutch and Latin but also in Greek and Hebrew, in French, Spanish, Italian and Danish, and especially in English. Just as this printing activity rose with Lutheranism, and happily embraced Calvinism and even Anabaptism, so it declined dramatically after 1545 with a massive counter-movement of censorship. Strasbourg's importance as a literary center was more local, although it, too, straddled different worlds. Strasbourg provided a route for dissident materials to reach an international market, and the city magistrates seem to have taken a liberal attitude. From here, German authors could reach France, Switzerland and the Netherlands. One of the striking facts to emerge from Chrisman's chapter is the diversity of authors emanating from Strasbourg presses, including the most radical, from the earliest years. Basel, in this respect, was more conservative, as Peter G. Bietenholz shows in his exceptionally detailed analysis. Although direct censorship was discretionary and light, voluntary self-regulation among the printers sometimes achieved the same results. Anabaptist writers who might be printed in Strasbourg in the 1520s or 1530s were not risked in Basel. On the other hand, despite the fury of their Genevan neighbours, Basel provided a haven for Anti-trinitarians in person if not in print. Basel remained a very different literary center from either Antwerp or Strasbourg. International in outlook, it was also an established episcopal and academic city with a prominent university. Its printers remained attached to the humanist markets through which they made their name. The reaction of the Basel firms to Luther was to try to turn him into a humanist reformer, as in Froben's immediate efforts to produce a collected works' edition. For a time, Luther provided a publishing boom in Basel as he did more or less everywhere, but after a while, the Basel printers lost enthusiasm. Their international markets did not mix well with Lutheran isolationism.

One general lesson to be drawn from the chapters on the three border cities is the importance of censorship to the historiography of books. Political control of the publication process is a subject that is integral to every one of the essays in this collection. The politics of printing ranges from the proliferation of printing centers in Germany, to the absolute monopoly in Vasa Sweden, which produced quite simply the most successful and least ambiguous Reformation in Europe. Gustav's control of the press was the envy of every budding autocrat in Europe. England, on the other hand, despite the best and most violent efforts of Henry VIII in the late 1520s or early 1540s, was vulnerable to subtle and ever more complex lines of dissemination, in particular through Antwerp. While to many bibliographers censorship remains a side issue, almost an occupational nuisance, it can reveal something about the whole dynamic of readership and how it works. It is usually seen (perhaps naturally) as an entirely negative force. Yet in the procedures of censorship—by which is meant something much larger than the formal interdiction or emendation of a particular book—may be found the faultlines of a whole cultural attitude to the processes of information and dissemination. The patterns of censorship show what happens when a book is passed from person to person, and how differently it may be interpreted in different literary acts. For this reason, some of the most interesting writing in the book concerns the wake of Inquisition, particularly the chapter on Italy. It may seem a paradox to find in Italy some of the most exciting evidence on the Reformation and the book, but the advantage here (and it is an area expanded since the publication of this volume by the opening up of the archive of the Office of Propaganda) lies in the copious records of trials involving books. .

If a criticism may be levelled at this powerful and excellent collection, it is that sometimes it is distracted from its intellectual arguments by the sheer volume of books, authors and printers to be catalogued and identified. Also, the tripartite division between printing, authorship and reception can sometimes be applied a little rigidly. The category that suffers here is the third one of readership, which is once or twice squashed into a couple of paragraphs. Rozzo and Menchi in their study of Italy have to be more inventive in their search for books and readers, and in the process reveal how diverse the processes of reception can be, and how different from the post-enlightenment model of the reader in his study, beginning (as this one did) at page one and going on to the end. As Gilmont remarks in his Conclusion, which by itself must rank as among the most incisive treatments of Reformation books ever penned, it is the history of reading that is expanding most rapidly and most excitingly in the field of bibliography. Books in this period are not always and only read: they are passed from hand to hand, often secretly; they are split into pieces so as to multiply readership; they are read aloud, sometimes in company; they are copied out and scribbled in and from.

On the basis of the research selected so carefully in this volume, and using its excellent lists of sources (although not the index, which is totally inadequate for such a complex area), many further projects could be built. More could be said about the inter-relationship between printed books and manuscript writing, and about the annotation of books in the margin. An equally promising area is the inter-relationship between the written and the oral. This applies not only to reading aloud in the household or in more open public spaces, but also to the oral dissemination of books in sermons, or even through conversation. Reading by and among women is a topic that has begun to receive much more attention since this collection was first written. The boundaries of the literate process are not so clear-cut as the bound covers of a printed book may suggest. The concept of literacy has often bedevilled Reformation studies, but it is becoming clearer all the time that literacy is a highly diverse and complex process.

This remains the deepest mystery, how a book is read, and how it comes to signify. This is not a question that looks the same for every reader or in different parts of society. To answer such a question would go beyond the scope of any collection of essays, but it remains the goal. It would require, for instance, going beyond the confessional boundaries of Protestantism. Near the end of this study, Gilmont asks the almost impossibly bold question, "Can one simply conclude that Protestants trusted books and Catholics feared them?" Yet no study of the Reformation and the book could be complete without examining the use of books in orthodox France or Italy or Spain, or for that matter the attitude to Catholic books in, for instance, Elizabethan England or the Calvinist Netherlands. This volume is largely conceived as a project about Protestantism, but books cross confessional as well as national borders. What this collection does show is that the early modern book is an object of extraordinary power, yet also of conflict and of division. It goes beyond its signification as a carrier of information to bear something of the burden of the fetish. In this respect, Foxe and Eisenstein were probably right in sensing that the culture of the book is a subject almost without limits.

Brian Cummings, University of Sussex

ANDREW HUNTER, ED.
Thornton and Tully's Scientific Books, Libraries and Collectors. 4th ed.
Ashgate: Aldershot, UK and Brookfield, Vermont, USA, 2000.

Since its first publication in 1954, "Thornton and Tully" has become a respected institution among historians of science, librarians and book collectors. While the first three editions—together with the supplementary volume added to the third edition in 1978—consisted principally of extensive lists of books, libraries and collections, this new edition attempts a different format that partially reflects our changing understanding of books and their historical significance. Those seeking information will not be disappointed, but some of the contributors to this volume have also written essays that engage recent developments in book history; in particular, they have analyzed the changing modes of production, distribution and reading. Likewise, some chapters achieve a high level of historical sophistication and deserve to be widely read by historians of science. For example, in the opening chapter, entitled "The Scientific Book as a Cultural and Bibliographical Object," two librarians—Henry E. Lowood and Robin E. Rider—problematize "the book" and identify some of the issues that need to be addressed if we are to understand science books in an historical framework. Unfortunately, several of the subsequent chapters fail to appreciate the implications of Lowood and Rider's analysis.

The majority of chapters are chronological in scope. Thus, Liba Taub provides a useful and thoroughly referenced essay on 'ancient science' which, as she realizes, is somewhat out of place since the terms 'book' and 'science' are thoroughly anachronistic when applied to her period. Do clay tablets, papyri and even manuscripts deserve a place in "Thornton and Tully"? Readers of this journal will be particularly interested in Sachiko Kusukawa's survey of incunabula and sixteenth-century books. Her chapter begins with an analysis of the different types of publication that drew on the various classical traditions, and she then directs attention to the new genres that expanded the domain of science, broadly defined. Thus, the innovation of printing offered new scope for accurately reproducing detailed information, as witnessed by the flurry of mathematical treatises containing numerical tables for the astronomer, the surveyor and the tradesman. Particularly fascinating is her discussion of books concerned with the design and construction of scientific instruments, such as sundials and astrolabes, some of which included cut-out paper models of these instruments.

Most of the later chapters are devoted to subsequent centuries. While many of these are highly informative, the project lacks consistency. Some authors attempt wide linguistic and geographical coverage, while others concentrate on English-language publications. Some deploy extensive notes and references while others have abandoned this essential apparatus. Likewise, bibliographies are an optional extra. The level of analysis is also very uneven. While these chronologically-arranged chapters are largely concerned with books, libraries and collectors are generally ignored but become the subject of the two concluding chapters, a division that, in the light of recent developments in historiography, should be minimized rather than accentuated.

Although it does not cohere well with the rest of the volume, W.H. Brock's chapter on scientific bibliography and bibliographers is a particularly welcome addition. This splendid essay should be required reading for all graduate students entering the history of science, since it not only contains a vast amount of useful information but it also provides a key to enable students to understand how the subject developed and is written by one of its most able and knowledgeable practitioners.

Despite the new "Thornton and Tully" making significant strides over its predecessors, it represents a missed opportunity since it could have usefully been written to incorporate recent innovations in book history. The lack of consistency between chapters is also a major defect. Will a fifth edition be required in twenty or thirty years' time? Possibly, particularly since the present one may not last that long: its binding is glued, not sewn.

Geoffrey Cantor, University of Leeds

ANN ELJENHOLM NICHOLS, MICHAEL T. ORR, KATHLEEN L. SCOTT, & LYNDA DENNISON, eds. *An Index of Images in English Manuscripts from the time of Chaucer to Henry VIII c.1380–c.1509.* Kathleen L. Scott, gen. ed. The Bodleian Library, Oxford. I: MSS Additional–Digby. Turnhout: Harvey Miller Publishers, 2000. 144 pp. 24 b&w pls.

This is the first volume in a continuing series of publications listing and identifying all illustrations contained in English manuscripts from c.1380–c.1509, which will appear under the general editorship of Kathleen L. Scott. Two further volumes will complete the present volume's coverage of illustrations in Bodleian manuscripts. Every illustration in a manuscript is described, "from full-page narrative miniatures and historiated initials to king's heads, marginalia and *nota bene* hands." The image-content of such famous manuscripts as the early fifteenth-century Li *romans du. . .Alexandre* (Bodley 264) is fully analyzed here, as well as such relatively unknown books as Ashmole 806, a mid-fifteenth-century manuscript of Upton's De *officio militari* with its unexpected Bestiary illustrations. Notationally, I applaud the convention of using superscript numbers 1-4 to indicate the quarter-century in question.

Before the descriptive indexes is an occasionally useful "Glossary of Subjects and Terms," which is, however, not entirely complete. When I looked up "Teaching Gesture" (a term listed in the "Index of Pictorial Subjects"), for example, the editors clearly expected me to understand what it was already [? = *Comput digital*], and I found no enlightenment. The same was true of several other terms that one might not immediately understand that are listed in the Index.

Building on the iconographical indexes of the same publisher's *Survey of English Illustrated Manuscripts* volumes, it is in the Index of Pictorial Subjects (sandwiched between the Index of Authors and Texts, and the Index of Manuscripts with Coats of Arms) in which the great usefulness of these volumes will reside. If bibliographers are the unsung heroes of scholarship, then indexers must surely be the unsung heroes of bibliography. As an index 'anorak' myself, I appreciate a good index when I scrutinize one, and this is, indeed, a good one, and satisfyingly minute!

An iconographical index is the home of *realia* and *irrealia* alike; it accommodates *pavement (cobblestone), pencase, salt cellar* and *shoe with loose lace*, along with *Dindimus (king of brahmans), Hydra* (but also—monstrously—making a second appearance between *York* and *Yun-nan!*) and *perpetual motion machine*. All rub shoulders in the glorious inconsequentiality of the alphabet. Modern methodological considerations rightly insist that iconographers should not impose their own interpretations on us, but should remain as objectively descriptive as possible, and thus the very proper appearance of *profile head with leaves in mouth* in the present Index, rather than the awful 'Green Man.'

Several of the marginal images in cat. no. 191, Peter of Blois's *Epistolae* (1375x1425), apparently depict a head with a forked tongue. I note that one of the *nomina reprehensibilium uirorum* from the seventh chapter of the fifteenth-century *Mayer Nominale* is that of the *bilinguis, qui habet binas linguas*, and that the *Catholicon Anglicum* (1483), defines *double-tongued* as 'Speaking contrary or inconsistent things; deceitful or insincere in speech': *Dubylletonged*, ambiloquus, bilinguis—clearly as figurative a usage as modern *two-faced*, or the (probably invented North American) *forked tongue*.

Having ten years ago written (with Charles Tracy) a piece entitled "A Medieval Choirstall Desk-End at Haddon Hall: The Fox-Bishop & the Geese-Hangmen," it was good to learn of another (late) preaching fox in Bodley 303. And, happily, the indexer has not spared us such entries as *profile head with hand picking nose* [from the late fourteenth-century *Decretals*, Add. D. 33] and *profile head with nose, with drops from* [from a mid-fifteenth-century manuscript of John of Gaddesden's *Rosa medicinae*, Bodley 362].

Writing from an English university Department of English Language, I am well aware that we live in the era of World English, and that that English is increasingly American. That said, however, and at the risk of sounding like a 'backwoodsman' (to use an increasingly popular British English Americanism), there are spellings and usages in the present Index that will bring the British English speaker up short. I can guess that *Pithagoras* is *Pythagoras*, of course, but what on earth are *blues*? On f.33v., the artist of Digby 227 painted in 1461 a branch of *blues*, apparently. Turning to my trusty OED, I find from Hakluyt's edition of Laudonnière's *Notable Histories* (1587): *There are Raspisses, and a little bearie which we call among us Blues, which are very good to eate*, which presumably suggests they are blueberries, but if so, how has our pre-Columbian English artist managed to paint this native American species? Harvey Miller may have shifted its local habitation from

London to Turnhout in Belgium, but what of its linguistic loyalties? I am no botanist, but the Index entry under Plants, *daisy(ies)*, *branch of*, gave even me pause. Do daisies grow on branches?

Nor am I sure that the archaic *jordan* [urinal bottle] in the present Index is a meaningful term to a Third Millennium readership; for different reasons, *man. . .nondescript* or. . .*ugly*, seems (to put it mildly) somewhat subjective as an indexing category. Otherwise, two of the very few errors I noted in the Index are the omission of a reference following the entry, W*oods, gathering flowers in* [it is, in fact, Bodley 264, f. 259v.], and the fact that no such miniature is listed in item no. 209, despite being so referenced at *Gestures, head in hand*.

A small criticism: the choice of plates strikes me as perverse. There are a disproportionate number of diagrams. Was the thinking, perhaps, that manuscripts like Bodley 264 are already over-familiar and available in facsimile?

The publishers, Harvey Miller (now an imprint of Brepols), are to be congratulated on having again espoused a project of such magnitude and importance to English medievalists, and the first volume to be issued bodes well for the future of this important undertaking.

Malcolm Jones, University of Sheffield

HELEN PHILLIPS.
An Introduction to the Canterbury Tales: Reading, Fiction, Context.
New York: St. Martin's Press, 2000. vi + 254 pp.

This book is an introductory textbook aimed at students and general readers and critics of Chaucer. The opening chapter provides background information about Chaucer's life and social setting and an introduction to the *Canterbury Tales* as a whole. The subsequent 22 chapters deal with individual tales, with some chapters containing discussions of pairs of tales such as those of the Friar and Summoner. Considering its breadth of coverage the book is relatively short and some of the tales are given rather brief treatment.

The organization of the chapters follows the order of tales as found in modern critical editions of the poem. In adopting this arrangement, Phillips differs from the thematic and generic organization familiar from Derek Pearsall's *The Canterbury Tales* (London, 1985). Her use of this ordering system encourages the author to draw links between tales and fragments which are often compelling and suggestive. However, certain interpretations appear to conflict with or ignore the evidence of the manuscripts. For instance, much is made of textual silences in the poem, where the tale-link-tale formula appears to break down. For example, Phillips considers the lack of comment that greets the conclusion of the "Second Nun's Tale," suggesting that this may represent a mark of respect for a religious tale, theological prudence, or a comment about narrative closure. No mention is made, however, of the many textual and scribal uncertainties concerning the positioning and integration of the "Second Nun's" and "Canon's Yeoman's Tales" within the poem's overall framework.

Treatment of the individual tales is extremely varied, and Phillips skillfully employs a wealth of critical approaches in her reading of the texts that is Chaucerian in its breadth and diversity. In addition to more formal, traditional modes of interpretation, Phillips makes frequent use of political, psychological, historicist and gender readings which create a series of richly textured interpretations. Each tale is treated as an independent text requiring individual treatment, in contrast to the more rigid structure adopted by Helen Cooper in the *Oxford Guide to the Canterbury Tales* (Oxford, 1989, 1996).

However, the rather more erratic coverage of aspects such as date, genre, sources and analogues may impair the overall usefulness of this book as a student reference work. In addition, there are a number of themes which recur throughout the study, including the question of authorship and audience, the use of stylistic register and Chaucer's narrative technique. In general, the use of critical terminology is sensibly employed and clearly explained. However, frequent reference is made to the technique of 'free indirect discourse,' which Phillips labels 'Chaucer's most original [stylistic] device.' This concept is not explained or defined in any detail. By contrast, linguistic terminology appears to have been suppressed and discussions of 'multiple senses' may have profited from some reference to lexical semantics.

In discussing Chaucer's narrative technique, Phillips makes frequent references to more modern English prose writers, such as Austen, Hardy and Defoe. These references serve to highlight Chaucer's place within an English narrative tradition and function as familiarizing reference points for beginning students. In some cases, however, the allusions seem too fleeting and too general to be of much relevance, e.g., 'Economics are not as dominant in Chaucer's social imagination as they are, say, with Defoe, but they are a recurrent element in his fictional creations in the Tales' (25). In summary, this is a stimulating and lively book which will make a welcome appearance on student bookshelves. It will not function as a replacement for classic introductions such as those by Pearsall and Cooper, but rather as a useful accompaniment.

Simon Horobin, University of Glasgow

Notes on Libraries and Collections

The Chapin Library
Stetson Hall, P.O. Box 426
Williams College
Williamstown, Massachusetts 01267
Wayne G. Hammond, Assistant Librarian
e-mail: Wayne.G.Hammond@williams.edu
Phone: (413) 597-2462
Fax: (413) 597-2929
Hours: M-F 10-12 and 1-5.
http://www.williams.edu/News/Map/B3.html
http://www.williams.edu/resources/chapin/History/history.html

In the Berkshire hills of western Massachusetts is a collection of manuscripts and early printed books which deserves to be more widely known. The Chapin Library was founded in 1923 on the campus of Williams College by Arthur Clark Chapin (Williams 1869) and is housed in Stetson Hall. The library has 51,706 volumes, including 32 medieval manuscripts, a collection of Oxyrhynchus papyri, and 525 incunables, nearly 100 of which are in their original bindings. One hundred items are Aldines. According to the terms of the orginal bequest, none of the rare books can ever leave the library building and so are not available for exhibitions elsewhere, though the Chapin Library does have several exhibitions of its own each year.

The quality and variety of the collection make it well worth a researcher's visit. In addition to the papyri, there is a Gospels (ca. 800) copied in Tours, a Greek New Testament, *Codex Theodori*, from Mt. Athos dated 1295 and a thirteenth-century French Vulgate Bible, several books of hours, psalters, a tenth-century copy of Bede's *De Arte Metrica* (former Phillipps MS 2166), a twelfth-century *Liber Genesis cum commentarius Bedae* copied in England, a mid-14th century copy of Jacobus da Voragine's *Legenda Aurea*, a copy of Dante's *Inferno* (Florence, 1427), and a fifteenth-century Ovid *Opera* in a very early cancelleresca bastarda. Among the early printed books are two editons of Christopher Columbus's letter to the Spanish court announcing his discovery of the New World (Rome 1493 and Basel 1494), Virgil (1501), Aristotle's *Opera* (1495-98), the *Hypnerotomachia Poliphili* (1499), and the first printed editions of Aesop, Aristophanes, and Homer.

There is, as yet, no published catalogue of the collection, though three published exhibition catalogues provide some details of specific items. Two of these, *Bookbindings in the Chapin Library* by Melanie Gifford

(1976) and *European Manuscripts IX-XV and the Williams College Museum of Art* by Deborah-Irene Coy (1977), are out of print. A third, *Finished by Hand: Decoration in Fifteenth-Century Printed Books* by Marguerite A. Keane (1995), is distributed by Oak Knoll Books. Permission to study manuscripts may be obtained by contacting the librarian.

Meradith T. McMunn, Rhode Island College.

Innerpeffray Library
Innerpeffray,
Crieff, PH7 3RF,
Scotland
Telephone: 01764 652819

Innerpeffray Library is the oldest free lending library in Scotland. It was established in 1680 by David Drummond, 3rd Lord Madertie, who founded his library in the loft of the collegiate chapel of St. Mary, the Drummond family burial place. The chapel is now maintained by Historic Scotland. The present library building, which is adjacent, was completed in 1762.

The collection comprises some 4,400 books, including 3,000 works which were printed before 1801. Although there are no *incunabula*, the library is rich in sixteenth-century books, of which the earliest is P. Reginaldetus, *Speculum finalis retributionis* (Paris 1502). There are many bibles, the earliest of which is a French version printed in Antwerp in 1530. There is also a copy of the sixth edition of the Great Bible (1541) containing a woodcut which is ascribed to Holbein, and another French bible of 1633 which belonged to James Graham, 5th Earl and 1st Marquis of Montrose, the so-called 'Great Marquis of Montrose.' Among the sixteenth-century books are items of Scottish interest such as the works of Hector Boece, Raphael Hollinshed, and Gavin Douglas.

The library's demise during the twentieth century may be attributed to multiple causes, including the growth of public libraries and changed reading habits, as well as a lack of financial resources and shelf space. After World War I, borrowings dropped to minimal levels, and the lending facility was finally dropped in 1968. Borrowing records have been preserved from 1747-1968, and the library has also kept its visitors' books. Following a successful bid for lottery funding, there are plans to computerize the library's contents and borrowing registers, and to establish a website, which will make Innerpeffray more of a public library once again.

The library is cared for by a private trust, the Innerpeffray Mortification; this has very limited funds and relies on donations, bequests, and visitor admission fees (which are very reasonable). The Friends of Innerpeffray Library (FOIL) holds regular meetings and produces a thrice-yearly newsletter. The library is situated on the bank of the River Earn with views over Strathearn and Crieff. It is five miles from Crieff, seven miles from Auchterarder. Opening times are currently as follows: daily, except Thursday, 10–12.45 and 2–4.45; Sunday 2–4pm. There is earlier closing during the winter (October–March), and the library is open in December–January by appointment only.

Margaret Connolly, University College Cork

Rare Books and Manuscripts Division
Special Collections Library
Penn State University Libraries
104 Paterno Library
University Park, PA 16802-1808
Telephone: (814) 865-1793
FAX: (814) 863-5318
http://www.libraries.psu.edu/crsweb/spcoll.htm
Hours: 8:00 to 5:00, Monday through Friday

The Department of Special Collections at the Pennsylvania State University Libraries recently moved into new quarters in the Paterno Library. Cataloging of the medieval manuscript holdings in the Rare Books and Manuscripts Division is underway, and we hope to have entries on-line by 2002. The medieval collection, assembled by the late Charles Mann, contains about a dozen more or less complete manuscripts, as well as some fifty manuscript leaves, ranging in date from tenth-century neumes to sixteenth-century antiphonal leaves. There are also more than fifty volumes of incunabula (recently edited for an updating of Goff) and some leaves, including a Caxton Chaucer leaf.

A Middle English *Prophetia Merlini* text (there is also a *Brut Chronicle* in the same hand) has been edited by Caroline Eckhardt, and Dennis Looney has written an article on a Petrarch *Trionfi*. Unstudied items include two leaves in Spanish from a Valencia confraternity volume; a variant version for lay readers of a pseudo-Bernard tract addressed to a nun and contained in a manuscript written by a noted humanist scribe; a Lenten sermon collection from 1489, rare in manuscript copies, though found in several printed editions; a fourteenth-century Florentine Boethius with glosses; several leaves with prayers in Dutch; and numerous decorated leaves from Books of Hours and breviaries. There are also eleven leaves from the unique Middle High German translation of Valerius Maximus.

The Special Collections Library also has good holdings in Italian books printed before 1601, a collection of early Bibles in many tongues, and an extensive list of manuscript facsimiles, which includes a near-complete run of Roxburghe Club publications. For those whose interests extend beyond the Early Book era, there are good collections in later periods, with particular strengths in art and architectural history; classical studies from 1500 to 1800; emblem books; English literature and history; history of photography; German literature in English translation; works of Joseph Priestley; utopian literature; and the Williamscote Library of English literature and history, a relatively intact 18th-century antiquary's working collection (especially strong in the classics and theology, with many Wing period books) assembled by John Loveday of Caversham.

Among other amenities at the Penn State Libraries, there is the complete STC on microfilm. The Special Collections Library is completely handicapped-accessible; if you can't reach the electrical sockets under the tables, an agile staff member will plug in your laptop for you. Fetching time is very quick.

      Jeanne Krochalis and Sandra Stelts
      Penn State University

About the Authors

Jennifer Britnell is Reader in French at the University of Durham, England. She works on sixteenth-century French literature, with special reference to *rhétoriqueur* poetry, polemic, prophecy, religious controversy and religious instruction. Her principal publications are her monograph *Jean Bouchet* (Edinburgh: Edinburgh University Press, 1986) and her two critical editions: Jean Bouchet, *La Déploration de l'Eglise militante* (Geneva: Droz, 1991) and Jean Lemaire de Belges, *Traité de la différence des schismes et des conciles de l'Eglise* (Geneva: Droz, 1997). She is co-editor and contributor to *Vernacular Literature and Current Affairs in the Early Sixteenth Century: France, England and Scotland*, edited by Jennifer Britnell and Richard Britnell (Aldershot: Ashgate, 2000).

Cynthia Brown, Professor of French at the University of California, Santa Barbara and specialist of late medieval and early modern French literature and culture, is the author of numerous books and articles, including the award-winning *Poets, Patrons, and Printers: Crisis of Authority in Late Medieval France* (Cornell University Press, 1995). Her critical edition of Pierre Gringore's early 16th-century French polemical works (1500-1513) is forthcoming from Librairie Droz in Geneva.

Brigitte Buettner teaches medieval art at Smith College. A specialist of late medieval secular visual culture, she is the author of *Boccaccio's Des cleres et nobles femmes: Systems of Signification in an Illuminated Manuscript* (Seattle: Washington University Press, 1996). Her article on New Year's gifts at the Valois courts around 1400 is forthcoming in *Art Bulletin*.

Geoffrey Cantor is Professor of the History of Science at the University of Leeds and co-director of the SciPer (Science in the Nineteenth-Century Periodical) Project.

Jacqueline Cerquiglini-Toulet is Professor of French literature of the Middle Ages at the University of Paris-Sorbonne and director of a research group (Centre National de la Recherche Scientifique, Paris). She is in charge of editing medieval texts. Her book *La Couleur de la mélancolie* (Hatier, 1993) was translated into English in 1997 [*The Color of melancholy. The Uses of Books in the Fourteenth Century* (The Johns Hopkins University Press)]. She has recently co-edited the *"Livre du voir dit" de Guillaume de Machaut* (Le Livre de Poche, Lettres gothiques, 1999), a volume that received a prize from the Académie des Inscriptions et Belles Lettres.

Margaret Connolly is a Lecturer in Medieval and Renaissance Literature in the English Department at University College Cork. Her research interests include devotional literature, textual criticism, and book history. Her most recent book is *John Shirley: Book Production and the Noble Household in Fifteenth-Century England* (Aldershot: Ashgate, 1998). She has edited *Contemplations of the Dread and Love of God* for the Early English Text Society (Oxford, 1994), and with Thomas G. Duncan, she is currently preparing an edition of *The Middle English Mirror: Sermons from Advent to Lent* for the Middle English Texts series.

Brian Cummings is a Lecturer in English in the School of European Studies at the University of Sussex. His book, *Grammar & Grace: the Literary Culture of the Reformation*, is forthcoming with OUP.

Martha Driver is Professor of English at Pace University in New York. A co-founder of the Early Book Society for the study of manuscripts and printing history, she writes and lectures about illustration from MS to print, book production, and the early history of publishing. In addition to publishing a number of articles, she has edited seven journals in four years, including *Film & History: Medieval Period in Film*, and with Deborah McGrady, a special issue of *Literary & Linguistic Computing*, "Teaching the Middle Ages with Technology" (1999). She is now at work on a book about fifteenth-century English text and illustration for British Library Publications.

Simon Horobin is British Academy Research Fellow in the Department of English Language, University of Glasgow. He is currently working (with M. Black and J.J.Smith) on *A Grammar of Middle English I: Transmission*, and on a study of the language of Chaucer's scribes.

Malcolm Jones is Lecturer in Folklore and Folklife Studies in the Department of English Language and Linguistics of Sheffield University. He works mainly in the area of late medieval and early modern iconography. Before entering academic life, he worked as a lexicographer and as a Research Assistant in the Department of Medieval and Later Antiquities of the British Museum.

Anne-Marie Legaré teaches Medieval and Modern Art History at Univerisity of Rennes Haute-Bretagne (France). She has received a Research Delegation (1999-2001) at the Institut de Recherche et d'Histoire des Textes (CNRS) in order to pursue her research on women's libraries in late medieval and early modern France and on manuscript illumination produced by the Master of Antoine Rolin and his associates in the Southern Netherlands in the time of Margaret of Austria. She is currently working on a monograph, "The Pèlerinage de Vie humaine in prose owmed by queen Charlotte de Savoie."

Jeanne Krochalis is Associate Professor of English and comparative literature at Penn State New Kensington, as well as palæography consultant for the Walters catalogue. Her current scholarly interests include manuscripts on rolls and texts associated with pilgrimage.

Deborah McGrady is an Assistant Professor in the Department of French & Italian at Tulane University. She has written on the role of patrons and readers in the works of Christine de Pizan, Guillaume de Machaut, and Jean Lemaire de Belges. She is currently writing a book-length study on *Rebellious Readers: The Changing Role of Audience in Late-Medieval French Literature* and editing Jean Lemaire de Belges's *Les Épitres de l'Amant Vert*.

Meradith T. McMunn is Professor of Medieval Literature in the Department of English at Rhode Island College in Providence. Her publications include *Beasts and Birds of the Middle Ages: The Bestiary and Its Legacy*, with Willene B. Clark (University of Pennsylvania Press), and a number of articles on the secular literature of the Middle Ages, word and image in medieval illustrated manuscripts, and the illustrated manuscripts of the *Roman de la Rose*. She is now completing a decade-long project to locate and describe the corpus of more than 9,000 illustrations in the manuscripts of the *Roman de la Rose* for a forthcoming descriptive catalogue and study.

Linne R. Mooney is Professor of English at the University of Maine and an officer of the Early Book Society. She works on late medieval English manuscripts, and is currently preparing a new electronic revision of *The Index of Middle English Verse* and writing a book about late medieval English scribes.

Jason O'Rourke is a member of the 'Traditions of the Book' research group at Queen's University Belfast. His research interests include patronage and book production in Wales and the Marches, and the activities of book owners and collectors both in Wales and further afield. He is especially interested in multilingual manuscripts (in English, Welsh, French and Latin) and their socio-literary context. He is currently working on a book of essays in collaboration with the other members of the 'Traditions of the Book' team, and an article on English texts in Welsh miscellanies for the *Yearbook of English Studies*.

Myra Dickman Orth is an independent scholar based in Boston. Since retiring from the Getty Research Institute, she has pursued her own research on

French sixteenth-century illuminated manuscripts, their artists, authors, and owners. Forthcoming articles and colloquium papers include "L'Enluminure au temps de Henri II," "Les Puys en images," "Reconsidering Radical Beauty: Marguerite de Navarre's Evangelical Catechism and Confession," "The Primacy of the Word in French Renaissance Psalm Manuscripts," "French Renaissance Manuscripts and *l'Histoire du livre*," and "Lyon et Rome à l'antique: les illustrations dans *Les Antiquités romaines* de Guillaume du Choul." Her *Survey of French Renaissance Illuminated Manuscripts* will be published by Harvey Miller Publishers/Brepols.

Oliver Pickering is Deputy Head of Special Collections in Leeds University Library and Associate Lecturer in English. He has published widely in the field of medieval English, and has recently compiled (with Veronica O'Mara) the *Index of Middle English Prose* volume for Lambeth Palace Library (1999). He is also the Editor of *The Library: The Transactions of the Bibliographical Society* [of London].

Susan Powell is a Senior Lecturer in English Language and Literature at the University of Salford, where she teaches the history of the English language, Chaucer and medieval Arthurian literature. Her research interests are in manuscripts and early printed books, with particular relation to late medieval and Tudor preaching and devotional texts.

Sandra Stelts is Rare Books Specialist at the Special Collections Library, Penn State University Libraries.

Jane H. M. Taylor is Fellow in Medieval French at St Hilda's College, Oxford, and Lecturer at the University of Oxford. She has worked extensively on late medieval French literature, and especially on the late medieval lyric. She has edited a part of the immense *Roman de Perceforest*, has edited a number of volumes on women in medieval art and literature, and her book on *François Villon: Text and Context* will appear in April 2001.

Carole Weinberg is a Senior Lecturer in the Department of English and American Studies at the University of Manchester where she teaches medieval literature. Her present area of research is medieval Arthurian literature, and among her publications she has co-edited a parallel text/translation of the complete text of Layamon's 'Brut.'

Mary Beth Winn is Professor of French Studies at the State University of New York at Albany. She has published articles on fifteenth- and sixteenth-century French literature, music, Books of Hours, and early printing. Having recently completed a study of the Parisian publisher Anthoine Vérard (Droz, 1997), she is currently collaborating on the critical edition of the *chansons* of Thomas Crecquillon (ca. 1557).

www.ingramcontent.com/pod-product-compliance
Lightning Source LLC
Chambersburg PA
CBHW021819300426
44114CB00009BA/236